EEC FISHERIES LAW

EEC FISHERIES LAW

by

R.R. Churchill

1987 **MARTINUS NIJHOFF PUBLISHERS**
a member of the KLUWER ACADEMIC PUBLISHERS GROUP
DORDRECHT / BOSTON / LANCASTER

Distributors

for the United States and Canada: Kluwer Academic Publishers, P.O. Box 358, Accord Station, Hingham, MA 02018-0358, USA
for the UK and Ireland: Kluwer Academic Publishers, MTP Press Limited, Falcon House, Queen Square, Lancaster LA1 1RN, UK
for all other countries: Kluwer Academic Publishers Group, Distribution Center, P.O. Box 322, 3300 AH Dordrecht, The Netherlands

Library of Congress Cataloging in Publication Data

```
Churchill, R. R. (Robin Rolf)
  EEC fisheries law.

  Bibliography: p.
  Includes index.
  1. Fishery law and legislation--European Economic
Community countries.  I. Title.
KJ6695.C48  1987          343.4'07892          87-12217
                          344.037892
```

ISBN 90-247-3545-9

Cover photograph: ANP, Amsterdam

Copyright

© 1987 by Martinus Nijhoff Publishers, Dordrecht.

PRINTED IN THE NETHERLANDS

Table of contents

Preface

In 1970 the EEC adopted its first legislation to implement its Common Fisheries Policy. Since that time the Policy has developed considerably, particularly after 1977 when EEC Member States extended their fishing limits to 200 miles: correspondingly, there has been a significant growth in the volume of EEC fisheries law. As a result there is now an extensive body of EEC law dealing with nearly all aspects of fishing, and the Community has largely, though not entirely, taken over from its Member States the responsibility for regulating the fishing industries of the EEC.

The aim of this book is to give a critical analysis of the whole body of fisheries law which has so far been adopted by the EEC. In particular, it seeks to determine the division of competence between the Community and its Member States in relation to the regulation of fishing, to describe the fisheries law which the Community has adopted, and to assess the effectiveness of that law in the light of its stated or presumed objectives. The first three chapters deal with a number of preliminary background and procedural matters. Chapter 1 considers the special characteristics which fisheries have which distinguish them from other economic activities as the object of regulation by public authorities. This is followed by a quick sketch of the fishing industries of EEC Member States and a brief account of the evolution of EEC fisheries law in order to facilitate understanding of the analysis of the substantive law which follows in later Chapters. Chapter 2 explains the processes by which EEC fisheries law is made, while Chapter 3 explores the scope of this law, seeking to ascertain to what kinds of aquatic creatures, geographical areas and persons it applies.

The substantive law is the subject of the remaining chapters. The waters of EEC Member States contain extensive fishery resources which are capable of making a permanent and important contribution to the EEC's food supplies if properly managed. Chapter 4 looks at the Community's system of fisheries management and asks how effective it is in practice. Apart from fishing in Community waters, EEC vessels also fish in the waters of third States or on the high seas: the extensive relationships which the Community has developed with third States and international fishery commissions to regulate such fishing are the subject of Chapter 5. Chapter 6 looks at various questions relating to the structure of EEC fishing fleets, in particular examining Community aid for modernising vessels and for adjusting the EEC's fish-catching capacity to the resources available, as well as considering the permissibility of national subsidies to the fishing industry. Chapter 7 looks at the measures the Community has taken to regulate the marketing of fish. The EEC is one of the world's largest traders in fish products: the law regulating such trade is the subject of Chapter 8. The final chapter attempts a general evaluation of EEC fisheries law, both in terms of its substance and considered more broadly as a regulatory system. From the latter viewpoint EEC fisheries law may have lessons for other areas of regulation by the EEC. In general, the law in this book is stated as at October 1, 1986.

It should be made clear that in describing and analysing the EEC's substantive fisheries law, this book is concerned only with the basic principles of the law and does not go into fine detail. Thus someone wishing to find out, for example, the minimum size of lemon sole which may legitimately be caught or the reference price for dogfish will look in vain for that information in this book.

In the past three or four years no less than three full-length books in English on the EEC's Common Fisheries Policy have appeared.[1] Some explanation is therefore owed as to why yet another book on EEC fisheries is being inflicted on students of EEC fisheries questions. The three books mentioned were written by political scientists and a geographer and were primarily concerned with tracing the political and economic factors governing the evolution of the Common Fisheries Policy to the point where a fully-fledged Policy was adopted at the beginning of 1983. As the summary of its contents given above suggests, this book is written from a rather different perspective and differs from the other books in a number of ways. First, it is devoted primarily to a legal analysis of the Common Fisheries Policy. The existence of the three books mentioned has meant that I have not had to say nearly as much about the political, economic and social background to EEC fisheries law as would otherwise have been necessary. A second difference is that this book discusses certain topics – such as marketing and trade – which are treated but scantily in the other books and indeed in the existing periodical literature – doubtless because these topics have less political appeal than resource management. Yet these matters are of equal concern to the fishing industry, and it will be argued

---

[1] M. Leigh, *European Integration and the Common Fisheries Policy,* Beckenham, 1983; J. Farnell and J. Elles, *In Search of a Common Fisheries Policy,* Aldershot, 1984; and M. Wise, *The Common Fisheries Policy of the European Community,* London, 1984.

in this book that management, structural policy, marketing and trade are all interlinked, so that one should not consider these topics in isolation from one another. A final point of difference is that while the other books cover events only up to the adoption of the revised Common Fisheries Policy at the beginning of 1983, this book is able to look at the subsequent operation in practic of the revised Policy and consider its effectiveness. It is also able to give an account of the arrangements that have been made in respect of Portugal and Spain, which became members of the EEC at the beginning of 1986.

Although this book is written from a legal perspective and is primarily concerned with legal questions, it is hoped that it will be of interest and accessible not just to lawyers but to those from other disciplines who are interested in EEC fisheries questions. It is also my hope that some parts of this book may be of interest to students of Community law generally. The way in which the EEC regulates the fishing industry and manages an important natural resource, and the relationship between its competence to do so and that of its Member States, is not without relevance for other areas of EEC law.

In writing this book I have had assistance from many people. First, I would like warmly to thank Professor E.D. Brown, my colleague in the Law Department at UWIST and the supervisor of the doctoral thesis of which this book is an updated and extensively revised version, for his unfailing encouragement and help over many years. Secondly, I am grateful for the knowledge and understanding of the Common Fisheries Policy which I have gained by talking over a period of years with many people (too numerous to mention individually) involved with the operation of the Policy: for any inaccuracies and limitations that appear in this book I am of course solely responsible. Last but not least I would like to thank Mrs. Zoë Selley and Mrs. Dawn Morgan for coping so cheerfully with all the typing involved in the production of this book.

Cardiff, December 1986   Robin Churchill

List of Abbreviations

A.F.D.I.	Annuaire Français de Droit International
A.J.I.L.	American Journal of International Law
Art.	Article
B.Y.I.L.	British Yearbook of International Law
Bull. E.C.	Bulletin of the European Communities
CCT	Common Customs Tariff
C.D.E.	Cahiers de Droit Européen
CECAF	Fisheries Committee for Eastern Central Atlantic
C.M.L.R.	Common Market Law Reports
C.M.L. Rev.	Common Market Law Review
Cmnd.	Command Paper (of the United Kingdom)
COM	Communication from the Commission to the Council
Dec.	Decision
Dir.	Directive
EAGGF	European Agricultural Guidance and Guarantee Fund
E.C.R.	European Court Reports
ECU	European Currency Unit
EEC	European Economic Community
EEZ	Exclusive Economic Zone
EFTA	European Free Trade Association
E.L.R.	European Law Review
E.P. Doc.	European Parliament Working Document
FAO	Food and Agriculture Organisation
GATT	General Agreement on Tariffs and Trade
GRT	Gross Registered Tonnes
G.U.	Gazzetta Ufficiale della Repubblica Italiana
H.C. Deb.	Debates of the House of Commons (of the United Kingdom)
H.C. Paper	House of Commons Paper
H.L. Deb.	Debates of the House of Lords (of the United Kingdom)
H.L. Paper	House of Lords Paper

ICES	International Council for the Exploration of the Sea
ICJ Rep.	Reports of Judgements, Advisory Opinions and Orders of the International Court of Justice
I.C.L.Q.	International and Comparative Law Quarterly
I.L.M.	International Legal Materials
J.C.M.S.	Journal of Common Market Studies
J.O.	Journal Officiel des Communautés Européennes
J.O.R.F.	Journal Officiel de la République Française
L.I.E.I.	Legal Issues of European Integration
MEY	Maximum Economic Yield
MSY	Maximum Sustainable Yield
NAFO	Northwest Atlantic Fisheries Organisation
NEAFC	North-East Atlantic Fisheries Commission
N.Y.I.L.	Netherlands Yearbook of International Law
O.D.I.L.	Ocean Development and International Law
OECD	Organisation for Economic Co-Operation and Development
O.J.	Official Journal of the European Communities
Reg.	Regulation
R.G.D.I.P.	Revue Générale de Droit International Public
R.M.C.	Revue du Marché Commun
R.T.D.E.	Revue Trimestrielle de Droit Européen
S.I.	Statutory Instrument (of Ireland and the United Kingdom)
Stb.	Staatsblad (of the Netherlands)
TAC	Total Allowable Catch
U.K.T.S.	United Kingdom Treaty Series
UN Legislative Series B/15	United Nations Legislative Series. National Legislation and Treaties relating to the Territorial Sea, the Contiguous Zone, the Continental Shelf, the High Seas and to Fishing and the Conservation of the Living Resources of the Sea (1970). ST/LEG/SER.B/15.
UN Legislative Series B/16	United Nations Legislative Series. National Legislation and Treaties relating to the Law of the Sea (1974). ST/LEG/SER.B/16.
UN Legislative Series B/19	United Nations Legislative Series. National Legislation and Treaties relating to the Law of the Sea (1980). ST/LEG/SER.B/19.
U.N.T.S.	United Nations Treaty Series
W.Q.	Written Question (asked by a member of the European Parliament)

List of Tables

Table of Cases

XVIII

B. CASES BEFORE OTHER COURTS

Table of Treaties

XX

XXII

XXIV

Table of Community Secondary Legislation

A. REGULATIONS

B. DIRECTIVES

C. DECISIONS

D. OTHER ACTS

CHAPTER 1

Introduction

The aim of this Chapter is to set out some background information which is necessary to an understanding of the Common Fisheries Policy and EEC fisheries law. Since such a body of law, by definition, seeks to regulate fisheries, the Chapter begins by considering some of the special characteristics fisheries have as the object of regulation. The Chapter then goes on to give a brief sketch of the EEC fishing industry. This is followed by a lightning account of the evolution of the Common Fisheries Policy and its accompanying body of law: such a bird's-eye view at this stage will, it is hoped, aid in following the detailed analysis of the various areas of substantive law in the later chapters. Finally, the Chapter considers the relationship of the specialised body of EEC fisheries law to Community law in general.

1. REGULATING MARINE FISHERIES – CHARACTERISTICS AND CONCERNS

In examining the EEC's Common Fisheries Policy and the law which forms an instrument of that Policy, this book is essentially concerned with the way in which marine fisheries in the EEC are regulated by governmental authority – be that authority one vesting in the Community institutions or in the Member States. As the object of regulation by governmental authority, marine fisheries have a number of characteristics which distinguish them from other kinds of economic activity based on the exploitation of natural resources, such as agriculture, forestry and mining. These characteristics all stem essentially from a fundamental feature of marine fish, namely that they are a common property natural resource. In other words, free-swimming fish in the sea are not owned by anyone: property rights only arise when the fish are caught and reduced into the possession of an individual fisherman.[1] It therefore follows that anyone can, in principle, fish in the sea. From the common property nature of marine fish, there follow four consequences of particular note as far as the regulation of marine fisheries is concerned – a tendency for fish stocks to be fished above biologically optimum levels; a tendency for more fishermen to engage in a fishery than is economically justified; a likelihood of competition and conflict between different groups of fishermen; and the necessity for any regulation of marine fisheries to have a substantial international component. Each of these consequences needs to be examined in a little more detail.[2]

Because fish are a common property resource, anyone can enter a particular fishery. It obviously follows that as more fishermen enter the fishery, more and more fish will – initially at least – be caught. If the quantity of fish caught, together with fish lost through natural mortality, exceeds the amount of fish being added to the stock through reproduction, then the size of the stock will start to decrease: in extreme cases the stock may even collapse, as has happened with the Antarctic whales and the California sardine. This phenomenon is known as overfishing. Moreover, in the absence of any regulation, an individual fisherman has no incentive to restrain his activities in order to prevent overfishing because there is no guarantee that other fishermen will follow his example: indeed, the opposite is more likely to occur, for with one competitor removed there is more fish for those that remain. Thus, just as common land was over-grazed before the enclosure movement, so an unregulated fishery will normally lead to overfishing.[3]

Thus to prevent overfishing it is usually necessary to regulate the amount of fish to be caught. To do this, it is necessary to know how much fish can be caught without overfishing resulting. As the result of research done by fisheries biologists, it is known that the growth of a particular fish stock is limited by environmental factors, such as the availability of food and the presence of natural predators, and that the stock will thus reach a particular size that cannot be exceeded. A stock which is not fished at all will tend to remain at this maximum size, and natural mortality and reproduction will balance out. Once the stock begins to be fished, however, its size will decrease. To recover its losses, the stock then starts growing at a rapid rate in an attempt to reach its original level. This rate of increase is greatest when a stock has been reduced to a particular size (which varies from stock to stock). It is at this level, which is known as the maximum sustainable yield (MSY), that the greatest quantity of fish can be caught year after year without the total size of the stock being adversely affected (assuming that environmental factors do not upset the balance).

Until thirty or so years ago MSY was frequently suggested as the principal objective of fisheries management, but over the past three decades its limitations have been increasingly revealed. First, ascertaining the MSY for a particular stock is by no means an easy task, even where the data exists (which is not always the case). Secondly, because of the inter-relationship of stocks (for example, one stock may feed upon another, as seals do upon cod) or because fishing directed at one species will often unavoidably result in other species being caught, it makes little sense to determine the MSY for each stock in isolation: if one stock is fished at the level of MSY, it may be impossible to achieve the level of MSY for a related stock. Thus it is desirable to establish fishing levels for inter-related stocks as a single exercise.

A second consequence of the common property nature of fish is that it leads to economic inefficiency. Typically a fishery will begin with few entrants, each of whom will make a profit. Other fishermen, seeing these profits, will be attracted to the fishery. As the number of fishermen participating in the fishery increases, so the size of catch – and hence economic return – per vessel will decrease. Thus, in the absence of any limitation on the number of fishermen entering a fishery, the economic return for each vessel will be below the optimum (or Maximum Economic Yield (MEY), as it is known)[4] and indeed in the long term total revenue from the fishery will tend to equal the total cost of fishing. In other words, the same quantity of fish is caught as could be caught with substantially fewer vessels than those acutally employed. This phenomenon is known as overcapacity (or over-capitalisation) and is found in most of the world's fisheries.

To reduce or prevent economic inefficiency it is necessary to limit the number of fishermen entering a fishery by mechanisms such as restrictive licensing schemes, individual vessel quotas and the scrapping and laying up of vessels (see further the discussion in Chapter 6). (Fisheries are thus an exception to classical economic theory that efficiency is best promoted by the free play of market forces). Limiting entry does of course raise fundamental problems of allocation, for it means denying or restricting the livelihood of established fishermen. As a result, and also for reasons of employment, social and regional policy which are often interlinked, most States have not appeared overly anxious to grapple with the problem of overcapacity and increase the economic efficiency of their fishing industries.

The third notable consequence of the fact that marine fish are a common property resource is the likelihood of competition and conflict between different groups of fishermen. It follows from the open access nature of fisheries that competition between fishermen is inevitable. Nor is such competition in itself necessarily harmful. Where it raises problems and may produce conflict is where competition is at such a level as to lead to overfishing and economic inefficiency. More directly, conflict may also arise between fishermen using different types of gear, notably where trawlers seek to fish in areas where there is stationary gear such as standing nets. Conflict may also arise between fishing and other uses of the sea, such as the offshore oil and gas industry and dredging for sand and gravel.

Finally, because much fishing takes place outside what has traditionally been regarded as the territory of States it follows that the problems discussed above must be regulated – in part at least – on the international level through co-operation between States and through the medium of international law. International law in this area has been concerned largely with delineating those areas of the sea subject to the jurisdiction of coastal States and with providing for co-operation in the regulation of fishing in the areas beyond, chiefly in the form of international fishery commissions.[5]

Up until the mid 1970s narrow zones of jurisdiction for coastal States were the norm – at least in Western Europe and North America, though elsewhere Latin American and some African States had been claiming zones of up to 200 miles in breadth since the end of the Second World War. In Western Europe the only jurisdiction originally enjoyed by coastal States was a 3-mile territorial sea (within which the coastal State had exclusive access to, and the exclusive right to regulate, fish stocks), but to this was added in the early 1960s, as a result partly of unilateral action by States like Iceland and Norway and partly of the 1964 European Fisheries Convention, a 12-mile fishing zone (within which the coastal State had the exclusive right to regulate, and priority access to, fish stocks). Beyond this zone fishing was largely regulated by international fishery commissions – in the North Atlantic the North-East Atlantic Fisheries Commission and the International Commission for the Northwest Atlantic Fisheries. These bodies were not very successful in managing the fish stocks under their jurisdiction. There were a number of reasons for this: first, political bargaining within the commissions over the allocation of quotas led to the total allowable catches prescribed being set at higher levels than was biologically defensible; secondly, the regulatory measures adopted by the commissions could legitimately be opted out of by any dissatisfied member State; and lastly, even where the regulations were accepted, they were often poorly observed and enforced.

The twin pressures of dissatisfaction with the work of international fishery commissions and the desire of coastal States (largely, but not exclusively, from the Third World) for greater control over the resources off their coasts, led the Third United Nations Conference on the Law of the Sea, which had been convened in 1973 to reconsider the whole of the Law of the Sea, to include in the Convention which it eventually adopted in 1982 provisions giving coastal States an exclusive economic zone (EEZ) of 200 miles in breadth. Within this zone each coastal State has sovereign rights for the purpose of exploiting, conserving and managing fishery resources, although it is under an obligation to allow other States to fish in the zone for any fish which it does not have the capacity to harvest itself. Although the Convention was not adopted until 1982 and even today is a long way from receiving the 60 ratifications necessary for it to enter into force, most coastal States (including, as we shall see in Chapter 3, EEC Member States) have already unilaterally claimed a 200-mile EEZ or fishing zone, so that it is safe to say that the right to a 200-mile EEZ has already passed into customary international law.[6] It is important to note, however, that the near universal introduction of 200-mile EEZs or fishing zones (which between them cover the areas where over 90% of commercial fishing currently takes place) have not altered the common property nature of fishery resources. What it has done is to reduce – though not eliminate – the international element in fisheries regulation and management. The reason why management in 200-mile zones is not purely a national matter is because fish in many cases (the North-East Atlantic is a prime example) migrate between the EEZs of neighbouring States (thus requiring co-operative management arrangements among such States) or between EEZs and the areas beyond (thus continuing the need for management by international fishery commissions, though usually in co-operation with the coastal States concerned). Thus even if the EEC Treaty did not require a Common Fisheries Policy (which it in fact does), the migratory patterns of fish stocks in the waters off the EEC would necessitate co-operation between the Member States.

From what has been said so far it follows that the concerns of marine fisheries regulation include controlling fishing effort so as to prevent overfishing and promote economic efficiency, and preventing conflicts between fishermen using different types of gear and between fishing and other uses of the sea. Other concerns, which may be no less important but which do not follow from the common property nature of marine fisheries, are prescribing conditions for the ownership and registration of fishing vessels (for the purposes primarily of order and control, though also as a means of restricting fishing effort); construction standards for vessels (for reasons of safety); the marketing of, and trade in, fishery products (in the interests partly of income support for fishermen and partly of the consumer); and the working conditions of fishermen.

These matters, in so far as they are the subject of regulation by EEC law (and most of them are), are discussed in Chapters 4–8. Here we must now turn to give a brief sketch of the object of such regulation, namely the fishing industry in the EEC.

2. THE EEC FISHING INDUSTRY[7]

In view of the high political profile which fisheries have had in the EEC over the past decade, the economic insignificance of fisheries may come as some-thing of a shock. In the Community as a whole fisheries account for about 0.14% of Gross Domestic Product: even in Portugal and Spain, the Member States in which fisheries are of the greatest relative importance, the figures are only 1.58 and 0.81%, respectively.[8] However, as with many other activities, percentage of Gross Domestic Product is a rather crude indicator of economic importance. First, this figure does not take any account of the value added in processing and distribution, nor of the industries dependent on fishing, such as boat building and fish processing. Secondly, the figures do not reflect the regional importance of the fishing industry. In a number of regions in the EEC, particularly its poorer regions, fishing makes an important contribution to the local economy, in particular offering jobs where the possibilities of alternative employment are often slight. Nor should it be forgotten that fishing is not an economic activity pure and simple but a vital source of food: worldwide, fish provide about 20% of animal protein, as well as being an important source of vitamins and certain minerals. As to why there should be such a disparity between the economic importance of fishing, and its political significance,[9] the explanation is probably because of the regional importance of fisheries and because disputes over fisheries frequently have an interna-tional character, and thus tend to encourage nationalistic attitudes, as seen, for example, in the Anglo-Icelandic 'Cod Wars'.

In recent years catches by the eleven EEC Member States (land-locked Luxembourg not surprisingly has no fishing industry) have averaged about 6.5 million tonnes a year. This represents about 10% of the total world marine fish catch; and the Community as a whole is the third largest fishing-catching power in the world, surpassed only by Japan and the Soviet Union. Of the Community catch, over 70% is accounted for by four Member States – Denmark, Spain, the United Kingdom and France – which in the period 1981–83 caught on average each year 1.86, 1.27, 0.87 and 0.77 million tonnes respectively.[10] In 1984 the Community catch had a value of US $4,145 million.[11] The most important grounds for Community fishermen are the North Sea and North Atlantic (from which about 75% of catches are taken), the Mediterra-nean (about 10%) and East Central Atlantic (about 8%). About 300,000 people in the Community are employed in fishing, well under 1% of the total

Community labour force, although perhaps twice as many jobs onshore (in fish processing, boat building, etc.) are directly dependent on the fishing industry. In spite of being such a large catcher of fish, the EEC is nowhere near self-sufficient in fishery products and therefore imports a large amount of fish. In 1984 these imports totalled US $4,697 million in value, against US $2902 million worth of exports, giving a trade deficit of some US $1795 million:[12] overall the Community accounted for something like a third of total world trade in fishery products.

The above picture may perhaps suggest that the fishing industry in the EEC, apart from differences in size between Member States, is relatively homogenous. This is in fact very far from being the case, either within individual Member States or as between Member States. Indeed it would have been more accurate to head this section 'the EEC fishing industries' rather than using the singular. First, there are differences in the structure of fishing fleets. Broadly speaking, there are three different types of vessel: distant-water (roughly over 110 feet in length), which tend to be company owned; middle- and near-water (80–110 feet); and inshore (under 80 feet), which tend to be owned by one individual or a small number of individuals in partnership. Over the past decade the size and significance of the Community's distant-water fleets have decreased dramatically as they have been forced out of waters they formerly fished as a result of countries like Canada, the Faroes, Iceland, Norway and the Soviet Union extending their limits to 200 miles: nevertheless, France, West Germany, the United Kingdom, Portugal and especially Spain still retain collectively a distant-water fleet of some size. On the other hand, the middle-water and inshore fleets have increased in recent years: inshore fishing is particulary important in Greece, Ireland, Italy and parts of Denmark, France, Portugal, Spain and the United Kingdom. These differences in fleet structure largely account for differences in productivity between Member States: thus, for example, Portugal with 16% of the Community fishing fleet (by tonnage) and 12% of Community fishermen accounts for only 3.8% of the Community catch by weight and 4.2% by value. The main consequences of different fleet structures as far as Community policy-making is concerned are, first, in deciding which type of fleet should have preferential access to the Community's fishery resources (the resource base being insufficient to support both the distant-water and near-water and inshore fleets in their totality), and, secondly, which fleets are to be the major beneficiaries of the Community's limited resources for restructuring – distant-water vessels requiring aid for conversion, laying-up or scrapping, or smaller vessels which require aid for modernisation.

Another area of difference in the Community's fishing industries relates to catches. First of all there are differences in the species of chief interest to the various Member States due to differences in fishing traditions, species availability and consumer preference. Thus, for example, British fishermen are particularly interested in white fish, such as cod, haddock and whiting; West Germany, alone of Member States, has a major interest in redfish; while in the southern part of the Community France and Spain are major fishers of tuna and Portugal and Spain of sardines. Such differences of interest have important implications both for marketing and trade and for management. As far as marketing and trade are concerned, differences of interest over species are likely to produce different views between Member States as to which species are most in need of price support arrangements and protective trading measures (as will be seen in Chapters 7 and 8). In relation to management, differences of interest between Member States become particularly significant when it comes to the Community regulating a multi-species fishery because, as was hinted above, in such a fishery one cannot set MSY as a management goal for all the species in the fishery: for some species the level of fishing will have to be very much less than the MSY. Such a problem can be seen – and has been particularly acute – in relation to an area of the northern North Sea where Denmark wishes to catch Norway pout for reduction to fish meal and oil (used particularly in the manufacture of animal feedstuffs and margarine – such so-called industrial fishing forms a very high proportion of the activities of the Danish fishing industry). However, because of the species mix in this area the Danes cannot fish for Norway pout without at the same time inevitably (because of the small mesh nets that industrial fishing requires) also catching significant quantities of immature cod and haddock. The United Kingdom, with a prime interest in these species, wishes to see Danish industrial fishing curtailed in this area in order to conserve the cod and haddock by allowing them to reach maturity and reproduce. Thus the Community, as the fisheries manager in this area, has to choose between allowing a high catch of Norway pout, thus giving effect to Danish interests, or curtailing fishing for Norway pout in order to conserve immature cod and haddock in the interests of British fishermen.

The differences in the species composition of the catches of the various Member States mean that there are significant differences in the value of each Member State's catch, as some species (e.g. sole, tuna, shellfish) fetch a much higher price than other species. Within the Community the value of the catch ranges from US $1970 per tonne in Greece to US $189 per tonne in Denmark (because the industrial species caught by Denmark have a low value).[13] Thus the weight of a Member State's catch is not necessarily proportionate to its value: for example, Italy accounts for 17.4% of the total Community catch by value, but only 6.6% by weight.

Finally there are differences in the fishing grounds of interest to Member States. Although there has been a great decline (as already mentioned) in access to the distant-water grounds off third States, some of these grounds still remain of some significance. France, West Germany and the United Kingdom still fish off Canada, Greenland, the Faroes and Norway; France, Italy, Portugal and Spain off West Africa and in the Indian Ocean; while Portugal and Spain (unlike other Member States) still retain a presence in many third State's waters through joint ventures. These differences of interest obviously affect the varying emphasis which different Member States place on negotiations over access with third States and with which third States (as will be seen in Chapter 5). For most Community vessels, however, it is the Community's own waters which are the main or exclusive area of interest, but here again there are differences of interest, both as to areas and within areas. The North-East Atlantic and North Sea are of no interest to Greece and Italy but of major or sole interest to the other Member States, while the Mediterranean is of interest only to France, Greece, Italy and Spain. Within the North-East Atlantic and North Sea there are differences of interest in particular areas, which are especially important as regards the fishing zones of individual Member States. Thus, for example, while France and the Netherlands take about 60% of their catches in the zones of other Member States, the United Kingdom takes less than 1%. Such differences affect the differing interest Member States will show in the need for management in different areas and over access arangements in such areas.

In studying the fishing industries of the EEC, it is necessary to know not only about the diversity of interests between and within Member States but also to appreciate that over the past decade or so the fishing industries in the EEC have been subject to a number of significant (and largely external) developments.[14] First, as already mentioned, the general world-wide introduction of 200-mile fishing limits in the late 1970s deprived EEC distant-water fleets of many of their traditional fishing grounds. While it is true that this loss has to some extent been offset by the gains resulting from the extension of EEC Member States' own fishing limits, these losses and gains do not neatly cancel each other out, not only because the sizes of catch for each are not the same, but also because different species are involved. The distant-water losses relate largely to demersal fish such as cod and haddock, whereas the near-water gains relate to commercially less valuable pelagic fish, such as mackerel, or to fish hitherto not having much commercial potential, such as blue whiting. Furthermore, distant-water vessels which have lost their traditional fishing grounds are not always easily adapted for fishing in near waters, nor is their use for such fishing usually economic. Secondly, the enormous increase in the price of oil since 1973 has dramatically increased the operating costs of fishing vessels, fishing being a very energy-intensive industry: for some vessels fuel represents about half of their running costs.[15] Another development is the overfishing that has taken place since the mid-1960s for many stocks in EEC waters, notably herring, as a result of the introduction of more technologically advanced methods of fishing. The decline in the size of many stocks means that the catch rates of most vessels have been reduced to well below the most economic levels. Then there has been a reduction in the demand for fish: fish consumption per head in the EEC (apart from Portugal and Spain) has been steadily declining since the 1950s. The uncertainty of supplies of fish resulting from the extension of limits and overfishing, coupled with a deline in demand, has led to fluctuating prices. The quayside price of fish has often been very low for long periods, especially at the end of the 1970s and beginning of the 1980s, while to the chagrin of fishermen, the retail price of fish has been very much higher, suggesting – at least to the fishermen – that the middlemen are making an unacceptably large profit. The fishermen's problems of low prices and high costs have been aggravated since 1979 by a flood of cheap, probably heavily-subsidised imports from countries outside the EEC, notably Canada, Iceland, Norway and the Faroes. Such imports have been encouraged by tariff reductions granted under various agreements with the Community (see Chapter 8) and the trend in marketing towards frozen or processed products; and in the case of the United Kingdom, in particular, by the high value of sterling during the early 1980s which made the British market a very attractive one.

These developments, all of which have unfortunately occurred over the same period of time, have led to serious difficulties, of varying degrees of intensity, for all sections of the EEC fishing industry. These difficulties have been exacerbated by the problems of adapting the original Common Fisheries Policy to the world of 200-mile limits. At the same time, and perhaps paradoxically, these difficulties have also, together with the diversity of Member States' fishery interests, been a major cause of the tortuous and protracted evolution of the Common Fisheries Policy and its accompanying body of law, which we must now turn to trace.

3. THE EVOLUTION OF THE COMMON FISHERIES POLICY AND EEC FISHERIES LAW[16]

The Treaty establishing the EEC not only authorises but actually requires the adoption of a Common Fisheries Policy. Articles 38–43 of the Treaty (discussed in more detail in the next Chapter) lay down the broad framework for the Policy and the legislation implementing it. These Treaty articles also provide that a Policy should be adopted by the Council, acting on a proposal from the Commission and after consulting the European Parliament and Economic and Social Committee, by the end of the transitional period for implementing the Treaty, i.e. December 31, 1969. Although the EEC Treaty was signed in 1958, it was not until 1966 that the Commission, prompted by the strains imposed on the then uncompetitive and inefficient French and Italian fishing industries by the increased liberalisation of trade in fish products which resulted from the progressive establishment of the EEC customs union and tariff reductions in GATT, took the first step towards the adoption of a Common Fisheries Policy by publishing a 'Report on the Situation in the Fisheries Sector of EEC Member States and the Basic Principles for a Common Policy'.[17] This Report was followed up two years later by the Commission with proposals for regulations (which were considerably less ambitious than the Commission's suggestions in its 1966 Report, notably by omitting all concern with social policy), and these proposals were adopted by the Council, after considerable debate, in October 1970. The measures adopted comprised two regulations.[18] The first dealt with what is known in the Community jargon as structural policy (that is, broadly speaking, the catching side of the fishing industry). It laid down what subsequently became the controversial principle of equal access for the fishing vessels of one Member State to the maritime zones of any other Member State. Further, it empowered the Council to adopt the necessary conservation measures to prevent a risk of over-fishing in Member States' maritime zones; promoted the co-ordination of Member States' structural policies; and provided for Community financial aid to be given for the restructuring of fishing fleets. The second regulation established a common organisation of the market in fishery products, the aim of which was to encourage the rational marketing of fishery products and ensure market stability. The common organisation of the market had five principal elements: a common pricing system; common marketing standards (whose aim was to improve the quality of fish marketed); encouraging the formation of producers' organisations (to operate the common pricing system and carry out marketing on their members' behalf); the right of equal access to any EEC port for the purpose of landing catches; and rules on trade with third States.

There is little doubt that agreement on these two regulations in the Council was hastened by the then impending first enlargement of the Community. It was desirable for the existing Member States to adopt a common position before negotiations with the four applicant States began, particularly as the latter had very different and much greater fisheries interests than the existing Member States. These differences of interest meant that the negotiations over the adaptation of the regulations to the applicant Member States were particularly tough. It was the failure to secure better terms which was one of the main reasons why a majority of Norwegians voted against EEC membership in their referendum. Nevertheless, the negotiations did lead to a number of minor changes to the Marketing Regulation and a major modification to the Structural Regulation. The latter concerns the equal access principle (the most contentious issue in the negotiations). Articles 100–103 of the Act of Accession provided that for a 10-year period (until the end of 1982) the equal access principle was not to apply to the 6-mile zone off Member States (extended in some areas to a 12-mile zone), although previous access to such waters obtained by virtue of historic rights was maintained. On the basis of a report from the Commission, the Council was to determine the regime which should follow the expiry of this 10-year derogation at the end of 1982.

In the event, the need for revision of the Common Fisheries Policy arose long before 1982 and was much more far-reaching than was contemplated by the Act of Accession. The reason for this was the move to extend existing fishing limits from 12 to 200 miles which a number of North Atlantic States (Canada, the USA, Iceland and Norway) began to undertake in 1976, prompted by the failures of the two international fishery commissions for the North Atlantic and the strong trend at the UN Conference on the Law of the Sea towards agreement on the 200-mile economic zone (see the discussion at p. 6 above).

The extension of limits off Iceland, the USA, Canada and Norway meant the closure of, or at least a reduction in fishing activities in, some of the most important distant-water fishing grounds for EEC vessels. Vessels from other States, too, were similarly affected, and there was a strong likelihood that such vessels would divert their activities to areas of the North Atlantic not subject to 200-mile limits, notably the waters off EEC Member States. Since most fish stocks in these waters were already fully exploited, there would have been a serious danger of over-fishing resulting. The Commission therefore began to consider how such a danger might be averted. From as early as the end of 1974, the Commission had published a series of reports,[19] examining the implications of the general introduction of 200-mile fishing limits for the Community.

In September 1976 the Commission produced a comprehensive package of proposals and forwarded them to the Council.[20] These proposals had four main elements. First, the Commission proposed that the Council should adopt a resolution calling on EEC Member States in concert to extend their fishing limits to 200 miles in the North Sea and North Atlantic from the beginning of 1977. The Commission felt this step was essential, first, to counter the threat of third States' fleets being diverted to Community waters, with the consequent danger of over-fishing, and secondly, to give the Community a better bargaining position to negotiate access arrangements for Community vessels to the waters of those States that had already extended their limits to 200 miles. The Commission's second proposal was that it, rather than the individual Member States, should negotiate with third States over the access of the latter's vessels to EEC Member States' 200-mile limits and the access of EEC vessels to third States' 200-mile limits (from which nearly a third of Community catches had come). In addition, the Commission proposed that the Community should replace individual Member States in membership of international fishery commissions. The Commission therefore requested the Council for the necessary negotiating mandate. Thirdly, the Commission proposed a draft Regulation to establish a system of Community management for the fishery resources within the 200-mile zones of Member States.[21] While the Commission proposed that the principle of equal access should apply to the waters embraced by Member States' 200-mile limits, it recognised that if overfishing were not to result, the principle needed to be accompanied by an effective conservation policy, since many of the fish stocks were fully or over-exploited. Finally, the Commission noted that the developments in fishing limits described above meant that the EEC fishing fleet contained more vessels than were required for taking available fish catches in EEC waters, as well as many distant-water vessels which no longer had any distant-water fishing open to them. The Commission therefore recommended that measures should be adopted to rationalise the EEC fishing fleet with the twofold aim of reducing its then catching capacity so as to conserve stocks and adapting the distant-water fleet (or at least part of it) for fishing in EEC waters.

Of these four sets of proposals, the Council quickly agreed on the first two. As far as the extension of fishing limits is concerned, the Council on November 3, 1976 adopted a Resolution which called on EEC Member States to extend their limits to 200 miles in concert on January 1, 1977.[22] In this Resolution the Council also gave the Commission its requested mandate to enter into negotiations with third States over the question of access to limits. The Commission has engaged in negotiations with over 25 States, with about half of whom agreements have so far been signed. In addition, the Community has become a member of a number of international fishery commisions. These matters are discussed in detail in Chapter 5.

It was the third element of the Commission's package of proposals that proved most difficult for the Council to agree on. Not until January 1983 did the Council agree on a revised version of the Commission's proposal for a Community system to manage fish stocks in EEC waters.[23] The main reason why it took the Council $5\frac{1}{2}$ years and more than 60 meetings before agreement was reached was, in general terms, the fact that there were insufficient fish available in Community waters to satisfy the catching capacity of Community vessels, and in particular because of the position taken by the United Kingdom. Motivated by its losses in the waters of third States, the fact that about 60 per cent of EEC fishery resources are found in its 200-mile limit, and the fact that fishermen from other Member States had far greater interests in its waters that its fishermen had in the waters of other Member States, the United Kingdom sought first an exclusive limit wider (though how much wider was never precisely specified) than the 12 miles proposed by the Commission, and when this appeared an unfruitful negotiating position, a higher share of the total allowable catch in Community waters than was being proposed by the Commission and a reduction of access to its 12-mile zone on the basis of historic rights. Eventually agreement on these two matters was finally reached. What undoubtedly acted as a powerful incentive in the later stages to reach agreement was the fact that at the end of 1982 the 10-year derogation to the equal access principle introduced by the Act of Accession was due to expire: the United Kingdom (and indeed several other Member States) had no desire to see unrestricted application of the equal access principle.

The Community management system has a number of elements. First, the Council each year establishes total allowable catches for the main stocks in Community waters, and divides them up into quotas allocated to each Member State. Secondly, there is a set of long-term conservation measures, including rules on closed seasons, closed areas, by-catches, minimum fish sizes and gear restrictions. Thirdly, a 12-mile exclusive national zone in derogation from the equal access principle has been laid down until at least 1992. Finally there are provisions aimed at securing effective observance of these measures.[24]

The fourth, and final, element of the Commission's package of proposals of September 1976, it will be recalled, was that structural measures to rationalise EEC fishing fleets should be adopted. In 1978 the Council adopted an interim programme for restructuring the inshore fishing industry.[25] Negotiations over long-term and more comprehensive restructuring measures, however, became linked to the negotiations over the Community management system. Thus it was not until October 1983 that the Council adopted the Commission's proposals.[26] Under these measures 250 million ECUs have been allocated to the laying-up and scrapping of vessels, modernising vessels, encouraging fishing in new areas and for new species, encouraging joint ventures with companies from third States, and developing aquaculture.

The extension of fishing limits to 200 miles by EEC Member States and many other States has altered the pattern of Community catches (as explained above). In 1978 the Commission began a review of the implications of this change for the marketing side of the Common Fisheries Policy, as well as a study of what other changes might be desirable to the common organisation of the market in fishery products as a result of experience gained from its operation in practice. In 1980 the Commission published its proposals for revision of the Regulation on the Common Organisation of the Market in Fishery Products.[27] The Commission was of the view that the basic form of the common organisation of the market was satisfactory, but that some changes of detail were required. These changes were adopted by the Council in December 1981 in a revised Regulation on the Common Organisation of the Market in Fishery Products.[28] The main changes made to existing marketing arrangements by the new Regulation, which came fully into operation on January 1, 1983, concerned arrangements to reduce the amount of fish withdrawn from the market, strengthening the role of producers' organisations and making the measures to protect Community fishermen from imports both more efficient and more flexible.

The Community has recently completed its second enlargement, Greece having become a member at the beginning of 1981 and Portugal and Spain at the beginning of 1986. Greece's accession posed few problems as far as fisheries were concerned because of the small size of the Greek fishing industry and because Greek vessels fish very little in the maritime zones of other Member States or in other areas where those States' vessels fish. With the expiry of a few transitional arrangements contained in the Greek Act of Accession, Greece is now fully integrated into the Common Fisheries Policy. In the case of Portugal and Spain, however, the situation has been very different because of the size of their fishing industries – the Spanish fleet being nearly three-quarters of the size of the combined fishing fleets of the 10 already existing Member States – and because their vessels fish – or wish to fish – many of the same grounds as the existing Member States. Not surprisingly, therefore, fisheries were one of the toughest issues in the entry negotiations, and the Act of Accession[29] contains some 50 pages dealing with fisheries questions. While in principle the *acquis communautaire* of the Common Fisheries Policy applies to Portugal and Spain, the special arrangements for the two new members are so extensive that in reality it will be many years before they are fully integrated into the Policy. Thus the access of Portuguese and Spanish vessels to the 200-mile zones of other Member States is on a restricted scale until 2002 (though some adjustments may be made after 1995), and it will be 1996 before Portugal and Spain are fully integrated into the common organisation of the market.

EEC fisheries law has now entered a period of consolidation. With the adoption of the basic management and structural regulations in 1983 and the revised marketing regulation in 1981, and no further enlargement of the Community in prospect, EEC fisheries legislation for the next few years is likely to consist largely of routine implementation of the basic regulations and the progressive adaptation of Portugal and Spain to the Common Fisheries Policy. Even so, as in many other fields, one must not underestimate the capacity of the Community remorselessly to churn out legislation: thus, for example, during the first six months of 1986 over 60 pieces of fisheries legislation were adopted, most of it, not unnaturally, of short-term interest.

4. THE APPLICATION OF GENERAL COMMUNITY LAW TO FISHERIES

As has been seen, since 1970 a substantial body of EEC law dealing specifically with fisheries has been developed. It is important to realise, however, that the general body of EEC law, particularly its provisions relating to the establishment of a common market, applies to fisheries, just as it does to any other sector of the economy. Only to the extent that specific rules are laid down in the EEC Treaty's articles on fisheries and implementing legislation adopted thereunder which derogate from the general provisions of the Treaty, do the latter not apply to fisheries.[30] It may be useful, therefore, to conclude this Chapter by giving an outline sketch of the more important provisions of the EEC Treaty, and explaining how they apply to fisheries.

Free Movement of Goods. Articles 9–37 of the EEC Treaty provide for the free movement of goods between Member States by eliminating customs duties and quantitative restrictions on trade between Member States, and establish a common customs tariff in trade with third States. The way in which these provisions apply to trade in fisheries products is discussed in Chapter 8.

Free Movement of Workers. Under Articles 48–51 nationals of one Member State are free to move to another Member State and take up offers of employment there: in addition, they must not be discriminated against because of their nationality in relation to the conditions of their employment.[31] Thus a fisherman of one Member State is free to move, with his family, and take up employment as a fishermen in another Member State.[32]

Right of Establishment. Under Articles 52–58 self-employed nationals of one Member State have the right to establish themselves in another Member State under the same conditions as nationals of the latter State. Similarly, companies of one Member State have the right to establish subsidiaries in another Member State.[33] These rights are facilitated by the provisions on free movement of capital (Articles 67–73). Thus a self-employed fisherman in one Member State is free to move to another Member State and set himself up in business as a fisherman there, subject to any rules which the latter State has laid down for its own nationals wishing to set up business as self-employed fishermen. Likewise a fishing company in one Member State may establish a subsidiary in another Member State, subject again to any relevant, non-discriminatory local legislation.[34]

Freedom to Provide Services. Articles 59–66 provide that an individual or company established in one Member State is free to provide services in another Member State.[35] This freedom would seem to have a limited application to activities connected with fishing. It would apply to such matters as trans-frontier activities of fish wholesalers and retailers (insofar as these activities were not covered by the Treaty provisions on free movement of goods), the chartering of fishing vessels by a company established in one Member State to a company in another Member State, and consultancy work done by an individual or company established in one Member State for an individual or company in another Member State.

Given the traditionally localised nature of much of the fishing industry, the fact that there is over-capacity in virtually every Member State's fishing industry and the principle of equal access under the Common Fisheries Policy, it seems unlikely that much use will be made in practice, or indeed has already been made, of the freedoms of movement, establishment and services, either by individual fishermen or by fishing companies.

NOTES

1. This, at least, is the position in modern law in all Western legal systems. It is possible that at other times and in other places the position has been and is different.
2. What follows is a very brief and simplified account. For full treatment, see – among a voluminous literature – F.T. Christy and A. Scott, *The Common Wealth in Ocean Fisheries,* Baltimore, 1965; C. Clark, *Bioeconomic Modelling and Fisheries Management,* Chichester, 1985; S. Cunningham, M.R. Dunn and D. Whitmarsh, *Fisheries Economics: An Introduction,* London, 1985; H.G. Knight, *Managing the Sea's Living Resources,* Lexington, 1977; A.W. Koers, *International Regulation of Marine Fisheries,* London, 1973; Chap. 1; and J-P. Troadec *Introduction to Fisheries Management: Advantages, Difficulties and Mechanisms,* FAO Fisheries Technical Paper 224, Rome, 1983.
3. See G. Hardin, 'The Tragedy of the Commons' (1968) 162 Science 1243.
4. The MEY for a fishery is in fact as difficult to calculate as the MSY. Apart from the same problems of the inter-relationship of stocks and possible inadequacy of data, the MEY also depends on the price at which the fish caught are sold and the unit costs of fishing, both of which vary over time and place.
5. The discussion which follows must inevitably be of the briefest. For a fuller treatment, see – again from a large literature – Knight, *op. cit.* in n. 2, and R.R. Churchill and A.V. Lowe, *The Law of the Sea,* Manchester, 1983, especially Chap. 13.
6. As was acknowledged by the International Court of Justice in the *Case concerning the Continental Shelf (Libya/Malta)* [1985] ICJ Rep. 13 at 33.
7. For a detailed account, see M. Wise, *The Common Fisheries Policy of the European Community,* London, 1984, Chap. 2.
8. Anon., *The European Community's Fishery Policy,* Luxembourg, 1985, European Documentation Series No 1/1985, p. 72. The figures are for 1981.
9. On this point, see also M. Shackleton, 'Fishing for a Policy? The Common Fisheries Policy of the Community' in H. Wallace, W. Wallace and C. Webb (eds.), *Policy-Making in the European Community,* Chichester, 1983, p. 349 at 353–4.
10. G. Pontecorvo, 'The Impact of the Law of the Sea Treaty on the Organisation of World Fishereis: Some Preliminary Observations on Production' in E.D. Brown and R.R. Churchill (eds.) *The U.N. Convention on the Law of the Sea: Impact and Implementation* (forthcoming). The catches of the other Member States were as follows: Netherland 0.48 million tonnes; Italy 0.43; West Germany 0.29; Portugal 0.25; Ireland 0.22; Greece 0.09; and Belgium 0.05.
11. OECD, *Review of Fisheries in OECD Member Countries 1984,* Paris, 1985, p. 56.
12. *Ibid.,* p. 60.
13. *Ibid.,* p. 56. The figures are for 1984.
14. For a fuller account, see J. Farnell and J. Elles, *In Search of a Common Fisheries Policy,* Aldershot, 1984, pp. 159–166.
15. House of Lords Select Committee on the European Communities, *EEC Fisheries Policy,* HL Paper (1979–80) 251, p. 123.

16. What follows is the briefest of surveys. For detailed accounts, see M. Leigh, *European Integration and the Common Fisheries Policy,* Beckenham, 1983; Wise, *op. cit.* in n. 7; and Farnell and Elles, *op. cit.* in n. 14. Shorter, but useful accounts an Shackleton, *op. cit.* in n. 9 and D. Freestone and A. Fleisch, 'The Common Fisheries Policy' in J. Lodge (ed.), *Institutions and Policies of the European Community,* London, 1983, pp. 77–84.

17. COM (66) 250, substantially reproduced in J.O. 1967, p. 862.

18. Reg. 2141/70 laying down a Common Structural Policy for the Fishing Industry and Reg. 2142/70 on the Common Organisation of the Market in Fishery Products, O.J.S. Ed. 1970 (III) pp. 703 and 707. These two Regs. were replaced by consolidating Regs. with the same titles in 1976 – Regs. 100/76 and 101/76, O.J. 1976 L20/1 and 19.

19. SEC(74)4400; SEC(75)3132; SEC(75)4503; and COM(76)59.

20. COM(76)500.

21. The text of the draft regulation is not in COM(76)500, but in O.J. 1976 C255/3.

22. O.J. 1981 C105/1. The extension of limits is discussed in more detail in Chapter 3.

23. In the period up to 1983 fishing in the Community's 200-mile limit was governed by a mixture of short-term Community conservation measures, a series of injunctions from the Council that Member States conduct their fishing activities in such a way as to take into account the Commission's proposals on total allowable catches, and a host of conservation measures adopted by Member States.

24. See Regs. 170 and 171/83. O.J. 1983 L24/1 and 14; and Reg. 2057/82, O.J. 1982 L220/1 – discussed in detail in Chapter 4.

25. Reg. 1852/78, O.J. 1978 L211/30.

26. Regs. 2908/83 and 2909/83, and Dir. 83/515, O.J. 1983 L290/1, 9 and 15 – discussed in detail in Chapter 6.

27. COM(80)540 and 724.

28. Reg. 3796/81, O.J. 1981 L379/1 – discussed in detail in Chapters 7 and 8.

29. O.J. 1985 L302/1.

30. Art. 38(2) of the EEC Treaty. See also Case 48/74, *Charmasson v. Minister for Economic Affairs and Finance* [1974] E.C.R. 1383 at 1393; [1975] 2 C.M.L.R. 208 at 224.

31. For extended treatment of this topic, see T.C. Hartley, *EEC Immigration Law,* Amsterdam, 1978, especially Chapters 4 and 5; and D. Wyatt and A Dashwood, *The Substantive Law of the EEC,* London, 1980, Chapters 13 and 14.

32. For the implications of Community Law relating to the free movements of workers for seafarers generally, see A.E. Bredimas, 'The Common Shipping Policy of the EEC' (1981) 18 C.M.L. Rev. 9 at 17–19.

33. For extended treatment of this topic, see Hartley, *loc. cit.* in n. 31; and Wyatt and Dashwood, *op. cit.* in n. 31, Chapter 15.

34. Problems might, however, arise in relation to the registration and nationality of fishing vessels: see Bredimas, *op. cit.* in n. 32, p. 21.

35. See n. 33.

CHAPTER 2

Community law-making in the fisheries sector: legal basis and legislative process

Having given a brief overview in the latter part of the previous Chapter of the main elements of EEC fisheries law, we turn in this Chapter to examine the processes by which that law is made. This examination covers both the making of legislation by the political institutions of the European Communities and judicial law-making by the European Court of Justice.

First, however, it is necessary to consider the legal basis for EEC fisheries law and a Common Fisheries Policy. This is because it is a fundamental feature of the legal system of the European Communities that the Community institutions can only adopt Community policies and legislation where, and to the extent that, the founding Community treaties so authorise: the founding treaties in the case of fisheries are the EEC Treaty and possibly also the 1972 Treaty of Accession. This fundamental rule is stated in Article 4(1) of the EEC Treaty,[1] and is reinforced by Articles 173, 177 and 184 of the EEC Treaty, under which the European Court of Justice must annul or declare invalid legislative acts of the Commission and Council which under the Treaty those bodies lack the competence to adopt. Further effect is given to the rule by Article 190, which requires all legislative acts adopted by the Commission and the Council to 'state the reasons on which they are based': these reasons include the provision or provisions of the Treaty on which the act in question is based.[2] Failure to state such reasons is a violation of an essential procedural requirement,[3] which is a further ground for the annulment or invalidity of Community legislation under Articles 173, 177 and 184.

It follows from these principles, therefore, that a Common Fisheries Policy and Community fisheries law can only be adopted if the founding treaties so authorise, and that the content of this Policy and law will be broadly determined and circumscribed by the provisions of these treaties. Thus we must turn to see whether the founding treaties do authorise the adoption of a Common Fisheries Policy and fisheries law, and if so, what they provide as to the range and content of such a Policy and law.

1. THE LEGAL BASIS FOR A COMMON FISHERIES POLICY AND EEC FISHERIES LAW

At first glance, it is not obvious that there is any provision in the EEC Treaty that could form the legal basis for a common fisheries policy or for fisheries legislation, since no article of the Treaty is overtly concerned with fisheries. On closer examination of the Treaty, however, it becomes clear that the legal basis for a common fisheries policy is to be found in the provisions of the Treaty dealing with agriculture.

After providing in Article 3(d) that the activities of the Community shall include 'the adoption of a common policy in the sphere of agriculture,' the Treaty goes on, in Articles 38–47, to spell out what this involves. Article 38(1) lays down that 'the common market shall extend to agriculture and trade in agricultural products'. 'Agricultural products' are defined as 'products of the soil, of stockfarming and of fisheries and products of first-stage processing directly related to these products.' In other words, the common market extends to trade in fisheries products. The Treaty goes on, in Article 38(3), to provide that the products listed in Annex II of the Treaty are subject to the provisions of Articles 39–46. The products listed in Annex II include fish, crustaceans and molluscs. It therefore follows that fish are subject to Articles 39–46 of the Treaty. These articles are concerned with four major matters: the common agricultural policy, the common organisation of agricultural markets, competition rules and trade.[4]

Article 38(4) provides that a common agricultural policy is to be developed by the Community institutions to accompany the operation and development of the common market for agricultural products. The objectives of the common agricultural policy are set out in Article 39(1). They are as follows:

a) to increase agricultural productivity by promoting technical progress and by ensuring the rational development of agricultural production and the optimum utilisation of the factors of production, in particular labour;
b) thus to ensure a fair standard of living for the agricultural community, in particular by increasing the individual earnings of persons engaged in agriculture;
c) to stabilise markets;
d) to assure the availability of supplies;
e) to ensure that supplies reach consumers at reasonable prices.

In working out the common agricultural policy and the special methods for its application, account is to be taken of:

a) the particular nature of agricultural activity, which results from the social structure of agriculture and from structural and natural disparities between the various agricultural regions;

b) the need to effect the appropriate adjustments by degrees;
c) the fact that in the Member States agriculture constitutes a sector closely linked with the economy as a whole. (Article 39(2)).

In addition, Article 41 provides that in order for the objectives set out in Article 39 to be attained, provision may be made within the framework of the common agricultural policy for such measures as effective co-ordination of efforts in the spheres of vocational training, research and the dissemination of agricultural knowledge, and joint measures to promote consumption of certain products.

As has been pointed out, Articles 39 *et seq.* apply to fisheries. The objectives and guidelines of the common agricultural policy, spelt out in Article 39(1) and (2), thus apply equally as the objectives and guidelines of a common fisheries policy. This may give rise to difficulties. The objectives set out in Article 39 have clearly been framed with agriculture, rather than fisheries, in mind, and it is not easy to see exactly how all of them may apply to fisheries. Take objective (a), for example. Productivity in fisheries, in the sense of increasing the catch per vessel, can certainly be increased. This can be done in the short term by reducing the number of fishing vessels operating. It can also be done in the longer term by building up depleted fish stocks; but measures to build up stocks may result in a temporary decline in existing productivity. Which method of increasing productivity does Article 39 have in mind, especially if a choice has to be made between them? Put another way, does 'rational' in Article 39(1) refer to biological rationality or economic rationality, i.e. is it concerned with Maximum Sustainable Yield or Maximum Economic Yield (cf. the discussion at pp. 4–5 above)? If the emphasis in objective (a) is biological rationality, then the objective in (b) – a fair standard of living for fishermen – may not be met. On the other hand, if the objective is economic rationality, it is likely that only certain fishermen (those whose vessels are not withdrawn from a fishery) will enjoy a fair standard of living. Again, objective (a) refers to increasing productivity by 'promoting technical progress'. Yet it is clear, as recent fishing history shows only too well, that technical progress, in the form of improvements in fishing gear and methods, can, if not sufficiently regulated, lead to overfishing and therefore a decline in productivity.[5] Objectives (c) to (e) raise fewer difficulties, and considered in isolation should be capable of fairly straightforward application to fisheries. However, objective (d) (assuring availability of supplies) might conflict with objective (a) if, as suggested, the latter can be interpreted as authorising a temporary decline in productivity in order to build up depleted fish stocks. Other conflicts between the objectives are possible e.g. between (c) (stabilising markets) and (e) (reasonable prices for consumers). The question of conflicts between the different objectives listed in Article 39(1) has been considered by the European Court of Justice, which has said that the Community institutions must seek to resolve any conflict between objectives, but where necessary they may allow one objective to have temporary priority.[6]

Just as the objectives of the common agricultural policy have been framed with agriculture rather than fisheries in mind, so too have the guidelines for working out the policy, set out in Article 39(2). Guidelines (a) and (b) are clearly directed at the problems of small, inefficient farms and farms in areas not naturally favourable to agriculture: it is difficult to see, however, exactly how they relate to fishing, though some comparison can perhaps be made between inshore fishing in certain parts of Scotland and Ireland, for example, and small, inefficient farms.

However the objectives and guidelines in Article 39 are interpreted in the context of fisheries, it is clear that the Community institutions in formulating a common fisheries policy are given a very wide set of objectives and guidelines within which to regulate fisheries. A more precise ambit of these powers will be suggested in later chapters, particularly in Chapter 4.

The second major matter with which Articles 39–46 of the Treaty are concerned, is the common organisation of agricultural markets. According to Article 40(2), a common organisation of agricultural markets is to be established in order to attain the objectives of the common agricultural policy. The expression 'common organisation of the market' is nowhere defined in the Treaty, and it may not be immediately obvious what it means. The European Court of Justice has defined an 'organisation of the market' as being 'a combination of legal institutions and measures on the basis of which appropriate authorities seek to control and regulate the market';[7] and has defined a 'common organisation of the market' as being an organisation of the market which provides 'safeguards for the standard of living of the producers concerned, contains arrangements designed to guarantee national producers a market for their product and ensures conditions for trade within the Community similar to those existing in a national market'.[8]

The exact form each organisation of agricultural markets is to take is left open in the EEC Treaty, but certain guidelines are laid down. First, the organisation must take one of the following forms, depending on the product concerned: common rules on competition; the compulsory co-ordination of the various national market organisations; or a European market organisation (Article 40(2)). In practice the last form of organisation has always been adopted. Secondly, the organisation may cover the regulation of prices, aids for production and marketing, storage and carry-over arrangements, and common machinery for stabilising imports and exports. Thirdly, the organisation may not go beyond the objectives of the common agricultural policy. Fourthly, it shall exclude any discrimination between producers and consumers in the Community. Fifthly, any common price policy shall be based on common criteria and uniform methods of calculation (Article 40(3)). In order to enable the common organisation to attain its objectives, one or more agricultural guidance and guarantee funds may be set up (Article 40(4)): in fact only one such fund has been established.

The power to establish a common organisation of the market in replacement for national organisations of the market may only be exercised, first, if the common organisation offers Member States which are opposed to it and which have a national organisation for the product in question equivalent safeguards for employment and the standard of living of the producers concerned; and, secondly, if the common organisation ensures conditions for trade within the Community similar to those existing in a national market (Article 43(3)). In fact, as was seen in the previous Chapter, a common organisation of the market for fishery products was established in 1970.

The third major concern of the articles of the Treaty dealing with agriculture is competition. Under Article 42 the Council is to determine how the competition rules in the Treaty are to apply to the production of and trade in agricultural products, taking into account the objectives of the common agricultural policy. In particular, the Council may authorise the granting of aid 'for the protection of enterprises handicapped by structural or natural conditions [or] within the framework of economic development programmes'.

Finally, the agricultural articles of the Treaty deal with trade. As has been seen, the normal EEC rules on trade in principle apply to agricultural products. Articles 44–46 deal with the regulation of trade in agricultural products between Member States during the transitional period (i.e. up to December 31, 1969) or before a common organisation of the market has been established for the product in question. Since the transitional period has expired and a common organisation of the market has been established for fisheries, it is not necessary to consider the provisions of Articles 44–46 any further.

Summing up the provisions of Articles 38–46 as they apply to fisheries, we can say that these articles provide the Community institutions not only with the power,[9] but also with a duty, to establish a common fisheries policy within the objectives laid down in Article 39, to establish a common organisation of the market in fisheries products, and to determine how EEC competition rules should apply to the production of and trade in fisheries products. According to Article 40(1) a common fisheries policy should have been adopted by the end of the transitional period, i.e. December 31, 1969: in fact, as was seen in the previous Chapter, the policy was not adopted until nearly a year after this date.[10] Although Articles 38–46 endow the Community with the competence (and the duty) to regulate fisheries, it does not necessarily follow that the Member States have lost all competence in this area. At this stage it need only be noted that the exact division of competence varies from one area of substantive law to another: a more precise demarcation of competence between the Community and its Member States will be attempted in Chapters 4–8 when dealing with the various areas of substantive law.

Although the provisions of the Treaty dealing with agriculture form the main legal basis for EEC fisheries policy and legislation, the Community institutions have also in practice based some of their fisheries legislation on other provisions of the Treaty – namely Articles 7, 235 and 103. It is therefore necessary to consider each of these articles briefly.

Article 7 provides that:

> Within the scope of the application of this Treaty, and without prejudice to any special provisions contained therein, any discrimination on grounds of nationality shall be prohibited.
>
> The Council may, on a proposal from the Commission and after consulting the Assembly, adopt, by a qualified majority, rules designed to prohibit such discrimination.

Article 7 is used as one of the legal bases for the Regulation laying down a Common Structural Policy for the Fishing Industry, and the exact scope of the Article in the context of fisheries will be discussed when that Regulation is considered in Chapter 4.

Article 235 reads as follows:

> If action by the Community should prove necessary to attain, in the course of the operation of the common market, one of the objectives of the Community and this Treaty has not provided the necessary powers, the Council shall, acting unanimously on a proposal from the Commission and after consulting the Assembly, take appropriate measures.

As has already been seen, a common agricultural (fisheries) policy is one of the objectives of the Community. Article 235 can therefore be used to attain the common fisheries policy where there are insufficient powers elsewhere in the Treaty. It should be pointed out, however, that according to the European Court of Justice, Article 235 can be used only as a supplementary legal basis and applies only where the Treaty has not provided the necessary powers for the realisation of the object in view.[11] On the other hand, as far as the latter point is concerned, the Court has admitted implicitly that even where a legislative act could have been based on other provisions of the Treaty, Article 235 can nevertheless be used as a basis in the interests of legal certainty.[12] Like Article 7, Article 235 is one of the legal bases for the Regulation laying down a Common Structural Policy for the Fishing Industry, and further discussion of its use as a legal basis for the Common Fisheries Policy will be deferred to Chapter 4.

The final provision of the EEC Treaty which has been used in practice as a legal basis by the Community institutions for fisheries legislation is Article 103. This reads:

1. Member States shall regard their conjunctural policies as a matter of common concern. They shall consult each other and the Commission on the measures to be taken in the light of prevailing circumstances.
2. Without prejudice to any other procedures provided for in this Treaty, the Council may, acting unanimously on a proposal from the Commission, decide upon the measures appropriate to the situation.
3. Acting by a qualified majority on a proposal from the Commission, the Council shall, where required, issue any directives needed to give effect to the measures decided upon under paragraph 2.
4. The procedures provided for in this Article shall also apply if any difficulty should arise in the supply of certain products.

The term 'conjunctural policy' used in this Article means, broadly, short-term economic policy. The question has arisen whether Article 103 can be used as a legal basis for adopting measures in the sphere of agriculture. In three cases coming before the European Court in 1973 it was argued that a Council Regulation concerned with Monetary Compensatory Amounts adopted on the basis of Article 103 was invalid because this Article could not be used as a legal basis for agricultural measures: instead the Regulation should have been based on Articles 40 and 43. The Court rejected this argument. It held that while Article 103 referred to conjunctural policy and thus in principle did not relate to those areas already subject to common rules, such as agriculture, the Council was nevertheless entitled to base the Regulation in question on Article 103, rather than on Articles 40 and 43 which would have been the normal legal basis, since there was no provision in the common agricultural policy for the adoption of urgent measures of the kind required. It would have taken appreciably longer to have acted under Articles 40 and 43 because of the need to consult the European Parliament. The Court also held that the Council, when acting under Article 103(2), can adopt measures in any form and is not limited to directives.[13]

It would therefore seem to be clear that Article 103 can be used as a legal basis for fisheries measures, even though fisheries is subject to common rules, provided the situation is one of urgency, not permitting time for consultation with the European Parliament as is required under Article 43, and provided that the measures adopted are of an interim nature. Thus the use by the Council on numerous occasions between 1977 and 1983 of Article 103 as the legal basis for short-term conservation measures and for short-term access arrangements for third States to Community waters was perfectly legitimate.

Before we leave the question of the legal basis for a Community fisheries policy, it is necessary to discuss one provision of the 1972 Act of Accession which could be construed as possibly providing a legal basis for Community fisheries legislation.

This is Article 102. It reads as follows:

From the sixth year after Accession at the latest, the Council, acting on a proposal from the Commission, shall determine conditions for fishing with a view to ensuring protection of the fishing grounds and conservation of the biological resources of the sea.

The first point is whether Article 102, placed as it is among the transitional measures of the Act of Accession, is capable of having 'primary' status (i.e. being equivalent in status to an article of the EEC Treaty) and therefore of serving as a legal basis for Community action, or whether it is purely 'secondary' and therefore equivalent in status to a regulation, directive or decision. It would seem to follow from Articles 6–8 of the Act of Accession that those parts of the Act which relate to secondary legislation have secondary status, whereas those that do not and stand independently have primary status. Since Article 102 does not relate to secondary legislation, either expressly or implicitly,[14] it would therefore seem to have primary status.

Even if Article 102 has primary status, this does not necessarily mean that it can serve as a legal basis for Community fisheries legislation. It has been argued that Article 102 is not so much a grant of power as a provision setting out an obligation to be fulfilled within a specific time scale.[15] It is suggested that the reason why Article 102 cannot be considered as a legal basis for fisheries legislation is, first, because the intention in adding Article 102 to the Act of Accession was that a specific time limit should be laid down, rather than a new power conferred on the Community, and secondly, because Article 102 contains no decision-making procedure as is required in the case of provisions constituting a legal basis for Community institutions to act. In response to the first of these arguments, it may well be that this was the intention of the drafters of the Act of Accession. On the other hand, no records of the *travaux préparatoires* of the Act of Accession exist to verify this intention, nor, according to the modes of interpretation used by the European Court, is the intention of the drafters necessarily conclusive as to the meaning of a provision of the treaties of the European Communities. It is, however, true that Article 102 does not give the Council any powers which it does not already have on a broad reading of Article 43 of the EEC Treaty. As far as the second argument is concerned, while it is true that Treaty provisions conferring a power of action on the Council normally specify the method of voting to be used and consultation with the European Parliament and/or the Economic and Social

Committee, this is not always the case. There are provisions of the Treaty (e.g. Articles 49 and 128) which say nothing about the voting procedure, even though mention is made of consultation, and there is even one provision (Article 153) which says nothing about either consultation or voting procedure.

The main argument against the view that Article 102 is not a legal basis for fisheries legislation is the fact that the Council has actually cited Article 102 as the legal basis for a number of fishery regulations.[16]

The European Court has also pronounced on the status of Article 102 in a number of the fisheries cases that have come before it. Its observations are, however, somewhat equivocal. While in both the *Kramer*[17] and *Irish Fisheries* cases,[18] there seems to be a suggestion that Article 102 is a separate legal basis for fisheries legislation, in the *Cap Caval* case[19] the Court said that Article 102 'specifically confirmed' the powers given in Articles 38 *et seq.* of the EEC Treaty, thus implying perhaps that Article 102 is not an independent legal basis. A similar implication is suggested by the Court in *Commission v. United Kingdom*, where the Court said that the purpose of Article 102, which recognises the Community institutions' competence to regulate fishing, is to open 'a new transitional period within which the Council was required to introduce the necessary conservation measures.'[20]

The arguments as to whether Article 102 of the Act of Accession has the status of a provision giving the Community institutions the legal basis to adopt fisheries legislation are therefore rather finely balanced. However, it is not now necessary to come to a firm conclusion on this question. This is because Article 102 in its terms only has effect up until the 'sixth year after Accession at the latest', i.e. the end of 1978.[21] Therefore even if Article 102 was an independent legal basis, it was so only up until the end of 1978.

Finally, it is conceivable that Article 100 of the EEC Treaty could serve as a basis for some kinds of EEC fisheries legislation. This Article provides that 'the Council shall, acting unanimously on a proposal from the Commission, issue directives for the approximation of such provisions laid down by law, regulation or administrative action in Member States as directly affect the establishment or functioning of the Common Market.' In practice the Council has not yet made any use of Article 100 for the purposes of fisheries legislation, although one commentator has suggested that the Article could have been used to harmonise the breadth of Member States' fishing zones.[22]

The EEC Treaty, both in its provisions on agriculture and in some other provisions, authorises and indeed obligates the Community institutions to adopt a common fisheries policy and fisheries legislation. These Treaty provisions are, however, only a framework: they contain no specific regulations for fisheries, but instead confer authority on the Community institutions to adopt detailed rules within the guidelines laid down in the Treaty. The

Community institutions have therefore had to adopt, and will continue to have to adopt, detailed rules by means of the three types of legislative measure set out in Article 189 of the EEC Treaty – regulations, directives and decisions. A regulation is a legislative act of general application, which is binding in its entirety and directly applicable in all Member States. Normally Member States are not required to take any action to implement regulations, and indeed such implementation is generally regarded as impermissible by the European Court:[23] exceptionally, however, regulations do require implementing action to be taken by Member States,[24] and, more commonly, by Community institutions. A directive, by contrast, lays down in binding form on Member States a result to be achieved, but leaves it up to the national authorities of each Member State to determine the choice of form and methods by which that result is to be achieved: in other words, unlike regulations, directives are not directly applicable, but require some implementing action to be taken by Member States. Decisions are acts, often of an administrative rather than a legislative character, which are binding on the usually limited class of person to which they are addressed, whether Member States or natural or legal persons. Which type of measure – regulation, directive or decision – is selected for Community legislation will depend to a large extent on the nature and object of the rules to be laid down. Where it is desired to lay down precise, uniform rules, a regulation will be used. Where a more flexible, less standardised legal regime is desired, a directive will normally be the instrument chosen. Another important factor governing the choice of legislative instrument is whether the Treaty provision on which the legislative act is based contains any limitations on the type of legislative instrument which may be used. As can be seen from Table 1, only in the case of acts adopted under Article 103(3) (or Article 100, should that ever be used by the Council as the basis for fisheries legislation), where the Council is restricted to using directives, is there any limitation on the type of legislative instrument open to the Community institutions. In practice, the overwhelming majority of legislative acts relating to fisheries which have so far been adopted, have been in the form of regulations.

This leads naturally on to a discussion of the procedure by which regulations, directives and decisions relating to fisheries are adopted.

2. THE EEC'S LEGISLATIVE PROCESSES IN RELATION TO FISHERIES[25]

In general there is in the EEC no single process by which legislation is adopted. It depends in each case on the provisions of the article of the EEC Treaty conferring legislative competence. The position under each of the EEC Treaty provisions relevant to fisheries is shown in Table 1. Thus it can be seen

Table 1. Powers and procedures for EEC legislation relating to fisheries.

EEC treaty article	Subject matter	Form of the legislation	Enacting body	Voting procedure	Proposal from	To be consulted
Article 43(2)(3)	Common agricultural (fisheries) policy; Common organisation of the market in fishery products	Regulations, Directives or Decisions	Council	Qualified Majority	Commission	Economic and Social Committee (first stage only); European Parliament
Article 42	Application of competition rules to agriculture (and fisheries)	Regulations, Directives or Decisions	Council	Qualified Majority	Commission	European Parliament
Article 7	Prohibition of discrimination	Not specified	Council	Qualified Majority	Commission	European Parliament
Article 235	Action to attain Community objectives	Not specified	Council	Unanimity	Commission	European Parliament
Article 103	Short-term fishery measures	Art. 103(2): Not specified Art. 103(3): Directives	Council	Art. 103(2): Unanimity Art. 103(3): Qualified Majority	Commission	None

that in every instance the measure is to be adopted by the Council, either unanimously or by qualified majority, acting on a proposal from the Commission. In all cases except acts adopted under Article 103, the Council is required to consult the European Parliament before adopting the Commission's proposal: in addition, during the first stage (i.e. 1958–61) the Council was obliged to consult the Economic and Social Committee in relation to proposals based on Article 43.

This, then, is the bare bones of the procedure. We will now proceed to examine each of the stages in rather more detail. All fisheries legislation begins life as a Commission proposal (although the stimulus for the proposal may have come from some other body or organisation). Within the Commission, fisheries matters are dealt with, and proposals for legislation originate from, Directorate-General XIV, the smallest of the 20 Directorates-General into which the Commission is divided.[26] As at present constituted, this consists of some 60 plus officials, under a Director-General, working in three main divisions. Directorate A is concerned with marketing and international questions; Directorate B with the management of the Community's fisheries resources; while Directorate C deals with structural policy. A separate, untitled, unit deals with legislation and national measures. Outside Directorate-General XIV the Commission's Legal Service and Statistical Office are also concerned with fisheries matters as part of their work. The Legal Service provides the Directorate-General with legal advice as and when requested, and is consulted on all proposals for legislation: in addition it represents the Commission in litigation before the European Court of Justice. The Statistical Office collects and publishes a variety of statistics relating to fisheries, of which the most important are the annual *Yearbook of Fishery Statistics* and the quarterly *Fisheries – Quantities and Values of Landings in the European Communities*.

Although all proposals for fisheries legislation are made by the Commission, the Commission does not act in isolation when formulating such proposals. Although not formally required by the EEC Treaty to consult with anyone in preparing proposals for legislation, the Commission in fact consults with a number of bodies. First, there are a number of Community committees which have been specifically set up to advise the Commission. In the field of fisheries these comprise the Advisory Committee on Fisheries, the Joint Committee on Social Problems in Sea Fishing and the Scientific and Technical Committee for Fisheries. The composition and functions of these three committees are briefly as follows.

Advisory Committee on Fisheries. This Committee was set up by the Commission in 1971.[27] It consists of 45 members, representing producers and co-operatives in the fishing industry, credit institutions involved in fisheries, traders in fishery products, fish processing industries, workers in the fishing industry, and consumers.[28] The function of the Committee is to give the Commission its views on 'any problem concerning the operation of the Regulations relating to the establishment of a common structural policy in fisheries or to the common organisation of the market in fishery products, and in particular on measures to be adopted by the Commission under those Regulations and also on all social problems arising in the industry, with the exception of industrial disputes.'[29]

Joint Committee on Social Problems in Sea Fishing. This Committee was set up by the Commission in 1974.[30] It consists of 44 members, divided equally between representatives of employers' associations and employees' associations. The Committee's function is to 'assist the Commission in the formulation and implementation of the Community social policy aimed at improving and harmonising the living and working conditions in sea fishing', in particular by issuing opinions and submitting reports to the Commission, either at the latter's request or on its own initiative.[31] The Committee is also, in respect of matters falling within the competence of certain listed employers' and employees' associations, to 'promote dialogue and conciliation and facilitate negotiations between these associations; arrange for studies to be carried; [and] participate in discussions and seminars.[32]

Scientific and Technical Committee for Fisheries. This Committee was set up by the Commission in 1979.[33] It consists of 28 fishery scientists sitting in an individual capacity. The Committee gives the Commission scientific advice on questions of fisheries conservation, and prepares an annual report on the state of fish stocks in Community waters and on ways and means of conserving them. The Committee clearly plays an important role when the Commission is drawing up proposals for Total Allowable Catches and other conservation measures for vessels fishing in Community waters.

In drawing up legislative proposals, the Commission also usually consults with civil servants from the various ministries of the Member States concerned with the subject matter of the proposal. Lastly, the Commission often consults with outside interests. For the purposes of such consultation the Commission prefers outside interests to be organised on a Community-wide footing, rather than being purely national in character. In relation to fisheries the following interest groups have been established at the Community level: the Association of National Organisations of Fishing Enterprises in the EEC (Europêche), representing fish producers; the Association of the Fish Industries of the EEC (AIPCEE) and the Union of the Associations of Fishmeal Manufacturers of the EEC, representing fish processors; the Federation of National Organisations of Fish Wholesalers, Importers and Exporters of the EEC (CEP), representing the wholesale fish trade; and the General Committee of Agricultural Co-Operatives of the EEC (COGECA) and the Specialised Committee for Fishing Co-Operatives in the EEC, representing fishermen's co-operatives. In practice these organisations have fewer resources (mainly because of mixed support from national fishing organisations), and therefore are not nearly as effective, as interest groups in most other fields of Community activity.

Once the Commission has formulated and adopted a proposal, it is sent to the Council. The Council then forwards the proposal to the European Parliament for its opinion where, according to the EEC Treaty, it is obliged to do so. Even if the proposal is based on a Treaty provision which does not require the Council to consult the European Parliament, in practice the Council often does consult the Parliament. In the case of fisheries proposals based on Articles 7, 42, 43 or 235 of the EEC Treaty, the Council is obliged to consult the European Parliament. In the case of proposals based on Article 103, the Council is not obliged to consult the Parliament, nor does it in practice do so, as this would defeat the object of using Article 103 as a legal basis, since, as explained above, the article is used for short-term measures which require urgent adoption.[34]

Once the European Parliament has received a request from the Council for its opinion on a Commission proposal, the normal practice is for the proposal to be referred to the appropriate committee of the European Parliament: in the case of fisheries this is the Committee on Agriculture, which has a Fisheries Working Group (effectively a sub-committee). The Committee will then discuss the proposal and produce a report, together with a draft opinion. This report and draft opinion are then debated by the European Parliament in plenary session. Parliament usually adopts the draft opinion, sometimes with modifications. Parliament's opinion on a proposal takes the form either of approving the proposal as it stands, or of recommending amendments to the proposal, or of recommending that the proposal be not adopted. Where the Parliament has recommended amendments, there is no obligation either on the Council to accept them if it decides to adopt the proposal, or on the Commission to include them in any revisions it may make of the proposal. Insofar as one can generalise from a considerable number of opinions, it seems that in general the amendments suggested by the European Parliament to draft fisheries legislation have not often been accepted by the Council or the Commission.[35] There would seem to be two main reasons for this. First, there was prior to 1983 considerable difficulty in securing agreement in the Council on the more important pieces of fisheries legislation, as was seen in the previous Chapter. In this situation the legislative process essentially consisted of lengthy negotiations between Member States at Council meetings in an attempt to resolve conflicting interests and positions, with the Commission acting as an honest broker by producing a succession of revised proposals aimed at achieving an acceptable compromise. Clearly in that kind of situation the European Parliament could not hope to exercise much influence. Secondly, the European Parliament's suggested amendments have often been rejected in the case of proposals concerned with external aspects of the Common Fisheries Policy. This is because many such proposals simply implement agreements with third States or measures adopted by international fisheries organisations: amendments to such proposals are only acceptable to the Council and Commission if these bodies are prepared to re-open negotiations with the third State or international organisation concerned, but obviously they are very rarely prepared to do so.[36]

From the above description, it appears that the European Parliament's powers are merely consultative and that it cannot effectively amend or prevent the adoption of draft legislation. It has, however, been argued by some that the effect of the judgment of the European Court in the *Isoglucose* cases[37] in 1980 has been to confer a power of veto over draft legislation on the European Parliament. In these cases the Court held that failure to consult the European Parliament was the violation of an essential procedural requirement justifying annulment of a Community act under Article 173 of the EEC Treaty, and the fact that in this case the Council had asked the European Parliament for its opinion but had adopted the Commission's proposal before receiving the Parliament's opinion, meant that there had been no consultation of the Parliament. As the Court put it, consultation 'implies that the Parliament has expressed its opinion. It is impossible to take the view that the requirement [of consultation] is satisfied by the Council's simply asking for the opinion.'[38] This dictum has led some commentators to argue that the Council cannot act until it has received the European Parliament's opinion (in cases where the Council is obliged to consult the European Parliament), and that by delaying in giving an opinion, or even refusing to give one, the European Parliament can effectively block the adoption of legislation – in other words, the Parliament has in effect acquired a power of veto. It is doubtful whether this is correct. First, the facts in the *Isoglucose* cases were somewhat exceptional. The delay in Parliament's giving an opinion was largely caused by the hiatus resulting from the change-over from the old, selected Parliament to the new, directly elected one. Furthermore, the Council failed to make use of the various procedures at its disposal for calling an emergency session of the Parliament in order to discuss the draft regulation in question. Secondly, it is clearly required by the spirit of the EEC Treaty, particularly Article 4(1),[39] that the Community institutions carry out their functions in good faith. If the European Parliament deliberately refused to give, or delayed quite unreasonably in giving, an opinion – as opposed to giving an adverse opinion – because it did not like a proposed measure, it would not be acting in good faith. In such a case the Council would surely be able to go ahead and adopt a proposed measure, even though it had not received an opinion from the European Parliament. If this is right, it suggests that the picture painted earlier of the European Parliament's role in the legislative process is still essentially correct. The *Isoglucose* cases are a warning to the Council to give the European Parliament adequate time in preparing its opinion on draft Community legislation.[40]

As well as consulting the European Parliament on draft legislation, the Council is often obliged to consult in addition or alternatively the Economic and Social Committee. As far as fisheries legislation is concerned, the only situation in which the Council is obliged to consult the Economic and Social Committee is when it is acting on the basis of Article 43 and then during the first stage (i.e. 1958–61) only. In practice, the Council has consulted the Committee on several pieces of draft fisheries legislation, even when not obliged to do so, and on a few occasions the Committee has given its opinion on draft legislation of its own accord, without being asked by the Council. Like the European Parliament, the Economic and Social Committee works largely through Committees (known as sections, that concerned with fisheries being the Section for Agriculture) in preparing its opinions. These opinions, like those of the Parliament, are in no way binding on the Council.

Having received the opinions of the European Parliament and/or the Economic and Social Committee, the Council then begins its deliberations on the Commission's proposal. This process invariably begins with the Council referring the proposal to the Committee of Permanent Representatives. (In fact this happens when the Council first receives the proposal from the Commission). The Committee in turn will refer the proposal to a Working Party, consisting of officials from national ministries, at whose meetings representatives of the Commission take part. When the proposal has been thoroughly discussed by the Working Party and the Committee of Permanent Representatives, it finally comes before the Council for a decision. The voting procedure by which the Council takes its decisions varies. Where the proposal is based on Articles 103(2) or 235 – or where the Council desires to amend a Commission proposal, whatever its legal basis – unanimity is required. Where it is based on Articles 7, 42, 43 or 103(3), a qualified majority is sufficient. For this purpose the votes are weighted: France, West Germany, Italy and the United Kingdom have 10 votes each, Spain 8 votes, Belgium, Greece, Netherlands and Portugal 5 each, Denmark and Ireland 3 each and Luxembourg 2. For a decision to be adopted by a qualified majority, there must be at least 54 votes (out of a possible 76) in favour.[41] The Treaty provisions on qualified majority voting must, however, be considered in the light of the Luxembourg Accords.[42] According to the latter, where a proposal subject to qualified majority voting affects 'very important interests' of one or more of the Member States, every effort must be made to arrive at a unanimous decision. France, and it seems also Denmark, Greece, Ireland and the United Kingdom, take the view that in these circumstances only a unanimous decision is acceptable, whereas the other Member States take a less rigid view. While the Luxembourg Accords do not have any formal legal validity, they are nevertheless a kind of Community constitutional convention which is observed in practice. As far as the adoption of proposed fishery measures subject to qualified majority voting is concerned, the Luxembourg Accords have been invoked on a number of occasions, notably by the United Kingdom.

Some doubt as to the continued existence of the Luxembourg Accords has been raised by the events of May 1982, when the Council in voting on a series of price measures for the then current agricultural year, disregarded the United Kingdom's invocation of the Luxembourg Accords.[43] Whether this was an isolated instance which will not be repeated remains to be seen. It is interesting to note, however, that at a Council meeting in December 1982 where all the Member States except Denmark were prepared to vote in favour of a draft regulation on a Community system for the conservation and management of fishery resources, a suggestion was made by the Commission that the invocation of the Luxembourg Accords by Denmark should be disregarded. This suggestion was not accepted.[44]

Although not a formal part of the legislative procedure, there is another stage which is sometimes found in the Council's decision-taking and which is worthy of brief mention. If the Council is unable to come to any decision on a Commission proposal, the matter is occasionally referred to the European Council – the thrice-yearly meetings of Heads of Government – to see whether at this exalted level a solution can be found. On one or two matters – such as direct elections to the European Parliament and the United Kingdom's rebate from the Community budget – the European Council has indeed been able to find a basis for agreement and has thus paved the way for a decision by the Council. In the case of fisheries, the long-continuing inability of the Council to agree on a Community system of fisheries management for EEC waters – described in the previous Chapter – was referred to the European Council on at least two occasions – the meeting at Maastricht in March 1981 and the meeting at Copenhagen in December 1982. On neither occasion, however, was the European Council able to make any effective contribution to a solution.

When the Council is deliberating on a Commission proposal, it is influenced not only by the arguments of the Commission and the opinions of the European Parliament and/or Economic and Social Committee, but also by the domestic political and sectional pressures to which each member of the Council – that is, each Minister – is subject. In the case of fisheries, each fisheries minister is sought to be influenced by a number of different bodies. First, opinions may be expressed in national parliaments and by parliamentary committees. For example, in the United Kingdom there have been numerous debates in Parliament on the Common Fisheries Policy. In these debates forceful and often critical views have been put forward. There have also been full and well-reasoned reports from Parliamentary committees, seeking to influence Government attitudes.[45] In Denmark, which is unique in this respect, the fisheries minister, like all his ministerial colleagues, cannot agree to a decision by the Council unless he has the support of the Danish Parliament's Market Relations Committee. Thus, at the December 1982 Fisheries Council previously referred to, there was the odd situation of the Danish fisheries minister wanting to agree with his fellow ministers but being prevented from doing so because of the opposition of the Market Relations Committee.[46] Secondly, fisheries ministers may be influenced by lobbying from representatives of the various sections of the fishing and fish-related industries. It is important to realise that such lobbyists do not necessarily speak with one voice. Often the interests of distant-water fishermen are quite different from those of inshore fishermen, while fish processors may have quite different concerns than fishermen. Thirdly, the minister may be exposed to pressure from various statutory bodies concerned with the fishing industry. For example, in the United Kingdom the White Fish Authority and Herring Industry Board (before their replacement in 1981 by the Sea Fish Industry Authority) often in their annual reports made quite forceful criticisms of the Common Fisheries Policy. Finally, a fisheries minister has to take into account not only the views of other Government departments concerned with some aspect or another of fisheries,[47] but also his Government's general strategy towards the EEC, which may involve making concessions in one area in order to obtain benefits in another area.

We have now looked at the Community's basic legislative procedure, with particular reference to fisheries, but that is not the end of the Community's legislative processes. We must now turn to consider the question of delegated legislation. In the case of fisheries there are two types of delegated legislation – a true delegation by the Council to the Commission and a pseudo-delegation by the Council to itself.[48] Both these require some explanation.

We will deal with the latter first. Some of the EEC's fisheries regulations – notably those that may be regarded as the three basic regulations, namely the Regulation laying down a Common Structural Policy for the Fishing Industry,[49] the Regulation on the Common Organisation of the Market in Fishery Products[50] and the Regulation establishing a Community System for the Conservation and Management of Fishery Resources[51] – provide for further implementing action to be taken by the Council. Sometimes the procedure specified for such implementing action to be taken is that set out in Article 43 of the EEC Treaty (which has already been considered.)[52] More commonly, however, the procedure specified is for the Council to take a decision by qualified majority, acting on a proposal from the Commission.[53] This procedure differs from that laid down in Article 43 – the basic grant-giving power for agricultural and fisheries legislation – by removing the requirement to consult the European Parliament. Is it lawful for the Council, in giving itself a power of implementation in a regulation adopted under Article 43, to provide that such a power is to be exercised in accordance with a process which is at variance with Article 43? This question was considered by the European Court in *Eridania v. Minister of Agriculture and Forestry*.[54] In this case there was a dispute as to the validity of a Council regulation which was based on an implementing power given by the basic regulation on the common organisation of the market in sugar. The implementing regulation had, in accordance with the basic regulation, been adopted by the Council on a proposal from the Commission without consulting the European Parliament. It was argued that the regulation was invalid because the requirements of Article 43 had not been complied with. The Court rejected this argument. It observed:

> It cannot be a requirement that all the details of the regulations concerning the common agricultural policy be drawn up by the Council according to the procedure laid down by Article 43; it is sufficient for the purposes of that provision that the basic elements of the matter to be dealt with have been adopted in accordance with that procedure; on the other hand, the provisions implementing basic regulations may be adopted by the Council according to a procedure different from that under Article 43.[55]

The Court went on to make it clear that there are limits on the Council's powers of implementation in this way, and suggested that these powers must not exceed the scope of an objective laid down by the basic regulation.

The Court's judgment in *Eridania* therefore makes it clear that there can be no objections to the non-Article 43 procedure provided for the adoption of implementing regulations by the basic fisheries regulations, provided such implementation does not exceed the limits suggested by the Court. In practice, none of the implementing regulations so far adopted does appear to exceed these limits. This special procedure for implementing regulations, as sanctioned by the European Court, seems reasonable, given that such regulations are concerned essentially with matters of detail. This, after all, is the classic role of delegated legislation in any legal system, although here it is not strictly accurate to talk of delegation, as the same body takes the decision, whichever procedure is used. That is why the term 'pseudo-delegation' was used at the beginning of this discussion. The major effect of this pseudo-delegation is a decreased role for the European Parliament.[56] With the adoption of the last of the basic regulations of the Common Fisheries Policy at the beginning of 1983, most EEC fisheries legislation for the next decade or so is likely to be of an implementing nature where generally there will be no obligation on the Council to consult the European Parliament, although of course it can do so in any particular case if it feels that this would be desirable.

Apart from this pseudo-delegation, there is also a true delegation of powers by the Council to the Commission. One of the features of the Common Agricultural Policy is that quite extensive powers have been delegated by the Council to the Commission to allow it to run the day-to-day management of that Policy. While the Common Fisheries Policy does not require quite the same day-to-day management as much of the Common Agricultural Policy, certain powers have been delegated to the Commission by the Council. This has been done notably in relation to marketing and trade arrangements,[57] and to a lesser extent as regards conservation measures,[58] as well as one or two other matters.[59]

In each sector of the Common Agricultural Policy where the Council has delegated powers to the Commission, a Management Committee has been set up. The function of these Committees is essentially to ensure that the Commission, in exercising the legislative powers delegated to it by the Council, takes into account the views of Member States.[60] A similar step has been taken in respect of the Common Fisheries Policy. Two management committees have been set up – a Management Committee for Fishery Products, which covers marketing and trade,[61] and a Management Committee for Fishery Resources, which is concerned with conservation and management questions.[62] Each Committee consists of representatives of the Member States, with a representative of the Commission acting as chairman. The Committees' functions and procedure follow the usual pattern. Thus, when the Commission intends to exercise the legislative powers delegated to it, it submits a draft measure to the Committee. The Committee gives its opinion on the draft, its opinion being adopted in accordance with the qualified majority voting procedure which applies in the Council (and here, it should be noted, the Luxembourg Accords do not apply). The Commission then adopts its original draft as a definitive legislative measure. However, if the Committee's opinion did not approve the Commission's draft, the Council may within one month reverse the Commission's measure. In practice, the Committee almost always approves the Commission's proposed measures.[63] Although in the early days of the Common Agricultural Policy, doubts were expressed as to whether this form of delegation involving management committees was permissible under Community law, this point has been resolved by the European Court which has held that this form of legislative delegation is lawful: the Court has stressed, however, that the delegation must relate only to the implementation of matters of detail, and not basic principles.[64]

In one or two situations, usually where urgent action is required, there is a departure from the Management Committee procedure. In these cases the

Commission adopts a measure and the Council has a month in which to adopt by qualified majority a decision varying the measure.[65]

While the Commission undoubtedly has delegated legislative powers, the question has arisen as to whether it has any autonomous legislative powers in respect of fisheries. It is clear that in principle, as the European Court has stressed,[66] the Commission does enjoy genuinely autonomous legislative powers where these have been conferred on it by the EEC Treaty. None of these powers, however, appear relevant to fisheries. Nevertheless, the Commission appears to have claimed such powers. In July 1981, after the Council had failed yet again to reach any agreement on the Commission's proposals, originally submitted four years previously, for the management of Community fish stocks, the Commission – no doubt in exasperation – issued a declaration in which it stated that in view of the Council's failure to adopt management measures, Member States should observe the Commission's proposals for total allowable catches and quotas for 1981. The Commission added that it considered these proposals 'in the present situation as being legally binding on the Member States.'[67] For the Commission to consider its proposals as legally binding seems to be tantamount to claiming a legislative power for itself. The Commission justified its view by recalling that it had, as the European Court, particularly in *Commission v. United Kingdom*,[68] had confirmed, certain rights and duties under Article 155 of the EEC Treaty, and it went on to refer to the 'overriding public interest' in it taking this step.

While the Commission's frustration at the Council's inability at that time to take any decision is understandable, there seems little, if anything, in either Article 155[69] or *Commission v. United Kingdom*,[70] which would justify the Commission in regarding its proposals as being legally binding, and thus effectively exercising autonomous legislative powers. The Commission's argument, it seems,[71] is as follows. Member States are under a duty to adopt conservation measures where the Council has not acted and where conservation measures are required for biological reasons. The corollary of this duty is that the Commission, as the body responsible for seeing that Member States observe their Community obligations, can require a Member State to adopt appropriate measures. The weakness of this argument is this: while it is true that according to the European Court Member States do have the duty described (see Chapter 4) – although it is perhaps doubtful whether this duty would embrace the setting of quotas – and that the Commission is responsible for seeing that Member States observe their Community obligations (Articles 155 and 169 of the EEC Treaty), it does not logically follow that the Commission can order a Member State to fulfil its obligations. According to Article 169 the Commission may point out to a Member State that it is failing to fulfil its obligations, and refer the matter to the European Court, but nothing in Article 169, either in its wording or its practical application, suggests that the Commission can order a Member State to take a particular course of action.[72]

A situation not dissimilar to that with which the Commission was faced in July 1981 has occurred in the operation of the Common Agricultural Policy. On at least two occasions where a vacuum has arisen as the result of the Council's failure to act, the Commission has responded by legislating where it apparently lacked any competence to do so – see Regulations 846/80 and 967/80[73] fixing monetary compensatory amounts after the Council had failed to fix such figures following the expiry of an earlier regulation, and Regulation 1390/80[74] where the Commission fixed import levies despite the absence of a Council regulation on prices which would normally have been necessary. In the case of the first two regulations, their validity was raised in Article 177 proceedings before the European Court in *Staple Dairy Products Ltd v. Intervention Board for Agricultural Produce*.[75] The Court found that it was not necessary to consider the validity of the Commission's Regulations because a later Council Regulation had retrospectively adopted the provisions of the Commission's Regulations for the period during which the Commission's regulations were operative. The Advocate General, while taking the same approach as the Court, did for the sake of completeness briefly discuss the validity of the Commission's Regulations. Emphasising that he was only dealing with the Commission's competence in relation to the particular facts of the case and not in relation to the Common Agricultural Policy generally, he said that he did not think that the Commission had the competence to adopt the disputed Regulations. Neither Article 155 nor the 'principle of continuity' (defined by the Commission as a principle whereby public authorities must ensure that the services for which they are responsible function regularly and continuously) gave the Commission sufficient competence. Although confined to the facts of the case, the Advocate General's views do nevertheless support the argument that the Commission cannot claim autonomous legislative powers as asserted in its July 1981 Declaration. If the Commission, according to the Advocate General, lacks the necessary competence to legislate in a situation where after a lengthy period of regulation by the Council a vacuum appears as a result of the Council's failure to act, it must *a fortiori* lack the competence where, as in the situation here, there has been no Council regulation at all.

It is noteworthy that the European Parliament has questioned the legality of the Commission's claims in its Declaration,[76] as have some members of the Council.[77] It seems probable that the Commission's claim is an isolated episode and that it is unlikely to be reasserted, given that at the beginning of 1983 the Council finally adopted management measures for Community waters.[78]

The better view, therefore, would seem to be that the Commission has no autonomous legislative powers as far as fisheries are concerned. The European Parliament certainly has no such powers, nor does it possess any formal power to initiate legislation. Nevertheless, apart from being consulted on Commission proposals, the European Parliament does often quite separately make suggestions for Community legislation, and has done so on several occasions in respect of fisheries,[79] as has the Economic and Social Committee,[80] and both bodies seek to monitor the implementation and effectiveness of the Community's fisheries legislation (the European Parliament *inter alia* through questions to the Commission and Council and its role in determining the Community budget).[81]

3. LAW-MAKING BY THE EUROPEAN COURT

Before we conclude discussion of the Community's law-making processes, it is appropriate to say something about the European Court. While the Court obviously is not formally a law-making body, nevertheless in its role of applying and interpreting Community law it does from time to time effectively create new law. This has happened in the field of fisheries. Thus, the law regarding the division of competence between the Community and Member States in both the internal and external spheres of fisheries management (discussed in Chapters 4 and 5) is essentially the creation of the Court.

By the end of 1985 the Court had given judgment in 28 cases involving some aspect or another of fisheries law. Although only a tiny fraction (about half-a-percent) of the Court's case load since its inception, these 28 cases represent a significant body of law. About three-quarters of the cases were references from national courts under Article 177 of the EEC Treaty (mostly concerned with requests for the interpretation of Community law rather than queries as to its validity), the remainder being actions against a Member State for failure to comply with its Community obligations brought by the Commission under Article 169 or in one case by another Member State under Article 170 (*France v. United Kingdom*[82]). Just over half of the cases concerned the validity of national conservation measures, the remainder involving a variety of questions relating to relations with third States, financial aid for the fishing industry, marketing and trade. From such a diversity of issues it is difficult to see that the Court has developed any distinctive philosophy of fisheries law or espoused any particular objectives for Community fisheries law, at least in terms purely of fisheries issues (cf. the discussion at the beginning of Chapter 1), except to stress a general need for the conservation of resources and to demonstrate a concern to avoid a vacuum in the regulation of fisheries, particularly where the Council has been paralysed in inactivity. This is scarcely surprising, given that the judges have no particular expertise in what is a rather specialised area of law and that it is not the function of the Court to determine the objectives of Community fisheries policy. What one can say of the Court's case law is that the Court has consistently sought to apply its general philosophy of Community law to the fisheries sector. Thus, it has promoted Community integration by strengthening and increasing the powers of the Community institutions at the expense of the powers of the Member States: what is remarkable is that this has usually been done by drawing the broadest, most concrete and communautaire conclusions from provisions of the EEC Treaty which are notable for their generality and vagueness (as will be seen, particularly in Chapters 4 and 5). The Court has also laid stress on certain fundamental principles of Community law, such as non-discrimination and the duty of Member States to co-operate. In turn, the Court's case law has undoubtedly given some stimulus to the Community's political institutions to develop the Common Fisheries Policy as well as constraining Member States from taking unilateral action or being over-obstructive in the Council.

NOTES

1. Art. 4(1) reads: 'Each institution shall act within the limits of the powers conferred upon it by this Treaty.'
2. See P.S.R.F. Mathijsen, *A Guide to European Community Law*, Fourth Edition, London, 1985, p. 91, and T.C. Hartley, *The Foundations of European Community Law*, Oxford, 1981, p. 111.
3. Mathijsen, *op. cit.*, p. 62; Hartley, *op. cit.*, pp. 433–435.
4. The inclusion of fisheries in agriculture is in many ways understandable since they have certain common characteristics e.g. a dependence on nature and fluctuating production of a perishable commodity. On the other hand, there are many significant differences: fishermen are much more dependent on chance, fish are a migratory common property resource, and there is a much greater international dimension to fisheries. Given these differences, and, with the benefit of hindsight, looking at the whole history of the evolution of the Common Fisheries Policy, the wisdom of the drafters of the EEC Treaty including fisheries with agriculture may be doubted.
5. For example, the introduction of purse-seining techniques by Norwegian fishermen in the 1960s had a drastic effect on North Sea herring stocks.
6. See Case 5/73, *Balkan-Import-Export GmbH v. Hauptzollamt Berlin Packhof* [1973] E.C.R. 1091; Joined Cases 63–69/72, *Wilhem Werhahn Hansamuhle v. Council and Commission* [1973] E.C.R. 1229; and Case 29/77, *Société Anonyme Roquette Frères v. France* [1977] E.C.R. 1835. For a discussion of the Court's case law in this area, see F.G. Snyder, *Law of the Common Agricultural Policy*, London, 1985, pp. 18–22.
7. Joined Cases 90 and 91/63, *Commission v. Luxembourg and Belgium* [1964] E.C.R. 625 at 634; [1965] C.M.L.R. 58 at 75.
8. Case 48/74, *Charmasson v. Minister for Economic Affairs and Finance* [1974] E.C.R. 1383 at 1395; [1975] 2 C.M.L.R. 208 at 225. For further discussion of this question, see Snyder, *op. cit.* in n. 6, pp. 91–92.
9. The power is to be exercised by the Council, acting on a proposal from the Commission and after consulting the European Parliament: see Art. 43(2).
10. Fisheries is by no means the only sector of agriculture where a common policy was not

adopted until after the end of the transitional period: for example, a common policy for sheepmeat was not adopted until 1980.

11. Joined Cases 73 and 74/63, *Rotterdam and Puttershoek v. Dutch Ministry of Agriculture and Fisheries* [1964] E.C.R. 1; [1964] C.M.L.R. 198.

12. Case 8/73, *Hauptzollamt Bremerhaven v. Massey Ferguson GmbH* [1973] E.C.R. 897. For a fuller discussion of Art. 235, see Hartley, *op. cit.* in n. 2, pp. 88–96.

13. Case 5/73, *Balkan-Import-Export GmbH v. Hauptzollamt Berlin-Packhof, op. cit.* in n. 6. Identical judgments on these points were also given in Case 9/73, *Schlüter v. Hauptzollamt Lörrach* [1973] E.C.R. 1135 and Case 10/73, *Rewe-Zentral v. Hauptzollamt Kehl* [1973] E.C.R. 1175.

14. E. Hiester, in 'The Legal Position of the European Community with regard to the Conservation of the Living Resources of the Sea' [1976] *Legal Issues of European Integration* 55 at pp. 63–64, argues that Art. 102 could be regarded as implicitly amending Art. 5 of Reg. 2141/70 (which is concerned with the taking of conservation measures by the Council – further discussed in Chapter 4), and therefore as having secondary status. This seems very unlikely, especially since Art. 5 is repeated *verbatim* in consolidating Reg. 101/76, adopted after the Treaty of Accession.

15. J. Bourgeois, 'The Field is Occupied.' Unpublished paper given at a conference on 'Fishing in European Waters', Edinburgh, 1978. See also the Commission's arguments in Case 804/79, *Commission v. United Kingdom* [1981] E.C.R. 1045 at 1055–6; [1982] 1 C.M.L.R. 543.

16. E.g. Reg. 350/77, O.J. 1977 L48/28, where both Art. 102 and Art. 103 of the EEC Treaty were cited as the legal basis.

17. Joined Cases 3, 4 and 6/76, *Officier van Justitie v. Kramer* [1976] E.C.R. 1279 at 1309–1311; [1976] 2 C.M.L.R. 440 at 469–471.

18. Case 61/77, *Commission v. Ireland* [1978] E.C.R. 417 at 443; [1978] 2 C.M.L.R. 466 at 511.

19. Case 141/78, *France v. United Kingdom* [1979] E.C.R. 2923 at 2940; [1980] 1 C.M.L.R. 6 at 22.

20. Case 32/79, *Commission v. United Kingdom* [1980] E.C.R. 2403 at 2434; [1981] 1 C.M.L.R. 219 at 262. It should also be noted that in Case 804/79, *Commission v. United Kingdom* [1981] E.C.R. 1045 at 1085; [1982] 1 C.M.L.R. 543 at 555–556 the Advocate General was quite emphatic that Art. 102 was not a legal basis for fishery measures. On the other hand, the Legal Affairs Committee of the European Parliament has considered Art. 102 to be a legal basis: see E.P. Doc. 80/78, pp. 9–11.

21. That the phrase quoted refers to the end, rather than the beginning, of 1978 was held by the European Court to be the case in Joined Cases 185–204/78, *Officier van Justitie v. Van Dam en Zonen* [1979] E.C.R. 2345; [1980] 1 C.M.L.R. 350.

22. D. Vignes, 'The EEC and the Law of the Sea' in R.R. Churchill et al. (eds.), *New Directions in the Law of the Sea*, Vol. III, London, 1973, 335 at 342–343. A similar view is taken by E. Peyroux, 'Problèmes juridiques de la pêche dans le Marché Commun' (1973) 9 R.T.D.E. 46 at 52.

23. Case 39/72, *Commission v. Italy* [1973] E.C.R. 101; [1973] C.M.L.R. 439. The Commission has several times had to remind Member States of this rule as far as Community fishery measures are concerned. See, e.g., O.J. 1981 C218/10 and 1983 C121/8.

24. E.g. Reg. 1463/70, Art. 21 (dealing with tachographs), O.J. S. Edn. 1970, p. 482. Failure by the United Kingdom to take the requisite implementing action led to its condemnation by the European Court – Case 128/78, *Commission v. United Kingdom* [1979] E.C.R. 419; [1979] 2 C.M.L.R. 45.

25. See also M. Leigh, *European Integration and the Common Fisheries Policy*, Beckenham, 1983, Chap. 8.

26. Directorate-General XIV was established in February 1977. Prior to this date, fisheries were dealt with by the Directorate-General for Agriculture.

27. Dec. 71/128, J.O. 1971 L68/18. Following the enlargement of the EEC in 1973, the composition of the Committee was altered and minor amendments were made to its functions – see Dec. 73/429, O.J. 1973 L355/61.

28. As to how members of the Committee are chosen, see the Commission's Answer to W.Q. 1004/80, O.J. 1980 C288/22.

29. Dec. 73/429, *op. cit.* in n. 27, Art. 2.

30. Dec. 74/441, O.J. 1974 L243/19, amended by Dec. 83/53, O.J. 1983 L44/21. This Committee replaces the Joint Advisory Committee on Social Questions arising in the Sea Fishing Industry, set up in 1968 by Dec. 68/252, O.J. S. Edn. 1968 (I), p. 125.

31. Dec. 74/441, Arts. 2 and 3(1)(a).

32. *Ibid.*, Art. 3(1)(b).

33. Dec. 79/572, O.J. 1979 L156/29. This Dec was amended by the Third Act of Accession so as to enlarge the membership of the Committee: see Annex I, XV, O.J. 1985 L302/241.

34. The frequent use made of Art. 103 by the Council between 1977 and 1983 was criticised by the European Parliament precisely because in this way Parliament was by-passed. See, for example, its Resolutions of June 15, 1978, March 15, 1979 and December 19, 1980, O.J. 1978 C163/41, 1979 C93/54 and 1980 C346/121. See also the Report of Parliament's Legal Affairs Committee on the Legal Basis and Procedures for Certain Legal Acts relating to the Community's Fisheries Policy, E.P. Doc. 80/78, especially pp. 13–14.

35. But for some examples of amendments being accepted, see Leigh, *op. cit.* in n. 25, p. 197.

36. This point is taken up again, and elaborated upon, at the end of Chapter 5.

37. Cases 138/79, *Roquette Frères v. Council* and 139/79, *Maizena v. Council* [1980] E.C.R. 3333 and 3393.

38. *Ibid.*, at pp. 3360 and 3424.

39. Quoted in n. 1.

40. For further discussion of these points, see the Editiorial Comment in (1980) 5 E.L.R. 431–2 (taking the broad view, i.e. that the cases give the European Parliament a power of near-veto); case note by T. Hartley in (1981) 6 E.L.R. 181 at 184–5; and F.G. Jacobs, 'Isoglucose Resurgent: Two Powers of the European Parliament upheld by the Court' (1981) 18 C.M.L. Rev. 219 at 221–2 (both of which take a narrow view). Note also that following the cases the European Parliament amended its Rules of Procedure in order to ensure that it does not formally give its opinions until it has fully exhausted the process of consultation: see Rules 32–37, O.J. 1981 C90/49. See also E. Kirchner and K. Williams, 'The Legal, Political and Institutional Implications of the Isoglucose Judgments 1980' (1983) 22 J.C.M.S. 173.

41. Art. 148(2) of the EEC Treaty, as amended.

42. Reproduced in B. Rudden and D. Wyatt, *Basic Community Laws*, Oxford, 1980, p. 71.

43. *The Guardian*, May 19, 1982.

44. *The Guardian*, December 22, 1982. See also Editorial Comments in (1983) 20 C.M.L. Rev. 7 at 8.

45. E.g. Fifth Report from the Expenditure Committee, 'The Fishing Industry', H.C. Paper (1977–78) 356; House of Lords Select Committee on the European Communities, 'EEC Fisheries Policy', H.L. Paper (1979–80) 351 and 'The Common Fisheries Policy', H.L. Paper (1984–85) 39.

46. *Loc. cit.* in n. 44.

47. Taking the United Kingdom again as an example, while the Ministry of Agriculture, Fisheries and Food is the main government department responsible for fisheries, no less than six other departments are concerned in one way or another with the fishing industry. See further R.R. Churchill, 'A Review of United Kingdom Fisheries Law' (1982) 2 *Derecho Pesquero* 7 at 12–13.

48. There is also a third type of delegation – from the Council to Member States. In the fisheries

48

field very limited use has been made of this type of delegation. So far it has only been applied to certain types of conservation measure. Since it is easier to understand this type of delegation in its substantive setting, discussion will be postponed to Chapter 4.

49. Reg. 101/76, O.J. 1976 L20/19.
50. Reg. 3796/81, O.J. 1981 L379/1.
51. Reg. 170/83, O.J. 1983 L24/1.
52. E.g. Arts. 4 and 7 of Reg. 101/76, and Arts. 4(2) and 8(2)(3) of Reg. 170/83.
53. E.g. Arts. 2(3), 5(3), 10(3) and 26(2) of Reg. 3796/81, and Arts. 2, 3, 4(1)and 7(2) of Reg. 170/ 83.
54. Case 230/78, *Eridania v. Ministry of Agriculture and Forestry* [1979] E.C.R. 2749.
55. *Ibid.*, p. 2765.
56. A role to which the European Parliament has strongly objected. See its Resolutions of March 16, 1984, O.J. 1984 C104/153, in which it 'protests strongly against the curtailment of its right of consultation', and calls on the Commission and Council to return to the practice of consulting it; and of February 20, 1986, O.J. 1986 C68/108, in which it calls on the Commission to submit to the Council a draft Regulation specifying the cases in which the European Parliament has to be consulted.
57. Reg. 3796/81, *op. cit.* in n. 50, Arts. 3, 4(4), 9(5), 11(4), 12(3), 13(7), 14(7), 15(4), 16(3), 17(6), 18(3), 20(2), 21(6), 22(5), 25(4) and 31. There is also delegation provided for in some of the subsidiary marketing regulations, as well as the Iberian Act of Accession.
58. Reg. 170/83, *op. cit.* in n. 51, Arts. 5(2) and 7(5); Reg. 171/83, O.J. 1983 L24/14, Arts. 6, 7, 8(1), 13(2), 15(2) and 18(1).
59. E.g. Reg. 2057/82, O.J. 1982 L220/1, Art. 13 (control and surveillance measures); and Reg. 2908/83, Art. 19; Reg. 2909/83, Arts. 2 and 12; Dir. 83/515, Arts. 9 and 10; O.J. 1983 L290/1, 9 and 15 (all concerned with structural matters).
60. For a detailed discussion of the role of management committees, see D. Lasok and J.W. Bridge, *Introduction to the Law and Institutions of the European Communities*, 3rd ed., London, 1982, pp. 213–219.
61. Originally set up by Reg. 2142/70, O.J. S. Edn. 1970 (III) p. 707, Arts. 28–30. See now Reg. 3796/81, *op. cit.* in n. 50, Arts. 32–34.
62. Reg. 170/83, *op. cit.* in n. 51, Arts. 13–15.
63. In the case of measures implementing Community legislation on structural matters (see n. 59 above), the Standing Committee for the Fishing Industry (on which see Chapter 6) is used instead of a Management Committee, but the procedure is the same.
64. Case 25/70, *Einfuhr- und Vorratstelle für Getreide und Füttermittel v. Köster, Berodt et al.* [1971] E.C.R 1161; [1972] C.M.L.R. 255, and Case 23/75, *Rey Soda v. Cassa Conguaglio Zucchero* [1975] E.C.R 1279; [1976] 1 C.M.L.R. 185. See also Hartley, *op. cit.* in n. 2, pp. 97–100. Note, too, that Art. 10 of the Single European Act (text in Bull. E.C., Supplement 2/86) will, when it enters into force, amend Art. 145 of the EEC Treaty and formally provide for a power of delegation by the Council to the Commission in terms which encompass existing practices.
65. E.g. Reg. 3796/81, Art. 24(2) and (3), and Reg. 171/83, Art. 18(4)–(6).
66. Joined Cases 188–190/80, *French Republic, Italian Republic and United Kingdom v. Commission* [1982] E.C.R. 2545 at 2572–2576; [1982] 3 C.M.L.R. 144 at 168–171.
67. O.J. 1981 C224/1.
68. Case 804/79, *op. cit.* in n. 20.
69. Art. 155 reads: 'In order to ensure the proper functioning and development of the Common Market, the Commission shall:
   – *ensure that the provisions of this Treaty and the measures taken by the institutions pursuant thereto are applied*;

- formulate recommendations or deliver opinions on matters dealt with in this Treaty, if it expressly so provides or if the Commission considers it necessary;
- *have its own power of decision* and participate in the shaping of measures taken by the Council and by the Assembly *in the manner provided for in this Treaty*;
- exercise the powers conferred on it by the Council for the implementation of the rules laid down by the latter.' (emphasis added).

In Joined Cases 188–190/80, *op. cit.* in n. 66, the European Court implicitly rejected the idea that the Commission derived any legislative powers from Art. 155 in itself: its powers derived from the various articles of the Treaty specifically providing for Commission legislative action.

70. The passage in the Court's judgment that the Commission presumably has in mind is ground 30, which reads: 'As [fisheries management] is a field reserved to the powers of the Community . . . a Member State cannot therefore, in the absence of appropriate action on the part of the Council, bring into force any interim conservation measures which may be required by the situation except as part of a process of collaboration with the Commission and with due regard to the general task of supervision which Article 155 . . . gives to the Commission.' Cf. also ground 28 which reads: "Article 5 of the [EEC] Treaty . . . imposes on Member States special duties of action . . . in a situation in which the Commission, in order to meet urgent needs of conservation, has submitted to the Council proposals which, although they have not been adopted by the Council, represent the point of departure for concerted Community action.' While this passage can be read as requiring the *Member States* to act, it cannot be regarded as authorising the Commission to take unilateral legislative action.

71. See R. Wainwright, 'Common Fisheries Policy – the Development of a Common Regime for Fishing' (1981) 1 *Yearbook of European Law* 69 at 83.

72. It is noteworthy that in two later Declarations by the Commission (of August and December 1982) the Commission said that the duty of Member States to take conservation measures in certain circumstances was one which it (the Commission) 'can ask them to accept' (see O.J. 1982 C199/21 and C343/2). This is a much weaker formulation than that discussed in the text, and is quite in accordance with the Commission's powers under Arts. 155 and 169.

73. O.J. 1980 L91/1 and L103/1, and see the Commission's Declaration in O.J. 1980 C87/12.

74. O.J. 1980 L136/1.

75. Case 84/81, [1982] E.C.R. 1763; [1984] 1 C.M.L.R. 238.

76. Resolution on Fisheries Policy of September 17, 1981. O.J. 1981 C260/82.

77. General Secretariat of the Council, *Twenty-Ninth Review of the Council's Work* (1983) p. 249. The Commission's declaration is also the subject of indirect challenge by three Member States in proceedings which at the time of writing were pending before the European Court: Case 325/85, *Ireland v. Commission*, Case 346/85, *United Kingdom v. Commission* and Case 348/85, *Denmark v. Commission*, O.J. 1985 C357/2, 5 and 6. It should also be noted that in Case 24/83, *Gewiese and Mehlich v. Mackenzie* [1984] E.C.R 817; [1984] 2 C.M.L.R. 409 the Advocate General assumed the Commission's Declaration was valid (p. 424), but the point was not elaborated or explained and in any case was very much *obiter*. Ironically, the Advocate General was the same as in the *Staple Dairy* case – Sir Gordon Slynn.

78. Note, however, that Commission Dec. 83/3, O.J. 1983 L12/50, provides that during the period January 5–26, 1983 'fishing in Community waters shall be carried out in compliance with the Commission's proposals' (Art. 1). This Dec. also predates the Council's adoption of management measures.

79. E.g. Resolutions in O.J. 1979 C67/25 and 1983 C68/74.

80. E.g. Own-Initiative Opinion on the Current Situation and Medium-Term Prospects of the Community Fisheries Sector, O.J. 1985 C104/12.

81. For fuller discussion of the work of the European Parliament in this area, see D.I.A. Steel, 'Fisheries Policy and the EEC: the Democratic Influence' (1984) 8 *Marine Policy* 350.

82. See n. 19.

CHAPTER 3

The scope of EEC fisheries law

The earlier part of the previous Chapter explained the general competence of the EEC to regulate fisheries. What the present Chapter seeks to do is to establish more precisely the scope of that competence as regards subject matter (to what kinds of fish and other aquatic resources does the competence extend); place (to which territories and marine areas does the competence extend); and persons (to which fishermen does the competence extend). In dealing with these three aspects of the scope of Community competence, the aim will be to consider the maximum possible reach of such competence and of legislative measures adopted by virtue of that competence – as provided by Community Law in general – rather than to examine the scope of each individual piece of EEC fisheries legislation. Such legislation often has a narrower scope than the theoretical maximum. Reference will be made in later chapters, where appropriate, to the scope of individual pieces of legislation.

1. MATERIAL SCOPE

The Community's competence obviously applies to fish. But does this mean both marine and freshwater fish, or only the former? Furthermore, does the Community's competence apply just to fish in the strict biological sense, or does it also cover other living aquatic resources, such as mammals, crustaceans, molluscs, corals, sponges etc? The starting point for discovering the answer to these questions is Article 38 of the EEC Treaty. As was seen at the beginning of the previous Chapter, this article provides that the Common Agricultural and Common Fisheries Policies are to apply to agricultural products. The latter are defined as 'products of the soil, of stock-farming and of fisheries and products of first-stage processing directly related to these products,' as listed in Annex II to the EEC Treaty. This Annex lists agricultural products according to the nomenclature used in the Brussels Convention on Customs Nomenclature 1950, as amended.[1] The following products in the list in Annex II relate to fisheries:

No. in the Brussels Nomenclature	Description of Products
Chapter 3	Fish, crustaceans and molluscs.
Chapter 5. 05.15	Animal products not elsewhere specified or included; dead animals of Chapter 1 or Chapter 3, unfit for human consumption.
Chapter 15. 15.04	Fats and oils, of fish and marine mammals, whether or not refined.
Chapter 16.	Preparations of meat, of fish, crustaceans or molluscs.
Chapter 23.	Residues and waste from the food industries; prepared animal fodder.

These brief descriptions provide but a limited answer to the questions asked above, and it is therefore necessary to resort to the Brussels Convention to see if an examination of the references to it in Annex II of the EEC Treaty provides any clarification. There is at the outset one slight problem in this regard. The Brussels Convention has been amended several times since the EEC Treaty was signed.[2] Should clarification of Annex II therefore be sought in the Brussels Convention in its original or its amended form? Here it is not really necessary to answer this question, since although some of the amendments to the Convention do relate to the provisions of Annex II under consideration, they do not make any changes of substance. In the discussion that follows references to the Brussels Convention will be to it in its original form.

As far as 'fish' are concerned, the Brussels Convention does not expand on Annex II in relation to the species of fish covered. It seems reasonable to assume that the Convention, and thus Annex II, cover all species of fish, whether marine or freshwater. This means, therefore, that the Community has the competence to regulate freshwater as well as marine fish. In practice, most EEC fisheries legislation applies only to marine fish, but the Regulation on the Common Organisation of the Market in Fishery Products does cover a few freshwater and diadromous species.[3] The Brussels Convention makes it clear that Annex II covers fish, whatever its form – whether fresh, frozen, chilled, salted, dried, smoked, preserved etc. (Chapters 03.01, 03.02, 05.15 and 16.04) – and also when converted into oils, fats and meals (Chapters 15.04 and 23). The Convention (Chapters 03.03 and 16.05) and Annex II and thus the Community's competence, also apply to crustaceans and molluscs, again in whatever form they happen to be.

Corals, sponges and shells other than molluscs fall within Chapters 05.12 and 05.13 of the Brussels Convention. Since these chapters of the Convention are not mentioned in Annex II of the EEC Treaty, it follows that these aquatic organisms fall outside the scope of EEC fisheries law.

Somewhat problematical is the position of aquatic animals, particularly marine mammals (notably whales and seals). Some products of aquatic animals fall within Annex II, namely the meat of such animals (see Chapters 02.04 and 02.06 of the Brussels Convention which, though not mentioned above, are listed in Annex II), and the fats and oils of marine mammals (Chapter 15.04). On the other hand, some products of aquatic animals are dealt with by Chapters of the Brussels Convention that are not included in Annex II: this is the case with whalebone (Chapter 05.09); walrus and narwhal tusks and other teeth/tusks of whales, seals etc. (Chapter 05.10); ambergris and other animal products of a kind used in the preparation of pharmaceutical products (Chapter 05.14); spermaceti (Chapter 15.14); and skins and furs (Chapters 41 and 43). As far as marketing and trade is concerned, the position is straightforward. Those products of aquatic animals listed in Annex II fall within the scope of the Community's competence under the Common Fisheries Policy,[4] while those products not listed in Annex II fall outside that competence – though this does not necessarily mean, of course, that they fall outside the field of the EEC altogether: they may well be governed by some other policy e.g. the Common Commercial Policy, which covers trade in these products. While the position as regards marketing and trade is straightforward, the position as regards the catching of aquatic animals is not so simple. Where an animal is being caught exclusively for the purposes of obtaining a product which falls outside Annex II, for example killing seals exclusively for their pelts, it would seem that the catching stage lies outside the ambit of the Common Fisheries Policy. On the other hand, where the catching is exclusively for the purpose of obtaining a product falling within Annex II, then it falls within the Policy. Often, however, aquatic animals are caught for the purpose of obtaining a number of products, some of which fall within Annex II and others outside. Does such an activity, of which whaling is a notable example, fall within the scope of the Common Fisheries Policy? This question arose in a direct and practical form in 1979 when the Commission proposed that the EEC should become a party to the International Convention for the Regulation of Whaling. The Commission took the view that whaling fell within the scope of the Common Fisheries Policy.[5] At subsequent Council meetings, however, this view was contested by some Member States, and the issue appears to remain unresolved within the Council.[6] The argument essentially turns on the question of whether something which in part undoubtedly falls within Community competence can or should be excluded from that competence because it is indissolubly linked with matters outside that competence, or whether it is permissible to bring within Community competence matters which strictly speaking lie outside that competence on the ground that they are linked to matters within Community competence. On balance, the latter view (that of the Commission) appears preferable: first the inclusion of the non-Community matter could probably be justified by having recourse to Article 235 of the EEC Treaty;[7] secondly, adoption of the former view would mean excluding matters from the Community's competence which are certainly within that competence, and this would seem to be contrary to Community law.[8]

To sum up: the material scope of the Community's competence to regulate fisheries under Articles 39 *et seq.* of the EEC Treaty is as follows. The Community's competence extends to all species of fish, whether freshwater or marine, and to crustaceans and molluscs. It does not cover corals, sponges or shells other than molluscs. As far as aquatic animals are concerned, the Community's competence covers marketing and trade in the meat of such animals and the fats and oils of marine mammals, as well as the catching of such animals exclusively for the purpose of obtaining such products. It probably also covers the catching of aquatic animals partially for the purpose of obtaining the above-mentioned products – although this point is not entirely free from doubt.

2. TERRITORIAL SCOPE

One writer on Community law has stated that 'for those with a taste for the obscure a consideration of the territorial application of the Treaty of Rome may afford a spree of intellectual satisfaction, involving as it does a glance at many a far-flung corner of the globe, both in Europe and beyond.'[9] Whether the reader will experience a 'spree of intellectual satisfaction' from the discussion that follows remains to be seen, but an inquiry into the territorial scope of EEC fisheries law is necessary in view of the extensive international aspects of fisheries (of which some indication was given in Chapter 1). Such an inquiry has two separate, but related, aspects: first, to which territories does EEC fisheries law apply; and secondly, how far off the coasts of such territories may such law apply.

A. To Which Territories does EEC Fisheries Law apply?

There is nothing in the provisions of the EEC Treaty dealing with agriculture which defines the geographical scope of EEC agricultural and fisheries legislation. Therefore the presumption must be – a presumption confirmed by the European Court in the *Irish Fisheries* case[10] – that the geographical scope of fisheries legislation is the same as for the Treaty generally. The starting point for any discussion as to the general geographical scope of the Treaty must be Article 227(1) (as amended). This reads as follows:

> This Treaty shall apply to the Kingdom of Belgium, the Kingdom of Denmark, the Federal Republic of Germany, the Hellenic Republic, the Kingdom of Spain, the French Republic, Ireland, the Italian Republic, the Grand Duchy of Luxembourg, the Kingdom of the Netherlands, the Portuguese Republic and the United Kingdom of Great Britain and Northern Ireland.

In the case of Belgium, the Federal Republic of Germany, Greece, Ireland, Italy and Luxembourg, the position is straightforward: the Treaty applies to all their territory.[11] With other Member States the situation is not so simple. This is because, as a result of other provisions, the Treaty does not apply to their territories in their entirety. There is also the question as to whether the Treaty applies to territories for the external relations of which Member States are responsible. It is therefore necessary to consider the extent of the application of the Treaty in relation to (i) certain parts of Member States' European territories; (ii) Member States' territories outside Europe; (iii) European territories for whose external relations a Member State is responsible; and (iv) non-European territories for whose external relations a Member State is responsible.

(i) *Certain Parts of Member States' European Territories. Denmark.* In the case of Denmark the question is the extent to which the Treaty applies to the Faroes. In relation to this isolated North Atlantic archipelago, which is part of Denmark but which since 1948 has enjoyed a substantial degree of self-government, Article 227(5)(a) provides that the Treaty:

shall not apply to the Faroe Islands. The Government of the Kingdom of Denmark may, however, give notice, by a declaration deposited by December 31, 1975 at the latest with the Government of the Italian Republic ... that this Treaty shall apply to those Islands. In that event this Treaty shall apply from the first day of the second month following the deposit of the declaration.

Such a declaration was never in fact made. Well before the expiry of the prescribed deadline, on January 24, 1974, the Parliament of the Faroes, largely influenced by apprehensions about the Common Fisheries Policy, particularly its provisions on equal access, voted against accession to the EEC, and in favour of the conclusion of a commercial agreement with the Community. This action led the Council on February 4, 1974 to adopt a Resolution in which it took note of the Faroese decision with regret, and expressed the intention of seeking a longer-term solution that would be acceptable to the Faroes. The Council stated that it would re-examine the situation in the light of the outcome of the Third United Nations Conference on the Law of the Sea: a subsequent revision of the Common Fisheries Policy might then make the accession of the Faroes to the EEC possible.[12] So far such a re-examination has not been carried out, and the position is, therefore, that at the present time the Faroes are not part of the EEC. The Faroes, however, do have a fisheries agreement with the EEC on reciprocal access to each other's waters (discussed in Chapter 5) and preferential access to EEC markets for their fishery exports (discussed in Chapter 8).

United Kingdom. The United Kingdom has sovereignty over certain military bases on Cyprus. Article 227(5)(b) of the EEC Treaty, however, provides that the Treaty does not apply to these bases.

(ii) *Member States' Territories outside Europe.* Five Member States – Denmark, France, the Netherlands, Portugal and Spain – have possessions outside Europe which are part of their territory in the strict sense and not simply territories for whose external relations they are responsible. These territories are Greenland; the French overseas departments of French Guyana, Guadeloupe, Martinique and Réunion (between 1975 and 1986 St. Pierre et Miquelon was also an overseas department); the Netherlands Antilles; the Portuguese archipelagos of Azores and Madeira; and Spain's Canary Islands and its two North African enclaves of Ceuta and Melilla.

Greenland and the Netherlands Antilles are dealt with by the provisions of Part IV of the EEC Treaty. These provisions are considered below, when discussing the position of non-European territories for whose external relations Member States are responsible. The Azores and Madeira are fully within the Treaty and thus the ambit of EEC fisheries law. On the other hand, the

Canary Islands and Ceuta and Melilla fall outside the Treaty as far as fisheries matters are concerned, although they enjoy certain advantages in exporting fish to the Community and the Community institutions are empowered to adopt a limited range of fisheries measures for these territories, should this prove appropriate at some future date.[13]

The position of the French overseas departments is more complex. Article 227(2) of the EEC Treaty provides that with regard to these territories:

> the general and particular provisions of this Treaty relating to:
> the free movement of goods;
> agriculture, save for Article 40(4);[14]
> ... shall apply as soon as this Treaty enters into force. The conditions under which the other provisions of this Treaty are to apply shall be determined, within two years of the entry into force of this Treaty, by decisions of the Council, acting unanimously on a proposal from the Commission.

As far as fisheries are concerned, the effect of this provision is that the French overseas departments come within the Treaty for the purposes of that part of EEC fisheries law adopted under the provisions of the Treaty dealing with agriculture (i.e. the common marketing policy and part of the common structural policy) and also for the purposes of trade in fishery products (insofar as such trade is not regulated by the common marketing policy). As far as EEC fisheries law adopted on the basis of provisions of the Treaty other than those dealing with agriculture (possibly part of the common structural policy) is concerned, a literal reading of Article 227(2) would suggest that the application of this area of EEC fisheries law to the French overseas departments is dependent on a determination by the Council, and that since no such determination has been made, this area of law does not apply. This literal approach must be rejected, however, in the light of the judgment of the European Court in *Hansen & Balle v. Hauptzollamt Flensburg*.[15] In this case the Court held that after the expiry of the two-year period laid down in Article 227(2):

> the provisions of the Treaty and of secondary law must apply automatically to the French overseas departments inasmuch as they are an integral part of the French Republic, it being understood, however, that it always remains possible subsequently to adopt specific measures in order to meet the needs of those territories.[16]

The consequence of this interpretation of Article 227(2) by the Court is that all EEC fisheries law applies to the French overseas departments: it is, however, possible for the Community institutions to adopt specific measures in order to meet the needs of these territories in fisheries matters.

As well as the French overseas departments, Article 227(2) also refers to Algeria. At the time the EEC Treaty was signed, Algeria was indeed part of France. But since Algeria became independent in 1962, it seems highly unlikely that Article 227(2) still applies to it, even though the Article has never formally been amended. It has been argued that the inclusion of Algeria in Article 227(2) was impliedly conditional on the status of the territory remaining unaltered.[17] In addition, it is almost certain that the doctrine laid down by the European Court in *Lensing v. Hauptzollamt Berlin-Packhof*[18] (where the Court held that the attainment of independence by a territory has the effect of automatically deleting it from the list of territories in Annex IV, discussed below) also applies to Algeria.

(iii) *European Territories for Whose External Relations a Member State is Responsible.* Article 227(4) of the EEC Treaty reads:

The provisions of this Treaty shall apply to the European territories for whose external relations a Member State is responsible.

There are several territories which are potentially subject to this provision. They are: Monaco, San Marino, Andorra, Gibraltar, the Channel Islands and the Isle of Man. Some of these, particularly land-locked San Marino and Andorra, have only a very limited interest as far as fisheries are concerned (principally in relation to trade). Each of these territories will be examined in turn, to see whether they do actually fall into the category of territory to which Article 227(4) refers.

Monaco. It is doubtful whether France can be said to be responsible for Monaco's external relations. Under a Treaty between Monaco and France of 1918, France assures to Monaco 'the defence of its independence and sovereignty and guarantees the integrity of its territory.'[19] Article 1 of Monaco's Constitution speaks of Monaco as being a 'sovereign and independent State.' Thus it seems unlikely that Monaco is within the general ambit of the Treaty.[20] It is, however, in the EEC customs territory.[21]

San Marino. It is doubtful whether Italy can be said to be responsible for San Marino's external relations. A treaty between San Marino and Italy of 1971[22] reaffirms that Italy regards San Marino as independent. Thus it seems unlikely that San Marino is within the general scope of the Treaty.[23] Like Monaco, however, it is within the EEC customs territory.[24]

Andorra. Andorra is subject to the joint control of the President of France and the Spanish Bishop of Urgel. It therefore seems unlikely that it is covered by Article 227(4).[25] Nor is Andorra in the EEC customs territory.[26]

Gibraltar. Gibraltar is a United Kingdom Colony and there is therefore no doubt that in principle it falls within the scope of Article 227(4). Article 28 of the Act of Accession, however, provides that:

Acts of the institutions of the Community relating to the products in Annex II to the EEC Treaty and the products subject, on importation into the Community, to specific rules as a result of the common agricultural policy . . . shall not apply to Gribraltar unless the Council, acting unanimously on a proposal from the Commission, provides otherwise.

Since, as has been seen earlier in this Chapter, the products listed in Annex II include fisheries products, the consequence of Article 28 is that EEC fisheries legislation does not apply to Gibraltar unless the Council decides otherwise. This the Council has not done.

The Channel Islands and the Isle of Man. The Channel Islands and the Isle of Man are British Crown dependencies. The United Kingdom is responsible for their defence and international relations. There is therefore no doubt that in principle these territories fall within the scope of Article 227(4). However, Article 227(5) provides that the EEC Treaty:

shall apply to the Channel Islands and the Isle of Man only to the extent necessary to ensure the implementation of the arrangements for these islands set out in the Treaty [of Accession].

These arrangements are set out in Protocol No. 3 to the Act of Accession. As far as fisheries are concerned, the following provisions of this Protocol appear to be relevant.

First, under Article 1 of the Protocol, the Channel Islands and the Isle of Man are effectively part of the EEC for customs and trade purposes. This means that trade in fish between these territories and EEC Member States and between these territories and third countries is governed by Community rules. However, Article 1 also goes on to provide in subparagraph 2 of paragraph 2, that:

such provisions of Community rules . . . as are necessary to allow free movement and observance of normal conditions of competition in trade in these products [i.e. agricultural products, which include fisheries products] shall also be applicable.

Under subparagraph 3 the Council is to determine the conditions under which these provisions are to be applicable. The Council made such a determination in Regulation 706/73.[27] This Regulation provides that that part of the Common Fisheries Policy concerned with the rules applicable to trade and the rules on quality and marketing standards applies to the Channel Islands and the Isle of Man. The fact that the Regulation says nothing about the other aspects of the Common Fisheries Policy does not necessarily mean that they do not apply to the Channel Islands or the Isle of Man: whether they do or not depends on the remaining provisions of the Protocol that are relevant.

The first of these is Article 2, which provides that 'the rights enjoyed by Channel Islanders or Manxmen in the United Kingdom shall not be affected by the Act of Accession'. An important point is whether the phrase 'in the United Kingdom' used in Article 2 includes not only the land territory of the United Kingdom but also its territorial sea and exclusive fishing zone. If it does, then among the rights which Channel Islanders and Manxmen enjoyed 'in the United Kingdom' before the latter's accession to the EEC was a right of access for their fishing vessels to the United Kingdom's territorial sea and its then 12-mile exclusive fishing zone.[28] On this reading of the phrase 'in the United Kingdom', the effect of Article 2 is that Channel Island and Manx fishing vessels continue to enjoy access to the United Kingdom's territorial sea and exclusive fishing zone, regardless of any provisions of Community Law contained in the structural side of the Common Fisheries Policy. On the other hand, if 'in the United Kingdom' excludes the territorial sea and/or exclusive fishing zone, Article 2 has no application as far as fisheries is concerned. It therefore becomes important to decide whether the phrase 'in the United Kingdom' includes maritime areas appurtenant to the United Kingdom. In the absence of any definition of 'in the United Kingdom' in the Protocol, the meaning of the phrase must be sought by reference to general principles of international law. 'In the United Kingdom' must, in the absence of any qualification of the phrase, be taken as meaning at least the territory of the United Kingdom. Since a State's territory includes its territorial sea,[29] it follows that the United Kingdom's territorial sea is included in the phrase, 'in the United Kingdom'. The exclusive fishing zone, on the other hand, is not strictly speaking part of a State's territory. It could therefore be argued that 'in the United Kingdom' does not include the exclusive fishing zone. Such an argument, however, would lead to the anomalous situation that Channel Islands and Manx fishermen had access to the United Kingdom's territorial sea, but not its exclusive fishing zone. It would therefore seem reasonable to construe the phrase 'in the United Kingdom' as including the exclusive fishing zone of the United Kingdom, as well as its territorial sea. On this construction the consequence of Article 2 is that Channel Island and Manx fishermen enjoy access to the United Kngdom's territorial sea and exclusive fishing zone.

The other relevant provision of the Protocol is Article 4. This provides that the authorities of the Channel Islands and the Isle of Man 'shall apply the same treatment to all natural and legal persons of the Community'. This appears to suggest that any rights which United Kingdom fishermen enjoy in Channel Island or Manx waters shall also extend to fishermen from other Member States. In trying to discover what rights, if any, United Kingdom fishermen do enjoy, or did enjoy, in Channel Island and Manx waters, it is helpful to trace the positions through the recent series of United Kingdom fisheries enactments. The Fishery Limits Act 1964 placed restrictions on the access of foreign fishing vessels to the fishing limits of the British Islands, which included the Channel Islands and the Isle of Man. In the absence of any other relevant provisions in the Act or elsewhere, it would seem to follow that United Kingdom vessels had in principle access to Channel Island and Manx waters. These provisions of the Fishery Limits Act were replaced by s.6 of the Sea Fisheries Act 1968. This section was concerned with limiting the access of foreign fishing vessels to United Kingdom waters only (and not the waters of the British Islands, as under the Fishery Limits Act). However, orders were made including the Channel Islands and the Isle of Man within the ambit of s.6.[30] The result of these orders would seem to be to make the position under the 1968 Act the same as it was under the 1964 Act.

S.6 of the 1968 Act has in turn been replaced by the Fishery Limits Act 1976, which is the current legislation governing the question. S.2 of this Act places restrictions on the access of foreign vessels to 'British fishery limits', which are defined as including the waters adjacent to the Channel Islands and the Isle of Man (see s.1(1)). It would therefore seem to follow, just as in the case of the 1964 Act, that United Kingdom fishing vessels have in principle access to the waters around the Channel Islands and the Isle of Man. Some doubt, however, is cast on this apparently clear reading of the 1976 Act by s.11 of the Act. This section provides that orders may be made for the Channel Islands and the Isle of Man as appear 'to be necessary in consequence of the extension of British fishery limits' by the Act. Such orders may in particular extend s.2(2)–(7) (which deals with restrictions on the access of foreign fishing vessels) to the Channel Islands and the Isle of Man. No such orders have yet been made. The existence of this power under s.11 suggests that s.2 does not apply to the Channel Islands and the Isle of Man. In this case the inference drawn above from the presence of s.2 would seem to be impermissible, and the position would be that United Kingdom vessels have no access to Channel Island and Manx waters. On the other hand, if the first reading of the Act is correct, then s.11 confers a power which is not needed, because s.2 applies to the Channel Islands and the Isle of Man automatically. If the first reading of the Act is correct, and United Kingdom fishing vessels do in principle enjoy access to Channel Island and Manx waters (and contemporary United Kingdom practice certainly suggests this is the position), the effect of Article 4 of the Protocol would seem to be that fishing vessels from other EEC Member States also enjoy in principle access to Channel Island and Manx waters. This consequence of Article 4 is, however, contradicted by United Kingdom practice. The Fishing Boats (European Economic Community) Designation Orders 1972 and 1983,[31] which regulate the access of vessels of EEC Member States to British waters, do not give these vessels any rights of access to

Channel Island or Manx waters. Other EEC Member States appear not to have objected to this legislation.

If the first interpretation of the 1976 Act and the effects of Article 4 of the Protocol is wrong, as this United Kingdom practice suggests, that is not the end of the matter as far as the access of EEC vessels to Channel Island and Manx waters is concerned. Under various orders made under the Fishery Limits Act 1964,[32] Belgian, French and Irish vessels enjoy certain rights in the 6–12 mile zone off the Isle of Man and French vessels enjoy certain rights in the 6–12 mile zone off the Channel Islands. The effect of Article 4 of the Protocol, it would seem, is that the vessels of all EEC Member States should enjoy the same rights as Belgian, French and Irish vessels (although it should be noted that, strictly speaking, these rights do not derive from the authorities of the Channel Islands and the Isle of Man, to which Article 4 refers, but from the authorities of the United Kingdom: if this distinction is significant, then that it is all the more reason why access should be non-discriminatory).

Even if EEC vessels do enjoy access to all or part of Channel Island and Manx waters, and Channel Island and Manx vessels enjoy access to United Kingdom waters, this does not necessarily mean that those parts of the Common Fisheries Policy falling outside the fields of trade and marketing standards (the subject of Article 1 of Protocol 3 and Regulation 706/73) and non-discrimination (dealt with by Article 4 of the Protocol) apply to Channel Islands and Manx waters. Indeed, Article 227(5), which speaks of the EEC Treaty applying 'to the Channel Islands and the Isle of Man only to the extent necessary to ensure the implementation of the arrangements' contained in the Protocol, suggests quite strongly that they do not. However, a different conclusion is suggested by the practice of the Council and the case law of the European Court.

As far as the former is concerned, the Council in 1977 adopted a short-term fishery conservation measure for Manx waters.[33] On the other hand, the present long-term conservation regulation is equivocal, defining the areas to which it applies as 'all maritime waters under the sovereignty or jurisdiction of Member States and situated' in *inter alia* the North-East Atlantic.[34]

More significant, perhaps, is the discussion in two cases brought by the Commission against the United Kingdom.[35] These case were concerned, *inter alia,* with whether a set of United Kingdom measures establishing a quota and licensing system for United Kingdom and Manx vessels fishing for herring in the Northern Irish Sea and around the Isle of Man, was contrary to Community law. A preliminary point was whether this legislation fell within the ambit of Community law at all. The United Kingdom argued that the effect of Article 227(5)(c) and Protocol 3 was that Community rules on fisheries (other than those concerned with the free movement of goods) did not apply to the Isle of Man. The Commission, on the other hand, argued that because of the close link as regards fisheries between the organisation of the market and structural measures, the effect of Protocol 3 was that Community rules on fisheries did apply to the Isle of Man. Furthermore, Regulation 706/73 did not specify exhaustively which provisions of Community law were applicable to the Isle of Man, but merely clarified some technical administrative matters. The Court, however, rather avoided the issue. It observed that

> it does not seem necessary to consider the constitutional position of the Isle of Man and the relationship of that territory to the Community. In fact, it is clear from the very wording of the order in question that it was adopted under the legislation of the Unted Kingdom by the British government, so that the United Kingdom must take responsibility for that measure vis-à-vis the Community.[36]

The Court's judgment on this point seems rather question begging, and its reasoning is not very satisfactory. The argument that if legislation has been adopted for the Isle of Man by the United Kingdom, that legislation automatically falls within the ambit of Community law does not seem tenable as a general proposition: for example, if the United Kingdom legislated for the Isle of Man in respect of a matter falling within an area of Community Law which unambiguously did not apply to the Isle of Man, it seems difficult to see how that United Kingdom legislation could be considered as being within the ambit of Community Law. The proposition put forward by the Court would therefore seem to depend on a prior, unspoken assumption having been made that the legislation in question does relate to an area of Community Law which does apply to the Isle of Man. In the present cases, the Court found that the United Kingdom legislation at issue infringed Community rules relating to non-discrimination and the obligation to consult the Commission about proposed national conservation measures: it would seem, therefore, that at the least the Court regards these rules as applying to Manx (and Channel Island) waters. While the non-discrimination rule might follow from Article 4 of Protocol 3 (as explained above), the rule on consultation with the Commission must follow because the Court considers that at least some part of the Common Fisheries Policy other than those following from Protocol 3 apply to Manx and Channel Island waters.It is also of interest to note what the Advocate General's views on the question were in the first case. (In the second case he adopted what the Court said in the first case). On the question of whether the United Kingdom measures were discriminatory, he observed that since other Member States had no rights to fish in Manx waters there could be no discrimination against them. This observation is quite erroneous, first because the premise on which it is based is false (as has been pointed out, Belgian, French and Irish vessels undoubtedly do have rights in Manx waters); and secondly because it completely overlooks the effects of Article 4 of Protocol 3. On the other hand, as far as those provisions of the United Kingdom measures requiring catches to be landed in the Isle of Man were concerned, the Advocate General opined that these were caught by Community law because they affected Community rules on the free movement of goods (which, as has been seen, undoubtedly do apply to the Isle of Man). While in this latter aspect the Advocate General's opinion is more satisfying than the Court's judgment, it must be regarded now as being of somewhat academic interest only, given that the Court has adopted a consistently different approach.

To sum up the position of the Channel Islands and the Isle of Man in relation to the territorial scope of EEC fisheries law is not easy. It is clear that EEC rules on trade in fisheries products, both within the Community and with third States, and the rules on quality and marketing standards apply to the islands. It is also clear that EEC fishing vessels enjoy certain rights of access to Channel Island and Manx waters – though the exact scope of these rights is uncertain because of the two apparently possible interpretations of the Fishery Limits Act 1976. As regards the remainder of EEC fisheries law, Article 227(5) suggests that it does not apply to the islands at all. However, the Court, and to some extent the Council, take the view that at least some – undefined – parts of this area of law do apply. Furthermore, according to the Court, if the United Kingdom authorities, rather than the Channel Island or Manx authorities, legislate for the islands in fisheries matters, such legislation is subject to Community law. As has been suggested, this proposition is highly debatable.

(iv) *Non-European Territories for Whose External Relations a Member State is Responsible.* There is a large number of such territories, many of which are of considerable practical importance as far as fisheries are concerned because of their capacity to generate extensive maritime zones, rich in fishery resources. The position of these territories is governed by Article 227(3) and Part IV of the EEC Treaty.

Article 227(3) provides that the special arrangements for association set out in Part IV of the Treaty shall apply to those territories listed in Annex IV of the Treaty. In relation to those non-European territories for whose external relations a Member State is responsible which are not listed in Annex IV, the Treaty does not apply. The only territories coming in this latter category are Hong Kong (a colony of the United Kingdom) and Macau.[37]

The overwhelming majority of non-European territories for whose external relations Member States are responsible are, however, listed in Annex IV. This list has not been amended since the EEC Treaty came into force in 1958, and as a result includes many territories which are now independent. However, as briefly mentioned above, the European Court in *Lensing v. Hauptzollamt Berlin-Packhof*[38] held that the attainment of independence by a territory has the effect of automatically excluding it from the list in Annex IV, unless provision to the contrary is made. Applying this principle, and therefore excluding all territories which are now independent (no special provisions to the contrary having been made), the list of territories in Annex IV now reads as follows:

- Territories for which Denmark is responsible: Greenland.
- Territories for which France is responsible: St. Pierre et Miquelon, Mayotte, New Caledonia, French settlements in Oceania,[39] and the Southern and Antarctic territories.[40]
- Territories for which the Netherlands is responsible: Netherlands Antilles.
- Territories for which the United Kingdom is responsible: Anguilla, Bermuda, British Antarctic Territory, British Indian Ocean Territory, British Virgin Islands, Cayman Islands, Central and Southern Line Islands, Falkland Islands, Montserrat, Pitcairn, St. Helena and Dependencies, and the Turks and Caicos Islands.

The arrangements for these territories are set out in Part IV of the EEC Treaty (Articles 131–136), supplemented by a series of implementing measures adopted under Article 136. The current such measure is Decision 86/283.[41] There are two features of these arrangements which are relevant to fisheries. First, in general there are no customs duties on trade between Annex IV territories and EEC Member States (Articles 133 and 134). Detailed rules on this topic are set out in Decision 86/283, and these will be discussed in Chapter 8. Secondly, under Article 176 of Decision 86/283 EEC Member States have limited rights of establishment in Annex IV territories. While there is no automatic right of establishment for nationals and companies of EEC Member States in Annex IV territories, if a right of establishment is granted it must be non-discriminatory: i.e. if a national of EEC Member State A is permitted to establish himself for a particular activity in Annex IV territory X, a national of EEC Member State B must also be permitted to establish himself for the same activity in the territory, provided, however, that State B grants a similar right of establishment to individuals and companies from territory X. The implications of this provision for fisheries are discussed in Chapter 4. Apart from the arrangements set out in Part IV, Annex IV territories are outside the scope of the EEC Treaty. These territories are therefore completely outside the field of the EEC fisheries law, and their only connection with fisheries in an EEC context is in relation to trade with the EEC and the limited opportunities for establishment by EEC fishermen and EEC fishing companies.

Before leaving Annex IV territories, special mention must be made of Greenland. Greenland is in fact a newcomer to the list of Annex IV territories. As part of Denmark, it became part of the EEC when Denmark joined in 1973. However, in February 1982 an advisory referendum on continued Greenland membership of the EEC was held. The result was a small majority in favour of leaving the EEC, a result that was probably the reflection of a certain amount of dissatisfaction with the Common Fisheries Policy and of the aspirations unleashed by the granting of home rule in 1979. In response to the referendum a Treaty amending the EEC Treaty so as to add Greenland to the list of Annex IV territories was signed in March 1984 and entered into force on February 1, 1985.[42] Accompanying the Treaty are a Protocol making special provision for the import of fishery products from Greenland (discussed in Chapter 8) and an Agreement and Protocol on Fisheries, which provide for fishing by Community vessels in Greenland waters (discussed in Chapter 5).[43]

We can sum up this discussion of the territories to which EEC fisheries law applies as follows. This law applies to the European parts of Belgium, Denmark (except the Faroes), France, the Federal Republic of Germany (including West Berlin), Greece, Ireland, Italy, Luxembourg, the Netherlands, Portugal, Spain and the United Kingdom, together with the Azores, Madeira and French overseas departments. On the other hand, EEC fisheries law does not apply to the Faroes, the United Kingdom's Sovereign Bases in Cyprus, the Canary Islands, Ceuta and Melilla, Monaco, Andorra, San Marino, Gibraltar, the territories listed in Annex IV, Hong Kong and Macao. Finally, the Channel Islands and the Isle of Man appear to be in a kind of half-way position: some parts of EEC fisheries law undoubtedly do apply to them, while there is doubt as to whether the remainder do.

Having reached these conclusions as to the territories to which EEC fisheries law applies, we must now turn to consider the other aspect of the territorial scope of this law, namely the question of how far off the coasts of these territories such law may apply.

B. *How far off the Coast may EEC Fisheries Law apply?*

As has already been seen in the previous section, Article 227(1) of the EEC Treaty states that the Treaty applies to 'the Kingdom of Belgium, the Kingdom of Denmark ...' etc. This must mean, at the very least, that the Treaty applies to the territories of those States. The territory of a State includes its territorial sea: this is the position both under Article 1 of the 1958 Geneva Convention on the Territorial Sea and the Contiguous Zone[44] (to which, of EEC Member States, Belgium, Denmark, Italy, the Netherlands, Portugal, Spain and the United Kingdom are parties), and under customary international law.[45] It therefore follows that the EEC Treaty, and legislation adopted under it, applies to the territorial sea of Member States, as well as – obviously – their internal waters.

But what about Member States' maritime zones beyond the territorial sea, such as the exclusive fishing zone, exclusive economic zone (EEZ) and continental shelf, which are not part of their territory? Does the Treaty, or may the

Treaty, extend to such zones, or indeed even beyond these zones to the high seas? The EEC Treaty contains no direct answer to this question. It has been argued by one writer[46] that Article 227 must be interpreted strictly: this would mean that the EEC has no competence outside the territory of its Member States. On the other hand, other writers[47] take the view that such a narrow interpretation of Article 227 would hinder the Community in achieving its objectives, and that a literal reading of the article must therefore be replaced by a more teleological approach. Furthermore, they point out that Article 227 does not refer to 'territories': the Treaty is declared to be applicable to Member States. This suggests that in principle the Treaty has the same geographical reach as the jurisdiction of Member States in relation to the differing subject matter of the EEC Treaty, unless the scope of the Treaty is specifically restricted, as it is in some articles: e.g. Articles 48 and 52 explicitly restrict the authority of the Community to the 'territory' of Member States.

This broader approach has been confirmed by the European Court as being the correct one. In the *Kramer* case [48] the Court said that it should be made clear that although Article 5 of the original regulation laying down a common structural policy for the fishing industry (Regulation 2141/70) was applicable only to a geographically limited area (the territorial sea and exclusive fishing zone):

> It none the less follows from Article 102 of the Act of Accession, from Article 1 of the said regulation and moreover from the very nature of things that the rule-making authority of the Community *ratione materiae* also extends – in so far as the Member States have similar authority under public international law – to fishing on the high seas.[49]

Thus Community fisheries law may apply beyond the territorial sea. Essentially the Community's competence in this matter is co-extensive with the legislative (or prescriptive) jurisdiction which its Member States have in fishery matters under international law. This means that Community fisheries law can apply to: (1) all vessels, whether registered in a Member State or a third State, engaged in fishing activities in the territorial sea, exclusive fishing zone or EEZ off one of the territories to which the Common Fisheries Policy applies, or fishing on the continental shelf of such a territory for sedentary species; (2) to all vessels registered in a Member State fishing on the high seas; (3) to all vessels registered in a Member State fishing in the territorial sea, exclusive fishing zone or EEZ of a third State, although here Community legislation will be concurrent with the legislative jurisdiction of the third State, and the latter will have the sole right to exercise enforcement jurisdiction in this area.

It is appropriate at this juncture to examine the precise extent of the maritime zones referred to in (1) in the previous paragraph, i.e. the extent of the territorial sea, exclusive fishing zone, EEZ and continental shelf claimed by each Member State. Between 1970, when the original Common Fisheries Policy was adopted, and 1976, the last year before the move to extend fishing limits to 200 miles, two Member States (France and Italy) claimed a 12-mile territorial sea, while the remaining Member States each claimed three miles. Three of the latter (Denmark, Ireland and the United Kingdom) claimed a 12-mile fishery zone, while an 80-mile fishery zone was claimed in respect of French Guyana. All Member States claimed sovereign rights over the sedentary species or 'natural resources' (which it is safe to assume include sedentary species) of the continental shelf, the extent of which was either defined in the terms of the Continental Shelf Convention[50] or not specified.

Since 1976 there has been no change in the territorial sea or continental shelf claimed by any Member State,[51] but as we saw briefly in the first chapter, there was a concerted move by Member States to extend their fishery limits to 200 miles at the beginning of 1977 as a result of the Hague Resolution adopted in November 1976. This action must now be examined in a little more detail.

The Council's Resolution of November 3, 1976 (The Hague Resolution).[52] In this Resolution the Council notes that:

> ... present circumstances, and particularly the unilateral steps taken or about to be taken by certain third countries,[53] warrant immediate action by the Community to protect its legitimate interests in the maritime regions most threatened by the consequences of these steps to extend fishing zones, and that the measures to be adopted to this end should be based on the guidelines which are emerging within the Third United Nations Conference on the Law of the Sea.

The Council then goes on to agree that:

> as from January 1, 1977, Member States shall, by means of concerted action, extend the limits of their fishing zones to 200 miles off their North Sea and North Atlantic coasts, without prejudice to similar action being taken for fishing zones within their jurisdiction such as the Mediterranean.

The first point of interest about this Resolution is whether it is a legally binding instrument. Resolutions as such are not mentioned in the category of acts which the Council is empowered to adopt under Article 189 of the EEC Treaty. Nevertheless, as the European Court has held, the title of an instrument is not necessarily conclusive as to its nature,[54] and so a Resolution may fall within one of the categories of act listed in Article 189, viz. regulations, directives, decisions, recommendations and opinions. Since the Resolution is not reasoned (an essential requirement for regulations, directives and decisions under Article 190), it cannot be regarded as being one of those types of act. It would therefore seem to fall into the category of a recommendation, which under Article 189 has no binding force. Nevertheless, this may not be the end of the matter. In *French Republic v. United Kingdom* the European Court held that the Hague Resolution made 'specific the duties of co-operation which Member States assumed under Article 5 of the EEC Treaty', and therefore was legally binding by virtue of that Article.[55] While the Court made this comment about the Resolution generally, it was in fact in that case only concerned with the nature of Annex VI of the Resolution (which is concerned with the competence of Member States to adopt national conservation measures and is discussed in detail in the next Chapter), and the Commission's argument, on which the Court appears in this respect to have based its judgment, was couched solely in terms of the binding nature of Annex VI. Had the Court been faced directly with the question as to whether the main part of the Resolution under discussion here was binding it is less certain that it would have reached the same, clear-cut conclusion.[56] In any case, the question of whether that part of the Resolution concerned with the extension of fishing limits is binding or not, is now more of theoretical than practical interest, since all EEC Member States have implemented the Resolution, although, as will shortly be seen, not all of them did so within the specified time-limit.[57]

Whether the Resolution is binding or not, the actual extension of fishing limits is a matter for the Member States and not for the Community, even if the consequences of any such extension are a matter for the Community.[58] This follows from the general scope of the EEC Treaty, which does not empower the Community to alter the maritime zones of its Member States,[59] and more specifically from Article 2(3) of Regulation 101/76[60] which provides that it is up to each individual Member State to define in its legislation the maritime waters coming under its sovereignty or within its jurisdiction. Nevertheless, on a matter as politically sensitive as national maritime zones, it is interesting to observe a Community institution addressing a recommendation to Member States for action.[61]

The Resolution, as we have seen, calls for an extension of Member States' fishing limits to 200 miles in the North Sea and North Atlantic, but adds that this is 'without prejudice to similar action being taken [by Member States] for other fishing zones within their jurisdiction such as the Mediterranean'. When it made its proposals in September 1976 for extending fishing limits, the Commission said that it would put forward in due course proposals for an extension around Member States' Mediterranean coasts.[62] No proposals have yet been made. However, as we shall shortly see, although fishing limits have not been extended in the Mediterranean, Member States have extended their fishing limits to 200 miles off coasts other than those bordering the North Sea and North Atlantic.

The final point of interest about the Council's Resolution of November 3, 1976 is that with its implementation, fishing limits of a uniform width have now been established off all Member States' coasts in the North Sea and North Atlantic, even if this uniformity is somewhat theoretical because limits cannot be extended as far as 200 miles off some coasts, particularly in the North Sea, because of the presence of neighbouring States. Prior to the implementation of the Resolution Member States' fishing limits were of varying width.

Implementation of the Council's Resolution. As far as implementation of the Council's Resolution goes, only four of the seven Member States concerned had enacted the necessary legislation and extended their fishing limits to 200 miles by the specified date of January 1, 1977. These were Denmark (both for its metropolitan coast and Greenland),[63] the Federal Republic of Germany,[64] Ireland [65] and the United Kingdom.[66] Although France had enacted enabling legislation for the creation of a 200-mile economic zone in July 1976,[67] it did not actually bring such a zone into operation for its North Sea and North Atlantic coasts until after January 1, 1977 – for its North Sea, English Channel and Atlantic coasts from the Belgian to the Spanish frontiers on February 12, 1977[68] and for St. Pierre et Miquelon (at the time an overseas department) on February 27, 1977.[69] The Netherlands was more tardy and did not extend its limits until Christmas Day, 1977,[70] while Belgium did not extend its limits until October 1978.[71]

As we have seen, under the Hague Resolution the agreement to extend fishing limits to 200 miles in the North Sea and North Atlantic was 'without prejudice to similar action being taken for other fishing zones within [Member States'] jurisdiction', and in fact there have been a number of extensions off coasts bordering seas other than the North Sea and North Atlantic. The two Member States which border the Baltic, Denmark and the Federal Republic of Germany, have each extended their fishing limits in that sea to as far as is possible in relation to neighbouring States – on March 1, 1978[72] and June 15, 1978,[73] respectively. Denmark also extended its fishing limits in the Skagerrak and Kattegat on January 1, 1978.[74] France has extended the fishing limits of its overseas departments situated outside the North Atlantic to 200 miles – for French Guyana on February 25, 1977;[75] for Réunion (in the Indian Ocean) on February 11, 1978;[76] and for Guadeloupe and Martinique (in the Caribbean) on March 11, 1978.[77] The result of these actions is that of the territories to which the Common Fisheries Policy applies, it is only off Mediterranean coasts that fishing limits have not been extended to 200 miles or to as far as is possible in relation to neighbouring States. The main reasons why fishing limits have not been extended in the Mediterranean are probably because the presence of neighbouring States would in most areas not allow zones of any great size to be generated beyond existing territorial sea limits (and in the case of Greece there would be formidable delimitation problems with Turkey); and because virtually no third States in the Mediterranean have extended their limits.[78]

Although it is a decade since fishing limits were extended to 200-miles, there are still a considerable number of unresolved boundaries, involving either the zones of adjacent States or the zones of States opposite each other but less than 400 miles apart. There are about 22 cases where it is necessary to draw a boundary between an EEC Member State and a third State, and about a dozen cases involving a boundary between two EEC Member States.[79] So far the only boundaries that have been agreed relate to the French overseas departments.[80] Boundaries have been established between the 200-mile limits of Réunion and Mauritius;[81] Guadeloupe and Martinique and Venzuela;[82] Martinique and St. Lucia;[83] and French Guyana and Brazil.[84] The fact that the majority of boundaries have not yet been agreed does not appear to have given rise to any great difficulties in practice. It need hardly be added that the negotiation of these boundaries is a matter for individual EEC Member States and not the Community.

Even though most of these boundaries have not been agreed, a number of them can be predicted with some certainty. First, there are some cases where the national legislation of each State concerned defines the boundary as the median line[85] (and in some of these cases the exact course of such a median line can be ascertained because a continental shelf boundary between the two States concerned has already been defined and drawn as a median line in an agreement). Secondly, there are some cases where existing continental shelf boundaries not delineated as median lines will almost certainly be utilised, because to have separate boundaries for the continental shelf and exclusive fishing zones would give rise to anomalies and difficulties.[86]

There remain, however, some cases where a boundary cannot be predicted and where it will probably be difficult for the States concerned to reach agreement on a boundary. Brief mention may be made of some of these cases. The fishing zones at present claimed by the United Kingdom and Ireland substantially overlap, as a result of a radical difference of views as to which islands may serve as base-points for the measurement of 200-mile limits.[87] A similar situation exists as regards the fishing zones of the United Kingdom and the Faroes.[88] Finally, as far as the boundary between St. Pierre et Miquelon and Canada is concerned, there are substantial differences of view between France and Canada over how large an exclusive fishing zone (and continental shelf) St. Pierre et Miquelon should be allowed to generate.[89] However, with the change in status in 1985 of St. Pierre et Miquelon from an overseas department to an Annex IV territory, this unresolved boundary is no longer of any concern to the Community as far as the application of its fisheries law is concerned.

3. PERSONAL SCOPE

The subjects of the Community legal system comprise the Community institutions, the Member States and individuals (including artificial legal persons). Rights and duties are conferred and placed on Community institutions and Member States both by particular provisions of the EEC Treaty and also to some extent by secondary legislation (regulations, directives and decisions): in later Chapters reference will be made to the relevant provisions of Community Law. Such provisions raise no difficulties of principle: it is merely a question of looking at the wording of a provision to see whether it creates a right or obligation (though obviously questions as to the exact meaning of a provision may arise). With individuals, however, the position is not quite so straightforward. This section therefore focuses on the scope of the EEC fisheries law as it relates to individuals. It examines two questions: first, which parts of such law confer rights and obligations on individuals; and secondly, insofar as this law does confer direct rights and obligations on individuals, to which individuals does it apply.

A. *Which Parts of EEC Fisheries Law Confer Rights and Obligations on Individuals?*

As was pointed out in the previous Chapter, EEC fisheries law is contained in certain articles of the EEC Treaty, together with the regulations, directives and decisions adopted by the Council under those articles. Not all these different types of legal instrument, however, directly confer rights and obligations on individual fishermen. In seeking to determine which instruments do confer such rights and obligations, it is desirable to make a distinction between the concepts of direct applicability and direct effect.[90] Applicability refers to the manner in which a particular type of Community legal instrument is introduced into the national legal systems of Member States. Where no form of implementing action is required by, or indeed even permitted to, the national authorities of Member States, the legal instrument in question is said to be directly applicable. Regulations and decisions addressed to individuals fall into this category. Where, however, it is necessary for the national authorities of Member States to take some action to implement the Community legal instrument in question, the latter is described as being indirectly applicable. Treaty provisions, directives and decisions addressed to Member States come into this category. The concept of direct effect, on the other hand, refers to the nature of the provisions of the Community legal instrument in question. Where these provisions are clear and precise, unconditional, with no further implementing measures to be taken by Member States or Community institutions, and no substantial discretion left to Member States, they are said to have direct effect. This means that they confer rights and obligations on individuals which can be invoked before the national courts of Member States. Where the provisions of a Community legal instrument are insufficiently precise, or are conditional, or require some implementing measure, or leave substantial discretion to Member States, then those provisions do not have direct effect. There is a presumption that all directly applicable Community law, i.e. regulations and decisions addressed to individuals, has direct effect: however, there are certain provisions of some regulations which do not meet the test of direct effectiveness, and therefore will not have direct effect. In the case of Community law which is not directly applicable, i.e. Treaty provisions, directives and decisions addressed to Member States, the European Court has held on numerous occasions that notwithstanding the fact that such law is not directly applicable, it may nevertheless have direct effect if it satisfies the tests set out above, and thus may be invoked by individuals before national courts.[91]

Thus to sum up: regulations and decisions addressed to individuals are directly applicable and will normally have direct effect. The EEC Treaty, directives and decisions addressed to Member States are not directly applicable: however, certain of their provisions may have direct effect if they satisfy the test as to precision, unconditionality etc. set out above. As far as fisheries legislation is concerned, the overwhelming bulk of this legislation, as will be seen in later Chapters, is in the form of regulations, and thus is binding automatically on individual fishermen, and confers rights and obligations on them which can be invoked before national courts. Very little fisheries legislation is in the form of directives and decisions, but if such instruments contain any provisions which satisfy the test of direct effect, these provisions, too, can be invoked by individual fishermen before national courts. As far as the provisions of the EEC Treaty dealing with fisheries are concerned, these provisions are not directly applicable and virtually all of them are by their very nature not capable of having direct effect.[92]

Another important source of Community law in the context of fisheries is the various fisheries treaties into which the EEC has entered with third States. The substantive provisions of these treaties are discussed in Chapter 5. What must be discussed at this point is the question of whether such treaties are directly binding on Community fishermen or confer on them rights and obligations which can be invoked before the national courts of Member States. The European Court has held in a number of cases,[93] most recently and emphatically in *Hauptzollamt Mainz v. Kupferberg,*[94] that those provisions of a treaty to which the EEC is a party that are precise and unconditional (viewed in the light of the spirit, general scheme and wording of the treaty) have direct effect, and thus can be invoked by individuals before national courts, unless the treaty in question stipulates otherwise.

The question posed at the beginning of this section – which parts of EEC fisheries law confer rights and obligations on individuals? – may therefore be answered as follows. Regulations, in which form the greater bulk of EEC fisheries law is cast, will normally be binding in their entirety on individual fishermen. Those parts of the EEC treaty, directives, decisions and treaties into which the EEC has entered with third States that satisfy the criteria for direct effect, confer rights and obigations which can be invoked by individual fishermen before the national courts of EEC Member States.

We have spoken of Community law as being binding on, or as being capable of being invoked by, 'individual fishermen', and we need to consider now exactly who these 'individual fishermen' are.

B. *To Which Individuals does EEC Fisheries Law Apply?*

Like the geographical range of EEC fisheries jurisdiction, discussed in the previous section, the personal range of the EEC's jurisdiction in fisheries matters is essentially coterminous with that of its Member States.[95] Thus the Community has legislative (or prescriptive) jurisdiction in respect of: (1) all nationals of, and vessels registered in, the territories to which the Common Fisheries Policy applies,[96] wherever they may be: in the case of such nationals fishing in the territorial sea or exclusive fishing or economic zone of a third State, the Community's jurisdiction will be concurrent with that of the third State; and (2) all other individuals and vessels, regardless of nationality, engaged in fishing activities in the territorial sea or exclusive fishing zone of a territory to which the Common Fisheries Policy applies. The Community also has enforcement jurisdiction in respect of individuals and vessels falling in both these categories (except in the case of its nationals fishing in the territorial sea, exclusive fishing zone or economic zone of a third State, where that State alone has enforcement jurisdiction): in practice, as will be seen in later Chapters, because of its limited capacity to take enforcement action, the enforcement jurisdiction of the Community is largely exercised through its Member States.

NOTES

1. Convention on the Nomenclature for the Classification of Goods in Customs Tariffs, Brussels, December 15, 1950, together with Protocol of Amendment, Brussels, July 1, 1955. Both in force on September 11, 1959. 347 U.N.T.S. 127; 1960 U.K.T.S. 29.
2. See 1965 U.K.T.S. 49 and 83; 1972 U.K.T.S. 11; 1978 U.K.T.S. 27; and 1979 U.K.T.S. 57.
3. Reg. 3796/81, O.J. 1981 L379/1, Annexes IV A and VI.
4. In practice the regulation of trade in the products of marine mammals falling within Annex II has not been done as a fisheries measure, but on the basis of the common organisations of the markets in oils and fats and in certain Annex II products: see Reg. 348/81, O.J. 1981 L39/1.

76

5. COM (79) 364. The Commission in this document gives no arguments to support its view but refers to an opinion of the Legal Service: the latter is not publicly available.
6. See *Bull E.C.* 1979, No. 10, p. 52 and the Commission's Answer to W.Q. 730/80, O.J. 1980 C312/5. According to Leigh, the United Kingdom, one of those Member States objecting to the view that whaling fell within the Community's competence, subsequently dropped its objection, but Denmark had (as of 1983) maintained its objection: see M. Leigh, *European Integration and the Common Fisheries Policy,* Beckenham, 1983, p. 157.
7. For discussion of this provision, see the previous Chapter.
8. While it may be difficult to point to a specific Community legal provision that would be infringed, it is likely that the Court would find such an action contrary to the whole spirit and system of Community law, and perhaps a breach of Art. 5 of the EEC Treaty.
9. P. Oliver, *Free Movement of Goods in the EEC,* London, 1982, p. 27.
10. Case 61/77, *Commission v. Ireland* [1978] E.C.R. 417 at 446; [1978] 2 C.M.L.R. 466 at 513.
11. But the following points should be noted: (1) the EEC Treaty applies to West Berlin; (2) the German territories of Heligoland and Büsingen and certain Italian communes are excluded from the EEC's customs territory (Reg. 2151/84, O.J. 1984 L197/1, Art. 1). The main significance of these points concerns trade in fishery products.
12. The text of the Resolution has not apparently been published. This summary of its contents is taken from *Encyclopedia of Community Law,* p. B 9203.
13. Third Act of Accession, Arts. 25 and 155 and Protocol 2.
14. Art. 40(4) is concerned with agricultural guidance and guarantee funds.
15. Case 148/77, [1978] E.C.R. 1787; [1979] 1 C.M.L.R. 604.
16. *Ibid.* at pp. 1805 and 623 respectively.
17. T.C. Hartley, *EEC Immigration Law,* Amsterdam, 1978, p. 29.
18. Case 147/73, [1973] E.C.R. 1543.
19. Treaty of Protective Amity between France and Monaco, Paris, July 17, 1918, Art. 1. *British and Foreign State Papers,* Vol. III, p. 727.
20. So, too, Hartley, *op. cit.* in n. 17, pp. 41–42 and A. Parry and J. Dinnage, *EEC Law,* 2nd edition, London, 1981, p. 59. For the opposite view, see the writers quoted in Hartley.
21. Reg. 2151/84, *op. cit.* in n. 11, Art. 2. This is because France and Monaco formed a customs union for many years before the EEC was established.
22. Referred to in G.H. Blaustein and G.H. Flanz (eds), *Constitutions of the Countries of the World,* Dobbs Ferry, 1975, Vol. XIII, pp. 7–8.
23. So, too, Hartley and Parry and Dinnage, *loc. cit.* in n. 20.
24. Reg. 2151/84, *op. cit.* in n. 11, Art. 2. This is because of the customs union between Italy and San Marino.
25. So, too, Hartley and Parry and Dinnage, *loc. cit.* in n. 20.
26. Note, however, that a Declaration attached to the Third Act of Accession says that an arrangement governing trade relations between the Community and Andorra will be finalised by 1988.
27. O.J. 1973 L68/1.
28. This follows from the Fishery Limits Act 1964 and the Sea Fisheries Act 1968. S.1(2) of the 1964 Act, replaced by s.6 of the 1968 Act, placed restrictions on the access of foreign fishing vessels to the United Kingdom's territorial sea and exclusive fishing zone. Since the definition of foreign fishing vessels excluded vessels registered in the Channel Islands and Isle of Man (see s.3 of the 1964 Act and s.19(1) of the 1968 Act) it follows that in principle there was no restriction on the access of Channel Island and Isle of Man vessels to the United Kingdom's territorial sea and exclusive fishing zone. These provisions of the 1964 and 1968 Acts have been replaced by similar provisions in the Fishery Limits Act 1976, ss. 2 and 8.
29. See the discussion in the text at n's 44 and 45 below.

30. Sea Fisheries (Isle of Man) Order 1971, S.I. 1971 No. 1747, and Sea Fisheries (Channel Islands) Order 1973, S.I. 1973 No. 1319.

31. S.I. 1972 No. 2026 and S.I. 1983 No. 253. The 1983 Order revokes the 1972 Order.

32. S.I. 1965 No's 1241, 1448 and 1569. In spite of the repeal of the provision of the 1964 Act on which they are based, these Orders have been preserved. See Fishery Limits Act 1976, Sched. 3, para. 1 and Fishing Boats (European Economic Community) Designation Order 1976, S.I. 1976 No. 2216, Art. 4 and Sched.

33. Reg. 1779/77, O.J. 1977 L196/4.

34. Reg. 171/83, O.J. 1983 L24/14, Art. 1(1).

35. Case 32/79, *Commission v. United Kingdom* [1980] E.C.R. 2403; [1981] 1 C.M.L.R. 219, and Case 804/79, *Commission v. United Kingdom* [1981] E.C.R. 1045; [1982] 1 C.M.L.R. 543.

36. [1980] E.C.R. 2403 at 2444; [1981] 1 C.M.L.R. 219 at 270. In the second case the Court merely repeated its first judgment.

37. This is expressly the case with Hong Kong (Article 227(3), which is limited in its wording to United Kingdom territories) and implicitly the case with Macau since it is nowhere mentioned in the Iberian Act of Accession (see Commission Answer to W.Q. 401/85, O.J. 1985 C251/26).

38. *Loc. cit.* in n. 18.

39. This includes French Polynesia, Wallis and Futuna Islands, and Clipperton Island.

40. What is not quite clear is whether the Islands of Tromelin, Glorieuses, Juan-de-Nova, Europa and Bassas-da-India, all in the neighbourhood of Madagascar, are included in Annex IV. Annex IV refers to 'Madagascar and dependencies'. Do these islands fall within the 'dependencies' of Madagascar even though the latter has become independent? This seems likely, since during the colonial period the islands came under Madagascar for administrative purposes. If the islands do not fall within the 'dependencies' of Madagascar, it is difficult to see how they come under Annex IV. On the other hand, it seems that the intention of Annex IV is to cover all French possessions which are not overseas departments (which the islands are not, even though administered from the department of Réunion), since there is nothing in the Treaty about French possessions not coming in one or other of these categories. Article 227(3), which deals with territories not listed in Annex IV, is limited by its wording to United Kingdom territories.

41. O.J. 1986 L175/1.

42. O.J. 1985 L29/1.

43. O.J. 1985 L29/7, 9 and 14.

44. 516 U.N.T.S. 205; 1965 U.K.T.S. 3. An identical provision is found in Art. 2 of the 1982 United Nations Convention on the Law of the Sea, (1982) XXI ILM 1261.

45. See *Yearbook of the International Law Commission*, 1956, Vol. II, p. 265; D.P. O'Connell 'The Juridical Nature of the Territorial Sea' (1971) 45 B.Y.I.L. 303.

46. C.A. Fleischer, 'L'accès aux lieux de pêche et le traité de Rome' (1971) 141 R.M.C. 148 at 151.

47. E.g. A.W. Koers, 'The External Authority of the EEC in regard to Marine Fisheries' (1977) 14 C.M.L. Rev. 269 at 274-5; Y. Van der Mensbrugghe, 'The Common Market Fisheries Policy and the Law of the Sea' (1975) 6 N.Y.I.L. 199 at 202; D. Vignes, 'The EEC and the Law of the Sea' in R.R. Churchill et al. (eds), *New Directions in the Law of the Sea,* Vol. III, London, 1973, p. 335 at 337–339; E. Hiester, 'The Legal Position of the European Community with regard to the Conservation of the Living Resources of the Sea' [1976] *Legal Issues of European Integration* 55 at 60–62; and M. Brouir, 'Le Réglement du Conseil de la CEE de 1970 sur les pêcheries' (1973) 9 C.D.E. 20 at 28–32.

48. Joined Cases 3, 4 and 6/76, *Officier van Justitie v. Kramer* [1976] E.C.R. 1279; [1976] 2 C.M.L.R. 440.

49. *Ibid.,* at pp. 1309 and 469 respectively. In the subsequent fisheries cases neither the parties nor the Court appear to have felt it necessary to discuss this point any further.

78

50. I.e. the seabed out to a depth of 200 metres or beyond that limit if the depth of water allows the resources of the seabed to be exploited. The Continental Shelf Convention gives coastal States the exclusive right to exploit the sedentary species (e.g. oysters, clams and mussels) of their continental shelves.

51. Since 1976 Greece, Portugal and Spain have of course become members of the EEC. Greece claims a 6-mile territorial sea, and Portugal and Spain each a 12-mile territorial sea.

52. Council Resolution on Certain External Aspects of the Creation of a 200-mile Fishing Zone in the Community with effect from January 1, 1977. (1976) XV I.L.M. 1425. Curiously this Resolution was not published in the *Official Journal* until 1981. See O.J. 1981 C105/1.

53. I.e. to extend their fishing limits to 200 miles. The third countries chiefly concerned were Canada, the Faroes, Iceland, Norway, USSR and USA. See further discussion in Chapter 1 at pp. 13–14.

54. See P.S.R.F. Mathijsen, *A Guide to European Community Law,* 4th Edition, London, 1985, p. 89, and cases quoted therein; T.C. Hartley, *The Foundations of European Community Law,* Oxford, 1981, pp. 83 and 352.

55. Case 141/78, [1979] E.C.R. 2923 at 2942; [1980] 1 C.M.L.R. 6 at 23. On this reading by the Court, the Resolution becomes one of the type of legally binding acts *sui generis* identified by Hartley. See Hartley, *op. cit.* in n. 54, pp. 83–85.

56. It may be noted that in Case 32/79, *Commission v. United Kingdom* [1980] E.C.R. 2403 at 2432; [1981] 1 C.M.L.R. 219 at 261, the Court observed simply that 'it is not contested that this resolution is binding on the Member States'. In this case, too, the Court in practice was only concerned with Annex VI of the Resolution.

57. According to the Belgian Foreign Minister, the Minutes of the Council meeting at which the Resolution was adopted contain a declaration stating that the date of January 1, 1977 for the implementation of the Resolution is subject to the fulfilment of the necessary constitutional procedures in each Member State. See (1978–79) 14 *Revue Belge de Droit International* 590.

58. This is why it was necessary that the actions of Member States should be co-ordinated.

59. For a possible contrary view, see D. Vignes, *op. cit.* in n. 47, at 342–343. He argues that since the exclusive fishing zone (unlike the territorial sea) is solely of an economic character, it would be possible for the Community institutions to determine its limits on the basis of Arts. 100 (harmonisation of laws) and 235 of the EEC Treaty. So, too, E. Peyroux, 'Problèmes juridiques de la pêche dans le Marché Commun' (1973) 9 R.T.D.E. 46 at 52. It is also interesting to note that Advocate General Reischl, in his opinion in Case 61/77, *Commission v. Ireland* [1978] E.C.R. 417 at 456; [1978] 2 C.M.L.R. 466 at 492, says that 'the extension of the [Irish fisheries] jurisdiction [to 200 miles] originated in an act of the Community.' This must, however, be taken as referring to a political or factual origin, rather than a legal origin.

60. O.J. 1976 L20/19.

61. Cf. also the proposal made by the Commission in 1978 (in the wake of the *Amoco Cadiz* disaster) for a Council Resolution which would 'call on those Member States which have not yet done so to extend the breadth of their territorial seas to a 12-mile limit' (O.J. 1978 C146/11). It is understood, however, that there is little likelihood of the Council adopting this draft Resolution.

62. COM (76) 500.

63. Law No. 597 of December 17, 1976 on the Fishing Territory of the Kingdom of Denmark; Executive Order No. 628 of December 22, 1976 on the Fishing Territory of Denmark; and Executive Order No. 629 of December 22, 1976 on the Fishing Territory of Greenland. *Lovtidende,* Pt. A, 1976, pp. 1631, 1694 and 1695. English translation in UN Legislative Series B/19, pp. 192, 194 and 195 and R.R. Churchill et al. (eds), *New Directions in the Law of the Sea,* Vol. V, London, 1977, pp. 109, 110 and 112. The last of these orders created a 200-mile fishing zone off Greenland's west coast as far north as 75° N and off its east coast as far north as

67° N. Executive Order No. 176 of May 14, 1980 (*Lovtidende,* Pt. A, 1980, p. 679) extended with effect from June 1, 1980 the 200-mile fishing zone to the remainder of Greenland's coast.

64. Proclamation of the Federal Republic of Germany on the Establishment of a Fishery Zone of the Federal Republic of Germany in the North Sea, December 21, 1976. *Bundesgesetzblatt,* Pt. II, December 29, 1976, p. 1999. English translation in UN Legislative Series B/19, p. 211 and Churchill, *op. cit.,* p. 118.

65. Maritime Jurisdiction (Exclusive Fishery Limits) Order 1976, S.I. 1976 No. 320. Reproduced in UN Legislative Series B/19, p. 213 and Churchill, *op. cit.,* p. 120.

66. Fishery Limits Act 1976. Reproduced in Churchill, *op. cit.,* p. 123.

67. Law No. 76–655 of July 16, 1976 relating to the Economic Zone off the Coasts of the Territory of the Republic, J.O.R.F. July 18, 1976, p. 4299. English translation in Churchill, *op. cit.,* p. 301. It should be noted that France is the only Member State to have extended its fishing limits by means of an economic zone, the other Member States claiming simply the more limited exclusive fishing zone. The reason for this is because the 200-mile fishing limit, together with the exclusive rights over seabed resources which they already had under the continental shelf doctrine, gave most Member States all that they at that time wanted from an EEZ. They were less certain about the other principal rights envisaged by the various UN Conference negotiating texts for the coastal State in the EEZ, namely the regulation of research and pollution control. It is noteworthy that even the French legislation is very cautious about these matters. For comment on the French legislation, see G. De Lacharrière, 'La zone économique française de 200 milles' [1976] A.F.D.I. 641.

68. Decree No. 77–130 of February 11, 1977, J.O.R.F., February 12, 1977, p. 864. English translation in Churchill, *op. cit.,* p. 303.

69. Decree No. 77–169 of February 25, 1977, J.O.R.F., February 27, 1977, p. 1102.

70. Law of June 8, 1977 concerning the Possibility of Establishing a Fishery Zone and Royal Decree of November 23, 1977. *Stb.,* 1977, No's 345 and 665. Partial English translation in (1978) IX N.Y.I.L. 385.

71. Law of October 10, 1978 establishing a Fishing Zone for Belgium, *Moniteur Belge,* December 28, 1978.

72. Executive Order No. 43 of February 1, 1978 on the Fishing Territory of Denmark. *Lovtidende,* Pt. A, 1978, p. 161.

73. Proclamation of the Federal Republic of Germany on the Establishment of a Fishery Zone of the Federal Republic of Germany in the Baltic Sea, May 18, 1978. *Bundesgesetzblatt,* Pt. II, June 13, 1978, p. 867.

74. Executive Order No. 639 of December 22, 1977 on the Fishing Territory of Denmark. *Lovtidende,* Pt. A, 1977, p. 1768.

75. Decree No. 77–170 of February 25, 1977, J.O.R.F., February 27, 1977, p. 1103.

76. Decree No. 78–148 of February 3, 1978, J.O.R.F., February 11, 1978, p. 687.

77. Decrees No. 78–276 and 78–277 of March 6, 1978, J.O.R.F., March 11, 1978, pp. 1048 and 1049.

78. Of those Member States which have joined the Community since the Hague Resolution, Portugal and Spain have each claimed a 200-mile economic zone (in 1977 and 1978 respectively), while Greece, as will be obvious from the discussion above, has made no claim. For text of Portuguese and Spanish legislation see UN Legislative Series B/19, pp. 93 and 250.

79. It might be thought that boundaries between EEC Member States would be unimportant, given the fact that fishing in Member States' waters is regulated primarily by the Community. In fact such boundaries are of some importance. First, they define the area within which each Member State (insofar as it has such competence) may prescribe its own fishery regulations applicable to all vessels. Secondly, they define the area within which Member States may enforce their own regulations and must enforce Community fishery measures.

80. The writer has also come across an unofficial report of a boundary between Denmark and Sweden, concluded in 1983: see *Bulletin of Legal Developments,* 1983, No. 21.

81. France – Mauritius. Convention on the Delimitation of the French and Mauritian Economic Zones between the Islands of Réunion and Mauritius, April 2, 1980. J.O.R.F., July 19, 1980, p. 1830.

82. France – Venezuela. Convention relating to the Delimitation of Economic Zones, July 17, 1980, J.O.R.F., March 16, 1983, p. 782.

83. France – St. Lucia. Convention on Delimitation, March 4, 1981. J.O.R.F., May 21, 1981, pp. 1608–1609.

84. France – Brazil. Treaty on Maritime Delimitation, January 30, 1981. J.O.R.F., December 3, 1983, p. 3496.

85. For example, the boundaries between Norway and the United Kingdom; Denmark and Norway; Denmark and the United Kingdom; the Netherlands and the United Kingdom; and Portugal and Spain.

86. For example, the Federal Republic of Germany's boundaries with Denmark, the Netherlands and the United Kingdom. On the other hand, one Member State – the United Kingdom – appears to take the view that it is not necessary for continental shelf and exclusive fishing zone boundaries to coincide. A semi-official map – the Admiralty Notice to Mariners No. 1766, published in July 1979 – shows the outer limit of the United Kingdom's fishing limit in the English Channel and the Western Approaches diverging quite significantly from the continental shelf boundary laid down by the Anglo-French Arbitral Tribunal in its decisions of 1977–78. For further details, see C.R. Symmons, 'British Off-Shore Continental Shelf and Fishery Limit Boundaries: An Analysis of Overlapping Zones', (1979) 28 I.C.L.Q. 703 at 711–712, 715–717.

87. For further details, see Symmons, *op. cit.* in n. 86, pp. 719–729.

88. For further details, see *ibid.,* pp. 730–731.

89. For further details, see C.R. Symmons, *The Maritime Zones of Islands in International Law,* The Hague, 1979, pp. 127–128, 196, and *ibid.,* 'The Canadian 200-Mile Limit and the Delimitation of Maritime Zones around St. Pierre and Miquelon' (1980) 12 *Ottawa Law Review* 145.

90. Among the voluminous literature on this topic see J.A. Winter, 'Direct Applicability and Direct Effect: Two Distinct and Different Concepts in Community Law' (1972) 9 C.M.L. Rev. 425; L. Collins, *European Community Law in the United Kingdom,* 3rd edition, London, 1984, Chapter 2; D. Wyatt and A. Dashwood, *The Substantive Law of the EEC,* London, 1980, Chapter 3; J. Usher, *European Community Law and National Law,* London, 1981, pp. 17–30; and Hartley, *op. cit.* in n. 54, Chapter 7. It must be admitted, however, that not all writers maintain the distinction between direct applicability and direct effect, and the European Court itself is not always consistent in the use of the two terms.

91. E.g. Case 26/62, *Van Gend en Loos v. Nederlandse Administratie der Belastingen* [1963] E.C.R. 1; [1963] C.M.L.R. 105; Case 9/70, *Grad v. Finanzamt Traunstein* [1970] E.C.R. 825; [1971] C.M.L.R. 1; Case 41/74, *Van Duyn v. Home Office* [1974] E.C.R. 1337; [1975] 1 C.M.L.R. 1.

92. The only provisions possibly having direct effect are the prohibitions on discrimination contained in Arts. 7 and 40(3): they are discussed in Chapter 4. On the other hand, many of the provisions of EEC law discussed at the end of the first Chapter which are only indirectly relevant to fisheries (free movement of goods and workers, rights of establishment and services) do have direct effect.

93. E.g. Joined Cases 21–24/72, *International Fruit Co. N.V. v. Produktschap voor Groenten en Fruit* [1972] E.C.R. 1219; [1975] 2 C.M.L.R. 1; Case 181/73, *Haegeman v. Belgian State* [1974] E.C.R. 449; [1975] 1 C.M.L.R. 515; and Case 87/75, *Bresciani v. Italian Finance Department* [1976] E.C.R. 129; [1976] 2 C.M.L.R. 62. For a very full discussion of this question, see G.

Bebr, 'Agreements concluded by the Community and their Possible Direct Effect: From International Fruit Company to Kupferberg' (1983) 20 C.M.L. Rev. 35. Dr. Bebr comes to a rather less clear-cut conclusion than that which follows.

94. Case 104/81, [1982] E.C.R. 3641; [1983] 1 C.M.L.R. 1.

95. For a fuller discussion of this point, see A. Bleckmann, 'The Personal Jurisdiction of the European Community' (1980) 17 C.M.L. Rev. 467, especially at pp. 474–478.

96. i.e. the nationals of Belgium, the Federal Republic of Germany, Greece, Ireland, Italy, Luxembourg; French nationals other than those domiciled in Annex IV territories; Dutch nationals other than those domiciled in the Netherlands Antilles; Danish nationals other than those domiciled in the Faroes and Greenland; Portuguese nationals other than those domiciled in Macau; Spanish nationals other than those domiciled in the Canary Islands, Ceuta and Melilla; citizens of the United Kingdom and colonies other than those domiciled in Annex IV territories, Hong Kong, Gibraltar or the Sovereign Bases in Cyprus; and vessels registered in EEC Member States (except the Faroes, Canary Islands, Ceuta and Melilla, Gibraltar, Hong Kong, Macau and Annex IV territories) and French overseas departments. The position of the residents of, and vessels from, the Channel Islands and Isle of Man is not very clear, but they would seem to fall into this category for the purpose of at least some aspects of the marketing side of the Policy, and possibly outside it for the remainder of the Policy.

CHAPTER 4

Fisheries management in Community waters

The waters of EEC Member States at present yield an annual catch of the order of 6 million tonnes. This is by any standard a sizable resource, and represents about nine per cent of the total world marine fish catch. If this resource is not to be squandered through overfishing, it is essential that it be properly managed (cf. the discussion in Chapter 1, at p. 3 above). For such management the Community, rather than its Member States, is primarily responsible: an attempt to demarcate more precisely the division of competence between the Community and its Member States will be attempted in the first part of this Chapter. The Chapter will then go on to examine the Community system of management.[1] The main elements of this system (which came into operation at the beginning of 1983) are the annual setting of Total Allowable Catches (TACs) for the principal fish stocks, the division of TACs into quotas allocated to individual Member States, a range of supplementary conservation measures, rules on access to fishing grounds, and provisions governing the enforcement of Community measures by the national authorities of Member States. As well as describing this system, an attempt will also be made to assess its effectiveness in practice. In doing this, and in considering the Community's management system generally, it is desirable at the outset to bear two things in mind: one is that the waters now subject to Community management had been poorly managed, mainly by the North-East Atlantic Fisheries Commission, before the Community assumed responsibility for management in 1977 when fishing limits were extended to 200 miles (see p. 5 above). The other thing to bear in mind is that the Community's fish-catching capacity is greater than the resources available so that both before and since the Community assumed responsibility for management most fish stocks in Community waters were and continue to be fully exploited, and in some cases over-exploited.

1. THE DIVISION OF COMPETENCE BETWEEN THE COMMUNITY AND ITS MEMBER STATES
IN RELATION TO FISHERIES MANAGEMENT

In seeking to determine how competence in fisheries management matters is divided between the Community and its Member States, it is helpful to begin by first establishing the ambit of the Community's competence in relation to fisheries management and thereafter to see what competence (if any) is left to the Member States. It should be stressed that in talking about competence, the discussion that follows is concerned only with legislative competence (or legislative jurisdiction), i.e. the competence to enact legal rules (as opposed to enforcing them). As far as enforcement jurisdiction is concerned, i.e. the competence to arrest and for courts to deal with alleged breaches of the law, since breach of fisheries legislation is normally a criminal rather than a civil matter and since there is no Community system of criminal justice (the Community possesses no powers of arrest nor does the European Court of Justice have the jurisdiction to try alleged breaches of fisheries legislation), enforcement jurisdiction is vested exclusively in Member States.[2] This is so, notwithstanding the fact that Member States' legislative jurisdiction is (as will be seen) very restricted. Turning first to the Community's competence to regulate fishing, there are three Treaty provisions which give it some competence in this matter – Articles 43 and 103 of the EEC Treaty and Article 102 of the 1972 Act of Accession. It will be assumed here that the last of these has the status of primary law, although this point is not free from doubt (see the discussion in section 1 of Chapter 2). There is no need at this stage to consider the various provisions of secondary legislation which define the Community's competence, since these derive from and therefore cannot exceed the primary provisions of the treaties referred to above.

Article 43 of the EEC Treaty, it will be recalled from Chapter 2, authorises the Council to implement the Common Agricultural (Fisheries) Policy within the objectives laid down in Article 39. Thus Article 43 authorises the taking of any fisheries measures which fall within the objectives listed in Article 39. The latter are so broadly framed that it would seem that almost any measure to regulate fishing could be based on Article 43. Thus, measures to conserve and promote the optimum utilisation of fish stocks, and to promote fisheries research, fall within the objectives of increasing productivity and assuring the availability of supplies; while measures to allocate catches, resolve conflicts between fishermen, promote economic efficiency in fishing operations and promote enforcement come within the objectives of increasing productivity, ensuring a fair standard of living for fishermen and ensuring that supplies reach consumers at reasonable prices. Nor, it must be noted, are there any restrictions on the geographical scope of Article 43. It can thus be used to regulate fishing both in Community waters and on the high seas. Turning next to

Article 103 of the EEC Treaty, this provision, it may be recalled from the discussion in Chapter 2, permits the Council to take short-term measures to regulate fishing. The scope *ratione materiae* of such measures would seem to be the same as that for measures adopted under Article 43. Finally, Article 102 of the Act of Accession gave the Council not only the competence but also the duty before the end of 1978 to 'determine conditions for fishing with a view to ensuring protection of the fishing grounds and conservation of the biological resources of the sea'. This, too, is (or rather was) a broad competence, though not perhaps as broad as Article 43. While the expression, 'conditions for fishing,' covers many regulatory matters, it may not cover measures to promote research or economic efficiency; the European Court, moreover, seems to regard Article 102 as being limited to conservation measures. Like Article 43, Article 102 is applicable to both Member States' waters and the high seas.

It thus appears that the Community has an extensive competence to regulate fishing. The next question is to consider whether any competence remains with the Member States. This question can only really be answered by tracing the position as it has evolved over recent years. Three distinct phases can be observed: first, the period prior to the extension of fishing limits to 200 miles at the beginning of 1977; secondly, the period from the beginning of 1977 to the expiry at the end of 1978 of the transitional period laid down in Article 102 of the Act of Accession; and thirdly, the period since then.

During the first phase, the period between the adoption in 1970 of the Community's first basic regulation relating to fisheries – the Structural Regulation[3] – and the beginning of 1977, when fishing limits were extended to 200 miles and the Community began adopting its own fishery measures, there was no regulation of fishing by Community institutions, even though Article 5 of the Structural Regulation empowered the Council to adopt conservation measures.[4] In such a situation it is clear from the general scheme of Community law[5] that the national authorities of Member States are permitted to adopt national measures. That this was the position in the case of fisheries during this period was specifically confirmed by the European Court in the *Kramer* case,[6] where the Court held, *inter alia,* that Dutch legislation laying down quotas for sole and plaice was valid.

The second phase to be considered is the period between the beginning of 1977, when the Community began taking fishery measures of its own – even though, as will be seen, such measures were of a fairly limited nature – and the end of 1978, when the deadline laid down in Article 102 of the Act of Accession, requiring the Council to 'determine conditions for fishing', expired. First it must be noted that when the Council adopted its Resolution of November 3, 1976 (the Hague Resolution), providing for concerted action in extending fishing limits to 200 miles, it adopted an Annex to that Resolution (Annex VI), which provided that pending the adoption of a Community regime for regulating fishing within 200-mile limits, Member States could adopt interim non-discriminatory unilateral measures to conserve resources. However, Annex VI added that 'before adopting such measures, the Member State concerned will seek the approval of the Commission, which must be consulted at all stages of the procedures.'[7]

The view of the Council expressed in Annex VI concerning the permissibility of national fishery measures was confirmed by the European Court in the *Irish Fisheries* case.[8] In this case the Court had to consider whether Ireland was entitled, in principle, in April 1977, to adopt unilateral fishery conservation measures. The Court held that Ireland was so entitled. The Court began by observing that 'the Community has the power to take conservation measures both independently and in the form of contractual commitments with non-Member States or under the auspices of international organisations.'[9] The Court then went on to explain that:

in so far as this power has been exercised by the Community, the provisions adopted by it preclude any conflicting provisions by the Member States. On the other hand, so long as the transitional period laid down in Article 102 of the Act of Accession has not expired and the Community has not yet fully exercised its power in the matter, the Member States are entitled, within their own jurisdiction, to take appropriate conservation measures without prejudice, however, to the obligation to co-operate imposed upon them by the Treaty, in particular Article 5 thereof.[10]

Since the Council had failed to adopt the necessary conservation measures, 'Ireland was entitled to adopt conservation measures for the maritime waters within its jurisdiction provided, however, that they conform to the requirements of Community law.'[11] The Court confirmed this holding on the competence of Member States in the subsequent cases of *Van Dam*,[12] *France v. United Kingdom*,[13] *Commission v. United Kingdom*,[14] and *Kerr*.[15] In *Commission v. United Kingdom* the Court explained that where Community conservation measures had been adopted for a particular area and then had lapsed, this neither deprived the Community of its powers nor restored to Member States the freedom to act at will in adopting measures for the area in question. 'In such a situation, it was for the Member States, as regards the maritime zones coming within their jurisdiction, to take the necessary conservation measures in the common interest and in accordance with both the substantive and the procedural rules arising from Community law.'[16]

During the period 1977–78, Member States not only had the right to take conservation measures that were in accordance with Community law, but also, in certain circumstances, a duty to take such measures. The existence of such a duty was first mentioned by the Court in the *Van Dam* case, but without any explanation being given as to the source or scope of this duty.[17] Such an explanation was, however, supplied in *Commission v. United Kingdom*. In this case the Court found that the United Kingdom was under a duty to take measures to conserve the Mourne herring stock off Northern Ireland, which was in direct danger of extinction. The legal basis for this duty derived from Article 102 of the Act of Accession, Regulation 101/76, Annex VI of the Hague Resolution and the Council Declaration of January 1978. These provisions, said the Court,

> are based on the two-fold assumption that measures must be adopted in the maritime waters for which the Community is responsible so as to meet established conservation needs and that if those measures cannot be introduced in good time on a Community basis the Member States not only have the right but are also under a duty to act in the interests of the Community.[18]

Thus, if a particular conservation measure was required and the Community was unable to act, the Member State concerned was under a duty to adopt such a measure, which had to be framed in such a way as to take account of the collective interests of the Community.

So much for the competence of Member States to regulate fishing in the period 1977–78. We must now consider what the position is in the third and present phase, the period since the beginning of 1979. This question was dealt with by the European Court in the second case of *Commission v. United Kingdom*.[19] The Court in this case began by declaring that the expiry of the transitional period referred to in Article 102 of the Act of Accession on December 31, 1978 meant that as from this date 'power to adopt . . . measures relating to the conservation of the sea has belonged fully and definitively to the Community. Member States are therefore no longer entitled to exercise any power of their own in the matter of conservation measures in the waters under their jurisdiction.'[20] On the other hand, in the present case this strict principle had to be qualified because at the time of the dispute the Council had not adopted the measures it was required to do under Article 102. But this did not mean, the Court stressed, that in this situation Member States' power and freedom to act unilaterally in this field were restored. All Member States could do was to maintain those national measures in force at the time of the expiry of the transitional period referred to in Article 102, and to amend such measures 'in case of need owing to the development of the relevant biological and technological facts in this sphere. Such amendments would be of a limited scope only and could not involve a new conservation policy on the part of a Member State.'[21] Such amendments must also be in accordance with Community law. The relevant provisions of the latter will be outlined below, following the conclusion of the discussion of Member States' competence in principle to adopt conservation measures. The Court has followed its ruling in *Commission v. United Kingdom* on the scope of Member States's competence in a number of subsequent cases,[22] so that what has been said above may be regarded as the Court's *jurisprudence constante* on the question.

The Court's ruling in these cases that the effect of the expiry of the transitional period laid down in Article 102 is to transfer legislative competence in fisheries matters from Member States to the Community would no doubt startle some of the drafters of that Article. For example, Mr. Rippon, the United Kingdom's chief negotiator, speaking immediately after agreement had been reached on the fisheries articles of the Act of Accession, stated in the House of Commons that the United Kingdom would 'retain full jurisdiction' in its then 12-mile fishing zone, including the power to enact conservation regulations.[23] And the Norwegian Government, in its White Paper on the results of its negotiations for entry to the EEC, speaking of Article 102, said that 'it must be assumed that the coastal State itself will have the greatest interest in conserving fish stocks off its coast and thus will adopt the regulations necessary'.[24] The Court's ruling thus illustrates how little weight it puts, in interpreting Community law, on the intentions of the draftsmen, and how much it adopts a dynamic, policy-oriented approach to promote the interests of the Community and the further integration of its Member States. The Court's interpretation of the effect of Article 102 should come as no very great surprise, partly because it was hinted at in the *Irish Fisheries* case (in the passage quoted earlier), and partly because it parallels its approach in some other areas of Community law.[25]

While the Court's judgment in *Commission v. United Kingdom* may not be all that surprising, the reasoning leading to its conclusions as to the consequences of Article 102 is not immediately obvious. Both the Court and the Advocate General assert that the expiry of the time limit in Article 102 results in Member States losing their competence in relation to conservation measures, but neither provides any real explanation as to why this is so. How then can this assertion be justified? One way of doing this is by the following line of reasoning. It is a general principle of Community law that if there is a conflict between Community law and national law, Community law must prevail:[26] as the European Court explained in *Costa v. ENEL*, in areas where the Community is competent Member States have transferred their law-making powers to the Community. As has been seen, the Community has the competence to adopt fishery conservation measures. Once such measures have been adopted, no conflicting national measures are possible. Since under Article 102 the Council is obliged to adopt *comprehensive* measures, it follows that once it has done so there is no room for national measures. Since the Council was in theory to act by the end of 1978, it follows that in theory the lack of scope for national measures also ensues from this date. This reasoning also explains why the Court held in the *Irish Fisheries* case that in the period prior to 1978 Member States retained competence to adopt conservation measures provided the Council had not acted under Article 102.[27] This leaves the question of how it is that notwithstanding the exclusivity of Community competence in principle after 1978, Member States retain some competence. From the Court's judgment, this would appear to be a pragmatic ruling in order to avoid having a vacuum in fishery conservation as a result of the Council's failure to adopt the requisite measures. The Advocate General, however, seeks to base this limited competence of Member States on firmer legal principle. He discusses, but ultimately rejects, the idea that such competence has been delegated to Member States by the Council in its series of so-called roll-over decisions.[28] Instead, he prefers to see this competence flowing from the duty of Member States (referred to earlier) to adopt conservation measures to meet established conservation needs where the Community has failed to act.

An important point is what exactly the exclusivity of competence obtained by the Community since the expiry of the transitional period in Article 102 covers. In *Commission v. United Kingdom* and other cases the Court refers to this exclusivity of competence as covering 'conservation'. This term would include total allowable catches, closed seasons and areas, minimum fish sizes, gear regulation and similar measures. But is Community competence limited to such measures? It would seem not. It appears that it must also include the allocation of resources among Member States (which is a matter quite separate from conservation). This is partly because the Court in various dicta (erroneously) includes allocation in its concept of conservation,[29] and partly because the Community institutions clearly envisage this as a Community matter, e.g. the Council's annual adoption of national quotas. In fact it would seem that the exclusivity of Community competence should be defined in the same terms as those of the article(s) of the Treaty endowing it with that competence, viz. Article 43. In other words, the Community has exclusive competence in relation to any matter covered by Article 43, which, as has been seen, can be practically any matter relating to fisheries management, including – apart from conservation *stricto sensu* – allocation and the regulation of conflicts between fishermen.

There are two arguments that can be raised against this conclusion. First, the Court has determined the Community's exclusivity in terms of time on the basis of Article 102. It could therefore be argued that the Community's exclusivity in terms of subject matter should also be taken from Article 102, i.e. it should be limited to exclusive competence in relation to determining 'conditions for fishing with a view to ensuring protection of the fishing grounds and conservation of the biological resources of the sea.' This, it was suggested earlier, is probably a less wide-ranging competence than that given by Article 43. In the light of the reasoning suggested earlier as to why the Community has exclusive competence, this argument clearly has some force. Nevertheless, it is one that is unlikely to be accepted by the Court, which in the later cases has laid stress on the function of Article 102 as being solely to set a time limit and not to be a source of Community competence. The second argument against the view that the Community's exclusivity of competence relates to all fisheries management matters is the fact that Articles 2 and 3 of Regulation 2141/70 (now Regulation 101/76)[30] envisage that Member States can and will enact rules governing fishing. If Community exclusivity of competence related to all fisheries management matters, there would be nothing left for Member States to legislate on and Articles 2 and 3 would therefore lack any point. Against this it can be argued, first, that the Community did not obtain exclusivity of competence until the end of 1978, thus from February 1, 1971 (when Articles 2 and 3 came into force) until December 31, 1978 Articles 2 and 3 did serve a purpose. Secondly, even after the latter date Member States retain some competence (as will be explained more fully shortly), and thus Articles 2 and 3 retain a purpose. On balance, therefore, the better view would seem to be that the Community's exclusivity of competence relates to all the fishery management measures that can justifiably be based on Article 43 of the EEC Treaty.

At the time of the facts which gave rise to the dispute in *Commission v. United Kingdom* the Council had not adopted the comprehensive conservation (management) measures required by Article 102. Since then the position has changed. At the beginning of 1983 the Council adopted comprehensive fishery management measures for most Community waters, including TACs and quotas, conservation measures, and regulations on access to coastal waters.[31] The various measures apply to different waters, and it is not clear which measures have to be taken into account when considering the Council's fulfilment of its obligations under Article 102 of the Act of Accession. If one takes the Court's pronouncements literally, it is only the regulation setting out conservation measures (other than total allowable catches) – Regulation 171/83 – that is relevant. This Regulation (like its temporary predecessor, Regulation 2527/80)[32] applies to all Community waters except those in the Baltic and Mediterranean. Subsequently, in June 1986, the Council adopted conservation measures for the Baltic.[33] Thus, it is only in the Mediterranean that the Council has not fulfilled its obligations under Article 102[34] and that Member States retain the competence described in *Commission v. United Kingdom,* that is to maintain those measures in force at the time of the expiry of the transitional period in Article 102 (i.e. December 31, 1978) and amend them where necessary. Moreover, following the Court's earlier case law, there is not only a right to do this but also a duty where it is necessary for action to be taken to meet established conservation needs. This will also be the position in other areas should Regulation 171/83 lapse without being replaced by something equally comprehensive,[35] and indeed this was the position between the lapse of Regulation 2527/80 on October 31, 1981 and the entry into force of Regulation 171/83 on January 27, 1983 (or June 1986 in the case of the Baltic).

At the present time outside the Mediterranean the Community has exclusive competence in relation to fishery management matters. However, both Regulation 2527/80 and one of the 1983 regulations – Regulation 171/83 – permit Member States in certain circumstances to take conservation measures. Article 18 of Regulation 171/83 (and Article 19 of Regulation 2527/80, which was almost identically worded) provide that a Member State may take 'appropriate non-discriminatory measures' in its waters 'where the conservation of certain species or fishing grounds is seriously threatened and where any delay would result in damage which would be difficult to repair.' In such cases the Commission must be informed immediately and shall then confirm, cancel or amend such measures: the Council may then subsequently, if it wishes, amend the Commission's decision. Under Article 19 of Regulation 171/83 (Article 18 of Regulation 2527/80 is fairly similar in content) a Member State may take 'measures for the conservation and management' of 'strictly local stocks of interest to the fishermen' of that Member State only: and a Member State may 'lay down any strictly local conditions or detailed arrangements, applying to [its] national fishermen only, designed to limit the catches by technical measures in addition to those defined in the Community regulations.' Before adopting such measures the Member State concerned must obtain the agreement of the Commission. Again the Commission's decision can be changed by the Council, this time via the management committee procedure. A provision similar to Article 19 of Regulation 171/83 is also found in the Baltic Conservation Regulation (Article 13).[36] Finally, Article 20 of Regulation 171/83[37] (which has no equivalent in Regulation 2527/80) provides that a Member State may adopt 'technical measures' going beyond the minimum requirements of the Regulation, which are applicable only to the fishermen of that Member State and which 'are intended either to ensure better management and better use of fish, crustaceans and molluscs in such a way as to limit the quantity and improve the quality of the species caught or to establish special measures not provided for by this Regulation for the species and areas concerned.' Nothing is said about requiring Commission approval for such measures, but this probably results from the general requirements of Community law (which are discussed below).

The question that arises is: is the power which Member States are given by these provisions compatible with the Court's findings on Community exclusivity of competence? Clearly, the only way in which these provisions could be reconcilable with the Court's case law is if the Community is considered to have delegated some of its powers to the Member States. Is this type of delegation permissible under Community law? In the few cases in which the question of delegation by Community institutions to non-Community bodies has arisen, the European Court has taken the view that such delegation is permissible provided that the powers delegated do not confer any substantial measure of discretion on the delegate and provided that the Community institutions retain a measure of supervision over the delegate.[38] Both these conditions are met here, so that the delegation of limited competence to Member States by Regulations 171/83 and 2527/80 appears to be lawful.

The Community has also delegated powers to its Member States in relation to one or two fisheries management matters other than conservation. Thus, under Article 5(2) of Regulation 170/83[39] 'Member States shall determine, in accordance with the applicable Community provisions, the detailed rules for the utilisation of the quotas allocated to them'. Under Article 14 of Regulation 2057/82[40] which deals with enforcement, Member States may adopt 'national control measures which go beyond any of [the Regulation's] minimum requirements, provided they comply with Community law and are in conformity with the common fisheries policy.' These two examples of delegation seem unobjectionable.

Apart from these delegated powers and the competence to adopt autonomous measures established in *Commission v. United Kingdom,* the Court has also recognised that on occasions national legislative measures are permissible, and indeed necessary, in order to fill various lacunae in Community law. In *Rogers v. Darthenay*[41] a French fisherman (Darthenay) was prosecuted before a British court for alleged infringement of Article 7 of Regulation 2527/80 and of a piece of British legislation, the Fishing Nets No. 2 Order 1980. Article 7 provided that the mesh of a net should not be obstructed by any device, subject to any exceptions which might be laid down in Community implementing rules. No such rules had been adopted at the time of the offence. The British Order provided for some exceptions to the general rule in Article 7. Darthenay was caught fishing with an obstructing device which was not permitted under the Order. He argued in his defence that Article 7 did not apply to him because no exceptions had been adopted by the Community and Member States were no longer competent to adopt exceptions. As to this last point about Member States' competence, which was one of the questions the British Court referred to the European Court under Article 177, the European Court first of all noted that the intention of Article 7 was that some exceptions should be permitted to the general rule so as to allow nets to be protected from wear. It would therefore be contrary to the scheme of the Regulation if such protection of fishing nets could not be taken into account simply because Community implementing rules had not been adopted. Such protection was required immediately. In the absence of Community rules 'it is for the *competent courts* to fill the resulting lacuna in a manner which is consistent with the aim of protecting fishing stocks and which also takes into account the fact that protection of fishing nets should be permitted' (emphasis added).[42] Among the means available to national courts to fill any lacunae are presumably any relevant national rules, provided such rules are consistent with the aims of the Community legislation in question.

A rather less ambiguous approach to the use of national legislation to fill gaps in Community law was taken by the European Court in the later case of *Officier van Justitie v. Bout.*[43] Here Bout was prosecuted before a Dutch court for having allegedly contravened Article 14(3) of Regulation 171/83 by fishing for sole and/or plaice with a beam trawl less than 12 miles from the Dutch coast with a vessel exceeding 70 Gross Registered Tonnes (G.R.T.). The European Court was asked how G.R.T. was to be calculated (the problem being that the tonnage of a vessel can be calculated in a number of different ways). The Court noted that Community law did not prescribe how G.R.T. was to be calculated and said that 'in the absence of Community regulations it is for Member States to determine the calculation method to be followed'.[44]

The Court's decisions in these two cases, though going against the Court's case law in other areas of Community law,[45] are much to be welcomed. Community fisheries management legislation, particularly the Conservation Regulation (Regulation 171/83), contains a number of lacunae and it is important that, until the Community takes the necessary action, they can be filled by Member States' legislation so as to allow fishing to proceed in an orderly fashion and to prevent fishermen exploiting potential loopholes in the Community rules. In some cases it is possible that such national legislation might also be justified under Article 20 of Regulation 171/83.

The discussion so far has concerned only Member States' competence in principle to take fisheries management measures. As has been seen, Member States' competence is limited to three situations: first, to take measures of the kind described in *Commission v. United Kingdom* at times and in places where there are no Community conservation measures in force – at the present time this competence concerns only the Mediterranean; secondly, to take measures based on the powers delegated by Regulations 2057/82, 170/83 and 171/83 and the Baltic Conservation Regulation – and in practice a large number of such measures have been adopted; and finally, to take measures to fill any lacunae in Community legislation. In each case – and also in the case of national measures adopted prior to the expiry of the transitional period in Article 102 – any measure taken must comply with the requirements of Community law. An attempt will now be made to establish, with the aid of the European Court's considerable case law on the subject, what these requirements are. The requirements are both substantive and procedural: the latter will be examined first.

(i) *Notification to the Commission and Member States.* Articles 2(2) and 3 of Regulation 101/76 require a Member State adopting or amending national measures to notify the Commission and other Member States. These provisions make it clear, as the European Court confirmed in *France v. United Kingdom*, that notification must be given *before* a measure is brought into force. Nevertheless, the practice of Member States is that more often than not (particularly before 1983) notification is given *after* the measure has been brought into force.[46] While notification given after a measure has been brought into force is clearly a breach of a Community obligation, it is not entirely clear whether it renders invalid the measure in question. Certainly the Commission has not objected to, and has treated as valid, measures notified to it after the date of their entry into force. The Court in *Gewiese and Mehlich v. Mackenzie*[47] took the view that the British measure at issue was not invalidated even though it had been notified to the Commission after its entry into force. However, the facts in this case were rather exceptional in that the measure in question did not require the Commission's approval (a requirement considered below). Had the measure required the Commission's approval, the Court would probably have reached a different conclusion as to the measure's validity because it said that a measure notified to the Commission after its entry into force would not fulfil the requirement of seeking the Commission's approval (a further requirement, discussed below).

In the case of national measures adopted by Member States under the powers delegated to them by Regulation 171/83 there are special notification procedures. In the case of urgent measures, the Member State concerned must send the text of those measures, together with an explanatory memorandum, to the Commission and other Member States by telex as soon as they are decided on (Article 18(3)). In the case of local measures, any measures taken prior to the entry into force of Regulation 171/83 were to be notified to the Commission by July 1, 1983. Any future measures must be notified to the Commission and other Member States when they have been taken – though the Commission will already have had to approve the draft of such measures (Article 19 (3)–(5)). It will be noted that in each case, contrary to Regulation 101/76, notification is to be given *after* the measures have been adopted.

(ii) *Seeking/Obtaining the Approval of the Commission.*

(a) **The position before 1979.** As was seen earlier, Annex VI of the Hague Resolution provides that a Member State wishing to take national measures[48] must 'seek the approval of the Commission'. Is this a binding obligation? Although, as was pointed out in the previous Chapter, Council Resolutions are not normally binding, the European Court in *France v. United Kingdom* held that Annex VI of the Hague Resolution does lay down a binding obligation because it 'makes specific the duties of co-operation which Member States assumed under Article 5 of the EEC Treaty when they acceded to the Community.'[49] According to the literal wording of Annex VI, the obligation is limited to *seeking* the Commission's approval, and does not extend actually to *obtaining* it. Nevertheless, in his Opinion in *France v. United Kingdom,* Advocate General Reischl was of the view that a Member State's duty was 'more than merely informing the Commission.'

It required:

> *collaboration* with the Commission, including a genuine readiness to seek out solutions which are acceptable to the Community ... [and] to accept modifications to the measures it intends to take ... Even if Annex VI does not expressly mention the necessity for the Commission's approval or a thoroughgoing right of veto ... the provision comes extremely close to such legal definitions (emphasis in the original)[50].

The Commission itself has said that discussions in the Council are no substitute for seeking the approval of the Commission,[51] and that it will not approve national measures which are submitted at such short notice that their impact cannot be properly assessed, or which deal with a problem on which the Council has not even attempted to reach a solution.[52] This standpoint of the Commission received support from the Court in *Commission v. United Kingdom.* Referring to a United Kingdom Order prohibiting fishing for the Mourne herring stock, of which the Commission was informed only two days before its entry into force, the Court observed:

> The fact that a draft measure, the details of which clearly raised problems from the point of view of Community law, was submitted to the Commission at a day's notice after a long period during which the United Kingdom had failed to act cannot be considered as being in accordance with the duties laid down in Annex VI to the Hague Resolutions which requires that the Commission should be consulted at all stages of the drawing-up of proposed measures allowing for the necessary time to study those measures and to give its opinion in good time.[53]

In the same case the Court took a similar view of the four days's notice given to the Commission by the United Kingdom Government of a measure restricting herring fishing in the Irish sea. Here not only was the notice too short, but the United Kingdom gave the Commission incomplete information about the proposed measure, and failed to give any justification for the measure on conservation grounds or to indicate how the interests of other Member States would be safeguarded. In these circumstances, the Commission was entitled to withhold its approval for a measure whose scope and justification it was unable to assess.[54]

The rationale for the requirement of Member States to consult the Commission and seek its approval was explained very well by Advocate General Reischl in *Commission v. United Kingdom*. As he put it:

A sensible Community policy in the field of the conservation and management of the resources of the sea . . . makes it essential that, in the absence of a comprehensive system of Community rules, the Commission be at least in a position to ensure that unilateral measures by Member States do not lead to an unjustified prejudicing of the interests of the Community and of other Member States. The active co-operation of the Commission is important in order to keep the differences between national fishery rules as small as possible.[55]

(b) **The position since 1979.** In the second case of *Commission v. United Kingdom* the Court said that the effect of the expiry of the transitional period in Article 102 of the Act of Accession was that the obligation in Annex VI of the Hague Resolution to 'seek the approval of the Commission' had become transformed into an obligation to 'undertake detailed consultations with the Commission' and 'not to lay down national conservation measures in spite of objections, reservations or conditions which might be formulated by the Commission.'[56] In other words, the Commission's approval is now required; or put more bluntly, the Commission can veto national measures. The Court, as is so often the case, does not explain the reasoning which led to its conclusion. Instead, one must look to the Advocate General's opinion for an explanation. According to Advocate General Reischl, a necessary consequence of the Community's having obtained exclusive competence to adopt fishery measures is that the '*Community interest can only be upheld* if the measures enacted by the Member States as representative of the Community are adopted . . . with the approval of the Community.'[57] It follows from Article 155 of the EEC Treaty and Annex VI of the Hague Resolution that it is the Commission which must represent the Community in this regard.[58]

In *Commission v. United Kingdom* the Advocate General also said that it was possible for the Commission's approval to be conferred not only expressly but tacitly. Tacit approval could result where consultation between a Member State and the Commission over a proposed measure had taken place, and the Commission had not expressly opposed the introduction of such measures. The question of what constitutes tacit approval arose directly in *R. v. Tymen*.[59] This case was concerned with the validity of a United Kingdom Order dealing with minimum mesh sizes. The Commission had objected to this Order, but the British Government argued that as this objection was not to the substance of the Order – since the Commission had proposed a Regulation to the Council very similar in content – but only as to the date of its entry into force – the Order came into force on July 1, 1979, whereas the Commission had proposed that the draft Regulation should come into force on September 1 following – it must follow that as from September 1 the Order had the Commission's tacit approval. The Court rejected this argument. To regard a Commission proposal similar in content to a national measure as constituting approval of the latter would be contrary to legal certainty and distort the division of powers between the community and Member States. In any case it was clear from the facts that the Commission, so far from approving the Order, maintained its objections to it.

On the other hand, in *Gewiese and Mehlich v. Mackenzie* the Court accepted that a national measure which simply re-enacted without substantive amendment an earlier measure which had received the Commission's approval did not require to be submitted to the Commission for approval. The Advocate General, while agreeing with this, added (*obiter*) that in the case of a measure extending a previously approved measure which was limited in time but not otherwise making any changes, fresh approval might be necessary.

It is clear that the pre–1979 law on the consultation process requiring the Commission to be informed fully and in good time of proposed measures applies equally, if not more strongly, to the post–1979 position. Nevertheless, in practice many Member States have often informed the Commission only a very short while before a measure has come into force and not infrequently until after a measure has come into force: in one extreme case the Commission was not informed until three months after a Dutch measure had come into force.[60] Although in these cases there is a breach of Community obligations concerning notification and the Commission would be entitled to withhold its approval, in practice it has approved nearly all these measures. While it is readily understandable that the Commission has given its approval – if it did not, there would have been very few conservation measures of any kind in existence for most of the time between 1979 and 1983 – there must be doubts as to the legal validity of such national measures. This is particularly the case during the period when a measure has come into force and before the Commission has given its approval. While it seems that the Commission's approval is retrospective in its effect, it is not desirable in this, as in any other area of law, that there should be widespread retrospective legislation. At the very least it creates considerable legal uncertainty. It seems doubtful whether the Commission's practice would be supported by the Court. In *Gewiese and Mehlich v. Mackenzie* the Court suggested, *obiter,* that a measure notified to the Commission after its entry into force could not by definition meet the requirement of seeking the Commission's approval.

A further point of some interest and uncertainty is whether the Commission, having originally approved a particular national measure, can withdraw its approval if that measure, as a result of changing circumstances, no longer meets required conservation needs. A Commission official, writing in a private capacity, has suggested that in this situation the Commission can withdraw its approval:[61] this seems reasonable. This view is also supported by the Advocate General's Opinion in *Gewiese and Mehlich v. Mackenzie* where it is suggested that the Commission could require a national measure to be repealed or amended in order to conform to the Community's conservation policy. In fact the British measure at issue in that case was subsequently revoked following an order from the Commission.

While the Commission has in fact approved most national measures submitted to it, its approval has been far from a formality. It has required measures to comply with all the substantive requirements of Community law (which will shortly be outlined), and has insisted on changes where those requirements were not observed. Its approval has tended to be most quickly and readily given where a national measure has simply implemented a Commission proposal to the Council. In some cases the Commission's approval has been provisional, pending further information from the Member State concerned or the Commission's being able to make a full assessment of the effect of the measure in question.

What has been said so far about approval relates very largely to the position before the adoption of comprehensive Community conservation measures in January 1983. Since that time it is only in the Mediterranean that autonomous national conservation measures have been possible and where, therefore, the provisions discussed above concerning Commission approval have current application. It is therefore odd that in the lists of national measures published since 1979 in the *Official Journal*[62] and *Bulletin of the European Communities* by the Commission, there are no measures relating to the Mediterranean. This is not because there have been no national measures since 1979 – there have been quite a number of Italian measures, for example.[63] If the Commission's lists are exhaustive (and there is nothing to indicate that they are not), it seems as though the obligations of notification and obtaining the Commission's approval – even though they undoubtedly apply to the Mediterranean – are simply not being observed by the Mediterranean Member States. If so, this means that all national fishery measures in the Mediterranean are in breach of Community law!

In relation to measures adopted by Member States in pursuance of the powers delegated to them by Regulation 171/83, there are special procedures for Community approval. As was pointed out above, in the case of urgent or local conservation measures, the Commission must give its approval, but unlike the position in respect of autonomous measures, any decision taken by the Commission can be changed by the Council (Articles 18 and 19). In the case of measures taken under Article 20, nothing is said about Commission approval being required. The Commission's practice is to take note of such measures (which must of course, like all national measures, be notified to it) and reserve its right to review such measures for their compatibility with Community law. On occasions the Commission has ruled that a Member State should withdraw or amend its measures. The justification for this action is presumably the Commission's role under Article 155 as guardian of the Community interest: and if a Member State did not comply with the Commission's ruling, the Commission would no doubt begin proceedings under Article 169. The result of the Commission's practice is that national measures adopted under Article 20 do *de facto* require its approval. The Commission has taken a similar approach to national measures adopted under Article 5(2) of Regulation 170/83 and Article 14 of Regulation 2057/82, as well as with national measures filling lacunae in Community rules.

(iii) *No conflict with Community measures.* National measures must not conflict with any existing Community fisheries measures. This follows from the general rule (mentioned earlier) that Community law prevails over any inconsistent national law.

(iv) *No jeopardising of the Common Fisheries Policy.* In the *Kramer*[64] and *Irish Fisheries* cases[65] the European Court held that national measures must not jeopardise the objectives, attainment or functioning of the Common Fisheries Policy. The Court's decision here is really a specific application of Article 5 of the EEC Treaty, which provides that Member States shall 'abstrain from any measure which could jeopardise the attainment of the objectives of this Treaty.'

(v) *Relationship of national measures to earlier Community measures.* As will be seen later in this Chapter, the Community adopted quite a number of conservation measures in 1977, all but one of which lapsed at the beginning of 1978. In *Commission v. United Kingdom* the question arose as to whether the fact that Community conservation measures had been adopted and then lapsed gave rise to any limitations on national measures concerned with the same matters. The Court held that it did. In relation to the United Kingdom Order restricting herring fishing in the Irish Sea, the Court noted that it appreciably departed from the lapsed Community legislation on this topic. It was therefore clear that the United Kingdom had unilaterally prejudiced the situation established by this Community legislation when it had undertaken to maintain it, without being able either to give reliable information as to the effects of its Order or to justify conservation needs which might warrant the changes introduced. As a result the United Kingdom was in breach of Community law. The Court also reached similar conclusions as regards the United Kingdom Order banning fishing for Norway pout. It follows, therefore, that a Member State may only introduce a measure departing from an earlier, lapsed

Community measure if it can justify the change on conservation grounds.

(vi) *Measures must be genuine conservation measures.* In its earlier case law the Court laid stress on the fact that any measures taken by the Member States must be conservation measures (using that term in its strictest sense): social and economic measures – and quotas, too, in the view of the Advocate General in *Commission v. United Kingdom*[66] – were not permissible. Thus, for example, in *Commission v. United Kingdom* the British measure temporarily exempting vessels under 35 feet from the ban on fishing for Mourne herring was contrary to Community law because it was not a conservation measure: in fact it was contrary to conservation requirements and was really adopted for reasons of regional and social policy.

In the later case of *Kerr,* however, the Court took a broader view of the type of measures which may be taken by Member States. It referred to such measures as being for the purposes of 'conservation and management';[67] and held that they included the power to allocate quotas among Member States, even where the basis of the allocation was in part the needs of the local population (*in casu* Greenland). The reasons why the Court found the Danish measure in this case permissible appear to be, first, that fixing quotas was the most effective way of ensuring observance of the total allowable catch (the establishment of the latter was undoubtedly a true conservation measure); and, secondly, that the criteria used in allocating quotas were based on Commission proposals.

On the other hand, in the later case of *R. v. Kirk*[68] the Court appears to have reverted to a more restrictive approach. The case concerned the validity of a United Kingdom Order which prohibited Danish vessels from fishing within a 12-mile zone around the United Kingdom. The Order had been adopted to deal with the situation arising upon the expiry at the end of 1982 of the derogation to the equal access principle of a 12-mile national zone introduced by the 1972 Act of Accession and before its renewal by the Council on January 23, 1983. The Order, it should be noted, had been approved by the Commission. The Court held, nevertheless, that the Order was not in conformity with Community law. It rejected the arguments of the United Kingdom and Commission that the expiry of the derogation meant that there was a vacuum that Member States were entitled to fill as trustees of the common interest by measures approved by the Commission as had been recognised by the Court in *Commission v. United Kingdom.* However, in that case, said the Court, it had been talking about conservation measures. That was not the case here. Although

> rules relating to access may in certain cases constitute a response to a
> concern to conserve fishery resources, it is clear that in this instance the

disputed measure was not intended to achieve such an objective. National rules which prohibit access to national waters and which are not intended to achieve an objective of conservation cannot be covered by the power of Member States, recognised in [*Commission v. United Kingdom*] to take the temporary conservation measures.[69]

The Court was possibly influenced in taking a stricter view in *Kirk* than in *Kerr* by the fact that the United Kingdom Order was in derogation of the fundamental Community principle of non-discrimination (of which equal access is one aspect). It may be that putting the dicta in *Kerr* and *Kirk* together the position is that a Member State can adopt fisheries management measures which are not strictly speaking pure conservation measures, provided such measures in some way are likely to further conservation requirements.

In relation to the powers delegated to Member States by Regulations 2052/82, 170/83 and 171/83, as well as powers relating to the filling of lacunae in Community rules, it is clear from the nature of these powers as described earlier that not all of them are principally (or in some cases at all) concerned with conservation.

(vii) *Non-discrimination.* It follows from Article 7 of the EEC Treaty in general, and from Article 2(1) of Regulation 101/76 in particular (discussed in detail in section 5 below), that national measures must be non-discriminatory, i.e. they must not apply different treatment to particular vessels or particular fishermen solely because of their nationality. The question of discrimination was one of the central issues in the *Irish Fisheries* case. Ireland had made two Orders banning all vessels over 33 metres in length or with engines in excess of 1,100 h.p. from fishing in certain parts of the Irish 200-mile fishing zone. The Commission argued that although these orders were based on apparently objective criteria, they were in fact discriminatory because Irish vessels were scarcely affected, only two being of the proscribed size, whereas a considerable number of Dutch and French vessels were affected. The Court agreed with this argument. Community law, it said, forbids 'not only overt discrimination by reason of nationality but also all covert forms of discrimination, which, by the application of other criteria of differentiation, lead in fact to the same result.'[70] The Court found that this certainly applied in the case of the criteria used in the Irish Orders, since their effect was to keep out of Irish waters a substantial proportion of the fishing fleets of other Member States which had traditionally fished in those areas, whereas no comparable obligation was imposed on Irish nationals.

The Court also found a similar form of covert discrimination in *Commission v. United Kingdom*. The United Kingdom Order banning fishing for Mourne herring temporarily exempted from the ban boats of less than 35 feet in length.

Although formulated in apparently objective terms, the measure was in fact discriminatory because the smallness of the vessels permitted to fish meant in practice that only Northern Irish vessels, and not vessels from the Republic of Ireland as hitherto, would engage in the fishery.[71]

The Court's judgments in the *Irish Fisheries* case and in *Commission v. United Kingdom* were undoubtedly the correct ones. Nevertheless, because conservation measures will usually have a different impact on different national fleets, due to the different structure and patterns of fishing of each fleet, it will not always be easy to see whether a measure which is objectively formulated does in fact lead to differences in treatment by reason of nationality and therefore is discriminatory.[72] The effects of a measure will not often be as obviously discriminatory as they were in the *Irish Fisheries* case.

On the other hand, in the first *Van Dam* case, the Court appears to have accepted that reverse discrimination (i.e. a Member State treating its nationals in a less advantageous way than the nationals of other Member States) is permissible under Community law, at least in certain circumstances. In this case the Netherlands had applied quotas for sole and plaice to its fishermen, but similar quotas were not applied to the fishermen of other Member States fishing in the Dutch fishing zone. It was argued that this difference in treatment amounted to a discrimination prohibited by Community law. The Court held that this was not so. It observed that:

> It cannot be held contrary to the principle of non-discrimination to apply national legislation, the compatibility of which with Community law is moreover not contested, because other Member States allegedly apply less strict rules. Inequalities of this kind, if they exist, must be eliminated by means of the consultations provided for by Annex VI to the Hague Resolution ..., but they cannot be the foundation of a charge of discrimination with regard to the provisions made by a Member State which applies equally to any person under its jurisdiction, the regulations which it had adopted for fishing quotas.[73]

An interesting problem of discrimination arose in the *Kerr* case. Here the Danish authorities had established a total allowable catch for shrimp in Greenland waters and allocated it among Greenland, Danish, French and Faroese vessels. Kerr, the captain of a British trawler, was arrested and fined for fishing for shrimp in Greenland waters, contrary to the Danish Order. On appeal, he argued that the quotas set for shrimp in Greenland waters were discriminatory. The question was referred to the European Court by the Danish Court under Article 177. In its judgment the Court held that the quotas were not discriminatory because they had been allocated on the basis of the same objective criteria (the needs of the local Greenland population and past fishing patterns) used by the Commission in its proposals for quotas for Greenland shrimp for the year in question (1978).

(viii) *Measures must be necessary.* The Council's Declaration of January 30–31, 1978 (which, it would seem, is binding for the same reasons as the Hague Resolution) stresses that national conservation measures may only be adopted where this is 'strictly necessary'. This requirement had already been suggested by Advocate General Reischl in the *Irish Fisheries* case. Without explaining the legal basis for this requirement,[74] he commented that 'the crucial condition with regard to conservation measures . . . is . . . that they are *necessary,* in other words that in a certain area the fish stocks have already been considerably reduced or that there is an immediate danger of over-fishing and without restrictions and measures of protection regeneration and thus future supplies are endangered.'[75] In *Commission v. United Kingdom* the Court found that the United Kingdom Order prohibiting fishing for Norway pout was, because of the size of the area and period of time to which the prohibition related, not strictly necessary.

This requirement, as formulated by the Advocate General, is a rather strict one. It would, for example, seem to exclude the taking of measures to restore a stock to the level of MSY (and these are undoubtedly conservation measures), in circumstances where the stock is not 'considerably reduced' or there is not an 'immediate danger of overfishing.' Furthermore, there is a risk that the complexities of species inter-relationships may be ignored. For example, the United Kingdom prohibition on fishing for Norway pout was certainly not necessary in order to conserve Norway pout (which were not under any threat of overfishing): but the Court arguably gave too little attention to the question of whether the prohibition was necessary in order to conserve immature haddock and whiting, which are caught as by-catches in Norway pout fishing.

It seems likely that the requirement of necessity is relaxed in the case of measures taken under Regulations 2057/82, 170/83 and 171/83 and to fill lacunae in Community rules.

(ix) *Measures must be proportionate.* This is a specific application of the general principle of proportionality[76] which the Court has held forms part of Community law. The question of proportionality has arisen in a number of the fisheries cases before the Court. In the *Irish Fisheries* case Advocate General Reischl was of the opinion that the Irish Orders prohibiting all vessels above a certain size from fishing in a substantial area of the Irish 200-mile fishing zone violated the principle of proportionality because these Orders went far beyond what was necessary from both a biological point of view (they covered all species of fish) and a geographical point of view (they applied to about a quarter of the Irish fishing zone). The Court, however, did not find it necessary to discuss this point. In *France v. United Kingdom* it was argued by both France and the Commission that a British Order that limited permissible by-catches to 20 per cent of the total catch violated the principle of proportionality because a Commission proposal on the same topic fixed a maximum permissible level of 40 per cent. Although the Court did not find it necessary to discuss the point, Advocate General Reischl was of the opinion that the British Order could not simply be compared with the Commission's proposals, and that otherwise there was insufficient data to determine whether the Order was excessive. In *Commission v. United Kingdom* the Danish Government (intervening) argued that the United Kingdom measure prohibiting fishing for Norway pout was contrary to the principle of proportionality because the gain obtained for British fishermen by thus conserving young haddock and whiting was out of proportion to the injury caused to Danish fishermen who were most directly affected by the ban. Neither the Court nor the Advocate General, however, found it necessary to consider this argument.

(x) *Measures must be interim.* Annex VI of the Hague Resolution states that national measures must be of an interim (i.e. temporary) nature. This obligation appears to derive from the fact that, as has been seen earlier, Member States' competence to adopt fisheries measures under the doctrine in *Commission v. United Kingdom* is essentially of a provisional character, only existing where the Council has not fulfilled its obligations under Article 102 of the Act of Accession. For this reason, therefore, the requirement would not apply to measures taken under delegated powers or to fill lacunae in Community rules.

An example of the practical application of the requirement that measures must be of an interim character is shown in *Commission v. United Kingdom,* where the Commission argued that the United Kingdom Order banning fishing for Norway pout violated this condition because it was stated to apply 'each year': it was thus not of a temporary nature and would apply irrespective of whether it was still necessary. Although the Court did not find it necessary to consider this argument, the Advocate General agreed with the Commission, rejecting the United Kingdom's counter-argument that the measure was temporary because it would automatically lapse, by virtue of the supremacy of Community law, when the Community adopted a measure dealing with the same matter.

(xi) *Measures must be limited to amending existing measures.* In the case of autonomous powers (as opposed to delegated and lacuna-filling powers) exercised after 1978, the Court has held, as has been seen earlier, that national measures may only 'amend' existing measures and may not 'involve a new conservation policy'. The scope of this obligation is not very clear. Does it mean that Member States may literally only amend existing legislation and nothing more? What is meant by a 'new conservation policy'? Does it mean conservation measures in respect of stocks for which no such measures have previously been taken; or does it mean rather a change in the objectives and types of measures of a previous conservation policy? The practice of Member States and the Commission does not support a strict reading of the Court's dicta. The Commission has approved many national measures which are not amendments of existing measures. Such measures have usually implemented Council roll-over decisions and/or Commission proposals, and in the Baltic, recommendations of the International Baltic Sea Fisheries Commission.

(xii) *Measures must be properly published.* The Court has laid down that, to be valid, national measures must be properly published. This obligation no doubt derives from the general principle of legal certainty, which the Court on numerous occasions has held forms part of Community law. In *Commission v. United Kingdom* the Court held that the United Kingdom violated Community law because it did not publish all the details of a licensing system it had introduced for herring fishing in the Irish Sea. Thus neither Member States nor individual fishermen could ascertain whether this licensing system was in accordance with Community law. The Court went on wisely to observe that:

> this obligation to introduce implementing measures which are effective in law and with which those concerned may readily acquaint themselves is particularly necessary where sea fisheries are concerned, which must be planned and organised in advance; the requirement of legal clarity is indeed imperative in a sector in which any uncertainty may well lead to incidents and the application of particularly serious sanctions.[77]

(xiii) *Observance of recommended TACs.* Where the Council has not laid down a total allowable catch (TAC) for a particular stock and where an autonomous national measure lays down a TAC for that stock (as, for example, happened in *Kerr*), that measure must comply with any Commission proposal for a TAC where there is in existence a Council roll-over decision so requiring. Between 1979 and 1983 there was a series of such decisions, all calling on Member States to 'take into account' TACs proposed by the Commission.

(xiv) *No relaxation within 12-mile limits.* Under Article 100(1) of the 1972 Act of Accession (as continued by Article 6 of Regulation 170/83) national measures governing fishing in a Member State's exclusive 12-mile zone must not be made less restrictive than they were at the time of accession, i.e. January 1, 1973. Member States, having obtained a 12-mile zone mainly or entirely for the benefit of their vessels, might possibly have been tempted to permit such vessels to increase their catches in the short-term by relaxing conservation and control measures. To have done so would have meant long-term detriment to fish stocks and to the Community as a whole. The aim of this provision in Article 100(1) is therefore to prevent that happening. On the other hand, it appears that where stocks improve, it is permissible to relax conservation measures if this is biologically justifiable.[78]

(xv) *Measures must not affect negotiations with third States.* In the *Irish Fisheries* case the Court held that national measures must not jeopardise or hinder negotiations on fisheries matters with third States. Relations with third States in fisheries matters are now exclusively within the competence of the Community (see Chapter 5), and this rule is therefore a specific application of Article 5 of the EEC Treaty.

(xvi) *Effect of measures on the functioning of the market in fisheries products.* This question was one of the main issues to be considered in the *Kramer* case. It was argued, following the Court's earlier decisions in relation to other sectors of agriculture that Member States must avoid taking any measures likely to derogate from or adversely affect common organisations of the market, that the Dutch measures imposing quotas on Dutch fishermen affected the operation of the common organisation of the market in fishery products and therefore were contrary to Community law. The Court rejected this argument. It pointed out that Community law gave the Community institutions the power to limit catches. Although the limiting of catches might affect the functioning of the common organisation of the market in fishery products, particularly its price system, such an effect, having been accepted by Community law itself, 'cannot be equated with the disruptive effects, prohibited by Community law, of national measures unrelated to the aim of Community rules.'[79] Thus, 'a Member State does not jeopardise the objectives or the proper functioning' of the common organisation of the market 'if it adopts measures involving a limitation of fishing activities with a view to conserving the resources of the sea.'[80] Nevertheless, the Court stressed, 'the existence of the common organisation of the market involves an obligation on the part of the Member States to ensure that catches should be limited in such a way as to keep the effects on the functioning of that organisation to a minimum.'[81]

(xvii) *Effect of measures on the free movement of goods.* Articles 30 *et seq.* of the EEC Treaty prohibit all quantitative restrictions and measures having equivalent effect on trade between Member States. The question as to whether national measures laying down quotas fell foul of this prohibition arose in the *Kramer* case. In earlier cases involving other sectors of agriculture[82] the Court had held that limitations on production amounted to quantitative restrictions or equivalent measures. In the *Kramer* case, however, the Court held that 'national measures involving limitation of fishing activities with a view to conserving the resources of the sea, do not constitute measures having an effect equivalent to a quantitative restriction on intra-Community trade which are prohibited under Articles 30 *et seq.* of the Treaty.'[83] This was because conservation measures, while restricting production in the short-term, are aimed in the long-term at building up production.[84]

There are thus a considerable number of rules of Community law – some procedural, some substantive – with which national fishery measures adopted by Member States must comply. In spite of the rather imposing, almost forbidding, nature of this list of requirements, the vast majority of national measures adopted since 1977 have complied with these requirements (although in giving its approval to such measures the Commission has probably adopted a rather less strict approach than the Court has done in its case law). If a national measure fails to satisfy one or more of these requirements, there will be a breach of its Community obligations by the Member State concerned, and the measure in question will be invalid (except possibly to some extent where the requirement not observed is a procedural one). The Court has held that a measure thus rendered invalid may not be enforced against Community fishermen by national courts, and any attempt to do so is contrary to Community law.[85] Although this is obviously common sense, it is not always easy to find a theoretical justification for the rule. In *Schonenberg* there was no problem because the Community rule breached – Article 2 of Regulation 101/76 (prohibiting discrimination) – was one that has direct effect and therefore can be relied on by an individual before a national court. In *Tymen,* on the other hand, the British measure in question was invalid as a result of the United Kingdom's failure to obtain the Commission's approval. One of the points undoubtedly troubling the Court of Appeal, which referred the case to the European Court under Article 177, was whether the requirement of obtaining the Commission's approval, which stems from Article 5 of the EEC Treaty, had direct effect and therefore could be relied on by Tymen before the English court. The European Court did not address itself to this problem, but the Advocate General did discuss it. He said that the question here was not whether the Community law in issue had direct effect, in the sense that individuals might rely on it before national courts, but whether it had direct applicability, in the sense that it must be fully and uniformly applied by national courts and thus a 'direct source of rights and duties for all those affected thereby, whether Member States or individuals, who are parties to legal relationships under Community law'.[86] The test of whether a provision of Community law is directly applicable in this sense is that it is sufficiently clear. In the case of the obligations flowing from Article 5 of the EEC Treaty in relation to the adoption of national fishery measures, the Advocate General thought that the test was satisfied beyond dispute. The Advocate General here seems to blur the distinction between direct applicability and direct effect. Might it not have been preferable to say that although Article 5 does not in general have direct effect,[87] the specific obligations deriving from it which the Court has attributed to Member States when enacting national fishery measures *do* have direct effect? On this basis most, if not all, the requirements discussed above could be regarded as having direct effect.

The Court has performed a useful service in clarifying the permissible scope of national fishery measures, given the absence of Community measures for so much of the time between 1977 and 1983. It has taken this opportunity to promote the role of the Community, and especially that of the Commission: there are times when reading the Court's case law one has the impression that the Court is more interested in this matter than in the good management of the fish stocks in Community waters. Undoubtedly by stressing the role of the Community and the Commission, the Court was seeking to put pressure on the Council to reach agreement on Community fishery management measures. The Court's judgments have been more important for this aspect and for elaborating Member States' future conduct, than for their practical effect on the national measures before it, most of which had expired or been replaced by the time the Court ruled on them: of course, in those cases which have arisen out of criminal proceedings before national courts (e.g. *Van Dam, Kerr, Tymen, Bout*), the European Court's ruling has usually been crucial in determining whether the individual concerned was convicted.

The cases that have arisen concerning national measures adopted since 1979, such as the second *Van Dam* case, *Bout* and *Tymen,* suggest that from now on when the Court is faced with assessing the compatibility of national fishery measures with Community law – and this will be mainly in Article 169 and 177 proceedings – its decision will largely turn on the question of whether there has been adequate consultation with the Commission and Commission approval for the measure in question. If there has been adequate consultation and the measure has been approved, it will be compatible with Community law: if not, not. If this prediction is right, it means that the Court will usually only be concerned with straightforward procedural questions of consultation and approval. All the substantive conditions with which national fishery measures must comply – such as non-discrimination, being genuine conservation measures etc. – which the Court elaborated in its case law on pre-1979 measures are now almost exclusively the concern of the Commission in deciding whether to give or withhold approval for a national measure, and are only likely to be considered by the Court in two situations. First, in Article 177 proceedings where a national court asks whether the Commission wrongly gave or withheld its approval, as was essentially the position in *Kirk* (the same point might also be raised in proceedings under Articles 169 or 170); and secondly, where a Commission decision giving or withholding approval is challenged by a Member State under Article 173[88] (or possibly by an individual fisherman, but it seems very doubtful whether the latter would have *locus standi*).

So far, the discussion has concentrated on the requirements which Member States' fishery measures must observe, but for the sake of completeness the requirements which Community measures must observe ought also to be sketched briefly. First there are two procedural requirements. Community measures must be reasoned (Article 190 of the EEC Treaty), i.e. they must state the legal provision on which they are based, mention any proposals or opinions received, and state the reasons which motivated the Community institution concerned to act. They must also be published (Article 191) – regulations in the *Official Journal,* decisions and directives to their addressees. On the substantive side, Community measures must not exceed the material competence given to the Community institutions by the EEC Treaty (on this see section 1 of Chapter 2); they must not discriminate between different groups of fishermen (Articles 7 and 40(3) of the EEC Treaty); and they must respect those general legal principles, such as proportionality and legal certainty, which the Court has held form part of Community law.[89]

Having seen that the Community is competent to adopt fishery management measures for Community waters – and since 1979 has in principle had exclusive competence in this area – we must now turn to look at the measures which it has actually adopted. But before doing so, it is necessary to say a few words about the objectives of Community management.

2. THE OBJECTIVES OF COMMUNITY FISHERIES MANAGEMENT

It is not entirely easy to ascertain what the objectives of Community fisheries management are. While the Commission has spelt out its views in various communications to the Council,[90] and the European Parliament and Economic and Social Committee have made their views known in various opinions and resolutions, it is difficult to know how far the Council, the most important body in the Community legislative process, shares these views. This is because there is no public record of discussions in the Council: the only guide to the Council's views is in the text of Community legislation, which on this matter is particularly laconic and elliptical.

According to the Commission, a Community system of fisheries management should have three fundamental objectives. The first objective should be, in the medium and long term, to optimise exploitation of the living resources in Community waters, taking into account economic restraints resulting from the diversity of technical and social structures and the multiplicity of market requirements to be met. In the shorter term, given the state of Community stocks, most of which are fully exploited and some of which are over-exploited, the aim should be, first, to take measures which will ensure the continuation of each stock as a commercially viable resource; secondly, to decrease the fishing effort on over-exploited stocks in order to ensure yields which are stable from year to year; and thirdly, to ensure the highest possible catches from the stocks, consistent with the first two aims and taking into account the inter-relationship of stocks. The second objective should be to maintain as far as possible the level of employment and income in coastal regions that are economically disadvantaged or largely dependent on fishing activities. But while a Community management system should take account of economic, social, regional and other aspects of fisheries, in the short term these must be strictly subservient to biological considerations. The third objective should be to adapt Community fishing fleets to catch potential. The matters to which this last objective relates are discussed in Chapter 6.

The objectives suggested by the Commission have been broadly endorsed by the European Parliament[91] and the Economic and Social Committee.[92] Insofar as any firm conclusions can be drawn from the elliptical provisions of Community legislation, they also appear largely to be shared by the Council. Article 1 of Regulation 170/83 establishing a Community System for the Conservation and Management of Fishery Resources[93] provides that the aim of this system is to:

> ensure the protection of fishing grounds, the conservation of the biological resources of the sea and their balanced exploitation on a lasting basis and in appropriate economic and social conditions.

Recital 9 of the Preamble to the Regulation says the system must also 'safeguard the particular needs of regions where local populations are especially dependent on fisheries and related industries.'

Referring back to the discussion of the objectives of fisheries management at the beginning of Chapter 1, it can be seen that the objective of the Community system is MSY, subject to the inter-relationship of stocks and taking into account the socio-economic needs of certain regions and the desirability of greater economic efficiency. Such objectives could be characterised as a form of Optimum Sustainable Yield (if such a term has any value). While such objectives may seem rather vague, it is doubtful whether they could be made much more precise, given that the matter to which they relate, the management of Community fish stocks, is not a static but a dynamic process, operating against a background of natural fluctuations in the size of fish stocks, a fishing industry which (as explained in Chapter 1) has recently been subject to a host of major changes, and a diverse range of fisheries.[94]

The Community seeks to achieve its objectives by a number of different measures – total allowable catches divided into individual Member State quotas, a wide range of supplementary conservation measures, and rules on access to fishing grounds. Each of these will now be examined in turn.

3. TOTAL ALLOWABLE CATCHES AND QUOTAS

In its proposals of September 1976, put forward shortly before the extension of Member States' fishing limits to 200 miles, the Commission suggested fish stocks in Community waters should be conserved by means of a system of total allowable catches (TACs) supplemented by a variety of more traditional measures such as gear regulations, minimum fish sizes, and closed seasons and areas. These proposals are incorporated in Regulation 170/83 establishing a Community System for the Conservation and Management of Fishery Resources (hereafter referred to as the Management Regulation), adopted by the Council on January 25, 1983. Articles 2 and 3 of the Regulation provide that the Council, acting by a qualified majority on a proposal from the Commission, and in the light of the available scientific advice, shall adopt the conservation measures necessary to achieve the objectives specified in Article 1 (quoted above). Such measures may include closed areas and seasons, gear regulation, minimum fish sizes and TACs. The Regulation goes on to provide that TACs are to be divided up into quotas allocated to individual Member States. This section looks at the question of TACs and quotas: the other conservation measures will be considered in the following section.

Total Allowable Catches

A TAC, which customarily is prescribed for a year at a time, lays down the amount of fish that may be taken from a particular stock for the year in question. The purpose of a TAC, put somewhat crudely, is to ensure that no more fish are taken from the stock than is biologically justifiable. A TAC is a conservation measure of considerable effectiveness provided that it is actually set at a level which will not lead to overfishing, and that once so set, it is observed. The latter is more likely to happen if the TAC is allocated among interested fishermen by means of quotas and/or licences. Such means are also essential to mitigate the economic disadvantages of using TACs. If a TAC is set but not allocated, it encourages fishermen to catch as much of the fish as quickly as possible before the TAC is exhausted. This stimulates the use of unnecessarily large amounts of capital and labour, shortens the fishing season with the result that fishing vessels may be made idle unless they can fish elsewhere, and floods the market, with the consequent likelihood of a marked drop in prices.

Even though the Management Regulation was not adopted until January 1983, the Commission has made proposals for TACs for Community waters for every year from 1978 onwards. Its proposals have been based since 1979 on advice from the Scientific and Technical Committee for Fisheries (as to which see pp. 34 above). The Committee has based its advice on the recommendations of the International Council for the Exploration of the Sea (ICES) and, when Greenland was within the Community, the Northwest Atlantic Fisheries Organisation.[95] The way in which the TAC is set by the Commission depends on the state of the stock.[96] For stocks which have been so heavily fished that they are not a commercially viable resource (e.g. many herring stocks until recently), a zero TAC is set. For stocks which are over-exploited the TAC is initially set at a level which will achieve a stabilisation of the fisheries at the existing level of fishing mortality rate: thereafter TACs are set which will gradually reduce the fishing mortality rate so as to produce relatively stable yields (presumably at or around the level of MSY). The reason for this gradualist approach is to protect the fishing industry from too sudden changes. In the case of fully exploited stocks the TAC is set at a level which will maintain stocks at a stable yield level (again presumably around the level of MSY). For stocks which are not (yet) fully exploited, a TAC is generally not set: however, in some cases a precautionary TAC is set. This will be done for one or more of three reasons: first, to 'prevent misreporting of catches to areas where catch restrictions would not otherwise operate, ... secondly, in the case of rapidly expanding fisheries, such as that for blue whiting, [to] provide a limit to overexpansion during the period in which scientific data are being accumulated and thus avoid the possible need to reduce the fisheries once sufficient scientific data, on which to base an analytical assessment, have been accumulated; thirdly, in the case of species fished mainly for reduction to meal and oil and with which there is a large by-catch of valuable human consumption species, they provide a calculable upper limit to the total by-catch.'[97] In the case of stocks for which insufficient scientific advice is available, mainly stocks in Portuguese and Spanish waters, TACs are 'established on the basis of average catches, setting them, in general, at a level which is higher than maximum catches in previous years.'[98] The levels of TAC (except for over-exploited stocks) are broadly of the same order from year to year, the variations that do occur reflecting mainly short-term changes caused by fluctuations in year-class strength.

While the Commission's point of departure in setting TACs is the advice it receives from scientists, the TACs recommended by the latter are from time to time varied for socio-economic reasons. This has mainly happened in relation to the TACs for over-exploited stocks, where the Commission has not always been prepared to reduce levels of fishing quite as quickly as the scientists have recommended. The Commission has argued that while rapid reductions in the amount of fishing will bring long-term benefits more quickly, less rapid reductions, while bringing long-term benefits less quickly, involve less short-term economic costs, and this is what the EEC fishing industry requires. Whether the Commission has struck the balance correctly between biological and socio-economic considerations is something which can only be judged in relation to specific TACs; but this is not a matter on which the writer feels competent to offer a judgment.[99]

In the case of stocks not wholly confined to Community waters, i.e. stocks which migrate between Community waters and the waters of third States and/ or areas beyond 200-mile limits (and probably the majority of stocks in Community waters come into this category), TACs are set by agreement between the Community and the third State(s) concerned. In such cases the Community has often had to modify the objectives described above. This matter is discussed further in the final section of the next Chapter.

Although the Commission has proposed TACs for every year since 1978, in view of the fact that the Council did not reach agreement on the Management Regulation until 1983 it is scarcely surprising that between 1978 and 1983 the Council only once – in 1980 – adopted TACs.[100] Although the Council succeeded in adopting the Management Regulation in January 1983, it enjoyed limited success in setting TACs for that year. Formally TACs for 1983 were not adopted, because of prolonged disagreement over the TAC and quotas for North Sea herring, until December 20, 1983 and did not come into force until December 30![101] This is not quite such a fiasco as it sounds, because the Council had adopted TACs for 1982[102] (admittedly in January 1983) and these were 'rolled-over' and effectively operated as the TACs for 1983.[103] Since then the position has improved enormously.From 1984 onwards the Council has adopted TACs either at the very beginning of, or at the end of the year preceding, the year to which TACs relate. TACs relate to all Community waters except the Mediterranean and the waters off the French overseas departments, and within the waters to which they apply cover most significant stocks of fish. In most years it has usually been found necessary to make minor adjustments, typically three or four times a year, to TACs in order to take account of new scientific advice or other relevant developments. In general, Community practice since 1984 has been such that EEC fishing industries have been able to plan properly for their fishing activities, in contrast to the situation before 1984.

Two important questions need to be asked about the Community's system of TACs. First, has the Council for reasons of political expediency increased TACs beyond the levels recommended by scientists, as so notoriously used to happen in the North-East Atlantic Fisheries Commission? Secondly, how well have TACs been observed? As regards the first question, as has been seen, the Commission has to some extent in its proposals increased TACs above the levels recommended by scientists for socio-economic reasons, but thereafter the Council has not, apart from a number of relatively minor instances, further increased TACs. For this the Council deserves considerable credit, given the ease with which TACs could have been increased to satisfy individual Member State demands for higher quotas. As regards observance of TACs, this question is better answered when considering how far Member States have observed the quotas (into which TACs are divided) allocated to them.

Quotas

Once an international fishery management body has decided to use TACs as a management tool, it is desirable to adopt further measures to improve the chances of TACs being observed and to avoid the economic disadvantages mentioned earlier. The method most commonly employed is to divide up the TAC into quotas allocated to the different States participating in the fishery. From the first the Commission had proposed that Community TACs should be divided up into quotas allocated to individual Member States and this was accepted by the Council (see Article 4 of the Management Regulation). The problem the Commission, and later the Council, faced was that which has been faced by all international fishery commissions attempting to use a quota system, namely on what criteria are quotas to be allocated among the States concerned. This problem was particularly difficult in the EEC, given the fact that for some years at least TACs would have to be lower than immediate past fishing levels, and given the substantial loss of access by EEC vessels to the waters of third States as a result of the general trend to 200-mile limits.

Article 4 of the Management Regulation, with wonderful imprecision, says that TACs are to be divided into individual Member State quotas 'in a manner which assures each Member State relative stability of fishing activities for each of the stocks considered'. More concrete criteria for allocation are set out in the recitals to the 1982 TAC and quota regulation.[104] There are essentially three criteria listed there:

1. Past fishing performance. This is taken as referring to 'average catches in the period 1973–78, less individual by-catches beyond permitted limits and human consumption species caught directly for reduction to meal and oil.'[105]
2. The needs of regions particularly dependent on fishing. These areas are considered to be Ireland, Northern Ireland, the Isle of Man, Scotland, the North-East coast of England between Bridlington and Berwick, and, before its departure from the Community, Greenland.[106]
3. Losses suffered as a result of the extension of fishing limits by third States.[107]

Even these criteria are not very precise, and from them one could not easily determine the exact allocation of any particular TAC. What happens in practice is that the quotas agreed for 1982 (which were derived from these criteria) are regarded as providing the 'key' for future years, at least until 1992.[108] In other words, the proportions into which the 1982 TACs were divided have been used (in some cases with small modifications) when adopting TACs for later years. For the seven main human consumption species (cod, haddock, saithe, whiting, plaice, redfish and mackerel) the division in 1982 (in percentage terms) was as follows: Belgium 1.9, Denmark 24.3, France 11.7, West Germany 12.1, Ireland 4.7, Netherlands 7.8, the United Kingdom 37.6, Greece, Italy and Luxembourg 0.[109]

Not all stocks for which TACs and quotas are currently set were covered by the 1982 TAC and quota regulation. For such stocks a 'key' has either been set subsequently, notably for North Sea herring,[110] or in some cases, for example horse mackerel, the basis of allocation is recent catches.[111] In the case of certain stocks of fish which are fished mainly for reduction to meal and oil (e.g. Norway pout), although a TAC is set, it has not (yet) been found necessary to divide the TAC into quotas: the reason presumably being that in most cases these stocks are large and that Member States' interest in them, apart from Denmark, is limited.

What has been said so far about quota allocation applies to the Community as constituted before its latest enlargement (referred to in this paragraph as the existing Community). In relation to the two new Member States, Portugal and Spain, rather different arrangements apply. Prior to its accession to the Community, Spain was allowed to catch specified tonnages of a limited range of species in existing Community waters under a bilateral agreement with the Community (which is discussed in the next Chapter). Article 161 of the Iberian Act of Accession sets out the percentages of various TACs which are to be allocated to Spain until the year 2002 (subject to the possibility of some adjustment after 1996). The TACs concerned relate to the same limited range of species to which Spain had access before (hake, monkfish, megrim and anchovy), together with two other species, Norway lobster and pollack (which Spain had previously been allowed to take as by-catches in hake fishing). The percentages set out in Article 161 correspond roughly to (though in some cases are larger than) Spain's previous share of the TACs concerned. In other words, the criterion for allocation of quotas to Spain in the existing Community's waters is essentially recent past fishing performance. Unlike Spain, Portugal had not fished in Community waters in the years immediately prior to its accession. Nevertheless Portuguese vessels are given limited quotas in existing Community waters. Article 349 of the Act of Accession provides that the Council is to fix annually the quotas available to Portugal of blue whiting and horse mackerel (species of no great interest to existing Member States), together with quotas of other species not subject to TACs if conservation requirements and the needs of other Community vessels so permit: in practice this latter provision has so far led to Portugal only being allocated quotas for tuna. The stocks of blue whiting and horse mackerel concerned are ones for which the Community has so far fixed TACs, but for which it has not divided up the TACs into quotas for existing Member States. Nevertheless, Portugal's access to these TACs is fixed in quantitative terms. The criterion for such allocation is not specified, but in 1986 Portugal's quotas were, as a proportion of the TAC, very small – about 1.1% of the blue whiting TAC, and 3.7% of the horse mackerel TAC.[112] Finally, in the case of fishing in Portuguese and Spanish (as opposed to existing Community) waters, the Community allocates quotas in its annual TAC regulations. The criteria for allocation are not specified, but they are probably based on past fishing performance.

It has sometimes been argued that a system of national quotas – where EEC Member States are allocated different amounts of fish – is contrary to the EEC's rules on non-discrimination (Article 7 of the EEC Treaty and, possibly also relevant here, Article 40(3)). At first sight this argument may seem to have some merit, but on further reflection it is clearly mistaken. In various cases involving other branches of EEC law, the European Court has defined discrimination as occurring when similar situations are subjected to dissimilar treatment or when dissimilar situations are treated in a similar manner; and the Court has stressed that it is possible to differentiate between situations, provided that this is based on objective factors.[113] Thus, it would be discriminatory to give the same size of quota to each Member State because this would be to treat Member States which have quite different fishing capabilities (e.g. Denmark and Luxembourg) alike. On the other hand, it is permissible to give different sizes of quota to Member States, provided that this is done on an objective basis. The criteria used by the Community institutions for the allocation of quotas would certainly seem to be sufficiently objective. In the case of *Kerr* discussed earlier (see p. 103 above) the European Court upheld the validity of a national measure which set a TAC and then allocated it between various Member States along the same lines as had been proposed by the Commission: *a fortiori* would it have upheld the validity of a similar Community measure.[114]

Article 5(1) of the Management Regulation provides that Member States may, if they so wish, exchange quotas provided that prior notice is given to the Commission. This is a useful provision as it enables a Member State which feels it is unable to use up all or part of a quota allocated to it, to allow another Member State to do so, thus preventing waste. It seems from the wording of Article 5 as though exchanges must be in kind only: i.e. it is not possible for a Member State to exchange all or part of a quota for cash. The latter might be desirable since it would facilitate the using up of quotas where one Member State had part of a quota it could not exploit but no other Member State had a quota which the first State was interested in obtaining in exchange. In any case, because of the criteria for allocation and the fact that in most cases quotas represent a significant reduction in previous fishing levels, there have not so far been, nor are there likely to be in the future, many 'quota swops' in practice. Where quota swops have taken place, the practice has been for this not to affect future quota allocations.

The setting of annual quotas is, in itself, and without further modification, a somewhat unrefined management tool. If a Member State simply accepts its quota, and then just leaves its fishermen to catch that quota, several undesirable consequences are likely to follow. In such a situation fishermen, being in competition with one another, are likely to concentrate their effort in catching the quota in the early part of the year; but if this happens, stocks disperse and yield per unit of effort decreases in the later part of the year. Furthermore, if most effort is concentrated at the beginning of the year this may disrupt the market, as well as being to the detriment of processors who require a regular, and not a highly fluctuating, supply of fish. Fortunately the Management Regulation does not just require Member States to take their quotas and leave it at that. Article 5(2) provides that 'Member States shall determine, in accordance with the applicable Community provisions, the detailed rules for the utilisation of the quotas allocated to them.' This therefore allows a Member State, if it so wishes, to utilise its quotas more efficiently, for example by dividing up the quota so that it is taken at different times of the year, or allocating its quota between different sections of the fleet so as to give smaller vessels some protection from competition from larger vessels. Most Member States have taken advantage of Article 5(2) to introduce measures to manage their quotas, such as allocating their quotas over particular periods of time and/or to particular vessels (and in some cases to producers' organisations), often by means of licensing. It is noteworthy that the European Court has upheld the validity of a national measure which limited the taking of a particular quota to certain kinds of vessel, regarding such a measure as being within a Member State's discretion under Article 5(2).[115]

Last, but certainly not least, it must be asked how well the quotas (and hence TACs) set by the Community have been observed. It is not altogether straightforward to find out the answer to this question. The EEC Statistical Office's annual reports used to contain sufficient information on Member States' catches to enable one to answer this question, but whether by design or coincidence the format of these reports changed in 1983 – which, of course, was the first year that the quota system was in existence – so that they no longer contain adequate information to check Member States' catches against the quotas allocated to them. The Commission has also been rather coy in this matter. Asked by a member of the European Parliament which Member States had exceeded their quotas, the Commission, in an answer more reminiscent of Whitehall than Brussels, refused to give the information, considering that 'it is better for it to take appropriate action on a bilateral basis to ensure that the Member States concerned apply Community rules.'[116] A few weeks later, however, the Commission was confronted with the figures by another member of the European Parliament, and was forced to agree that the figures were accurate.[117] The figures show that 40 of the 230 or so quotas set for 1983 were exceeded, most by fairly insignificant amounts, though in some cases by as much as 50% (the United Kingdom's monkfish quota, Denmark's haddock and saithe quotas and the Netherlands' cod and plaice quotas). According to the Commission, taking all the quotas as a whole, excess fishing amounted to about one per cent. Assuming the catch figures on which this information is based are correct (and this may not be a valid assumption), this is an insignificant excess in general terms. However, it disguises the fact that TACs for some stocks were exceeded: for example TACs for saithe were exceeded by about 10%.[118] Figures for 1984 have been published by *Eurofish Report,* and show that 16 quotas were exceeded (which is an improvement on 1983).[119] Again most excesses were insignificant; the worst excesses were committed by West Germany (20% over its saithe quota), Denmark (25% over its prawn quota) and especially the Netherlands (100% over its cod and sole quotas, and nearly 200% over its plaice quota). Unfortunately the *Eurofish Report* figures do not show what the total overrun (if any) was on TACs.

Faced with this overfishing of quotas in 1983 and 1984, the Commission began proceedings against the seven Member States concerned under Article 169. The Commission subsequently discontinued these proceedings, apparently taking the view that an Article 169 action was not the best way of dealing with the problem and that 1983 and 1984 should be regarded as an experimental period: instead it sent a letter to all Member States asking for a guarantee that measures to prevent further over-fishing would be implemented.[120]

This episode does, however, raise the question of what sanctions are available against Member States which exceed their quotas. Clearly an action under Article 169 is of limited effect: all that the European Court can do is to declare that the Member State concerned has broken its Community obligations; but the overfishing having already occurred, there is no way in which the Member State can remedy the breach (unless the Court's declaration took the form of saying, for example, that the Member State lacked an adequate catch-reporting system). A more effective sanction would be to penalise a State that exceeded its quotas by reducing its quotas for the following year, but this is something which does not appear to be acceptable to the Council and Commission, although it has been advocated by the European Parliament.[121] In the absence of a willingness to use quota reductions as a sanction, the only effective sanction available to the Community at present is a financial one. Under Community rules on fish marketing, it is possible for Community funds for price support to be withheld where quotas have been exceeded. This matter is discussed in more detail in the context of price support measures in Chapters 7 and 8 (see pp. 240–241 and 270–271), but it may be noted that this sanction cannot be used if the quotas exceeded relate to species for which no price support arrangements exist or in cases where such arrangements do exist, they are not actually utilised. Ultimately the most effective way to improve observance of quotas is to tighten up arrangements for enforcing Community fisheries regulations generally. This is a matter which is discussed in section 6 below.

4. TECHNICAL CONSERVATION MEASURES

As mentioned earlier, Articles 2 and 3 of the Management Regulation provide that apart from TACs, the Council is to adopt a variety of other conservation measures such as closed seasons and areas, minimum fish sizes etc. (known in the Community jargon as technical conservation measures). Even before agreement on the Management Regulation was reached in January 1983 the Council had adopted a number of short-term conservation measures, mainly concerned with prohibiting fishing for herring:[122] one of these measures – a ban on the fishing and landing of herring for purposes other than human consumption – still remains in force.[123] Then between October 1980 and October 1981 there was in force a general set of conservation measures similar in content to the measures contained in Regulation 171/83 (discussed below).[124]

At the same time as adopting the Management Regulation, the Council also adopted Regulation 171/83[125] which contains a comprehensive set of technical conservation measures of indefinite duration. There is no space here to describe these measures in detail, and in any case their technical complexity is such that their details are unlikely to be of much interest to most readers. Broadly what these measures do is to prescribe minimum mesh sizes, maximum permitted by-catch levels and minimum fish sizes; prohibit fishing for salmon beyond 12-mile limits in most areas; establish closed seasons and closed areas for redfish and herring in order to protect spawning grounds and nursery areas; and prohibit the use of certain types of gear or vessel in certain areas and/or for certain species. Minimum mesh and fish sizes are largely aimed at preventing the catching of immature fish so as to allow stocks to grow, while the by-catch regulations are principally aimed at limiting the amount of human consumption species taken when fishing for industrial species such as Norway pout.

Like TACs, these measures are based on scientific advice, principally from ICES, channelled through the Scientific and Technical Committee for Fisheries. In many cases the measures reflect, with appropriate modifications, the recommendations of the two international fishery commissions formerly primarily responsible for what are now Community waters, the North-East Atlantic Fisheries Commission and the International Commission for the Northwest Atlantic Fisheries.

Since its adoption Regulation 171/83 has been amended at intervals in order to take into account changing conservation requirements and experience gained in its practical implementation.[126] Although such changes are based (or allegedly based) on scientific recommendations, they have not been immune to political pressures, or at least political controversy. Thus, for example, a temporary, six-month relaxation of by-catch limits in the Norway pout fishery in 1984–85 provoked considerable opposition from the British fishing industry and moved the House of Lords' Select Committee on the European Communities to express 'considerable disquiet.'[127] While the Council has amended Regulation 171/83 on a number of occasions, it has failed to adopt all the Commission's proposals for amendment and has also made a practice of deferring decisions required by the Regulation to increase minimum mesh sizes. The Commission has expressed resigned regret over this inactivity and blamed the Council's procrastination on the latter's unwillingness to confront the fishing industry with the short-term losses which occur when larger mesh sizes are introduced.[128] The Council's procrastination creates considerable uncertainty for the fishing industry, making it difficult to know when to invest in new gear and when existing gear needs to be replaced.

Regulation 171/83 provides for certain implementing action to be taken by the Commission by means of the Management Committee procedure. In some cases such action is to deal with conservation needs as and when they arise, but in two cases at least implementing action is necessary for the Regulation to function effectively. Thus, under Article 6 of the Regulation the Commission is to determine how mesh sizes are to be measured, while under Article 7 the Commission is to draw up permitted exceptions to the prohibition on attaching obstructing devices to nets (the absence of such implementing regulations under the equivalent provision in Regulation 2527/80, it may be recalled, was one of the points at issue in *Rogers v. Darthenay*: see p. 93 above). Given the necessity for such implementing action, and the long period of gestation of Regulation 171/83, it is rather unsatisfactory that although the Regulation was adopted in January 1983, it was not until July 1984 and December 1984 respectively that the Commission adopted the necessary implementing measures.[129] The Commission can scarcely complain about the Council's inactivity, when it is so dilatory itself. The other implementing measure which the Commission has so far taken under Regulation 171/83 is to lay down a sampling procedure for measuring by-catches.[130]

Regulation 171/83 applies to all Community waters (including the waters of Portugal and Spain) except such waters in the Baltic and Mediterranean. In

June 1986 the Council adopted a set of comprehensive technical conservation measures for the Baltic.[131] These measures are based on the recommendations of the International Baltic Sea Fisheries Commission and are concerned with the same kinds of matters as Regulation 171/83. Unlike Regulation 171/83, the Baltic Regulation does not require implementing measures to be taken as regards mesh sizes and obstructing devices to nets: detailed rules on these matters are contained in the Regulation itself. With the adoption of this Regulation it is only in the Mediterranean that no Community technical conservation measures (or TACs and quotas) exist. This absence of any Community fisheries management measures in the Mediterranean is something that will be commented on in more detail at the end of this Chapter.

Both Regulation 171/83 and the Baltic Regulation contain technical conservation measures which are intended to be permanent (subject, of course, to periodic amendment). Further technical measures, which are short-term in character, are found in the annual TAC and quota regulations. These are mainly concerned with closed areas, closed seasons and permissible by-catch levels.

An important question is how far Community conservation measures have been complied with by the vessels of Member States. According to a Report published by the Commission in June 1986 breaches of these measures are frequent and in some cases 'so widespread that they are endangering conservation.'[132] The action the Commission intends to take to remedy this situation is outlined in the discussion on enforcement below (see section 6).

It will be apparant from the discussion in the first section of this Chapter that since 1977 Community conservation measures have been supplemented by a considerable number of national conservation measures adopted by Member States. Even after the adoption of Regulation 171/83 national measures have been numerous. From 1983–85 inclusive 224 measures were notified to the Commission: most of these were taken under Articles 19 and 20 of Regulation 171/83 (no measures were taken under Article 18, the provision concerning urgent measures). A further 512 pre-existing local measures were notified to the Commission as required under Article 19(5).[133] It is obviously beyond the scope of this book (and no doubt most readers' curiosity) to give any details of this vast amount of legislation, most of which is of very local application and interest.

5. ACCESS

Before 1970 an EEC Member State could grant access to its waters to whichever vessels it liked, subject to any existing treaty obligations (of which the most notable were those arising out of the 1964 European Fisheries Convention, which required a State party to permit the vessels of other States parties to fish in the outer six miles of its 12-mile exclusive fishing zone if such vessels had traditionally fished in those waters). In 1970, in its very first piece of fisheries legislation, Regulation 2141/70 laying down a Common Structural Policy for the Fishing Industry,[134] the Council introduced a principle of equal access, under which a Member State had to admit the vessels of any other Member State to its waters on the same conditions as its own vessels. This principle has subsequently proved very controversial, especially in those States which applied for EEC membership in 1970 and during the ensuing enlargement negotiations (see pp. 12–13 above), not least because the principle goes against the general international trend since 1945 of granting coastal States exclusive or preferential fishing rights in wider and wider zones off their coasts.

The equal access principle had its heyday between 1977 and 1983 when there was equal access to the 200-mile zones of all Member States, unrestricted by any TACs (except in 1980) or quotas. The principle was less important in practice (if not politically) before 1977 because fishing limits were only 12 miles in breadth, so the principle applied to a much smaller area (and beyond 12 miles there was free access under the doctrine of the freedom of the high seas), and also because much of the area which in theory was subject to the principle was in fact excepted from its application by the 6- and 12-mile zones reserved to local vessels laid down by the 1972 Act of Accession

The principle has also been less important in practice since 1983 when the Community system of TACs and quotas was introduced. TACs and quotas are set in terms of ICES and CECAF (Fisheries Committee for the Eastern Central Atlantic) Statistical Areas. The equal access principle means that within such an area (which is usually quite large: for example, the whole of the North Sea is a single ICES Area, though subdivided for some quotas) the vessels of a Member State can fish anywhere for the quotas allocated to that Member State, regardless of which State's (or States') fishing zone(s) that area happens to occupy, apart from the limited areas excepted from the principle (discussed below). In the case of those few areas (the Mediterranean and the waters off the French overseas departments), or in other areas those few stocks (e.g. sandeel and most species of shellfish), for which no TACs are set, the equal access principle has its unbridled pre-1983 application. Although the equal access principle is less important in practice since the introduction of a Community regime of TACs and quotas, it still remains very important in theory because without it such a Community regime would not be possible. If the equal access principle did not exist, the vessels of one Member State would have no automatic right of access to the fishing zones of other Member States: they would either have no access at all or access based on some such principle as historic rights. In either case, a Community quota system, if one applied, would look very different from the present system: quotas would be set in terms of Member States' fishing zones (not ICES and CECAF areas) and the basis of allocation would not be the criteria discussed above but some other formula which would presumably give much more weight to the interests of the coastal State concerned.

This section will first examine in more detail the scope and rationale of the equal access principle, and then look at the three exceptions to it – the 12-mile zone reserved to local fishermen, the Orkney/Shetland box, and the transitional arrangements concerning Portugal and Spain.

The Equal Access Principle

The principle of equal access is now to be found in Article 2(1) of Regulation 101/76,[135] which replaced and consolidated Regulation 2141/70. This provision reads as follows:

> Rules applied by each Member State in respect of fishing in the maritime waters coming under its sovereignty or within its jurisdiction shall not lead to differences in treatment of other Member States.
>
> Member States shall ensure in particular equal conditions of access to and use of the fishing grounds situated in the waters referred to in the preceding sub-paragraph for all fishing vessels flying the flag of a Member State and registered in Community territory.

Article 2(1) does two things. First, it provides that the regulations laid down by each Member State governing fishing in the maritime waters coming under its sovereignty or within its jurisdiction must be non-discriminatory; i.e. such regulations must not distinguish between different fishing vessels or different fishermen on the basis of their nationality. If different vessels are treated differently by such regulations, it must be on the basis of objective factors, such as the size of vessels or the type of gear they use, and not on the basis of their nationality. However, Article 2(1) does not mean that national fishing regulations must be harmonised. The existence of different national laws naturally entails factual inequalities between Member States, but these differences are not caught by Article 2(1) as long as they do not amount to overt or disguised discrimination. In any case, as the Community has taken an increasing role in fisheries management, there has been a substantial decline in the number and scope of such national fishery laws.

The second thing that Article 2(1) does is to provide that access to the maritime waters coming under the sovereignty or within the jurisdiction of a Member State cannot be restricted on the basis of nationality. Thus the United Kingdom, for example, could not ban all French vessels from its waters. It is, however, possible, subject to the general scope of Member States' competence to adopt fisheries management measures (discussed above), to restrict access on the basis of objective factors, for example by prohibiting the access to certain waters of all vessels above a particular size or all vessels using a particular type of gear.

Article 2(1) provides that the principle of equal access applies to 'the maritime waters coming under [the] sovereignty or within [the] jurisdiction' of Member States. This phrase does not use the customary international law terminology for describing and defining States' maritime zones; but taking each of its component parts – 'sovereignty' and 'jurisdiction' – the phrase, in the customary terminology of the International Law of the Sea, would appear to cover Member States' internal waters, territorial seas, exclusive fishing or economic zones, and continental shelves (in respect of sedentary species such as clams and oysters), as such zones are from time to time determined by Member States' national legislation.[136] It is not, of course, to the maritime zones of all Member States' territories that the Common Fisheries Policy and the principle of equal access apply. Those territories subject to the Policy (and thus the equal access principle) were spelt out in the previous Chapter. As was pointed out there, the Policy does not apply (among other places) to the territories listed in Annex IV to the EEC Treaty. Nevertheless, although the principle of equal access does not apply, a limited right of establishment, as explained in the previous Chapter, may apply. If an Annex IV territory permits companies or nationals of the EEC metropolitan territory to establish themselves in that territory for the purpose of fishing, including exploitation of that territory's exclusive fishing zone or territorial sea, then a similar right must be accorded to companies or nationals of any other EEC Member State, provided that the latter grants a similar right of establishment to individuals or companies from the Annex IV territory in question.[137] A somewhat similar provision is found in the Lomé Convention as regards establishment in the sixty or so African, Carribean and Pacific States parties to that Convention.[138] This limited right of establishment may be an avenue worth exploring for EEC fishing companies looking for new fishing grounds, since many of the Annex IV territories and Lomé Convention States have extensive 200-mile fishing zones.

The next point to consider is who are the beneficiaries of the right of equal access. The beneficiaries are not, strictly speaking, fishermen who are nationals of the Member States, but 'all fishing vessels flying the flag of a Member State and registered in Community territory.' It is up to each Member State to determine the conditions on which it grants the right to vessels to fly its flag. There are at present no Community rules on this question (although there are provisions of Community law, such as those on establishment, that have a bearing on the matter).[139] The legislation of Member States varies, but every

Member State requires some form of connection between it and the owners of vessels flying its flag. However, in some cases this requirement does not seem to be sufficiently strict to have prevented a form of flags of convenience occurring among fishing vessels (even though it is not in the interests of any Member State – except possibly Luxembourg! – to permit flags of convenience because of the overcapacity in EEC fishing fleets). The insufficient strictness of some Member States' legislation was revealed in the early 1980s, particularly as regards the United Kingdom. Under the Merchant Shipping Act 1894, to qualify as British, a vessel must either be wholly owned by British subjects or wholly owned by companies incorporated and having their principal place of business in the United Kingdom or some other part of Her Majesty's dominions. Taking advantage of the second alternative, a number of companies have been incorporated in the United Kingdom, the beneficial owners of which are foreign (mainly Spanish), and have registered ex-foreign vessels as British. It is thus possible by this means for third country fishing vessels to get unrestricted backdoor access to Community waters, when otherwise (as will be seen in the next Chapter) their access is very curtailed. By 1982 this problem had become serious. Over 60 ex-Spanish and a few ex-Norwegian vessels had re-registered as British. The ex-Spanish vessels operated out of ports in South-West England, catching mainly hake and exporting it to Spain.[140] The response of the British Government, after having being warned about this problem for some years,[141] was to rush through Parliament in a matter of days in March 1983 the British Fishing Boats Act. Under this Act and its implementing legislation[142] British fishing vessels may not fish in the United Kingdom's 200-mile fishing zone nor land fish, wherever caught, in British ports unless at least 75 per cent of the crew has an EEC nationality. Thus it is still possible for ex-foreign British vessels to fish in the waters of other Member States, provided they do not land their catch in a British port (and any fish so caught would, of course, count against British quotas). The Government rejected extending the legislation to cover this situation on the grounds that it would be difficult to enforce and that it would be more appropriate for other Member States or the Community to legislate for this situation. In fact, the governments of the United Kingdom and France (which at the time was considering introducing similar legislation to that of the United Kingdom) approached the Commission with a suggestion for Community legislation in this area.[143] Under the British legislation it is still possible for flag of convenience fishing vessels to register as British and fish in British waters provided they observe the conditions concerning crew nationality. It is somewhat surprising that the British authorities did not seek to prevent flags of convenience altogether by providing that a certain proportion of the shares of companies owning British vessels should be owned by British (or Community) nationals. The not entirely convincing reasons given by British Government ministers for not taking such a step were that it would be difficult to enforce and would be inconsistent with the Government's long-term approach to international shipping questions.[144]

Apart from the United Kingdom, Ireland has also had to deal with the problem of flag of convenience fishing vessels. Faced with the threat of companies operating flag of convenience vessels in the United Kingdom moving their operations to Ireland following enactment of the British legislation, the Irish Parliament (the Oireachtas) in July 1983 passed the Fisheries (Amendment) Act. Under section 2 of the Act Irish fishing vessels, wherever they fish, require a licence: a licence may be refused to vessels which are not under the control of and/or beneficially owned by EEC nationals. Section 3 empowers the Minister to make regulations requiring any boat fishing in Irish waters, landing its catch in an Irish port or transshipping fish in Irish waters to have a crew all or a fixed proportion of whose members are of a prescribed nationality.[145]

Elsewhere flag of convenience fishing vessels do not seem to have been a problem, although one or two Member States, such as Belgium, have legislation relating to the nationality of ships similar to that of the United Kingdom. The matter clearly needs to be kept under observation, although with Spain, whose nationals have hitherto been the major operators of flag of convenience vessels in Community waters, now a member of the Community the problem from the Community's point of view has clearly lessened. For individual Member States, however, there may still be cause for concern, for any fishing done under their flags by what are in reality Spanish vessels, will count against their quotas. And with access of Spanish vessels to Community waters seriously restricted until at least the year 2002 (see below), re-registering their fishing vessels under the flag of another Member State must still seem quite an attractive option for a number of Spanish shipowners. It is probably not possible for a Member State such as the United Kingdom to prevent Spanish shipowners from re-registering their vessels as British because this would offend against the Community's rules providing for freedom of establishment and prohibiting discrimination on the ground of nationality. Nor does the British legislation of 1983 any longer provide any practical limitation on Spanish shipowners' freedom of action. Instead the United Kingdom has sought to counter the threat of what are in reality Spanish vessels fishing against United Kingdom quotas by laying down as from the beginning of 1986 (the date of Spanish accession) new licence conditions for vessels fishing for United Kingdom quotas (all vessels over 10 metres fishing for United Kingdom quotas must have a licence). Under the new conditions, which are 'aimed at ensuring that licensed vessels have a real economic link' with the United Kingdom, a vessel to be eligible for a licence must: (1) be registered as a British fishing boat under the Merchant Shipping Act 1894; (2) normally operate from the United Kingdom, Channel Islands or Isle of Man: evidence of regular landings and/or visits to ports in these territories will be expected; (3) at least 75 per cent of the crew must be British or EEC nationals ordinarily resident in the United Kingdom, Channel Islands or Isle of Man: during the transitional period relating to the free movement of Spanish workers (i.e. until the end of 1992) Spanish nationals are not to be regarded as EEC nationals; and (4) the skipper and all the crew must contribute to a national insurance scheme in the United Kingdom, Channel Islands or Isle of Man.[146]

Apart from flying the flag of a Member State, a fishing vessel, to benefit from the right of equal access, must also be registered in 'Community territory'.[147] In practice under the legislation of some EEC Member States fishing vessels below a certain size are exempt from registration.

So much for the scope of the equal access principle. Before turning to examine the exceptions to the principle, it is worth pausing – since the principle has been so controversial and forms the theoretical underpinning of the Community management system (as was explained above) – to consider its legal basis and rationale. As regards the legal basis of the principle, while most Community fishery management measures can clearly be based on Article 43 (as was seen at the beginning of this Chapter), it is doubtful whether the equal access principle can be so based. This is because the principle does not easily correspond with any of the objectives of the Common Fishery Policy laid down in Article 39. The principle seems unrelated to the first of these objectives, increasing productivity: indeed equal access is likely to lead to an increase in the number of vessels fishing for particular stocks of fish, the most likely result of which is a decrease in productivity. This increase in competition for fish is similarly likely to decrease, rather than increase, the return to individual fishermen, and thus will tend to contradict the objective of ensuring a fair standard of living for fishermen. The principle is unlikely to have much effect on the stability of markets, and what effect it does have is more likely to be destabilising than stabilising. In some marginal cases, where stocks are under-exploited (and there are practically no such stocks in the waters to which the principle applies), equal access could lead to a better supply of fish of certain species (the fourth objective of Article 39). If equal access leads to an increase in the catches of certain species (as it well may), then the normal laws of supply and demand would suggest that prices for those species will fall, thus giving effect to the final objective listed in Article 39 (ensuring a reasonable price for fish for the consumer). On balance, however, the principle of equal access would not seem to accord with the objectives laid down in Article 39, and indeed it can be argued that the operation of the principle in practice is likely to be contrary to some of those objectives. Thus Article 43 cannot be regarded as the legal basis for the equal access principle. Its legal basis must therefore be sought elsewhere. The most likely place is in Article 7 and/or Article 235 of the

EEC Treaty, both of which are referred to in the preamble to Regulation 101/ 76 as being among the legal bases for that Regulation.[148]

Article 7 of the EEC Treaty, it may be recalled from Chapter 2, provides that 'within the scope of application of this Treaty . . . any discrimination on grounds of nationality shall be prohibited. The Council may . . . adopt . . . rules designed to prohibit such discrimination.' Article 235 provides that 'if action by the Community should prove necessary to attain, in the course of the operation of the common market, one of the objectives of the Community and [the EEC] Treaty has not provided the necessary powers, the Council shall . . . take the appropriate measures.' There are essentially two questions to be considered. First, is the equal access principle authorised by Articles 7 and/or 235, i.e. are these articles a sufficient legal basis for the principle? Secondly, if Articles 7 and/or 235 do authorise the equal access principle, do they go further and not merely permit the Community institutions to have adopted the equal access principle, but actually require them to have done so? If the answer to both questions is yes, then clearly the equal access principle is an immutable part of the Common Fisheries Policy. If, on the other hand, the answer to the first question is yes but the answer to the second question is no, then this would mean that the Community institutions could, if they so wished, abolish the equal access principle.

To deal with the first question: under Article 7 the Council may adopt rules designed to prohibit discrimination on the grounds of nationality. To ascertain whether such rules could include the equal access principle, and therefore whether Article 7 could serve as a legal basis for the adoption of this principle, it would seem to be necessary to consider three points: (1) is the area of operation of the principle – fishing by the vessels of one Member State in the territorial sea or exclusive fishery zone of another Member State – 'within the scope of application' of the EEC Treaty?: (2) can nationality, removal of discrimination on the ground of which is the concern of Article 7, relate not only to the nationality of individuals but also the nationality of vessels (which is the type of nationality with which the equal access principle is concerned)?: (3) is the equal access principle an example of, and no more than, a prohibition of discrimination on the grounds of nationality? If the answer to all three questions is yes, it would seem that Article 7 can serve as a legal basis for the equal access principle. As far as (1) is concerned, it would seem that fishing by the vessels of one Member State in the waters of another Member State does fall 'within the scope of application' of the EEC Treaty because by reason of its objectives set out in Article 39, the Common Fisheries Policy is concerned with the production of fisheries, and such fishing can be regarded as falling within the concept of the production of fisheries.[149] As for (2), there is nothing to suggest that Article 7 is limited in the types of entity having nationality with which it deals. (3) is less easy to answer. It has been suggested by one writer[150] that it is only the subject matter of the first paragraph of Article 2(1) of the Structural Regulation – regulations relating to fishing – that fall within the prohibition of discrimination dealt with by Article 7: the adoption of positive rules such as the equal access principle, in the second paragraph of Article 2(1), goes beyond a mere prohibition of discrimination. This seems a rather artificial distinction. It may be helpful to consider the matter thus. Supposing a Member State maintained an exclusive fishery zone to which its own fishing vessels, but not the vessels of other Member States, had access. This would be discrimination on the basis of nationality. The removal of such discrimination – the prohibition of such discrimination – would in practice lead either to equal access or possibly a regime based on freedom of establishment. This suggests, therefore, that it is possible to regard equal access as simply a form, and a consequence, of the prohibition of discrimination on the ground of nationality. This view is supported by the judgment of the European Court in the *Irish Fisheries* case, where the Court appears to have implicitly accepted that Article 2(1) of the Structural Regulation is no more than a specific application of Article 7.[151] It would seem, therefore, that Article 7 is an effective legal basis for the equal access principle. Since Article 7 contains the necessary powers, it would thus not be necessary to have recourse to Article 235 in this connection.

Even though Article 7 does appear to authorise the equal access principle, the matter is not wholly free of difficulties. First, as pointed out earlier, the operation of the equal access principle in practice is likely to conflict with many of the objectives of the Common Fisheries Policy set out in Article 39. It seems unlikely, however, that if a case on the point came before it, the European Court would hold that this conflict, based as it is on a possibly arguable projection of a rule in operation rather than on the manifest and logical incompatibility of two rules, invalidated the use of Article 7 as a legal basis for the equal access principle. The second point of difficulty is that Article 7 has not been used in an analogous fashion to secure equal access to freshwater fisheries or agriculture. There are good reasons for this. Access to freshwater fisheries and agriculture derives from private property rights (unlike sea fisheries where there are in general no private property rights). Thus, it is the individual landowner who enjoys access to any particular freshwater fishery or agricultural holding. As long as a Member State does not restrict the possibility of owning land to its own nationals – and the EEC Treaty's provisions on freedom of establishment are designed to prevent this – there can be no discrimination on grounds of nationality. A more liberal access to freshwater fisheries or agricultural land other than through the individual property owner would involve changing Member States' existing property legislation. This, however, would not be possible, since under Article 222 of the Treaty the EEC is precluded from making any changes to its Member States' systems of property ownership. Even though there are thus good reasons why freshwater fisheries and agriculture should be treated differently, it has nevertheless caused a good deal of resentment among most British and some Irish fishermen that there should be a so much more liberal access to sea fisheries than to freshwater fisheries (and some freshwater fish are, after all, subject to the common organisation of the market in fishery products), agriculture or indeed any other economic activity.

Having concluded that Article 7 permitted the Community institutions to adopt the equal access principle, we must now consider the question of whether Article 7 or Article 235 actually required the Community institutions to adopt this principle. The answer to this question is not very clear. The first sentence of Article 7 says 'discrimination on grounds of nationality *shall* be prohibited.' On the other hand, the second sentence appears to give the Council a discretion as to what action it takes to remove discrimination since it says the Council '*may* . . . adopt . . . rules designed to prohibit' discrimination. There is some logical inconsistency between these two sentences. This inconsistency may perhaps be resolved by the following approach. The first sentence of Article 7 can be regarded as the statement of a goal – the removal of discrimination on the grounds of nationality. But it is more than a mere goal – it imposes an obligation on Member States not to discriminate, an obligation which can be enforced by the Commission in proceedings taken under Article 169 (as was done, for example, in the *Irish Fisheries* case) and probably also by individuals before national courts (although there is some doubt about this because the European Court has not yet held unequivocally that Article 7 on its own has direct effect). The second sentence of Article 7 can be seen as a corollary of and subordinate to the first sentence. The Council can take the action it deems appropriate to achieve the goal of non-discrimination, and to eliminate such discrimination as has not been removed through Article 169 or individual proceedings. This would explain why it was possible not to introduce the equal access principle, or, alternatively, a régime based on freedom of establishment, until 1970 (although reserved national waters might have been the subject of an action on the basis of the first sentence of Article 7 before 1970, had the idea occurred to anyone). On the other hand, it may seem difficult to explain, in terms of strict law, how it is that the Council, some years after having adopted the equal access principle, was able to make the major exceptions to it contained in the two Treaties of Accession and the Management Regulation (discussed below). At first sight the Council appears to be re-introducing discrimination, which it surely cannot be permitted to do. The answer, however, is that the 12-mile zones in derogation of the equal access principle contained in the Treaties of Accession and Management Regulation are not discriminatory because they are not national reserved zones, which would be discriminatory, but zones reserved to local vessels.[152]

This discussion suggests, therefore, that although Article 7 did not require the Council to introduce the equal access principle (a régime based on freedom of establishment, which would have been more restrictive than the equal access principle, could probably have been introduced as an alternative),[153] once the principle had been introduced, the Council was and is precluded from returning to the régime of reserved national zones (which are discriminatory), but it may modify and make exceptions to the equal access principle provided such modifications and exceptions do not lead to discrimination on the grounds of nationality. Again, it would appear superfluous for the Council to have had recourse to Article 235.[154]

Although Article 7 appears to be an adequate legal basis for the equal access principle, two other possible bases for the principle have been suggested – the provisions of the EEC Treaty on freedom to provide services and Article 40(3). As regards the former, it has been argued that the freedom of services includes the right of a fisherman established in one Member State freely to go and fish in the territorial sea or exclusive fishing zone of another Member State, and then land his catch either at a port of that State or of his home State.[155] This argument seems far-fetched. The activity contemplated here seems to be quite outside the concept of services as defined in Articles 59 and 60, which appear to relate only to situations where there is a transaction for remuneration between two separate persons, the supplier and the recipient of the service.[156] In the case of a fisherman of one Member State fishing in the waters of another Member State, there is clearly no such transaction. Furthermore the fact that the Community institutions did not seek to rely on Articles 59–66 as the basis for introducing the equal access principle suggests that the argument has no merit. As regards Article 40(3), this provides that 'the common organisation [of agricultural markets] . . . shall exclude any discrimination between producers . . . within the Community'. It seems unlikely that this can serve as a legal basis for the equal access principle. First, Article 40(3) relates to measures taken in connection with the common organisation of the market: but equal access does not appear to come within the latter. Secondly, Article 40(3) is concerned with discrimination between groups of producers, not solely or probably even primarily with discrimination on grounds of nationality. Finally, the obligation in Article 40(3) is laid on the Community institutions rather than the Member States, whereas the obligation to provide equal access is directed at Member States.

Lastly, it may be worth considering for a moment what the rationale for the equal access principle is. Apart from the desire to remove discrimination on grounds of nationality and thus promote further integration in the EEC,[157] the equal access principle is also a product of the idea that the liberalisation of access to fishing grounds is the *quid pro quo* for the liberalisation of trade in fishery products and the opening up of national markets which has resulted from the establishment of the EEC.[158] To some extent, also, the equal access principle follows from the traditional view in all Member States that fish in the sea do not belong to anyone: only when they are caught and reduced into possession are they considered capable of being owned. On the other hand, had fish been regarded as being the property of the coastal State while in the natural state, it might – because of Article 222 of the EEC Treaty – have been impossible to introduce a régime of equal access.

The equal access principle, as pointed out earlier, is clearly contrary to the general trend of international law, which is to vest in coastal States more and more control over their adjoining waters.[159] Furthermore, the effect of the equal access principle and Community fisheries legislation generally is that marine fishery resources have been communitised, a treatment which has been accorded to no other natural resource in the EEC.

Having examined, possibly at excessive length, the legal basis of and rationale for the equal access principle, we must now turn to look at the three exceptions to the principle: the 12-mile limit reserved for local fishermen, introduced by the 1972 Act of Accession and continued by the 1983 Management Regulation; the so-called Orkney/Shetland box, introduced by the Management Regulation; and the special arrangements for Portugal and Spain laid down by the 1985 Iberian Act of Accession.[160]

The 12-Mile Limit

As already mentioned, the equal access principle was one of the most controversial matters during the Community's first enlargement negotiations. By way of a compromise between the original and applicant Member States, the Act of Accession provided for a 10-year partial derogation from the equal access principle. Under Article 100 Member States could, if they so wished, restrict fishing in a six-mile zone off their coasts to 'vessels which fish traditionally in those waters and which operate from ports in that geographical coastal area'. Although the claiming of such a zone was optional, in practice all Member States, existing and new, claimed such a zone with the exception of Belgium and the Netherlands. Off Greenland, much of the coast of Ireland and the United Kingdom, part of the west coast of Jutland, and Lower Normandy and Brittany, the six-mile limit was extended to 12 miles (Article 101). Although these six- and 12-mile zones were in principle reserved for local fishermen, it was also provided that the rights which other Member States had previously enjoyed in these zones, notably by virtue of the 1964 European Fisheries Convention and bilateral agreements made thereunder, should be preserved (Article 100(2)).

Although fisheries were not a contentious matter during the Greek entry negotiations, the Greek Act of Accession also provided for a derogation from the equal access principle, modelled on that contained in the earlier Act of

Accession. Under Article 110 Italy and Greece were authorised, until the end of 1985, to restrict, as between each other, fishing in certain areas to local vessels, the areas concerned being a six-mile zone off all Greek coasts and a six-mile zone off all Italian coasts, extended to 12 miles in certain areas. Like the 1972 Act of Accession, the Greek Act made provision for pre-existing fishing rights of one party in the waters of the other party subject to the derogation to be preserved: in practice there do not appear to have been any such rights.

The derogation to the equal access principle contained in the 1972 Act of Accession expired at the end of 1982, but has subsequently been continued, in a slightly modified form, by Article 6 of the Management Regulation. Since this provision raises several questions of interpretation, its wording should be quoted in full. The article provides as follows:

1. As from 1 January 1983 and until 31 December 1992, Member States shall be authorised to retain the arrangements defined in Article 100 of the 1972 Act of Accession and to generalise up to 12 nautical miles for all waters under their sovereignty or jurisdiction the limit of six miles laid down in that Article.

2. In addition to the activities pursued under existing neighbourhood relations between Member States, the fishing activities under the arrangements established in paragraph 1 of this Article shall be pursued in accordance with the arrangements contained in Annex I, fixing for each member State the geographical zones within the coastal bands of other Member States where these activities are pursued and the species concerned.

In other words, EEC Member States may – but, it would seem from the language of Article 6, are not obliged[161] – to establish a 12-mile zone around all their coasts, access to which is limited to 'vessels which fish traditionally in those waters and which operate from ports in that geographical coastal area.' The aim of this provision, according to the Preamble of the Management Regulation, is to enable the inshore fishing industry 'to cope with the new fishing conditions resulting from the institution of 200-mile fishing zones.'[162]

The position as regards Greece is not entirely clear. Article 6 of the Management Regulation refers only to the 1972 (and not the Greek) Act of Accession, and provides for the new arrangements to begin on January 1, 1983 whereas the derogations to the equal access principle contained in the Greek Act of Accession did not expire until the end of 1985. On the other hand, Article 6 is not expressly limited in its wording to the other nine Member States, and the Iberian Act of Accession certainly assumes Article 6 applies to Portugal and Spain. The article is therefore probably applicable also to Greece. The only question perhaps is whether it was applicable from January 1, 1983 or January 1, 1986 (when the arrangements of the Greek Treaty of Accession expired).

The beneficiaries of the 12-mile zone – those for whom the zone is reserved – are not directly identified in Article 6. Instead the article cross-refers to Article 100 of the 1972 Act of Accession. Article 100 provides that the beneficiaries of the six- and 12-mile zones established by that article are 'vessels which fish traditionally in those waters [i.e. the six and 12-mile zones] and which operate from ports in that geographical coastal area'. Such vessels are thus the beneficiaries of the 12-mile zone provided by Article 6 of the Management Regulation. However, the meaning of the phrase used in Article 100 to qualify the benefiting vessels is far from clear. First, what is meant by 'traditionally'? Over how long a period does fishing have to take place before it becomes 'traditional'? The European Fisheries Convention laid down a period of 10 years. Is it to be regarded as the same here? Furthermore, does each individual vessel have to show it has fished in the waters 'traditionally', or is it sufficient if a particular category of vessel from the area in question can show that it has fished the waters 'traditionally'? The latter interpretation would seem to be the more reasonable.

Secondly, what does 'that geographical coastal area' mean? Grammatically, 'that' appears to refer to the (six- or) 12-mile zone of waters coming under Member States' sovereignty or jurisdiction. This would mean that where a Member State had a (six- or) 12-mile zone around all its coasts, 'that geographical coastal area' would apply to the whole coast: as a result, all vessels of that State which had traditionally fished in the (six- or) 12-mile zone could fish anywhere within that limit. An alternative interpretation would be to say that taking any particular area, only vessels operating from ports in that area could fish there. For example, taking the 12-mile limit around Devon and Cornwall, this would mean that fishing vessels from Devon and Cornish ports could fish in the 12-mile limit, but not vessels from other parts of the United Kingdom. One problem with this interpretation is how such a 'geographical coastal area' is to be ascertained – by reference to general administrative divisions, or special fishing districts or what? Can a 'geographical coastal area' stretch across frontiers? Can, for example, Devon Cornwall and Brittany be regarded as a single 'geographical area'? Or the frontier areas between Denmark and West Germany?

The first interpretation suggested of 'that geographical coastal area' is supported by the practice of some Member States. United Kingdom legislation[163] excludes all fishing by other Member States from its (six- or) 12-mile zones (apart from the historic rights exceptions referred to above). In addition, Scottish vessels which have not traditionally fished for mackerel off Devon and Cornwall have been permitted to do so within the 12-mile limit for the past few years. Danish,[164] Irish[165] and Italian legislation[166] also appears to take the same approach as United Kingdom legislation.

On the other hand, some support for the second interpretation comes from Article 100(1) itself. This provides that as an exception to fishing being restricted in the six-mile zone to vessels which have traditionally fished in those waters and 'which operate from ports in that geographical coastal area', 'vessels from other regions of Denmark[167] may continue to fish in the waters of Greenland until 31 December 1977 at the latest.' This provision therefore suggests, since it is an exception, that the main rule is that put forward as the second interpretation of 'that geographical coastal area'. If the first interpretation were correct, there would be no need for this special provision concerning Greenland, since Danish fishermen who had traditionally fished in Greenland waters could fish there anyway according to that interpretation. On the other hand, if the first interpretation were correct, this provision could be regarded as an exception, taking away a right that would otherwise have existed until the end of 1982. This view is not very convincing because of the wording – 'however', 'may continue' – used in Article 100(1). In either case, it is curious that 'vessels from other regions of Denmark' are not limited expressly to vessels which have 'traditionally' fished in Greenland waters, although this may follow automatically from the first part of Article 100(1). In addition, the French text appears slightly more in support of the second interpretation than the English text: the rights in Article 100(1) are accorded to vessels 'dont l'activité de pêche s'exerce traditionellement dans ces eaux et à partir des ports de la zone géographique riveraine.'

On balance, the second interpretation of the phrase, 'that geographical coastal area', suggested above is probably the correct one, particularly since it is most in accordance with the spirit of non-discrimination of the EEC Treaty and of Regulation 101/76. According to this interpretation, access is restricted to the (six- and) 12-mile zones, not on the basis of nationality, but of objective factors such as traditional fishing and vessels operating from local ports. In fact, this access could be regarded as being based on quasi-establishment principles. If the first interpretation were correct, access would be restricted to all intents and purposes on the basis of nationality. The second interpretation is also more in accordance with one of the aims underlying the derogations in the Acts of Accession and Management Regulation, namely to promote the interests of inshore fishermen, particularly in disadvantaged regions.[168]

If the second interpretation is the correct one – and if it is, it means that United Kingdom and probably Italian, Danish and Irish practice in this area is contrary to Community Law – it is nevertheless unfortunate that the provision is not more clearly drafted and the beneficiaries of the 12-mile zone more precisely identified.

Whichever local vessels are the intended beneficiaries of the 12-mile zone, a limited number of other vessels enjoy access to the zone in a similar manner to the position under the 1972 Act of Accession. Article 6(2) provides for such access, either on the basis of 'existing neighbourhood relations' (such as, for example, the Danish-German Agreement of 1958[169] or the Dutch-German Treaty of 1960[170]), or on the basis of the rights set out in Annex I of the Management Regulation (as amended by the Iberian Act of Accession). As regards the latter, in the case of the 12-mile zone off Denmark, France, Ireland, Spain and the United Kingdom the rights are based on those deriving from the European Fisheries Convention and arrangements made thereunder, but they are by no means always identical. In some cases the earlier rights have been curtailed, apparently because they had not been exercised in practice to any significant extent in the past[171] (this is especially true of other States' rights in Irish waters), in other cases new rights have been added to those existing under the earlier arrangements. In all cases rights are confined to the outer six miles of the 12-mile limit. Unlike the five States just mentioned, Belgium, the Netherlands and West Germany never claimed a 12-mile fishing zone so that no arrangements under the European Fisheries Convention for access to their waters were ever made. Nevertheless, Annex I gives other Member States certain rights of access to these three States' 12-mile limits. This access is no doubt based on existing fishing practices, and in the case of Belgium and the Netherlands on the Benelux Treaty's provisions on equal access.[172] Annex I gives no rights of access to the 12-mile limit off Greece, Italy, Portugal or the French overseas departments: in these territories, therefore, local fishermen enjoy exclusive access to the 12-mile limit.

The derogations to the equal access principle contained in Article 6 of the Management Regulation continue until the end of 1992. Article 8 provides that on the basis of a report from the Commission on the fisheries situation in the Community, the Council, acting on a proposal from the Commission and after consulting the European Parliament, is to decide on any 'adjustments' that may be required to be made to the present 10-year derogation arrangements.[173] A further report from the Commission is to be submitted to the Council during 2002, when the Council is to decide on the arrangements which 'could follow' those laid down for the decade 1992–2002. At the present time it is impossible to predict whether the reviews in 1992 and 2002 will be largely a formality, the present arrangements simply being continued, or whether they will be the occasion for renewed tough bargaining.

As has been seen, since the beginning of 1983 there has been a system of quotas in operation which covers the waters embraced by the 12-mile limit as well as those beyond that limit. Thus the point of the 12-mile zone is not so much to give inshore fishermen a certain preference in taking the catch – this is partly provided for in the way the quotas are calculated – but to give these fishermen some protection from competition from larger vessels from further afield (although the more a Member State treats its 12-mile zone as a national zone for all its vessels, the less such protection there will be).

The Orkney/Shetland Box

This box, which is the result – and only result – of United Kingdom demands for preferential access in areas beyond its 12-mile zone, is an area around the Orkneys, Shetlands and north of Scotland, extending beyond the 12-mile limit for some way, which is regarded as 'sensitive' because of the pressures on stocks and the needs of local fishermen. Special arrangements are laid down for this area in Article 7 and Annex II of the Management Regulation. Under these provisions all vessels over 26 metres in length fishing for demersal species other than Norway pout or blue whiting require a licence issued by the Commission. The number of such vessels which can fish in the box at any one time is limited to two Belgian vessels, 62 British, 52 French and 12 German. These vessels must report by radio when entering or leaving the box.[174] If the activities of other vessels are likely to 'jeopardise the satisfactory development of the stocks,' the size of vessels requiring a licence may be reduced or specific measures adopted to monitor their activities. No such measures have yet been taken, but in any case, the review procedures which apply to the 12-mile limit (discussed above) apply in the same way here. The criteria for restricting access to the Orkney/Shetland box are essentially preference for local inshore fishing vessels and past fishing performance in the case of other vessels. These criteria would seem to be sufficiently objective so as not to offend against the Community's rules on discrimination.[175]

Arrangements relating to Portugal and Spain

The equal access principle means that each Member State can have as many vessels as it likes fishing for its quota in the ICES or CECAF Area concerned (apart from in the Orkney/Shetland box). Before the Community's latest enlargement most Member States were fearful of the effects on the well-being of stocks of the access of the enormous Spanish fleet to Community waters, even if limited to prescribed quotas: it was felt in some quarters that the Spanish fleet, with its poor record of observing fisheries regulations, would exceed its quotas or damage stocks not subject to quotas if the number of vessels having access to fish for those quotas or for stocks not subject to quotas was not restricted. To meet these fears, Articles 156–160 of the Iberian Act of Accession provide that a maximum of 300 named Spanish vessels may fish in existing Community waters, of which not more than 150 may fish at any one time. These figures are an increase on the numbers of Spanish vessels permitted to fish in Community waters before enlargement: in 1984 and 1985 the number of vessels which could fish at any one time were 118 and 106 respectively. In addition, a further number of vessels are permitted to engage in certain specialised forms of fishing, such as anchovy, sardine and tuna fishing.

Where one of the listed vessels is laid up and deleted from the list, it may be replaced by a vessel of the same category having half the engine power of the vessel deleted from the list, until the list 'is established at such a level with respect to the allocated fish resources as to ensure normal exploitation' (Article 159(2)). In all cases Spanish vessels are limited to fishing in certain areas of Community waters: notably, as was the case before enlargement, they are excluded from the North Sea and Baltic. The above arrangements are to apply to 2002 subject to the possibility of some adjustment being made in 1992 (Articles 162 and 166). Similar arrangements apply to Portugal, except that the number of Portuguese vessels allowed access is to be determined by the Council each year, rather than being specified in the Act of Accession. Given that Portuguese vessels were not permitted access to Community waters before accession, and the restricted quotas which Portugal enjoys in existing Community waters (see above), it is not surprising that in 1986 only 11 vessels were given access, of which six could fish at any one time.[176]

As regards fishing in Portuguese and Spanish waters, the number of existing Community vessels which may fish in these waters is to be specified by the Council each year (Articles 164 and 351). Given that there has been little fishing by Community vessels in Iberian waters in the past, it may be expected that few vessels will be granted access in the future: in 1986 only 106 existing Community vessels (mainly French) were granted access to Spanish waters, and 110 vessels (all of which were French) to Portuguese waters.[177] Access of Portuguese and Spanish vessels to each other's waters is also restricted, Articles 165 and 352 setting out the numbers of vessels which may fish, and the areas in which and the conditions under which they may do so.

6. ENFORCEMENT

However fine conservation and other management measures may look on paper, it is obvious that unless they are effectively enforced they are of little value. At the beginning of this Chapter, it was pointed out that only the Member States – and not the Community – have the jurisdiction to enforce Community fishery management measures, i.e. to arrest vessels and try those alleged, for example, to have broken Community conservation measures or exceeded quotas. Nevertheless, the Community has adopted various measures aimed at persuading Member States effectively to enforce Community regulations. These measures have taken a 'carrot and stick' approach.

The 'carrot' is financial assistance from the Community. It is recognised that as far as the inspection and boarding of vessels at sea is concerned, the effort required by Member States to carry out this task varies enormously because of differences in the size of Member States' fishing zones and in the levels of fishing activity in these zones. At one extreme, the United Kingdom has a zone of about 275,000 square nautical miles, in which a high proportion of all fishing activities in Community waters occurs, while at the other extreme, the Belgian zone is only about 800 square nautical miles in area and comparatively little fishing takes place there. It has been agreed that the Community should make a financial contribution to those Member States which bear a disproportionately large share of the costs of surveillance at sea. So far concrete action in this regard has been taken only in respect of Ireland and Greenland: these countries were chosen because the costs of surveillance in their waters were out of proportion to the contribution made to their economies by fishing in their waters and because they did not have sufficient facilities for inspection and surveillance. In July 1978 the Council adopted a decision under which for the six-year period from January 1, 1977 to December 31, 1982 the Community reimbursed Greenland and Ireland for their expenditure on fisheries inspection and surveillance up to a limit of 10 million ECU and 46 million ECU respectively.[178] According to this decision, the Council was to decide before 1983 on participation by the Community in the financing of inspection and surveillance in other Member States' waters, but it has not in fact done so; neither – regrettably – does the Commission appear yet to have made any proposals in this regard. All that has been done, and it is not much, is that the Community attached a declaration to the Iberian Act of Accession in which it is stated that 'Community support for monitoring and supervising waters falling under the sovereignty or within the jurisdiction of Portugal, *may* be envisaged' (emphasis added).

Should more comprehensive action be taken by the Community, as is to be hoped, the United Kingdom would seem to be a prime candidate for Community aid in view of the size of, and the level of fishing activities in, its fishing zone, and in view of the fact that it is one of the Community's poorer Member States. If the Community budget is eventually to be restructured, as many hope, with less money being spent on agricultural price support and more money on the poorer regions of the Community, aid for fisheries enforcement to the United Kingdom and possibly other Member States would fit well into such a new pattern of Community expenditure. After all, a Member State's surveillance activities are very far from being solely for its own benefit: they are carried out very much for the good of the Community as a whole.

So much for the 'carrot' to influence effective enforcement: now we must look at the 'stick'. In March 1980 the Council adopted a Regulation which laid down rules aimed at ensuring that catches taken by Community vessels did not exceed the permitted levels, even though such levels (i.e. quotas) had not at that time been established.[179] Skippers were to inform the national authorities of the State where the catch was landed of the size, composition and location of the catch. These authorities were to take 'appropriate measures' to verify the accuracy of this information, and pass it on to the Commission. Once catches so recorded reached the level of quotas laid down, fishing was to cease. This Regulation was almost wholly ineffective, partly because no quotas were laid down until January 1983, and partly because the Council never adopted the implementing measures which were required if the Regulation was going to be of any effect, even though such measures were proposed by the Commission.

Not surprisingly, therefore, this Regulation was revoked in 1982 and replaced by a rather more effective and ambitious Regulation.[180] The new Regulation begins by imposing a general obligation on Member States to inspect Community vessels in their ports and waters to ensure compliance with Community fishery management regulations, and to prosecute or take administrative action wherever a violation is detected. Member States are to co-ordinate their control measures and report to the Commission on the results of their inspections.[181]

Much of the Regulation is taken up with measures to control catches. Skippers of larger vessels (generally those over 10 metres in length) fishing for a stock for which a TAC has been set must keep a logbook of their operations in which are to be entered the quantities of the species caught, the date and location of such catches, and the type of gear used.[182] Member States must take appropriate measures to verify the accuracy of entries in log books. When he lands his catch, a skipper of a vessel over 10 metres in length must inform the authorities of the State of landing of the amount of fish landed and where it was caught. The authorities must again take appropriate steps to verify this information. Similar information must be provided by a skipper of any size of vessel to the authorities of his flag State where a catch is transshipped to another vessel or landed in a non-Community State: in the case of transshipment the information must also be provided by the skipper of the receiving vessel to the authorities of the Member State in whose waters or port the transshipment takes place. Again the authorities must take appropriate measures to verify the accuracy of the information provided concerning transshipments or landings in third States. Member States must also ensure that all landings of stocks subject to TACs are recorded, and must notify the Commission each month of the quantities of fish landed and where they were caught. The above provisions, it should be noted, apply not only to fishing for stocks subject to TACs in Community waters, but also to fishing for quotas allocated to the Community in the waters of third States.

On the basis of the information which it has obtained as a result of the provisions described above, a Member State must determine when a quota allocated to it has been completely fished. It shall then provisionally prohibit fishing for the stock concerned: a definitive decision is to be taken by the Commission. The reason why a Commission decision is necessary is to enable other Member States to enforce a prohibition on fishing in cases where the quota is being taken from their waters. Typically the Commission makes about fifty such decisions (by way of Regulations) a year. This system is not without its problems. There is inevitably some delay, because of the time-lag between fish being caught and landed and because of the intervals at which Member States pass on landed catch figures to the Commission, between a Member State's quota becoming exhausted and the Commission issuing a regulation prohibiting fishing for that quota. In September 1985 the Commission proposed that this delay should be reduced by providing that the adoption by a Member State of a national measure prohibiting fishing for a particular quota would automatically bring into effect a Community prohibition on such fishing.[183] Although nearly all the other amendments to Regulation 2057/82 proposed at the same time by the Commission were adopted by the Council,[184] this particular proposal was not adopted. It is unfortunate, whatever the reasons may be, that the Council did not act to reduce this delay. The effect of the delay is not only the likelihood that quotas will be exceeded – and it is noteworthy that all the quotas exceeded in 1984 had been the subject of orders prohibiting fishing by the Commission – but also that the order by the Commission to stop fishing will be given at extremely short notice. Often an order enters into effect on the date of its publication in the *Official Journal*: it is obviously unrealistic to expect immediate compliance by vessels engaged in fishing at that date, particularly where, as is not uncommonly the case, the Member State has not in fact issued a provisional prohibition order. Even worse than short notice is the case where, as happens from time to time, the Commission's order is retroactive, sometimes by as much as three weeks. This is particularly regrettable, especially if there has been no national prohibition order, as it is likely to entail criminal liability on the part of fishermen who have fished for the quota in question during the period of retroactivity. Indeed, not only are such Commission regulations regrettable, they are also almost certainly invalid, as the European Court has held that Community legislation entailing retrospective criminal liability is contrary to the general principles of law which it is the Court's function to uphold.[185]

As well as catches, the Regulation also deals with the control of fishing gear. Article 11 provides that a vessel which has on board gear which is of a smaller mesh than that allowed in the area or at the time of year in question, must keep such gear stowed.

One of the most important provisions in the Regulation is Article 12. This provides that in order to ensure that Member States comply with the Regulation, the Commission through authorised officials may verify implementation of the Regulation on the spot. Such Community inspectors, it is important to realise, do not have any right to enforce Community regulations against individual fishermen. Rather their function is to oversee national fisheries inspectors to ensure that the latter carry out their functions with the necessary vigour and consistency. Community inspectors began work at the end of 1983. So far there are 13 of them. The Commission would like to increase their number (and this would seem particularly necessary after the Community's latest enlargement, especially given the poor record of Spanish fishermen in observing conservation regulations), but is apparently unable to do so for lack of funds. In spite of their modest number, Community inspectors have made a significant contribution to the enforcement of Community fisheries law during their so far brief existence. Thus, for example, Community inspectors have uncovered a substantial 'grey market' operated by the Dutch fishing industry, where two sales notes were issued, one 'official' note being sent to Brussels (and generally understating the catch), the other 'grey' indicating the actual catch.[186] Although Community inspectors have no sanctions of their own, they are in a position to embarrass – and have embarrassed – national authorities into modifying existing practices where these run counter to Community rules. An indirect benefit of Community inspectors is the increased contact between the Commission and the fishing industry, and the greater awareness thereby gained by the Commission as to the response of the fishing industry to the Common Fisheries Policy.

Nevertheless there are drawbacks in the present powers of Community inspectors. Not all national inspectors inspect or are empowered to inspect all activities whose inspection is useful to ensure compliance with Community measures, such as the books of fish buyers. Since Community inspectors operate by accompanying national inspectors, it follows that they cannot inspect such activities. In its package of proposals to amend Regulation 2057/ 82 referred to earlier, the Commission proposed plugging this gap by providing that Community inspectors could carry out inspections on their own into such activities, but this proposal was not accepted by the Council. The Commission reiterated this proposal in a fresh package of proposals to amend Regulation 2057/82 put forward in September 1986.[187]

In addition to on-the-spot verification through Community inspectors, Article 12 also provides that if the Commission thinks a Member State has been guilty of 'irregularities' in implementing the Regulation, that Member State must 'conduct an administrative inquiry in which Commission officials may participate'. The Commission must be informed of the progress, results and report of the inquiry. The Commission has already made use of this provision on a number of occasions, notably in respect of Ireland, France and the Netherlands.

In June 1986 the Commission published a report on the working of Regulation 2057/82.[188] This report revealed serious deficiencies in the application and observance of the Regulation by virtually all Member States. Some Member States – Belgium, Denmark, Ireland, the Netherlands (against whom the Commission began but subsequently dropped Article 169 proceedings in respect of the matter) and the United Kingdom – do not have a system which allows them to record catches accurately: as a result actual catches must frequently be higher than those recorded. This is particularly unfortunate, as the cornerstone of the Community management system – TACs and quotas – is dependent on accurate catch statistics to operate effectively. Moreover, whether the figures for landed catches are accurate or not, they are usually not reported to the Commission by the specified date. After four months of Community membership neither Portugal nor Spain had sent to the Commission a single set of the catch figures due each month. Some Member States, especially Belgium, France, Ireland, the Netherlands and West Germany, have made little or insufficient effort to enforce Community technical conservation measures. Some Member States – Belgium, France, Ireland and the United Kingdom – are unable to issue provisional orders prohibiting fishing after exhaustion of a quota for all part of their fleet and/or in sufficient time. Finally, on some occasions Member States (notably France) have not co-operated sufficiently with Community inspectors.

The Commission naturally does not regard this situation as satisfactory. It is prepared to regard the first three years of the operation of the Regulation as a transitional period which has now ended. It therefore intends to take a tougher line in future in seeing that Member States comply with their obligations under the Regulation: in particular the Commission will call for inquiries under Article 12 where necessary, make proposals for improving Community legislation, and institute proceedings under Article 169 where the circumstances so require.

The Commission has made a start with the second of these measures – proposals for improving Community legislation – by publishing a package of draft amendments to Regulation 2057/82 in September 1986.[189] Apart from the proposal to increase the powers of Community inspectors mentioned above, the Commission has proposed that Regulation 2057/82 should be tightened up by Member States being required to monitor all activities which might be relevant to enforcement, including for example fish auctions; by Member States ensuring that all landings by their vessels, wherever they take place, are recorded; and by vessels keeping records of their landings and of related first-hand sales. In addition, the Commission would obtain the power to close fishing for a particular stock once the TAC had been exhausted, as opposed to its present power of only prohibiting those Member States that have actually exceeded their quotas.

While Regulation 2057/82 is the main Community measure relating to enforcement, there are a number of other provisions which are aimed at ensuring compliance with Community rules relating to fisheries management. First, as has already been seen, vessels over 26 metres fishing for demersal species in the Orkney/Shetland box require a licence and must report by radio when entering and leaving the box. Secondly, Article 15(1) of Regulation 171/ 83 (on technical conservation measures) provides that the skipper of a vessel intending to enter the 'mackerel box' (an area off south-west England) to fish must notify the authorities of the Member State in whose fishing zone he intends to fish of his estimated time and place of arrival in the area and of how much mackerel he has on board. Also under Regulation 171/83 the Commission has adopted various control measures related to the sampling of by-catches.[190] Lastly, there is a variety of measures designed to control the fishing activities of Portuguese and Spanish vessels; their range and complexity is no doubt a reflection of the apprehensions felt by most Member States at the entry of this enormous fleet (of questionable orderliness) into the Community. In relation to Spanish vessels fishing in existing Community waters, Regulation 3531/85[191] provides that the Spanish authorities must send to the Commission periodic lists of those Spanish vessels permitted to fish under the access arrangements described earlier: in most cases the Spanish authorities must specify on which days their vessels will fish and must ensure that such vessels do not leave port before the time required for them to reach the specified fishing area on the prescribed day. Licences for most types of specialised fishing are required. Vessels must radio to the relevant national authorities when they enter and leave the 200-mile fishing zone and when they begin and finish fishing. In addition, they must inform the Commission of how much fish they have and where it was caught. Similar arrangements apply to Portuguese vessels fishing in existing Community waters (except that there is no requirement for licences);[192] to existing Community vessels fishing in Spanish and Portuguese waters;[193] to Portuguese vessels fishing in Spanish waters;[194] and to Spanish vessels fishing in Portuguese waters.[195] Further measures to control Portuguese and Spanish fishing are provided by Regulation 3781/85.[196] Under this Regulation Member States must report to the Commission and the flag State any infringement in their waters of Community rules by Portuguese and Spanish vessels, and any penal or administrative measures taken in response to such infringement. 'On the basis of a judicial decision notified or in any other case of recorded infringement of the rules' the offending vessel may be struck off the list of vessels allowed access for a period of two to 18 months, depending on the type of fishing and the nature of the offence. While removal from the list is fair enough following a judicial hearing, it is questionable whether removal simply on the say-so of the national control authorities, without a hearing, is in accordance with Community law. The European Court has held on several occasions that the general principles of Community law require that when an administrative body adopts a measure which is liable to prejudice the interests of an individual, it must allow him to express his point of view.[197] It is interesting to note that an action challenging the validity of Regulation 3781/85 on *inter alia* these grounds has been brought up by a group of Spanish fishermen under Article 173: an application for interim relief was unsuccessful.[198]

It is of course obvious that proper enforcement of Community management measures is necessary. The reasons have been explained very well by the Commission.

> Without proper enforcement, conservation would be threatened and the Community's international fisheries relations would suffer. Moreover, the many restrictions which Community fisheries legislation places on fishing activities in order to conserve resources in the general interest will only be accepted by fishermen in the longer term on the understanding that they will be equally enforced by all the Member States concerned. A proper level of enforcement is thus not only a legal duty laid upon the Member States but also a political necessity in whose absence the conservation component of the common fisheries policy would lose credibility and respect.[199]

On the other hand enforcement is not just – as the Commission and the European Parliament give the impression of believing – a matter of devoting sufficient and effective resources to inspection and control of fishing activities. As with the enforcement of the criminal law generally, the ability to enforce fisheries regulations is also a function of the acceptability, complexity, comprehensibility and knowledge of such regulations.[200] The more Community fisheries regulations are accepted by and known to fishermen, the more likely it is that they will be observed: this is a point which is developed more fully in the final Chapter. As to complexity, there is no doubt that the Community's rules are extremely extensive and detailed (as to which it is hoped Table 2 gives some indication). Obviously the more complex the rules, the harder they are to enforce, especially where the method of enforcement is inspection at sea.[201] Also the more complex the rules, the more likely it is that the evidential burden will be greater in order to obtain a conviction in court proceedings. Observance of the rules is also a function of the capacity of the fleet. Where, as in the Community, there is excess capacity, the more likely it is that TACs and quotas will be exceeded and that fishermen, aware of the extremely competitive situation they are in, will cut corners in observing technical conservation measures.

Finally, in considering enforcement, it is also necessary to remember that it is an extremely costly business. The costs of enforcement can easily amount to a sizable proportion of the value of the catch: in the United Kingdom for example, the costs of enforcement in 1981 were calculated to be about 10 per cent of the value of the catch.[202] Clearly there is a limit as to how much should be spent on enforcement. Member States could possibly effect some savings by co-ordinating their inspection and surveillance activities, as Regulation 2057/

82 calls on them to do.[203] While the bulk – and cost – of enforcement falls on the Member States, present Community arrangements must also put considerable strain on the limited manpower of the Commission. Vast quantities of information have to be sent to the Commission and processed – monthly catch statistics, information on enforcement action taken by Member States, reports of inquiries under Article 12 of Regulation 2057/82, lists of Iberian vessels fishing in existing Community waters and of existing Community vessels fishing in Iberian waters, applications for licences from such vessels and from vessels wishing to fish in the Orkney/Shetland box, and radio reports from the latter vessels and Iberian vessels in existing Community waters. It would be interesting to know how (or even whether) the Commission copes with this vast flow of information.

Table 2. Factors to be taken into account in the observance/enforcement of EEC fisheries regulations.

1.	Nationality of the vessel	if British, what is the nationality of the crew?
		if Portuguese or Spanish, is that particular vessel allowed where it is?
2.	Location of the vessel	is the area closed to fishing at the time for any species?
		is the vessel observing particular requirements for special areas such as the Orkney/Shetland, Norway pout and mackerel boxes?
		if in the 6–12 mile zone of a non-flag State, are vessels of the flag State allowed there? to fish for species for which the vessel is fishing?
3.	Species being fished for	does the flag State have a quota for that species in that area which is not exhausted?
		is it observing other restrictions, e.g. no salmon fishing beyond 12 miles?
4.	Gear being used	are minimum mesh sizes (which vary from area to area and species to species) being observed?
		do the vessel's nets have attachments? if so, are they of the permitted kind?
		are other gear restrictions being observed?
5.	By-catches	are by-catch levels (which vary with the area and species fished) within the permitted limits?
6.	Minimum fish sizes	are there any fish on board below the permitted size?
7.	Log books	is the vessel required to carry a log book? if so, is it doing so? is the log book correctly completed?
8.	Licence	if Portuguese or Spanish, or in the Orkney/Shetland box, does the vessel require a licence? if so, does it have a valid licence?
9.	Reporting	if Portuguese or Spanish, or in the Orkney/Shetland or mackerel boxes, is the vessel required to report? if so, has it done so correctly?

7. SCIENTIFIC RESEARCH

It is obvious that any system of fisheries management can be effective only if it is based on adequate scientific knowledge of the fish stocks to be managed. In 1976, when it was first formulating its proposals for a Community system of fisheries management, the Commission had no expertise of its own in fisheries science; nor was there any point in its developing such expertise or establishing its own programme of fisheries research as this would largely, if not entirely, have duplicated the existing work of other international organisations and of Member States' fisheries research institutions. Instead the Commission relies on its Scientific and Technical Committee for Fisheries for scientific advice: the Committee, in turn, bases its advice on the work done by national institutions and especially the work of the International Council for the Exploration of the Sea (ICES). ICES, to which all EEC Member States except Greece, Italy and Luxembourg belong, was founded as long ago as 1902, and has attained a pre-eminent position among marine scientific inter-governmental organisations on account of the quality of its work and the impartiality of its advice. Its functions include the promotion and co-ordination of research relating to fisheries and to some extent pollution in the North Atlantic, North Sea and Baltic; the compilation and publication of statistics relating to fish catches; and, through its Advisory Committee on Fisheries Management, the formulation of recommendations for the management of the fish stocks found within its area of operation (which covers most Community waters).[204] If the Community institutions adopt a more active management policy for those Community waters lying outside the ICES area (namely, the Mediterranean and the waters off the French overseas departments of French Guyana, Guadeloupe, Martinique and Réunion), then it will be both desirable and necessary for the Scientific and Technical Committee for Fisheries to have recourse to the scientific work being done by international organisations in those areas.

Although the Community institutions have so far relied on the fisheries research being done by outside bodies, Article 8 of the original Structural Regulation (now Article 7 of Regulation 101/76) provides that the Council, acting on a proposal from the Commission after consulting the European Parliament, is to adopt 'measures to co-ordinate the policies of Member States on research and scientific and technical assistance for the fishing industry'. No proposals for action in this area were put forward by the Commission until 1980, when it published a draft regulation, which would provide for the co-ordination of fisheries research undertaken by Member States and its promotion at Community level.[205] Member States would be required to inform the Commission of all fisheries research being carried out. The Commission would keep the trend and development of scientific research in Member States under review and would organise exchanges of information. The Commission would also be authorised to co-ordinate national research activities in order to rationalise the facilities and resources utilised, and would adopt joint research programmes financed by the Community (the Community's financial participation being limited to about 5 million ECU over three years).

The Commission's proposal has evoked a very limited response from the Council. In a Resolution adopted on January 25, 1983 the Council stated that it was 'aware of the usefulness of a co-ordinated development of research in order to achieve the full realisation of the objectives of the common fisheries policy. With this in mind and in line with the orientations of common policy in the field of science and technology, the Council will re-examine, as soon as possible,' the draft Regulation 'with the aim of taking the appropriate measures.'[206] In spite of the fact that over three years have elapsed since the adoption of this Resolution, no measures, appropriate or otherwise, have been adopted by the Council (apparently because of financial reservations by some Member States and fears of duplication of research effort by others). Nevertheless, undaunted the Commission in November 1985 published a revised version of its draft Regulation with more specific proposals for research and co-ordination programmes and a suggested increase in expenditure to 27 million ECU over a five-year period.[207] The Commission's draft Regulation is a useful proposal. It envisages that co-ordination and research will involve not so much purely biological research (which is already fairly well co-ordinated through ICES and the Scientific and Technical Committee for Fisheries), as research on matters not being tackled, or adequately tackled, elsewhere and would cover the management of resources, aquaculture, fishing techniques and improvements in processing. Since the proposal would not lead to the duplication of existing work and could make a useful, if modest, contribution to improving the lot of European fishing industries, it is very much to be hoped that the Council will soon take some positive action and adopt the proposal.[208]

8. RESOLUTION OF CONFLICTS INVOLVING FISHERMEN

It was suggested in Chapter 1 that one of the objectives of fisheries management should be the resolution of conflicts involving fishermen. Although this is not one of the stated objectives of the Community's fishery management system, it is worthwhile looking to see what legal provisions there are for the resolution of conflicts involving fishermen in Community waters. As was seen in Chapter 1, such conflicts may be of two basic types, conflicts between fishing and other uses of the sea, and conflicts involving fishermen only: the latter mainly comprise disputes over access to fishing grounds and collisions between different types of fishing gear.

To take the second type of conflict first, conflicts involving only fishermen, the question of access to fishing grounds is comprehensively regulated by Community law through the principle of equal access, modified by the 12-mile exclusive zone for local fishermen, the Orkney/Shetland box and the special arrangements relating to Portugal and Spain. On the other hand, there are no provisions of Community law dealing directly with the resolution of gear conflicts, although some Community measures, such as the Orkney/Shetland box and the restrictions on certain types of gear laid down by Regulation 171/83 (on technical conservation measures) indirectly contribute to the avoidance of gear conflicts.[209] Furthermore, the Convention on Conduct of Fishing Operations in the North Atlantic[210] (to which all EEC Member States except Greece, Ireland and Luxembourg are parties), which applies to Community waters in the North Atlantic and North Sea, is aimed at preventing collisions between vessels while fishing and conflicts between trawling and the users of fixed gear, and at facilitating the resolution of disputes arising out of such collisions and conflicts. It is also possible for Member States, by virtue of the powers delegated to them under Regulations 171/83 and 2057/82, to adopt legislation designed to prevent gear conflicts, provided that such legislation complies with all the requirements of Community law outlined in section 1 above.

As far as conflicts between fishing and other uses of the sea are concerned, the uses of the sea which are most likely to conflict with fishing are the exploitation of the seabed for mineral resources (oil, gas, sand and gravel) and the use of the sea as a convenient disposal area for pollutants. In the case of the exploration and exploitation of offshore oil and gas, conflicts with fishing may arise in a number of ways. First, the presence of offshore oil and gas production and exploration installations, together with the safety zones around them, reduce the areas of sea open to fishing. Such installations are also a navigational hazard to fishing and other vessels. Thirdly, the presence of pipelines reduces the areas where trawling can take place. Finally, debris from the oil and gas industry is a hazard to fishermen and their nets. Such conflicts are at present resolved almost entirely by national law. The authorities of Member States decide, subject to their obligations under the Continental Shelf Convention not to interfere with recognised sea lanes or to interfere unjustifiably with other uses of the sea, whether offshore installations may be erected and pipelines laid. National fishing industries may, and in fact do, make representations as to the emplacement of installations and pipelines, but so far the Community does not appear itself ever to have made representations on behalf of Community fishermen generally in such cases: the matter is regarded no doubt as being too politically sensitive. The disposal of debris is also regulated by national law, although the latter in part reflects and implements the international conventions on dumping.[211]

In the case of dredging offshore for sand and gravel, which not only reduces the areas where fishing can take place but may also damage spawning and nursery areas for fish, the position is again that it is up to the national authorities of Member States to balance the interests of the fishing and sand and gravel industries in deciding whether to allow dredging to proceed in any particular area. The Community does not appear yet to have intervened in such cases to put forward the views and interests of Community fishermen.

As far as marine pollution is concerned, competence in this area is divided between the Community and Member States. There is a wealth of both Community and national legislation on this topic. It is beyond the confines of this book to give any details of this legislation or to suggest how successful it is in preventing pollution which may prove deleterious to fish stocks in Community waters.[212]

9. CONCLUSIONS

Community waters contain considerable fishery resources for whose management the Community, rather than its individual Member States, has been primarily responsible since 1979. There was no proper or effective management of these resources between 1979 and January 1983, when agreement was reached on a Community system of fishery management. How effective has this management system been, particularly in the light of its objectives?

The first major objective of the Community system of management, it will be recalled, is broadly speaking to reduce fishing effort gradually so as to generate relatively stable yields from stocks at around the level of MSY. The means of achieving this aim are a combination of TACs, quotas and technical conservation measures. How effective these means have been, and will be, in guaranteeing the long-term health of fish stocks in Community waters it is probably too early to say, because the rebuilding of stocks takes several years. Certainly there have been some successes, notably in respect of North Sea herring, where Community action has saved the stocks from what might well have been terminal collapse. On the other hand, some other North Sea stocks, notably cod and haddock, are currently in a state that gives cause for concern. The present poor state of these stocks, however, may be as much due to poor recruitment in recent years as to the failings of the Community management system. But whatever the reason, there is in any case a general question mark hanging over the future effectiveness of the Community management system because of the rather poor record of compliance with and enforcement of the system during its first three years.

Apart from its practical observance hitherto, the Community system of TACs and quotas gives rise to other difficulties which have probably not been sufficiently aired in the Community. TACs are set every year (and are also subjected to minor adjustments several times during the course of a year). This has several drawbacks. It involves a lot of time and effort by scientists to produce the advice on which TACs are based (which is costly). As a result scientists spend so much time on producing short-term advice that there is little time for long-term research. Once the scientists have given their advice, the Commission and Council are put under a great deal of pressure of time to get TACs adopted by the beginning of the year to which they relate. Finally, annual variations in TACs make it harder for the fishing industry to make long-term plans. TACs could be set at less frequent intervals than a year for long-lived fish such as cod, stocks with low exploitation rates and stocks where recruitment does not vary much, especially if the Community were to be satisfied with catches somewhat below MSY. If this were done, pressure on scientists and Community fishery managers would be reduced, longer-term planning by the fishing industry would be possible, and greater stability would be given to markets for fish products.[213]

There are other drawbacks with TACs and quotas. If fishermen are limited to a set quota, they will tend to keep the bigger fish (which fetch a better price) and throw away the smaller fish in the hope of replacing them later with bigger fish. Secondly, once the quota for a particular species has been caught, fishermen will discard fish of that species caught later as a by-catch in some other fishery. Obviously both these tendencies are inimical to the needs of conservation. Quotas are also difficult to enforce. There is a tendency to under-report catches, it is difficult to check the weight of a catch either at sea (because of vessel movement) or on land (because of loss of part of the fish through filleting, ice in fish boxes, etc.).[214] Undoubtedly the continuing Community emphasis on TACs and quotas, in spite of the drawbacks mentioned, is due to their political acceptability – they continue the familiar (if unsuccessful) approach of NEAFC.

The second objective of the Community management system is to aid poorer regions where fishing is of particular economic importance. Such regions are primarily, but not exclusively, those where inshore fishing predominates, and it is only in respect of the latter that specific Community management measures have been taken (although Community financial assistance has been provided to the fishing industry as a whole in the poorer regions, as will be seen in Chapter 6). These measures comprise the 12-mile limit, the criteria used for allocating quotas, the Orkney/Shetland box and (as will be seen in Chapter 6) financial aid for structural measures. How effective these measures are in helping the inshore fishing industry in poorer regions depends very much on the action taken by individual Member States, particularly in relation to the first two of these matters. A Member State which treats its 12-mile zone as a national zone, allowing all sizes of vessel to fish there, will not be doing very much to assist the inshore fishing industry in disadvantaged regions. Secondly, if a Member State decides to allocate its quotas among different sections of its fleet (as it is entitled to do under Article 5(2) of the Management Regulation), then it can do much (or very little) for the inshore industry.

The third objective of the Community management system (which may to some extent conflict with the second objective) is to adapt the Community fishing fleet to catch potential. This matter is dealt with in Chapter 6 (this and the following chapter being concerned with biological aspects of management), but it is worth making two points briefly here. First, although for reasons of convenience and to break up the material into chapters of not excessive length, the economic and biological aspects of management are considered in separate chapters in this book, the two matters are closely related. The more excess capacity there is, and therefore the more competition there is between fishermen to catch a limited quantity of fish, the more likely it is that quota restrictions and technical conservation measures will not be observed. Thus eliminating excess capacity (or in other words, adapting the Community fishing fleet to catch potential) would lead to improved observance of Community measures related to biological management. Doing this would also allow the Community to place less emphasis on quantitative restrictions on catches (TACs and quotas) which, as pointed out above, have certain drawbacks as management tools. The second point worth making here is that the Management Regulation itself, in Article 5(2) (which provides that Member States are to determine the detailed rules for utilising the quotas allocated to them), allows individual Member States, if they so wish, to set about adjusting their fleets to their catch potential, and some Member States have begun taking steps in this direction. Whether this is likely to prove adequate to adapt the Community fleet to catch potential, or whether there is a need for more Community action in this regard is something that is discussed in Chapter 6.

As has been pointed out at various places in this Chapter, no Community fishery management measures have yet been adopted for the Mediterranean (apart from the 12-mile limit). The Commission and Council have been urged by the European Parliament and Economic and Social Committee several times to adopt such measures.[215] With the entry of Spain into the EEC, there would now seem to be some urgency for the Commission to come forward with proposals. It is likely that in considering such proposals the Commission will move away from the kinds of regulatory technique so far used in North-East Atlantic waters. Many of the more important stocks in the Mediterranean are of short-lived, schooling, pelagic species; nearly all fisheries are mixed-species; and scientific knowledge and fisheries statistics are less developed than in the North-East Atlantic. For these reasons, therefore, TACs and quotas are a less suitable form of management than other forms of effort limitation such as restrictive licensing (as the European Parliament has suggested). With a vast number of small concerns in the Mediterranean, the implementation and enforcement of any management scheme would be far more difficult and complex than in the North-East Atlantic. Co-operation would also be necessary with other Mediterranean States over the management of shared stocks.

As well as evaluating the management system agreed in 1983, it is also worth making a few comments about the continuing role of the Community as a fishery manager. First, the Community does not always take decisions with the necessary speed, as was pointed out earlier when discussing the action (or inaction) of both the Council and Commission in respect of various matters concerning technical conservation measures. Another example of Community inactivity is the failure of the Commission by November 1985 to have submitted a single one of the annual reports called for by Article 9(2) of the Management Regulation on the working of the Regulation.[216] Thirdly, it may be questioned (as was done in section 6 above) whether the Commission has adequate manpower effectively to process the vast amount of information submitted to it. Finally, questions can be asked about the costs of running the Community management system. The writer has never found any figures giving such costs, but the costs must be high. First, there are the high costs of obtaining the scientific advice on which Community TACs are based (although these costs are borne largely by ICES and its Member States, rather than the Community). Secondly, numerous individuals, both at the Community and national level, are involved in the drawing up and implementation of Community regulations: costs here include considerable travel, servicing Community meetings, and translating Community documents. Finally, there are the high costs of enforcement, which have already been referred to earlier in this Chapter. It would be an interesting exercise for an economist to attempt to calculate the costs of the Community management system and compare them with the income derived from fishing by Community fleets.

The Community system of fisheries management agreed in 1983, whatever its failings and limitations, has produced a period of stability which allows long-term planning and investment decisions in the fishing industry to be made. In this it compares very favourably with the period before 1983, which was one of considerable uncertainty and unpredictability for the fishing industries of the Community. The present period of stability should last at least until 2002, when major reviews are scheduled of the criteria for quota allocation, the 12-mile limit, the Orkney/Shetland Box, and the arrangements concerning Spain and Portugal. The difficulty of predicting what will happen then, in 16 years' time, can best be illustrated by pointing out how difficult (if not impossible) it would have been for anyone 16 years ago, in 1970 (before the world of 200-mile limits), to have predicted the situation in European fisheries as it is today in 1986.

NOTES

1. This Chapter focuses primarily on the biological aspects of management: socio-economic aspects of management, such as the adjustment of fish-catching capacity to catch potential, are discussed in Chapter 6. This Chapter is also confined to looking at the regulation of Community vessels in Community waters: the regulation of non-Community vessels in Community waters and of Community vessels in third States' waters is discussed in the next Chapter.

2. Although the Community possesses no enforcement jurisdiction in fisheries matters, it does play a supervisory role in law enforcement. See section 6 below.

3. Reg. 2141/70, O.J. S. Edn. 1970 (III) p. 703.

4. There is one exception to this statement. Reg. 811/76, O.J. 1976 L94/1, temporarily authorised national measures implementing quotas set by international fishery commissions. This was done in order to avoid any doubt as to the legality of such measures. The *Kramer* case, *op. cit.* in n. 6, effectively resolved these doubts.

5. And from Reg. 2141/70, *op. cit.* in n. 3 (and its successor, Reg. 101/76, O.J. 1976 L20/19) and Art. 100 of the Act of Accession, which all refer to the permitted existence of national regulations. At the time Reg. 2141/70 was adopted, it was apparently envisaged that fishing would continue to be regulated primarily by international fisheries commissions and by the national authorities of Member States.

6. Joined Cases 3, 4 and 6/76, *Officier van Justitie v. Kramer* [1976] E.C.R. 1279: [1976] 2 C.M.L.R. 440.

7. The text of Annex VI has not been published in the O.J. It is, however, reproduced in the *Irish Fisheries* case, *op. cit.* in n. 8, at pp. 444–445 and 468–469 respectively. The Council confirmed the provisions of Annex VI in a Declaration of January 30–31, 1978. Again, this Declaration has not been published in the O.J. It is reproduced in Case 32/79, *Commission v. United Kingdom* [1980] E.C.R. 2403 at 2408–9; [1981] 1 C.M.L.R. 219 at 223.

8. Case 61/77, *Commission v. Ireland* [1978] E.C.R. 417; [1978] 2 C.M.L.R. 466.

9. *Ibid.,* pp. 448 and 515 respectively.

10. *Ibid.,* pp. 448–449 and 515 respectively.

11. *Ibid.* 'The requirements of Community Law' will be outlined below, following discussion of the scope of Member States' competence in principle to adopt conservation measures.

12. Joined Cases 185–204/78, *Officier van Justitie v. Van Dam en Zonen et al.* [1979] E.C.R. 2345 at 2360; [1980] 1 C.M.L.R. 350 at 363.

13. Case 141/78, *France v. United Kingdom* [1979] E.C.R. 2923 at 2940–2942; [1980] 1 C.M.L.R. 6 at 22–23.

14. *Op. cit.* in n. 7, pp. 2431–2434 and 260–262 respectively.

15. Case 287/81, *Anklagemyndigheden v. J. Noble Kerr* [1982] E.C.R. 4053 at 4073; [1983] 2 C.M.L.R. 431 at 451.

16. *Op. cit.* in n. 7, pp. 2434 and 262 respectively.

17. Although Advocate General Reischl suggested that the duty in that case arose from an agreement in the Council, which, even though it was not published, had the character of a decision and therefore was binding.

18. *Op. cit.* in n. 7, pp. 2437 and 265 respectively. Cf. also the Opinion of Advocate General Reischl, who bases the duty more directly on Art. 5 of the EEC Treaty: he describes the provisions mentioned by the Court as '*leges speciales* in relation to the basic provision laid down in Article 5.' See pp. 2460–2462 and 236–238 respectively.

19. Case 804/79, [1981] E.C.R. 1045; [1982] 1 C.M.L.R. 543.

20. *Ibid.,* at pp. 1072–1073 and 570 respectively.

21. *Ibid.,* at pp. 1073–1074 and 571 respectively. But note that in *Gewiese and Mehlich v.*

Mackenzie, op. cit. in the following note, the Court suggests that the initiative to amend existing measures must come from suggestions by the Community authorities.

22. See Case 124/80, *Officier van Justitie v. Firma J. Van Dam & Zonen* [1981] E.C.R. 1447; [1982] 2 C.M.L.R. 93; Case 269/80, *R v. Tymen* [1981] E.C.R. 3079; [1982] 2 C.M.L.R. 111; Case 21/81, *Openbaar Ministerie v. Bout* [1982] E.C.R. 381; [1982] 2 C.M.L.R. 371; Case 87/82, *Rogers v. Darthenay* [1983] E.C.R. 1579; [1984] 1 C.M.L.R. 135; Case 24/83, *Gewiese and Mehlich v. Mackenzie* [1984] E.C.R. 817; [1984] 2 C.M.L.R. 409.

23. H.C. Deb., December 13, 1971, Vol. 828, col. 51.

24. St. meld. nr. 50 (1971–72) *Om Norges tilslutning til De Europeiske Fellesskap* Annex I, p. 26 (translation by the writer).

25. Usher argues that there have in general been two approaches by the Court to the question of whether Member States have any competence in areas where the Community has competence. One is that the Community is exclusively competent (as with, for example, fisheries and commercial policy), the other that Member States retain competence to enact measures which are compatible with Community measures (as in agriculture). Usher argues further that in its most recent case law the Court is moving from the compatibility approach in agriculture to the principle of Community exclusivity. See J.A. Usher, 'The Scope of Community Competence – its Recognition and Enforcement' (1985) XXIV J.C.M.S. 121 at 123–7. See also *ibid., European Community Law and National Law. The Irreversible Transfer?,* London, 1981, Chapter 3.

26. See, for example, Case 6/64, *Costa v. ENEL* [1964] E.C.R. 585; [1964] C.M.L.R. 425; and Case 106/77, *Amministrazione delle Finanze dello Stato v. Simmenthal* [1978] E.C.R. 629; [1978] 3 C.M.L.R. 263.

27. Usher, *op. cit.* in n. 25, p. 125, suggests that the Court may also have been influenced by the fact that the Community has exclusive treaty-making powers in fisheries matters, and that the internal and external sides of fisheries are closely inter-linked.

28. See n. 100 below.

29. See, for example, the *Kramer* case, *op. cit.* in n. 6, pp. 1309 and 469 respectively.

30. *Op. cit.* in n's 3 and 5.

31. Regs. 170–172/83, O.J. 1983 L24/1, 14 and 30.

32. O.J. 1980 L258/1. This Reg., as prolonged by a number of subsequent Regs., was in force between October 1, 1980 and October 31, 1981.

33. Reg. 1866/86, O.J. 1986 L162/1.

34. There is nothing in Art. 102 to suggest that it does not apply to all Community waters, even though Community efforts to adopt fishery management measures have concentrated on Member States' 200-miles zones in the North Sea and North Atlantic.

35. Reg. 171/83 is of indefinite duration.

36. *Op. cit.* in n. 33.

37. As amended by Reg. 2178/84, O.J. 1984 L199/1.

38. See Case 9/56, *Meroni and Co. Industrie Metallurgiche Sp A v. High Authority* [1958] E.C.R. 133 and Case 23/75, *Rey Soda v. Cassa Conguaglio Zucchero* [1975] E.C.R. 1279; [1976] 1 C.M.L.R. 185. See also the Advocate General in *Commission v. United Kingdom, op. cit.* in n. 19, pp. 1088 and 559 respectively. It is also interesting to note that in Case 151/78, *Sukkerfabrieken Nykobing Limiteret v. Ministry of Agriculture* [1979] E.C.R. 1 the Court, while observing that the regulation of sugar production fell exclusively within the competence of the Community so that Member States no longer were in a position to adopt unilateral measures, nevertheless accepted that the Council could authorise Member States to take national measures to deal with certain problems encountered in sugar regulation (though admittedly the Court did not talk of this in terms of delegation, but this is what it would seem to be). The situation in this case and discussed in the text should be distinguished

from that where, as often happens, Community legislation requires Member States to take measures to implement that legislation.

39. O.J. 1983 L24/1.
40. O.J. 1982 L220/1.
41. Case 87/82, [1983] E.C.R. 1579; [1984] 1 C.M.L.R. 135.
42. *Ibid.,* at pp. 1592 and 146 respectively.
43. Cases 86–87/84, [1985] 3 C.M.L.R. 218.
44. *Ibid.,* p. 221. Since this judgment the Council has adopted a Reg. defining vessel characteristics, including tonnage: see Reg. 2930/86, O.J. 1986 L274/1.
45. See Usher, *op. cit.* in n. 25, p. 127.
46. See the lists of national measures in O.J. 1978 C154/5, 1979 C119/5, 1980 C133/2 and C237/2, 1981 C218/2, 1982 C142/2 and C315/2, and 1983 C121/3.
47. *Op. cit.* in n. 22.
48. These include not only autonomous measures, but also national measures giving effect to the recommendations of international fishery commissions (see *France v. United Kingdom, op. cit.* in n. 13, pp. 2942–2943 and 23–24 respectively), as well as national measures merely implementing Community conservation measures (see *Commission v. United Kingdom, op. cit.* in n. 7, pp. 2445 and 271 respectively). According to the strict wording of Annex VI, national measures must be limited in their geographical scope to the exclusive fishing zone of the Member State concerned. The Court, in the first passage from the *Irish Fisheries* case quoted above, took a broader view and said that national measures could be adopted within a Member State's 'own jurisdiction'. Thus, according to the Court, it is possible for a Member State to adopt measures not only for its own fishing zone, but also – as in fact was the case with the national measures at issue in the first *Van Dam* case and *France v. United Kingdom* – for its fishermen fishing in waters beyond this zone.
49. *Op. cit.* in n. 13, pp. 2942 and 23 respectively. See also the Commission's arguments in the case, which elaborate this point. In *Commission v. United Kingdom* the Court simply observed: 'It is not contested that this resolution [i.e. the Hague Resolution] is binding on the Member States' (*op. cit.* in n. 7, pp. 2432 and 261 respectively).
50. *Op. cit.* in n. 13, pp. 2951 and 18 respectively. Note, too, that in his Opinion in *Commission v. United Kingdom, op. cit.* in n. 7, pp. 2476–2478 and 254–256, the Advocate General suggested that express approval would be required in the case of measures that were neither appropriate nor absolutely essential.
51. In a note of February 11, 1977, referred to in the *Irish Fisheries* case, *op. cit.* in n. 8, pp. 440 and 509 respectively.
52. In a letter sent by Commissioner Gundelach to the United Kingdom Minister of Agriculture, Fisheries and Food. See *The Guardian,* August 23, 1978, p. 4.
53. *Op. cit.* in n. 7, pp. 2439 and 266 respectively.
54. *Ibid.,* pp. 2446 and 272 respectively.
55. *Ibid.,* pp. 2468 and 245 respectively.
56. *Op. cit.* in n. 19, pp. 1076 and 573 respectively.
57. *Ibid.,* pp. 1090 and 561 respectively (emphasis in the original).
58. In *Gewiese and Mehlich v. Mackenzie* the Court appears to suggest that the obligation to obtain the Commission's approval flows from Art. 155.
59. *Op. cit.,* in n. 22.
60. See O.J. 1983 C121/10, and more generally the list of national measures referred to in n. 46 above.
61. See R. Wainwright, 'Common Fisheries Policy – the Development of a Common Regime for Fishing' (1981) 1 *Yearbook of European Law* 69 at 82.
62. See n. 46 above.

158

63. See L. Amato *et. al.* (eds), *La Legislazione Italiana sul Diritto del Mare,* Milan, 1981, pp. 155–169; and subsequently various issues of *Italy and the Law of the Sea Newsletter.*
64. *Op. cit.* in n. 6, pp. 1311 and 471 respectively.
65. See particularly the Court's Interlocutory Order of May 22, 1977, [1977] E.C.R. 932; [1978] 2 C.M.L.R. 478.
66. *Op. cit.* in n. 7, pp. 2471 and 248 respectively.
67. *Op. cit.* in n. 15, pp. 4074 and 452 respectively.
68. Case 63/83, [1984] E.C.R. 2689; [1984] 3 C.M.L.R. 522.
69. *Ibid.,* at pp. 2718 and 538 respectively.
70. *Op. cit.* in n. 8, pp. 450 and 517 respectively.
71. Although not discussed by the Court, the Advocate General found two other United Kingdom measures in this case discriminatory, although formulated in apparently objective terms. First, a measure which banned herring fishing in the Irish Sea after a particular date was discriminatory. At the date chosen, because of different fishing patterns, the fishing season for British vessels was nearly over while for vessels from other Member States it was just beginning. Secondly, a measure banning fishing for Norway pout was discriminatory because British vessels scarcely caught any of this fish, whereas for Danish vessels it was an important species.
72. Cf. the various tests suggested by the Commission in the *Irish Fisheries* case for determining whether the Irish measures were discriminatory.
73. *Op. cit.* in n. 12, pp. 2361 and 364 respectively. The Court's reasoning is open to criticism because of its confusion between personal jurisdiction and territorial jurisdiction, and because its reference to the compatibility of the national legislation with Community law not being contested is question begging. See further the case-note by Churchill in (1979) 4 E.L.R. 391. The Court's judgment was no doubt influenced by the fact that had it held that the Dutch measures were discriminatory and thus contrary to Community law, it would have penalised a State which had adopted more effective conservation measures than most of its fellow Member States and which, unlike them, had carried out undertakings agreed to in the Council.
74. This rule probably follows from Art. 5 of the EEC Treaty and the general principle that Member States must exercise their powers to take conservation measures in good faith.
75. *Op. cit.* in n. 8, pp. 459 and 495 respectively. Emphasis in the original.
76. I.e. the principle that individuals may only have imposed on them for purposes of the public interest obligations which are strictly necessary for those purposes to be attained: or, to borrow the more graphic definition once given by Lord Diplock, you must not use a sledgehammer to crack a nut, when a nutcracker will do!
77. *Op. cit.* in n. 7, pp. 2445 and 271–272 respectively.
78. Norwegian Government, *Rapport om De Europeiske Fellesskap i aret 1971,* Oslo, 1972, p. 48.
79. *Op. cit.* in n. 6, pp. 1312 and 471 respectively.
80. *Ibid.*
81. *Ibid.*
82. See, for example, Case 190/73, *Officier van Justitie v. Van Haaster* [1974] E.C.R. 1123; [1974] 2 C.M.L.R. 521.
83. *Op. cit.* in n. 6, pp. 1313 and 472 respectively.
84. See also the fuller discussion of this point in Chapter 8.
85. Case 88/77, *Minister for Fisheries v. Schonenberg* [1978] E.C.R. 473; [1978] 2 C.M.L.R. 519; *R. v. Tymen, op. cit.* in n. 22.
86. The Advocate General is quoting here from *Amministrazione delle Finanze dello Stato v. Simmenthal, op. cit.* in n. 26, pp. 643 and 282 respectively. Note that in this case the Court was referring to *Regulations,* which undoubtedly are directly applicable.

87. See, e.g., Case 9/73, *Schlüter v. Hauptzollamt Lörrach* [1973] E.C.R. 1135 and Case 44/84, *Hurd v. H.M. Inspector of Taxes* [1986] 2 C.M.L.R. 1.

88. Apparently the Danish Government contemplated Art. 173 proceedings against the Commission's decision approving the British measure at issue in *Kirk*: obviously once the Council reached agreement on continuing the derogation and the British measure was consequently revoked there was no point in instituting proceedings. See Editorial Comment in (1983) 20 C.M.L. Rev. 7 at 9.

89. On these general principles of law, see T.C. Hartley, *The Foundations of European Community Law,* Oxford, 1981, pp. 119–144.

90. See, in particular, COMs (76) 500; (77) 164; and (79) 612 and 687.

91. See, for example, Resolution of March 12, 1979 on the Common Fisheries Policy, O.J. 1979 C67/25, para. 1; and Resolution of November 21, 1980 on the Common Fisheries Policy, O.J. 1980 C327/84, para. 7.

92. See its opinion on the Draft Management Regulation, O.J. 1977 C56/73.

93. O.J. 1983 L24/1.

94. For a fuller discussion of the argument that it is better if management objectives are defined fairly generally, see J.A. Gulland, 'Introduction: Some Notes for the Consultation on the Regulation of Fishing Effort' in FAO, *Expert Consultation on the Regulation of Fishing Effort,* FAO Fisheries Report No. 289, Supp. 2 (1985), p. 1 at pp. 2–3.

95. For details of how ICES formulates and gives its advice to the Community, see M.J. Holden, 'The Procedures followed and Problems met by the European Economic Community in Implementing the Scientific Recommendations of the International Council for the Exploration of the Sea on Total Allowable Catches' in FAO, *op. cit.* in n. 94, Supp. 3(1985), p. 231 at 232–3.

96. The Commission's policy in this area is explained in COM (79) 687. See also COMs (83) 740, (84) 591 and (85) 709; Commission's Answer to W.Q. 2314/85, O.J. 1986 C150/17; and Holden, *op. cit.,* p. 233.

97. COM (82) 340, p. 2.

98. COM (85) 720. See also the Commission's Answer to W.Q. 593/85, O.J. 1985 C259/35.

99. The difficulties of making such a judgment can be illustrated by reference to the Commission's proposals for TACs in 1981. The European Parliament criticised the Commission for not striking a 'real balance between biological, social and economic requirements' (it thought the Commission had given insufficient weight to social and economic requirements) (Resolution of March 26, 1981, O.J. 1981 C90/109); whereas the British Government thought the Commission had got the balance about right (HC Paper (1980–81) 32-iv, p. 11).

100. Reg. 754/80, O.J. 1980 L84/37. But note that between 1979 and 1983, apart from a hiatus in 1981, the Council adopted a series of so-called 'roll-over' decisions in which it called on Member States 'to conduct their fishing activities in such a way as to take into account' the TACs proposed by the Commission.

101. Reg. 3624/83, O.J. 1983 L365/1.

102. Reg. 172/83, O.J. 1983 L24/30.

103. Reg. 198/83, O.J. 1983 L25/32.

104. Reg. 172/83, O.J. 1983 L24/30.

105. M.J. Holden, 'Management of Fisheries Resources: the Experience of the European Economic Community' in OECD, *Experiences in the Management of National Fishing Zones,* Paris, 1984, p. 113 at 117.

106. *Ibid.*

107. For details as to how these criteria were developed and their rationale, see J. Farnell and J. Elles, *In Search of a Common Fisheries Policy,* Aldershot, 1984, pp. 107–118.

108. See Art. 4(2) of the Management Regulation and Commission Answer to W.Q. 1077/83, O.J. 1984 C38/4.

160

109. General Secretariat of the Council of the European Communities, *31st Review of the Council's Work January 1 – December 31, 1983* (1985), p. 217.
110. See Dec. 83/653, O.J. L371/39.
111. COM (83) 740.
112. Reg. 3780/85, O.J. 1985 L363/24.
113. See, for example, Case 13/63, *Italy v. Commission* [1963] E.C.R. 165; [1963] C.M.L.R. 289 (free movement of goods); Case 152/73, *Sotgiu v. Deutsche Bundespost* [1974] E.C.R. 153 (free movement of workers); Case 11/74, *L'Union des Minotiers de la Champagne v. France* [1974] E.C.R. 877; [1975] 1 C.M.L.R. 75 and Case 139/79, *Maizena v. Council* [1980] E.C.R. 3393 (both on agriculture). See also B. Sundberg – Weitman, *Discrimination on Grounds of Nationality,* Amsterdam, 1977, pp. 39–92 and C. Vajda, 'Some Aspects of Judicial Review within the Common Agricultural Policy' (1979) 4 E.L.R. 244 at 250–261 and 341–346.
114. Note, too, that the Court has upheld the validity of the quota system for sugar production in the Community and the differences in the quotas allocated to Member States which are based on objective factors (past production levels and structural differences in the industry); see Case 230/78, *Eridania v. Ministry of Agriculture and Forestry* [1979] E.C.R. 2749 and Case 250/84, *Eridania v. Cassa Conguaglio Zucchero,* Judgment of January 22, 1986 (not yet reported).
115. Case 207/84, *De Boer v. Produktschap voor Vis en Visprodukten,* Judgment of October 3, 1985 (not yet reported).
116. Commission's Answer to W.Q. 1067/84, O.J. 1985 C93/13.
117. Commission's Answer to W.Q. 1425/84, O.J. 1985 C135/13.
118. This information has been obtained from *Eurofish Report,* No. 181, June 21, 1984, pp. BB/2 *et seq.*
119. *Eurofish Report,* No. 199, February 28, 1985, pp. BB/1 *et seq.* These figures can only be partial ones, it seems. In COM (86) 301 the Commission refers in passing to 17 quota breaches each by the Netherlands and the United Kingdom: regrettably figures are not given for other Member States except Ireland.
120. *Eurofish Report,* No. 207, June 20, 1985, p. BB/1 *et seq.* See, too, COM (86) 301, p. 27.
121. Resolution of December 13, 1985, O.J. 1985 C352/315.
122. For details see R. Churchill, 'Revision of the EEC's Common Fisheries Policy' (1980) 5 E.L.R. 3 at 29.
123. Reg. 2115/77, O.J. 1977 L247/2.
124. Reg. 2527/80, O.J. 1980 L258/1.
125. O.J. 1983 L24/14.
126. Regs. 2931/83, 1637/84, 2178/84, 2664/84, 3625/84 and 3782/85, O.J. 1983 L288/1, 1984 L156/1, 199/1, 253/1 and 335/3, and 1985 L363/28; and Iberian Act of Accession, Annex I, XV, point 9. The Commission has proposed a revised and consolidated version to replace Reg. 171/83: see COM (85) 710.
127. See House of Lords' Select Committee on the European Communities, *The Common Fisheries Policy* HL Paper (1984–85) 39, pp. xiv and 171–6.
128. Commission's Answer to W.Q. 2037/85, O.J. 1986 C182/10.
129. Regs. 2108/84 and 3440/84, O.J. 1984 L194/22 and L318/23.
130. Reg. 3421/84, O.J. 1984 L316/34.
131. Reg. 1866/86, O.J. 1986 L162/1.
132. COM (86) 301, p. 21.
133. 17th, 18th and 19th General Reports on the Activities of the European Communities, pp. 195, 186 and 228 respectively.
134. O.J. S. Edn. 1970 (III) p. 703.
135. O.J. 1976 L20/19.

161

136. Art. 2(3) of Reg. 101/76. In the *Irish Fisheries* case the European Court decisively rejected the Irish Government's far-fetched suggestion that the principle of equal access applied only to the zones in existence at the date Reg. 101/76 was adopted: *op. cit.* in n. 8, at pp. 446 and 513–514 respectively.

137. Dec. 86/283, O.J. 1986 L175/1, Art. 176, replacing similar provisions in earlier Decs. For a full discussion of the equivalent provision in an earlier Dec., see T.C. Hartley, *EEC Immigration Law,* Amsterdam, 1978, pp. 30–37.

138. Second Lomé Convention, Art. 160, O.J. 1980 L347/1; Third Lomé Convention, Art. 252, O.J. 1986 L86/1.

139. On this point, see A.E. Bredimas, 'The Common Shipping Policy of the EEC' (1981) 18 C.M.L. Rev. 9 at 21–22.

140. H.C. Deb., March 7, 1983, cols. 645–646.

141. As long ago as 1976 concern was expressed about the possible consequences of the Merchant Shipping Act on the ownership of British fishing vessels. In the debates in the House of Lords on the Fishery Limits Act (which extended the United Kingdom's fishery limits to 200 miles), Lord Kennet introduced an amendment aimed at ensuring that the beneficial owners as well as the legal owners of U.K. fishing vessels were British. Lord Kennet withdrew his amendment on being told that the Department of Trade was then currently reviewing the whole question of vessel registration criteria (H.L. Deb., December 21, 1976, cols. 1231–1235). Whether such a review was completed the writer does not know, but if it was, it seems that its conclusions must either have been complacent or not acted upon.

142. British Fishing Boats Order 1983. S.I. 1983: 482.

143. *Op. cit.* in n. 140, cols. 647 and 676. Although the Commission has examined the situation to see whether action at the Community level is desirable (see its Answer to W.Q. 282/83, O.J. 1983 C212/30), it has not (yet) made any proposal for Community action. It is also of interest to note that in its original proposals of 1966 on the basic principles of a Common Fisheries Policy, the Commission had suggested that national rules relating to the nationality of vessels should be harmonised. See J.O. 1967 p. 876.

144. *Op. cit.* in n. 140, col. 674 and H.L. Deb., March 15, 1983, col. 669.

145. The question of the compatibility of this Irish legislation with Community law is currently before the European Court under Art. 177 proceedings: see Case 223/86, *Pesca Valentia Ltd v. Minister for Fisheries and Forestry, Ireland* O.J. 1986 C242/8.

146. H.C. Deb., December 9, 1985, W.A. col. 482.

147. This expression presumably covers the territories to which the Common Fisheries Policy applies. The requirement of registration in one of these territories is necessary, because if the right of equal access applied simply to vessels flying the flag of a Member State, this would mean that vessels registered in the Faroes and Greenland or a French overseas territory (i.e. an Annex IV territory), which fly the Danish and French flags respectively, would have a right of equal access.

148. Curiously, however, Reg. 170/83, which continues certain derogations to the equal access principle, cites only Art. 43 as its legal basis.

149. Vignes takes a broader view, and says that fishing concerns the exercise of an economic activity, a matter which by Art. 2 of the EEC Treaty is within the Community's sphere of application: see D. Vignes, 'La réglementation de la pêche dans le marché commun au regard du droit communautaire et du droit international' [1970] A.F.D.I. 829 at 834–5.

150. *Ibid.,* p. 835.

151. *Op. cit.* in n. 8, pp. 451 and 517 respectively. The Court took a similar view in *Minister for Fisheries v. Schonenberg, op. cit.* in n. 85, and in *Commission v. United Kingdom, op. cit.* in n. 19, pp. 1075 and 572 respectively.

152. On this point, see further D. Vignes, 'The Problem of Access to the European Economic

Community's Fishing Zone as the Cornerstone for the Adoption of a Common Fisheries Policy' in C.L. Rozakis and C.A. Stephanou (eds.), *The New Law of the Sea,* Amsterdam, 1983, p. 83 at 89.

153. In the negotiations concerning the Community's first enlargement the Norwegian Government argued very strongly, but with no success, that the regime of equal access should be replaced by one based on freedom of establishment. See (1971) 8 C.M.L. Rev. 509.

154. Although the Structural Reg. cites Art. 235 as one of its legal bases, the discussion here and earlier in this Chapter suggests that it was in fact superfluous to do so. However, the European Court, in Case 8/73, *Hauptzollamt Bremerhaven v. Massey Ferguson GmbH* [1973] E.C.R. 897, suggested that even if a reg. can be based on other provisions of the Treaty, the Council is nevertheless entitled to base a reg. on Art. 235 in the interests of legal certainty. Since the use of Arts. 7, 42 and 43 as the legal bases of the Structural Reg. is not wholly free of difficulties, the Court's approach in the above case would suggest that the Council was justified in citing Art. 235 as an additional legal basis for the Structural Reg. in the interests of legal certainty.

155. See U. Everling, *The Right of Establishment in the Common Market,* Chicago, 1964, pp. 165–166; and K. Winkel, 'Equal Access of Community Fishermen to Member State Fishing Grounds' (1977) 14 C.M.L. Rev. 329.

156. The requirement for a transaction between two separate persons has been stressed by the European Court: see, for example, Joined Cases 286/82 and 26/83, *Luisi and Carbone v. Ministero del Tesoro* [1984] E.C.R. 377 at 401–3; [1985] 3 C.M.L.R. 52 at 76–8.

157. The view of the Commission in its *Principes de base pour une politique commune dans le secteur de la pêche,* J.O. 1967 p. 862 at 865.

158. The idea of a linkage between access to fishing grounds and access to markets was fairly widespread in Western Europe in the early 1960s: see E.D. Brown, 'British Fisheries and the Common Market' (1972) 25 *Current Legal Problems* 37 at 46–47 and 53; and D.H.N. Johnson, 'European Fishery Limits' in British Institute of International and Comparative Law, *Developments in the Law of the Sea 1958–64,* London, 1965, p. 48 at 56–61.

159. But note that the equal access principle is found in the Benelux Treaty, *op. cit.* in n. 172. Under Art. 61(1)(d) of the Treaty the parties may reserve fishing in their internal waters to their nationals.

160. It is also worth noting that Regulation 2141/70 provided that by way of exception to the equal access principle a three-mile zone could be reserved for local inshore fishermen for a five-year period. However, this provision required implementing action to be taken by the Council to be effective: since no such action was ever taken, the provision had in practice no application.

161. At the time of writing, the following Member States – at least – had established a 12-mile zone: Denmark and the Federal Republic of Germany (see *Bull. E.C.* 1983 No. 5, p. 44); France (Arrêtés ministeriels of March 4, 1983, J.O.R.F., March 18, 1983, pp. 2870–1); Ireland (*Bull. E.C.* 1984 No. 4, p. 43); Italy (Decree of the Minister for the Merchant Navy of November 20, 1984, G.U. No. 344 of December 15, 1984); Netherlands (*Bull. E.C.* 1983 No. 10, p. 46); and the United Kingdom (Fishing Boats (European Economic Community) Designation Order 1983, S.I. 1983 No. 253).

162. In fact many vessels fishing in the 12-mile zone, at least in the United Kingdom, are not inshore vessels at all: see House of Lords Select Committee on the European Communities, *EEC Fisheries Policy* H.L. Paper (1979–80) 351, p. 65.

163. Fishing Boats (European Economic Community) Designation Orders 1972 and 1983, S.I. 1972 No. 2026 and 1983 No. 253.

164. Notice No. 57 of February 7, 1973 on the Relaxation of Nationality Requirements etc. in Fisheries Legislation, Art. 1, *Lovtidende,* Pt. A. 1973, p. 71.

165. European Communities (Sea Fisheries) Regulations, 1973, S.I. 1973 No. 1. Replaced by the European Communities (Fishery Limits) Regulations, 1973, S.I. 1973 No. 127.

166. Decrees of February 21, 1975, May 8, 1981 and November 20, 1984, G.U. No. 60 of March 4, 1975, No. 140 of May 23, 1981 and No. 344 of December 15, 1984.

167. I.e. metropolitan Denmark and the Faroes.

168. The view just put forward is, however, rather contradicted by two members of the Commission writing in a personal capacity. Booss (of the Directorate-General for Fisheries) states bluntly that the 12-mile zone is a national zone, while Sack (of the Legal Service) says that although the 12-mile zone is not strictly speaking a national zone, it is often so treated by Member States because of the difficulty of defining clearly the vessels which are the beneficiaries of the zone. See D. Booss, 'La politique commune de la pêche: quelques aspects juridiques' (1983) 269 R.M.C. 404 at 410, and J. Sack, 'La nouvelle politique commune de la pêche' (1983) 19 C.D.E. 437 at 439.

169. Denmark – Federal Republic of Germany. Agreement concerning Common Fishing in the Inner Flensborg Fjord, May 29, 1958. 684 U.N.T.S. 119. Under the Agreement local fishermen from Denmark and West Germany have the right to fish in each other's waters in the Flensborg Fjord.

170. Federal Republic of Germany – Netherlands. Treaty concerning Arrangements for Co-Operation in the Ems Estuary, April 8, 1960, Art. 41. 509 U.N.T.S. 64. Under the Treaty Dutch fishermen have the right to fish along the German shores of the Ems-Dollard estuary.

171. M. Leigh, *European Integration and the Common Fisheries Policy,* Beckenham, 1983, pp. 86–7.

172. Treaty instituting the Benelux Economic Union, 1958, 381 U.N.T.S. 165, Art. 2. The right did not become effective until 1965. See Art. 3 of the Convention containing the Transitional Provisions, 381 U.N.T.S. 283.

173. According to Booss, *op. cit.* in n. 168, p. 411, there is a statement in the Council minutes in which the Council and Commission declare that Annex I could be amended at any time following a request from the Member States directly concerned, by the Council adopting a regulation on the proposal of the Commission.

174. The details of this licensing system are set out in Reg. 2166/83, O.J. 1983 L206/71.

175. While the reasons given by the Community for the Orkney/Shetland box are conservation needs and the interests of local fishermen, a more cynical view would be that the box is largely symbolic. First, the number of licences available for vessels over 26 metres is greater than the number of such vessels fishing there before the box was established (see House of Lords Select Committee on the European Communities, *The Common Fisheries Policy* H.L. Paper (1984–85) 39, pp. 171 and 177). Secondly, no effort is made to control fishing by vessels under 26 metres, which in practice catch the largest proportion of demersal species in the box.

176. Reg. 3780/85, O.J. 1985 L363/24. The number of tuna vessels which can fish with troll line is, however, unlimited.

177. Regs. 3778 and 3779/85, O.J. 1985 L363/20 and 22. Tuna fishing in some areas is unrestricted.

178. Dec. 78/640, O.J. 1978 L211/34. In 1982 the Dec. was amended by extending the time limit for contributions to Ireland to December 31, 1984: Dec. 82/892, O.J. 1982 L378/55. For action taken under this measure, see Commission's Answer to W.Q. 2000/83, O.J. 1984 C144/15. In spite of this assistance Ireland's performance in inspection at sea was regarded by the Commission in June 1986 as 'disappointing': see COM (86) 301, p. 15.

179. Reg. 753/80, O.J. 1980 L84/33.

180. Reg. 2057/82, 1982 L220/1, as amended by Regs. 1729/83 and 3723/85, O.J. 1983 L169/14 and 1985 L361/42. The Reg. came into force on January 1, 1983.

181. Detailed rules on the information to be sent by Member States to the Commission con-

cerning the results of their inspections are set out in Reg. 3561/85, O.J. 1985 L339/29.

182. Detailed rules as to how log books are to be completed are set out in implementing Commission Reg. 2807/83, O.J. 1983 L270/1. Although Reg. 2057/82 came into force at the beginning of 1983, the Commission did not succeed in distributing Community log books until the end of 1984, and the system of Community log books did not become operational until April 1, 1985: see O.J. 1985 L24/21.

183. COM (85) 490.

184. Reg. 3723/85, *op. cit.* in n. 180.

185. *R. v. Kirk, op. cit.* in n. 68.

186. See E.P. Doc A2–34/85, p. 11.

187. O.J. 1986 C245/5.

188. COM (86) 301.

189. COM (86) 474; largely reproduced in O.J. 1986 C245/5.

190. Reg. 3421/84, O.J. 1984 L316/34.

191. O.J. 1985 L336/20.

192. Reg. 3715/85, O.J. 1985 L360/1.

193. Regs. 3716 and 3719/85, O.J. 1985 L360/7 and 26.

194. Reg. 3717/85, O.J. 1985 L360/14, as amended by Reg. 1482/86, O.J. 1986 L130/21.

195. Reg. 3718/85, O.J. 1985 L360/20, as amended by Reg. 1483/86, O.J. 1986 L130/23.

196. O.J. 1985 L363/26.

197. See, e.g., Case 121/76, *Moli v. Commission* [1977] E.C.R. 1971 and Case 85/76, *Hoffman La Roche v. Commission* [1979] E.C.R. 461; [1979] 3 C.M.L.R. 211. See further R.R. Churchill and N.G. Foster, 'The Spanish Fishermen's Cases – the European Court of Justice at Sea?' (at present unpublished), pp. 33–36.

198. Case 55/86, *ARPOSOL v. Council,* O.J. 1986 C122/3 and C139/6.

199. COM (86) 301, p. 1.

200. For fuller development of this point, see G.N. Munro, 'Fisheries Enforcement: the United Kingdom Experience' in OECD, *op. cit.* in n. 105, p. 39; P.J. Derham, 'The Implementation and Enforcement of Fisheries Legislation' in G. Ulfstein, P. Andersen and R. Churchill (eds.), *Proceedings of the European Workshop on the Regulation of Fisheries* (forthcoming); and D.B. Thomson, 'Fishermen and Fisheries Management' in FAO, *op. cit.* in n. 94, Supp. 2 (1985), p. 21.

201. For the problems involved in enforcing the regulations at sea, see Derham, *op. cit.* For an excellent analysis of the general problems involved in enforcing quota regulations, see P.J. Derham, 'The Problems of Quota Management in the European Community Concept' in FAO, *op. cit.* in n. 94, Supp. 3 (1985), p. 241.

202. Munro, *op. cit.,* p. 43.

203. The European Parliament has called for Community centres of co-ordination – see its Resolution of May 13, 1982, O.J. 1982 C149/94. In general the European Parliament has pushed – so far rather unsuccessfully – for a much more communautaire system of enforcement than at present exists: e.g. it has suggested a Community coastguard service and that all fines for breaches of fishing regulations should go directly into the Community's 'own resources'. See its Resolution of January 19, 1979, O.J. 1979 C39/62. See also its Resolution of December 13, 1985, O.J. 1985 C352/310, and EP Doc A2–162/85.

204. For further information on the work of ICES, see H. Tambs-Lyche, 'Monitoring Fish Stocks. The Role of ICES in the North-East Atlantic' (1978) 2 *Marine Policy* 127; and K. Hoydal, 'ICES Procedures in Formulating Management Advice' in FAO, *op. cit.* in n. 94, Supp. 3 (1985), p. 215.

205. O.J. 1980 C243/12, as amended by COM (81) 25.

206. O.J. 1983 C28/1 at p. 2.

207. COM (85) 590 (partially reproduced in O.J. 1985 C312/5).

208. As the Economic and Social Committee has also urged: see its Own-Initiative Opinion of February 27, 1985, O.J. 1985 C104/12.

209. The European Parliament has called for Community legislation to 'prevent disputes and lost catches arising from incompatible fishing methods by designating areas open only to long-liners and trawlers respectively': see its Resolution of December 13, 1985, O.J. 1985 C352/310.

210. 1977 U.K.T.S. 40.

211. For a fuller account of the conflicts between fishing and the offshore oil and gas industry and the way such conflicts are resolved in English law, see J.P. Grant, 'The Conflict between the Fishing and Oil Industries in the North Sea: A Case Study' (1979) 4 *Ocean Management* 137 and R.R. Churchill, 'The Conflict between Oil and Fisheries: A Survey of Norwegian and United Kingdom Law and Practice' in Ulfstein, Andersen and Churchill (eds.), *op. cit.* in n. 200.

212. For an account of Community legislation on marine pollution, see D.J. Cusine and J.P. Grant (eds.), *The Impact of Marine Pollution,* London, 1980, pp. 253–292; C.M. Mason (ed.), *The Effective Management of Resources,* London, 1979, pp. 202–211; and P.W. Birnie, 'EEC Environmental Policy' in E.D. Brown and R.R. Churchill (eds.), *The UN Convention on the Law of the Sea: Impact and Implementation* (forthcoming). For a survey of Member States' legislation, see J. McLoughlin, *The Law and Practice relating to Pollution Control in the Member States of the European Communities: A Comparative Survey,* London, 2nd edition, 1982, pp. 182–228.

213. In general, management measures ought to take more account of the needs of the market. For example, the complete ban on herring fishing for several years, though successful in preventing collapse of the stock, was arguably too drastic. When herring fishing reopened, much of the human consumption market for herring had gone and many processors had gone out of business or converted processing plant to other species. Allowing a small, but strictly controlled, catch, instead of a complete ban, would have avoided these consequences (although it would probably have taken longer to build up herring stocks). For a full discussion of the relationship between management measures and marketing, see I. Mac-Sween, 'The Interaction between Fisheries Management and the Marketing of Fish' in FAO, *op. cit.* in n. 94, Supp. 2 (1985), p. 9.

214. For further discussion of these points, see Derham, *op. cit.* in n. 201.

215. See the European Parliament's Resolutions of February 10, 1983 and March 16, 1984, O.J. 1983 C68/74 and 1984 C104/121; and the Economic and Social Committee's Own-Initiative Opinion of February 27, 1985, O.J. 1985 C104/12. Furthermore, according to *Eurofish Report,* No. 198, February 14, 1985, p. BB/3, the Scientific and Technical Committee for Fisheries published a report on fisheries management in the Mediterranean in December 1984.

216. According to EP Doc A2–162/85, p. 15.

CHAPTER 5

External relations in fisheries management matters

The previous Chapter looked at the internal aspects of Community fisheries management, that is the regulation by the Community institutions of fishing by Community vessels in Community waters. However, Community fisheries management is not and cannot be purely an internal affair: the regulation of fishing in Community waters and of fishing by Community vessels inevitably also involves third States. Such involvement may arise in a number of ways. The vessels of third States may wish to fish in Community waters: conversely Community vessels may desire access to the waters of third States. Secondly, the Community naturally wishes to be represented in any international fisheries commission which has management responsibilities in areas traditionally fished by Community vessels. Thirdly, many fish stocks ignore man-made jurisdictional boundaries and migrate between Community waters and the waters of third States: the successful management of such stocks obviously demands co-operation between the Community and the third States concerned. It is these external questions in relation to fisheries management with which this Chapter is concerned. It will examine successively the three matters just mentioned – the access of vessels from third States to Community waters and the access of Community vessels to the waters of third States; Community membership of international fisheries commissions; and the management of joint stocks.[1] Since all these matters require the creation of treaty relationships between the Community and various third States, it is necessary to begin by looking at the Community's treaty-making powers in relation to fisheries.

1. THE COMMUNITY'S TREATY-MAKING POWERS IN RELATION TO FISHERIES

The Community's treaty-making powers are of two kinds – those expressly conferred by the EEC Treaty and those which may be implied from the Treaty. The only express treaty-making power which is in any way relevant to fisheries is Article 113 of the EEC Treaty. This provision gives the Community the competence to enter into agreements relating to trade and other aspects of the common commercial policy. Clearly, therefore, Article 113 gives the Community the power to enter into agreements with third States relating to trade in fishery products. In the *Kramer* case[2] the Commission argued that Article 113 also gave the Community the competence to negotiate international agreements on quotas and fishing effort limitation, since although such matters were concerned with conservation, they also had an economic aspect which brought them within the sphere of the common commercial policy. The Court by implication rejected this argument, since it said that the Community's treaty-making competence in relation to fisheries was based on implied powers.

Thus, in the absence of any express treaty-making powers,[3] the Community has had to rely on implied treaty-making powers in order to enter into agreements relating to the management and regulation of fisheries. The idea that treaty-making powers can be implied from the EEC Treaty is one that has been developed by the European Court. The doctrine was first enunciated by the Court in the *ERTA* case,[4] where it held that 'in its external relations the Community enjoys the capacity to establish contractual links with third countries over the whole field of objectives defined in Part One of the Treaty.'[5] Apart from express powers, treaty-making power may 'flow from other provisions of the Treaty and from measures adopted, within the framework of these provisions, by the Community institutions.'[6] That these implied powers apply to fisheries was affirmed by the Court in the *Kramer* case. Having examined Articles 38–46 of the EEC Treaty, Regulations 2141 and 2142/70 and Article 102 of the Act of Accession, the Court concluded that 'the Community has at its disposal, on the internal level, the power to take any measures for the conservation of the biological resources of the sea.' It follows from this internal power that 'the Community has authority to enter into international commitments for the conservation of the resources of the sea.'[7] This view of the Court has been followed by the Council which, in its Hague Resolution of November 3, 1976,[8] agreed that fishing by vessels of third States in Community waters and fishing by Community vessels in the waters of third States should be governed by agreements between the Community and the third States concerned; and it instructed the Commission to begin negotiating such agreements.

Having established that the Community has implied treaty-making powers

in relation to fisheries, it is necessary to consider three further questions:
1. When did the Community obtain this treaty-making power?
2. What is its scope *ratione materiae*?
3. Is it an exclusively Community power?
As to the first question, when did the Community obtain its treaty-making power in relation to fisheries, one must begin by considering the *ERTA* case. In that case the Court held that the Community did not obtain implied treaty-making powers until it had actually adopted its own internal rules relating to the subject matter of the proposed treaty. This view was followed, perhaps somewhat ambiguously, in the *Kramer* case. However, in the later *Rhine* case,[9] the Court has made a significant and potentially far-reaching modification to its original approach. In the *ERTA* and *Kramer* cases the Court had held that:

> whenever Community law has created for the institutions of the Community powers within its internal system for the purpose of attaining a specific objective, the Community has the authority to enter into the international commitments necessary for the attainment of that objective,

particularly in

> all cases in which internal power has already been used to adopt measures which come within the attainment of common policies.[10]

In the *Rhine* case, however, the Court went on to add that it is 'not limited to that eventuality'. Community treaty-making power 'flows by implication from the provision of the Treaty creating the internal power and in so far as the participation of the Community in the international agreement is . . . necessary for the attainment of one of the objectives of the Community.'[11] In other words, it is not essential that the Community should have adopted its own internal rules on a particular subject before it becomes a party to a treaty relating to the same matter.

How do these principles apply to fisheries? From the *ERTA* and *Kramer* cases it would seem that the Community could not enter into a treaty relating to fisheries conservation until it had actually adopted its own internal rules relating to fisheries conservation: in the *Kramer* case the Court appears to suggest that the Community does not obtain treaty-making powers until the Council has adopted measues under Article 102 of the Act of Accession. However, if one applies the principles in the later *Rhine* case, treaty-making powers could arise before measures are adopted under Article 102. Such powers flow 'by implication from the provisions of the Treaty creating the internal power' to take fishery conservation measures, viz. Article 43 of the

EEC Treaty and possibly also Article 102 of the Act of Accession. However, for there to be treaty-making powers, it must also, according to the *Rhine* case, be necessary for the Community to participate in the treaty in order to achieve one of the objectives of the Community. As was seen in Chapter 2, the objectives of the Community include the adoption of a common agricultural (fisheries) policy (see Article 3(d) of the EEC Treaty). According to the principles of the *Rhine* case, therefore, it would seem that the Community has had treaty-making powers in relation to fisheries at any time since the entry into force of the EEC Treaty (when the necessary internal power in the shape of Article 43 was created) when it has been necessary for the Community to enter into a fisheries agreement in order to achieve one of the objectives of the Community (i.e. the adoption of a common agricultural (fisheries) policy). It has not been necessary for the Community to adopt internal fishery measures before obtaining treaty-making powers. The actual practice of the Community accords with this view, since fisheries agreements were negotiated, and the first of them signed, before the Council had adopted any internal Community fishery management measures.

The second question, what is the scope *ratione materiae* of the Community's implied treaty-making powers in relation to fisheries, can be answered more shortly. The *ERTA, Kramer* and *Rhine* cases all assume that the scope *ratione materiae* of implied treaty-making powers corresponds to the scope of the internal powers from which the former powers flow. Thus, in relation to fisheries, the implied treaty-making powers correspond to the scope of Article 43 of the EEC Treaty. As was seen in the last Chapter, this Article is broadly enough framed to cover virtually any regulation of fisheries, not just conservation measures. Thus the Community's treaty-making powers cover all aspects of fisheries regulation, and not merely, as the Court suggested in the *Kramer* case, conservation matters. Again the practice of the Community bears out this view: the fisheries agreements into which the Community has so far entered deal with much more than simply conservation.

We must now consider whether the Community's treaty-making powers in relation to fisheries are exclusive; in other words, whether EEC Member States still retain any competence in this area. In the *ERTA* case the Court said that:

each time the Community, with a view to implementing a common policy envisaged by the Treaty, adopts provisions laying down common rules ... the Member States no longer have the right, acting individually or even collectively, to undertake obligations with third countries which affect those rules. As and when such common rules come into being, the Community alone is in a position to assume and carry out contractual obligations towards third countries affecting the whole sphere of application of the Community legal system.[12]

Later in its judgment, the Court observed that:

> ... These Community powers [to negotiate and conclude the ERTA Agreement] exclude the possibility of concurrent powers on the part of Member States, since any steps taken outside the framework of the Community institutions would be incompatible within the unity of the Common Market and the uniform application of Community Law.[13]

The Court applied these principles in the *Kramer* case, and held that since the Council had not adopted common fisheries measures at the time in question, Member States retained their competence to enter into international fisheries agreements. This competence only lasted, however, as long as the Council had not acted (and under Article 102 of the Act of Accession the Council was under an obligation to act before the end of 1978, although as was seen in the last Chapter, that obligation was not in fact observed).

Since the *Rhine* case, however, there is reason to doubt whether the principles enunciated in the *ERTA* and *Kramer* cases still epresent the correct legal position. The reason for this is as follows. In the *ERTA* and *Kramer* cases the Court said that Community rules must be adopted before the Community has treaty-making powers: once such rules have been adopted, however, the Member States no longer have the competence to conclude treaties in the area in question. In the *Rhine* case the Court says that it is not necessary for Community rules to be adopted in order for the Community to have treaty-making powers. Could one therefore argue that by analogy it is not necessary for Community rules to be adopted before the Member States lose their competence to conclude treaties? In other words, this would amount to saying that as soon as the Community in theory obtains treaty-making powers, Member States lose their own powers. One of the difficulties with this view is the uncertainty that it produces. As we have seen, it is in practice difficult under the *Rhine* doctrine to say exactly at what point the Community assumed treaty-making powers. It would therefore be correspondingly difficult to know at what point Member States lost their treaty-making powers. The uncertainties produced by the *Rhine* case have led writers to formulate the answer to the question of when the Community's treaty-making powers become exclusive in somewhat different ways. Thus Hartley, for example, suggests that the Community obtains exclusive competence once it has taken action either internally (i.e. by the adoption of Community legislation) or externally (i.e. by concluding a treaty) in relation to the subject matter in question.[14] Louis and Brückner, perhaps taking the *Rhine* case more into account, argue that the Community's competence is exclusive when common rules have been adopted or when external Community action appears necessary 'pour mettre en oeuvre une compétence que le traité reconnaît aux institutions.'[15]

Applied to fisheries, these views produce slightly different answers to the question of when the Community became exclusively competent to act on the external plane. According to Hartley's view, the competence of the Community became exclusive when the Community began exercising its powers in relation to the conservation and management of fisheries. On both the internal and external plane this happened in the early part of 1977 when the Council adopted various – though admittedly temporary – conservation measures and the Community signed a number of agreements (with the U.S.A., Sweden and the Faroes) on the access of fishermen to 200-mile zones. On the other hand, according to the view put forward by Louis and Brückner, the Community's competence became exclusive in November 1976 when the Council recognised the need for the Community to negotiate fisheries agreements in its Hague Resolution.[16] Today, of course, the question of when the Community became exclusively competent is academic – there is no doubt that the Community is, and has been for several years, exclusively competent to enter into treaties for the regulation and management of fisheries, although one slight uncertainty remains. This is whether the Community has exclusive treaty-making powers in relation to all matters connected with fisheries. Supposing in relation to an aspect of fisheries for which there were no Community internal rules and no Community external action had been taken or was contemplated, e.g. the resolution of gear conflicts or scientific research, would the Member States not have any treaty-making capacity? In the light of the Court's case law, it is at least arguable that they would retain such capacity, provided that its exercise did not affect any existing Community rules.

In general, Member States have in practice respected the Community's exclusive competence to conclude treaties in the field of fisheries. Since early 1977 only two instances have come to the writer's notice where a Member State has concluded a fisheries treaty with a third State: these are a treaty between France and Equatorial Guinea, signed in September 1982, on the access of French tuna vessels to the waters of Equatorial Guinea;[17] and a treaty of 1984 between France and Monaco, providing for the reciprocal access of each party's vessels to the territorial waters of the other party.[18] Since these treaties represent a denial, albeit an isolated one, of the Community's exclusive competence in respect of an area of fisheries where there can be no doubt that the Community's competence is exclusive, they amount to a breach of Community law by France.

Although the Community's treaty-making competence is in principle exclusive as far as fisheries are concerned, there may in practice be situations where the Member States retain a treaty-making competence which is exercised jointly with that of the Community. Under general Community law, where a treaty covers both matters which fall within the Community's competence and matters outside its competence, as for example the United Nations Convention on the Law of the Sea does, both the Community and the individual Member States can – and indeed must – become parties to the treaty in question. Such treaties are known as mixed agreements. As will be seen later, there are one or two treaties dealing both with fisheries and with other matters where the Community does not have treaty-making competence, where the mixed agreement procedure has had to be used.

A temporary exception to the principle of Community exclusivity in relation to fisheries treaties has been granted to Portugal and Spain by the Iberian Act of Accession. While in principle Portugal and Spain have accepted Community exclusivity and are included in and bound by the fisheries treaties which the Community has already concluded with third States (Article 4), the existing fisheries agreements which Portugal and Spain have with third States are to continue provisionally (though managed by the Community), until the Council decides what action is to be taken (Articles 167 and 354): such action will presumably be either to incorporate Portugal and Spain into existing agreements with third States (as has already been done in relation to the Community's agreements with Guinea Bissau and Senegal), possibly with some modification, or in cases where the Community does not already have an agreement with the third State concerned, to negotiate an agreement between the Community and such third States.

At this point it is appropriate to say a few words about the procedure by which the Community negotiates, signs and ratifies treaties concerning fisheries.[19] Article 228 of the EEC Treaty provides that treaties are to be negotiated by the Commission and concluded by the Council. Arguably this provision applies only in the area of the Community's express treaty-making powers, but it is generally followed where implied powers are concerned, and certainly has been in the case of fisheries. The treaty-making procedure begins with the Commission requesting a mandate from the Council to negotiate with a particular third State(s) or international organisation. Once it has received its mandate, the Commission begins negotiations, its room for manoeuvre generally being indicated in the mandate. If the negotiations are successful, the treaty will be initialled by the Commission and forwarded to the Council. The latter then consults the European Parliament. Having received the European Parliament's opinion, or sometimes earlier, the Council decides whether to sign the treaty on behalf of the Community. As far as fisheries are concerned, the Council has always signed each treaty negotiated, although, as will be seen, there have frequently been lengthy delays in coming to a decision. Finally, as a separate and subsequent stage, the Council ratifies the treaty, this action being done on the internal Community plane by adopting a regulation or decision.

As well as being a party to treaties in its own right, the Community can also under certain conditions become bound by a treaty to which its Member States are parties but which it itself has neither signed nor ratified. This is the so-called 'substitution principle' (or principle of succession, to use a more familiar international law term), first expounded by the Court in the *International Fruit Company* case.[20] For the principle to apply, and the Community to be bound by a treaty in place of (or perhaps in addition to) its Member States, the following conditions, according to the Court in the *International Fruit Company* case, must be satisfied: (i) the Community must have taken over from its Member States competence relating to the subject matter of the treaty; (ii) the Member States must have been bound by the treaty before the EEC Treaty was signed;[21] (iii) the Member States must desire to bind the Community by the obligations of the treaty; (iv) the EEC's institutions must have acted as though bound by the treaty; (v) third States parties to the treaty must have recognised the transfer of powers from the Member States to the Community; and (vi) it seems that all, or a high proportion of, the Member States must be parties to the treaty in question.[22]

In the *International Fruit Company* case the Court held that these conditions were satisfied in respect of the treaty at issue in that case, GATT. The Court has also applied the substitution principle to one or two other treaties.[23] Are there any fisheries treaties to which the principle might apply? There are in fact 30 or 40 fisheries treaties still in existence between one or more Member States and third States, concluded before the Community obtained exclusive treaty-making powers in relation to fisheries. While clearly all these treaties fulfil condition (i) above, it is unlikely that any of these treaties fulfils the other conditions necessary for the substitution principle to apply.[24]

If the substitution principle does not apply to these 30 or 40 treaties this raises the question of the legal position of these treaties at the present time. There are a number of possible answers to this question. First, some of these treaties have been expressly preserved by the agreements the EEC has concluded with the third States concerned: this has happened in the case of the Community's agreements with Canada, Norway and Sweden. In these cases the Community would seem to be under an obligation to respect the individual Member States' prior treaty obligations, in particular by not legislating contrary to such obligations. Secondly, in one case – that of Spain (prior, obviously, to its accession to the Community) – the EEC-Spain Agreement expressly states that it replaces prior treaties between Spain and individual EEC Member States. Thirdly, in the case of those treaties concluded before the EEC Treaty (or in the case of the six non-original members of the EEC, the date of their entry to the EEC), Article 234 of the EEC Treaty (or Article 5 of the three Acts of Accession) applies. Under these provisions, which reflect general principles of international law, the rights and obligations arising from agreements concluded before the EEC Treaty (or in the case of the new Member States, the Acts of Accession) are not 'affected by the provisions of' the EEC Treaty: on the other hand, 'to the extent that such agreements are not compatible with [the EEC] Treaty, the Member State or States concerned shall take all appropriate steps to eliminate the incompatibilities established'. It is not unreasonable to suppose that compatibility relates not only to the EEC Treaty as such, but also to measures taken under the Treaty. In *Burgoa* the Court said that Article 234 also implies:

> a duty on the part of the institutions of the Community not to impede the performance of the obligations of Member States which stem from a prior agreement. However, that duty of the Community institutions is directed only to permitting the Member State concerned to perform its obligations under the prior agreement and does not bind the Community as regards the non-member country in question.[25]

Finally, in the case of fisheries agreements concluded since the entry into force of the EEC Treaty or the Acts of Accession but before the Community obtained exclusive treaty-making powers in relation to fisheries (other than those coming in the first two categories above), it would seem that such agreements continue in force: but where any such agreement is incompatible with Community fishery measures, it would seem to follow from the obligations contained in Article 5 of the EEC Treaty that the Member State concerned is under an obligation to remove any such incompatibilities. A more radical approach has, however, been suggested by the European Court. In *Arbelaiz-Emazabel,* where a Spanish fisherman prosecuted for fishing in French waters before the entry into force of the EEC-Spain Agreement sought to rely on a Franco-Spanish Agreement of 1967 which gave Spanish vessels the right to fish in the area concerned, the Court held that the fishing relations which had developed between the Community and Spain 'replaced the prior international obligations existing between certain Member States, such as France, and Spain.'[26] The Court's doctrine here could only be justified if the EEC-Spain Agreement were regarded as applying retrospectively, or if the earlier treaty had terminated by reason of a fundamental change of circumstances or the emergence of a new rule of customary international law. None of these possibilities seems likely.[27]

2. ACCESS OF FISHING VESSELS FROM THIRD STATES TO COMMUNITY WATERS AND ACCESS OF COMMUNITY FISHING VESSELS TO THE WATERS OF THIRD STATES[28]

It was pointed out in Chapter 1 that the UN Convention on the Law of the Sea provides that within its 200-mile fishery or economic zone the coastal State is to make available to third States that part of the total allowable catch which its own vessels are unable to harvest. Since the Community is to be considered for fisheries purposes as a single coastal State, the general trend to extend fishing limits to 200 miles in the late 1970s meant that the Community was concerned with obtaining access for Community fishermen to any surpluses that might be available within 200-mile limits in areas where Community fishermen had traditionally fished before the extension of such limits. Conversely, the Community should have made available to third States any surpluses available in the 200-mile limits of its Member States. In practice, it was unlikely that there would ever be any surpluses in Community waters, since Community vessels were more than capable of taking the whole of the total allowable catch. Nevertheless the Community was interested in giving some access to its waters to the vessels of third States whose waters had traditionally been important for Community fishermen in order to try to improve the chances of access for Community fishermen to the waters of those States. The latter was desirable for two reasons: first, to minimise the dislocation suffered by the Community's distant-water fleets as a result of the world-wide trend to 200-mile limits, and secondly, to maintain access to species which might not be found, or which might not be so plentiful, in Community waters.

This group of third States will be described as reciprocal fisheries States. The arrangements that have been concluded with such States will be examined in some detail. First, however, it is necessary to look at those non-reciprocal fisheries States
(i) to whose waters Community fishermen desired to have access and
(ii) whose vessels aspired to access in Community waters.

(i) *Access of Community fishermen to non-reciprocal third States' waters*

There are four main areas, of a non-reciprocal nature, where Community fishermen have traditionally fished and where continued access has been obtained or sought. These areas are the North-West Atlantic; West Africa and the South-West Indian Ocean; the Mediterranean; and the Caribbean. Each area will be considered in turn.

North-West Atlantic. The Community has concluded fisheries agreements for the access of its vessels (in practice it is mainly French, German and to a lesser extent British and Italian vessels that are involved) with each of the three countries of the North-West Atlantic – the U.S.A.,[29] Canada and Greenland (after its withdrawal from the EEC). The agreement with the U.S.A.[30] is the standard type of agreement that the United States has concluded with third States wishing to fish in its waters. The Agreement permits Community vessels to fish under licence in the U.S.A.'s 200-mile fishing zone for a portion of any surpluses that may be available, this portion to be determined by the U.S.A.

each year.[31] Under the 1984 successor to the original agreement, continued Community access to the U.S.A.'s zone is conditional on the Community facilitating access for US fishery products to Community markets. This again is in accordance with recent US practice relating to foreign fishing in its waters, following the introduction of its so-called 'fish and chips' policy.

Canada was originally regarded as a reciprocal fisheries State, but with its unwillingness to regard St. Pierre et Miquelon as generating a fishing zone of any real size in the absence of a boundary agreement with France and the withdrawal of Greenland from the EEC in 1985, Canada has no fisheries interest in Community waters apart from some small-scale local fisheries off St. Pierre et Miquelon (which are regulated under a 1972 agreement between France and Canada.[32]). A short-term agreement[33] between Canada and the Community providing for fishing by Community vessels in Canadian waters was signed in 1979, and replaced by a long-term agreement in 1981.[34] Under the latter Community vessels are permitted to fish under licence in Canadian waters for a portion of the surplus catch. In reality the reference to the surplus is purely notional, because a second agreement[35] fixes the quotas to be awarded to the Community each year: moreover, these quotas are contingent upon the Community continuing to maintain the tariff quotas for Canadian fishery exports to the Community specified in the agreement. In their first two years the 1981 agreements did not work well, essentially because the Community failed to import the quantities of fishery products specified in the agreements, whereupon Canada reduced Community fishing in Canadian waters.[36] To try to remedy the situation, a further modifying agreement was concluded in 1983[37] and this appears to have made fisheries relations between Canada and the Community much less strained.

As noted earlier, Greenland left the EEC in 1985. Among the arrangements governing its withdrawal is a fisheries agreement.[38] This Agreement permits Community fishermen to fish under licence in Greenland waters for specified tonnages of fish in return for the payment of financial compensation by the Community and the admission of fishery exports from Greenland free of customs duties. The tonnages for which the Community may fish are fixed by a Protocol to the Agreement. It is fairly safe to assume that the Community's quotas will, for most stocks in most years, come from that part of the TAC which is surplus to the harvesting capacity of the indigenous population of Greenland. In addition to the tonnages guaranteed in the Protocol, the Community is also to have priority access to that part of the TAC which exceeds Greenland's harvesting capacity and the amounts already allocated to the Community in the Agreement.

West Africa and the South-West Indian Ocean. In these regions the Community's main, but not exclusive, interest is in tuna. Access agreements have been signed with Senegal,[39] Guinea-Bissau,[40], Guinea,[41] Equatorial Guinea,[42] Sao Tome e Principe,[43] Seychelles[44] and Madagascar.[45] All these agreements are broadly similar. They permit a limited number of Community vessels to fish under licence in the 200-mile zones of the above-mentioned States. The agreements do not say whether the amount of fish which the Community can catch (which is generally not precisely specified) comes from the surplus in these States' zones, but it is likely that this is the case. The conditions on which Community vessels have access include an obligation on these vessels to land part or all of their catches in the ports of, and to employ as crew fishermen from, the third States concerned. In return for the access described, the Community pays financial compensation to each of the States concerned. This compensation is used for financing projects connected with fishing and fisheries research, and is in addition both to licence fees and to any financial and technical aid under the Lomé Conventions. Although the obligations on the Community and Community vessels may appear rather onerous,[46] it is not uncommon to find such obligations contained in fisheries agreements between developed and developing countries, and indeed they are envisaged both by the UN Convention on the Law of the Sea and by the second and third Lomé Conventions which the EEC has concluded with some 66 developing States of Africa, the Caribbean and Pacific.[47]

In addition to the States mentioned above, the Community has also held negotiations on access arrangements for Community vessels with a number of other African States – Mauritania, Gambia, Sierra Leone, Gabon, Cape Verde, Congo, Angola and Mauritius. At the time of writing none of these negotiations seemed likely to lead to agreements being concluded in the near future. However, with the accession of Portugal and Spain to the Community, the need for such agreements has intensified as Portugal and Spain have agreements with Angola, Cape Verde and Mauritania. Furthermore, the Community will need to widen its negotiations to include Morocco, Mozambique and South Africa, with each of which Portugal and Spain have fisheries agreements. It may prove difficult to adjust Portuguese and Spanish agreements to Community agreements as the former are often more complex than the existing Community agreements and offer greater financial compensation.

Mediterranean. In the Mediterranean there are two States to whose waters Community (in practice Italian) fishermen are interested in having access – Tunisia and Yugoslavia. Some negotiations have been held with Tunisia, but the Tunisian authorities have informed the Community that they are not prepared to negotiate a fisheries agreement until they have reliable scientific information as to the state of stocks in their waters.[48]

The situation with regard to Yugoslavia is that since 1949 Italian fishermen, under a succession of bilateral agreements between Italy and Yugoslavia, have enjoyed access to Yugoslav waters in return for the payment of financial compensation by the Italian Government. The Yugoslav government has so far declined the EEC's suggestion that its agreement with Italy should be replaced by one with the Community (although it has indicated that it would be prepared to enter into broader-based negotiations which would include co-operation on fisheries).[49] The Council authorised Italy to extend the life of its agreement with Yugoslavia (due originally to expire at the end of 1976) to the end of 1980, and during this period the Community reimbursed Italy for 80 per cent of the financial compensation Italy paid to Yugoslavia.[50] Since 1981 Italian fishermen have not fished in Yugoslav waters.[51]

Caribbean. The Community has engaged in negotiations with certain Caribbean States over the access to their waters of fishermen from the three French overseas departments of French Guyana, Guadeloupe and Martinique, but so far none of the negotiations have resulted in agreements.

Although the Community now has exclusive competence to enter into treaties regulating the access of Community fishermen to the waters of third States, in the view of the Commission this does not prevent individual Community fishermen from entering into their own private arrangements for access to the waters of third States, provided that such arrangements are not contrary to any Community agreements with third States or 'interfere with any action or commitments undertaken by the Community in its relations with' such States.[52] This is particularly important given the extensive use made by Portugal and Spain of joint ventures to obtain access to the waters of third States: Spain, for example, in 1983 had 63 joint ventures in 14 different States.[53]

(ii) *Access of vessels of non-reciprocal third States to Community waters*

Those third States which desired access for their vessels to the Community's 200-mile limits but which were not in a position to offer the Community reciprocal access were Bulgaria, Cuba, Japan, Romania, German Democratic Republic, Poland and Portugal. As already pointed out, there was no Community surplus to offer these States. Of these States, the first four were excluded from Community waters as soon as limits were extended to 200 miles at the beginning of 1977, on the grounds that their vessels had only recently begun fishing in Community waters.[54] Vessels of the other three States had traditionally fished in Community waters and it was therefore decided that they should be phased out gradually. Negotiations began on agreements to embody phase-out arrangements, but in the case of the German Democratic Republic and Poland these negotiations broke down over the unwillingness of these two States to recognise the EEC as a negotiating partner.[55] In the case of Portugal negotiations became so protracted that its vessels were phased out before the negotiations could be concluded. Thus by the end of 1977 vessels from all three States had been phased out of Community waters – a very swift phase-out compared with most fishery phase-out arrangements.

It has already been said that there is no surplus in the 200-mile limits of the Community's Member States, but two small qualifications must be made to this statement. First, the 200-mile limit off French Guyana has a surplus of certain stocks (notably shrimp and tuna), and since limits were extended in early 1977, vessels of a number of third States – South Korea, United States of America, Japan, Suriname, Venezuela, Barbados, Guyana, Trinidad and Tobago and, for a time, Brazil – have been given access to this surplus. These vessels require a licence (issued by the Commission), and limits are set on the number of licences, the size of catch and number of fishing days. Foreign fishing vessels must also carry a log book, observe all applicable fisheries legislation and transmit certain information to the Commission. In most cases all or part of the catch must be landed in French Guyana for processing. These arrangements are enforced by the French authorities, who must report all infringements detected to the Commission.[56]

Secondly, a limited number of Japanese vessels have been given temporary access to parts of Portugal's 200-mile zone to fish under licence for tuna. In return Japan must carry out a scientific and technical fisheries co-operation programme to benefit Portugal's coastal population.[57] This arrangement continues the access Japan enjoyed prior to Portugal's accession to the Community under a bilateral fisheries agreement between Portugal and Japan.

(iii) *Arrangements with reciprocal fisheries States*

At the time of the extension of fishing limits to 200 miles in the late 1970s these States comprised, in rough order of importance, Norway, Iceland, U.S.S.R., Faroes, Canada, Spain, Sweden and Finland. Subsequently a number of these States ceased to be considered as ones with which the Community had a reciprocal fisheries interest – Canada (for the reasons mentioned earlier), Iceland (with the withdrawal of Greenland from the Community) and of course Spain when it became a member of the Community. Negotiations took place with all these States with the aim of arriving at long-term reciprocal access arrangements. In all but two cases – U.S.S.R. and Iceland – these negotiations were successful. In the case of the U.S.S.R., negotiations broke down in September 1977 over the unwillingness of the U.S.S.R. to recognise the EEC: neither party has fished in the waters of the other since. In the case of Iceland, there was originally no real basis for negotiations, as Iceland was of the opinion that there was no surplus in its waters that could be offered to the Community.[58] By 1980 attitudes had changed, and negotiations began on a reciprocal agreement, but failed to reach a conclusion before Greenland withdrew from the Community. With all the other States mentioned, however, negotiations were successfully concluded, and agreements signed with Sweden,[59] the Faroes,[60] Norway,[61] Spain[62] and Finland.[63] Although these agreements were initialled and/or signed in 1977 or 1978, because of opposition, first from Ireland and later from the United Kingdom,[64] the Council was unable to ratify and bring into force any of the agreements until 1981. There was also in most cases considerable delay (up to two years in some instances) between an agreement being initialled and its being signed. The delay in the entry into force of the agreements led to access being regulated by a succession of temporary arrangements (discussed below).

The agreements themselves are all framework ones, providing the structure and procedures for fisheries arrangements, but leaving the details as to quotas, conservation measures, licences etc. to be established in subsequent negotiations between the parties. All the agreements provide that each party is to grant access to its 200-mile zone to vessels of the other party to fish for allotments determined by the first party: such allotments are to be determined so as to achieve a balance between the fishing effort of each party in the waters of the other. In the case of the EEC-Norway Agreement, it is an understanding that the balance relates, not to the quantity of catches, but to their value.[65] All the agreements provide that each party may require the vessels of the other party fishing in its waters to carry a licence, and such vessels are subject to the fisheries jurisdiction (both prescriptive and enforcement) of the other party while fishing in its waters. Disputes relating to the interpretation or application of the agreements are to be settled by consultations and, in the case of the agreement with Sweden, where such consultations fail, by arbitration. The agreements with the Faroes, Finland, Norway and Sweden are to remain in force for 10 years (that with Spain was to remain in force for five years): in all cases, the agreement is renewable at the end of the specified period.

As has been pointed out, prior to the entry into force of the agreements access to Community waters by vessels from the above States was governed by a series of temporary regulations. Even after the entry into force of the agreements, which as has been pointed out are of a framework nature, the details of access have continued to be regulated by Community regulations (which in part implement the measures agreed in annual consultations between the Community and the third State concerned). All these regulations (of which there have been literally dozens) are broadly similar, though naturally there are variations both over time and as regards the different States concerned. The basic pattern of the regulations is as follows. They set out the quotas which may be caught by the vessels of each State.[66] In determining the areas where such quotas may be caught, the regulations (except in the case of Spain) take into account any historic rights which third States may enjoy in the waters of EEC Member States. Foreign vessels are normally required to carry a licence, issued by the Commission on behalf of the Community. In the case of some types of fishing, the number of licences is limited. Foreign vessels must also 'comply with conservation and control measures and all other provisions governing fishing' in Member States' 200-mile limits.[67] Foreign vessels must keep a log book in which information as to the size of catch and the time, place and method of fishing must be entered, and certain information relating to the vessel's movements and fishing operations must be transmitted by radio to the Commission. As far as the enforcement of these provisions is concerned:

> The competent authorities of the Member States shall take appropriate steps, including the regular inspection of vessels, to ensure the enforcement of [these provisions]. Where an infringement is duly established, the Member States shall, without delay, inform the Commission of the name of the vessel involved and of any action they have taken.[68]

In the case of the access of Community vessels to the waters of third States, this has been regulated by the legislation of the third States concerned. Acting under the framework agreements, these States have each year granted quotas to the Community, and the Community has by means of regulations allocated these quotas among Member States. The criteria for such allocation are past fishing performance and, in the case of less popular species such as blue whiting, Norway pout and sandeel, the actual interest of Member States in the species concerned.[69] It goes without saying that Community vessels are subject to the jurisdiction of the third State concerned while fishing in its waters, and this may include a requirement to obtain a licence.

The result of these access arrangements has been a steady reduction of both Community fishing in the waters of third States and of third States' fishing in Community waters: it seems now, though, that a level of stability has been reached. At the same time, at least in the case of Norway, the Faroes and Sweden, a balance of fishing effort, either in terms of quantity or value, has largely been achieved, and this, it will be recalled, is one of the objectives of the reciprocal framework agreements.

It must be admitted, however, that the agreements and the arrangements made thereunder have not always functioned entirely smoothly. The responsibility for this state of affairs has lain largely with the Community. Before 1983 arrangements for the access of third States' vessels to Community waters were often adopted by the Council after considerable delay and for short periods, usually because of differences between Member States: for example, a Member State would block adoption of arrangements with one third State until achiving satisfaction on some other aspect of fisheries being considered.[70] The result was uncertainty for foreign fishermen, and at times an interruption of their fishing, sometimes for several months at a time. In the case of Norway,

Community fishermen on several occasions exceeded the quotas allocated to them in Norwegian waters. Furthermore, the Community at times failed to supply Norway with catch statistics, in spite of an agreement to do so. Since 1983, however, with the adoption of the management regime for Community waters, arrangements for third States' vessels fishing in Community waters have operated much more smoothly and effectively.

Before leaving the topic of reciprocal access agreements, mention must briefly be made of a number of supplementary agreements concerning salmon which the Community has concluded with the Faroes and Sweden. The Community's agreements with the Faroes stem from its concern at the recently greatly increased catches of salmon, many of Community origin, by Faroese fishermen. Since 1982 a series of annual agreements[71] have been concluded under which the Faroese have undertaken to limit their salmon catches to prescribed tonnages. It is intended that these bilateral arrangments should be replaced by measures adopted by the North Atlantic Salmon Conservation Organisation (discussed below), but so far the Organisation has failed to agree on such measures.

The EEC's agreement with Sweden[72] is of a rather different character. Under the agreement the Community is to make an annual contribution to the Swedish Government towards its costs incurred in carrying out measures to promote the reproduction of salmon in the Baltic. The Community's contribution is determined 'so as to cover the actual cost to the Swedish authorities of breeding, tagging and releasing a quantity of smolts necessary to produce a quantity of salmon equal to the non-reciprocal quota allocated to the Community in the Swedish exclusive fishing zone for the year during which the contribution is to be paid.' In accordance with this formula, the Community's contribution was determined, for example, as SKr. 2 million for a quota of 325 tonnes of salmon in 1979, and SKr. 2.92 million for a quota of 220 tonnes in 1980.[73] In 1981, however, the Agreement fell into abeyance,[74] and has not apparently been revived subsequently.

3. COMMUNITY MEMBERSHIP OF INTERNATIONAL FISHERY COMMISSIONS[75]

With the general, world-wide introduction of 200-mile fishing limits, international fishery commissions are no longer as important in the regulation of fisheries as they once were. Nevertheless, they continue to have a significant, if reduced, role to play in fisheries management: first, to regulate fishing taking place beyond 200-mile limits; and secondly, to co-operate with coastal States in the management of stocks which migrate between coastal States' 200-mile zones and the area beyond. Negotiations are currently in progress, or have recently been completed, to adapt the constitutions and powers of many of the existing fishery commissions to this new role. EEC Member States between them belong to over a dozen such commissions. The question arises whether their individual membership of these commissions should be replaced by a collective Community membership.

In the *Kramer* case the European Court said that it follows from Articles 5 and 116 of the EEC Treaty that:

> Member States participating in the [North-East Atlantic Fisheries] Convention and in other similar agreements are now not only under a duty not to enter into any commitment within the framework of those conventions which could hinder the Community in carrying out the tasks entrusted to it by Article 102 of the Act of Accession, but also under a duty to proceed by common action within the Fisheries Commission. It further follows therefore that as soon as the Community institutions have initiated the procedure for implementing the provisions of the said Article 102, and at the latest within the period laid down by that Article, those institutions and the Member States will be under a duty to use all the political and legal means at their disposal in order to ensure the participation of the Community in the Convention and in other similar agreements.[76]

How far does this dictum represent an accurate statement of the position? First, it should be noted that the Court's holding that the Community should become a member of international fishery commissions is heavily influenced by its view of Article 116 (which provides that Member States shall 'proceed within the framework of international organisations of an economic character only by common action'). It seems unlikely, however, that Article 116 is relevant here because international fishery commissions are not primarily of an 'economic character'.

To consider how far the Court's dictum in the *Kramer* case represents an accurate view of the position, it is helpful to distinguish between those fisheries commissions whose constituent conventions are the subject of proposed or actual amendment, and those which are not. In the case of the former, it would now seem to be clear, particularly after the Court's judgment in the *Rhine* case, that under Community law only the Community may enter into negotiations to establish new or amend existing fisheries commissions and to become a party to any resulting treaty. Member States no longer have any competence to take part in such negotiations or become parties to such treaties.[77] In the case of fisheries commissions whose conventions are not undergoing amendment, it would seem the question is one of compatibility. If membership of a commission is compatible with, and does not in any way adversely affect the functioning or scope of, the Community's fisheries policy, then it would seem that it is permissible for a Member State to retain its membership of that commission, without being replaced by the Community. If, on the other hand, membership is incompatible with the Community's fisheries policy or would adversely affect it, then a Member State is under an obligation (flowing from Articles 5 and 234 of the EEC Treaty) to cease to be a member of such a commission. It would therefore seem that the Court's dictum in the *Kramer* case, while largely representing an accurate statement of the law, needs to be modified in the case of existing fisheries commissions where continued membership by a Member State is fully compatible with Community obligations.

There is a further point relating to the Community's competence to become a member of international fishery commissions which also needs to be considered. Nearly all these commissions have some form of quasi-legislative power, that is they can adopt measures such as minimum mesh and fish sizes, closed seasons and areas, and quotas, which are binding on their members unless objected to within a certain time-limit. Is Community membership of an international organisation having such powers compatible with the EEC Treaty? In the *Rhine* case the Court held that Community membership of an international organisation having decision-making powers of an executive character was compatible with the EEC Treaty, but left open the question of whether membership of an organisation having legislative powers would be. Nevertheless, it would seem that the kind of quasi-legislative powers possessed by international fishery commissions should raise no problems. First, if any quasi-legislative measures were adopted by a fishery commission which were felt to be incompatible with the EEC Treaty or any Community fisheries measures, the Community could object to them (and in fact would be obliged to do so) and thus would not be bound by them. Secondly, fishery commission measures do not have automatic effect in the Community legal system: in practice they are implemented by means of regulations. The institutional nature of the Community – particularly its legislative powers – is therefore not in any way called into question.

Having discussed the question of Community membership of international fishery commissions in theory, we must now look at the position in practice, and consider – for reasons of space, very briefly – the dozen or so existing commissions to which one or more of the EEC Member States belong and where, therefore, the question of their replacement by Community membership has arisen, as well as some recently established bodies which the Community has joined or is likely to join.

International Commission for the Northwest Atlantic Fisheries (ICNAF)/ Northwest Atlantic Fisheries Organisation (NAFO). Following the extension of fishing limits to 200 miles by all the coastal States of the Northwest Atlantic in early 1977, it was decided that ICNAF (of which a number of EEC States had been members) should be replaced by a new body, limited to regulating fisheries beyond 200 miles. As a result, NAFO was set up by a convention,[78] signed on October 24, 1978, which came into force on January 1, 1979. The NAFO Convention provides that the Community as such (instead of its Member States) may become a member of NAFO, and this possibility has been exercised by the Community. It is noteworthy that four East European States – Bulgaria, the German Democratic Republic, Romania and the U.S.S.R. – are also parties to NAFO. In the past these States have always refused to recognise the EEC as an international person. While becoming parties to the same treaty does not necessarily amount to recognition (cf. the Arab States and Israel), it will make it more difficult in future for the Eastern European countries to refuse to have dealings with the Community as such.[79]

Apart from co-ordinating scientific research, NAFO's main functions, exercised through its Fisheries Commission, are to manage the fishery resources of the Northwest Atlantic found beyond 200-mile limits and to co-operate with coastal States over the management of stocks that migrate between their 200-mile limits and the waters beyond. To this end the Fisheries Commission has adopted quotas, conservation measures such as minimum mesh sizes and by-catch levels, a scheme of joint international enforcement and an international scientific observer programme, all of which are binding on the Community. The Community implements such measures for its fishermen by means of regulations.[80] Before 1983 there was often considerable delay in this implementation – in most cases measures were not implemented until between six months and one year after they became binding on the Community, while NAFO's quotas for 1979 were never implemented at all. Apart from being in breach of its treaty obligations and causing uncertainty for Community fishermen, the Community's tardiness in taking implementing acion was hardly calculated to foster a spirit of co-operation with its NAFO partners. Since the adoption at the beginning of 1983 of the management regime for resources in Community waters, the Community has by and large implemented its NAFO obligations on time.

North-East Atlantic Fisheries Commission (NEAFC). Following the extension of fishing limits to 200 miles by most coastal States of the North-East Atlantic at the beginning of 1977, it was decided that NEAFC (which had been established by a Convention of 1959 and to which most EEC Member States belonged) should be modified and confined largely to regulating fisheries beyond 200-mile limits. The first efforts to revise NEAFC ended in deadlock at a diplomatic conference held in February-March 1978 because of the refusal of the Eastern European States taking part to accept the EEC as a party to a revised NEAFC convention. However, two years later their attitude had changed, and a conference held in February 1980 led to a convention modifying NEAFC (to which the Community could become a party in place of its

Member States) being approved and subsequently opened for signature in November 1980.[81] The Convention has been ratified by the Community,[82] and came into force on March 17, 1982. It establishes a new NEAFC, having functions and powers similar to those of NAFO. Although NEAFC is similar to NAFO, it has in practice adopted far fewer regulatory measures: only one measure seems to have been adopted so far – a minimum mesh size for fishing for capelin beyond 200 miles.[83]

International Baltic Sea Fishery Commission (IBSFC).[84] As a result of the fact that since 1977 the Baltic has fallen entirely within national fishing limits, it was proposed that the IBSFC's functions should be amended to take account of this fact. At the same time the EEC Commission proposed that the Community should replace its two Member States, Denmark and the Federal Republic of Germany, which were members of the IBSFC.[85] Although these two proposals were made as long ago as 1977, because of initial opposition from the Eastern European States members of the IBSFC to the second of these proposals, it was not until November 1982 that agreement was reached on a Protocol to the IBSFC's Convention embodying these proposals.[86] In relation to the former proposal, the Protocol defines the IBSFC's functions as the co-ordination of fisheries management and research in the Baltic and provides that any regulatory measures adopted by the IBSFC relating to the fishing zones of one or more Member States shall enter into force for those States only where they give their affirmative vote thereto. The Protocol entered into force on April 18, 1984 and thus since that date the Community has been a member of the IBSFC. The Community is bound by any regulatory measures adopted by the IBSFC to which it has not objected (though measures applying to Community waters require the Community's affirmative vote). Not until June 1986 did the Community implement the existing measures adopted by the IBSFC even though these measures had been binding on the Community since the date of its accession to the IBSFC over two years previously.[87]

Commission for the Conservation of Antarctic Marine Living Resources.[88] This is one of the newest international fishery commissions and, because of its ecosystem approach, in many ways the most advanced. Its functions are to co-ordinate research on Antarctic marine living resources and adopt conservation and management measures for such resources (such as the establishment of quantities to be harvested, the designation of protected species and closed seasons, and the regulation of gear). The Convention establishing the Commission provides that certain types of international organisation (including the EEC) may become members of the Commission, and this possibility has been exercised by the Community.[89] In addition, five EEC Member States – Belgium, France, the Federal Republic of Germany, Spain and the United

Kingdom – are also members of the Commission: i.e. the Convention setting up the Commission is a mixed agreement. The reason for this appears to be twofold. First, the subject matter of the Convention includes all marine living resources, not just fish but also, for example, birds; some of these resources (such as birds) fall outside the Community's present competence. Secondly, the Convention applies to areas in respect of which France exercises fisheries jurisdiction (the 200-mile economic zone around Kerguelen and Crozet islands), which are outside the ambit of the EEC Treaty (see Chapter 3, section 2): this fact affects the Commission's competence in taking conservation measures.[90] So far one set of measures adopted by the Commission has been implemented by the Community.[91]

International Commission for the South-East Atlantic Fisheries (ICSEAF).[92] The Convention establishing ICSEAF is at present open to accession only by States. In October 1980 the Federal Republic of Germany requested that the Convention should be amended in order to allow the Community to become a member in place of those EEC Member States who were members of ICSEAF.[93] Not until five years later – in December 1985 – did the 17 members of ICSEAF approve an amendment to the Convention enabling the Community to accede.[94]

North Atlantic Salmon Conservation Organisation (NASCO).[95] The Convention for the Conservation of Salmon in the North Atlantic Ocean broadly implements the principles on anadromous species contained in Article 66 of the UN Convention on the Law of the Sea. Thus it bans fishing for salmon on the high seas (as well as between 12 and 200 miles except off the Faroes and West Greenland) and provides for co-operation in the management of salmon between the States of the North Atlantic through the establishment of NASCO. The latter has a complex structure, designed to provide a careful balance between the interests of the states of origin (i.e. those States in whose rivers anadromous species spawn) and those States which catch salmon at sea, and comprises a Council, three regional commissions and a secretariat. The Community has ratified the Convention,[96] and is a member of the Council and of one of the three regional commissions (that for the North-East Atlantic: it was also a member of the West Greenland Commission before Greenland's withdrawal from the Community). The importance of the role of the Community in the negotiation and operation of the Convention is shown by the fact that the Council of the Community is the depositary for the Convention and that NASCO's headquarters are in an EEC Member State (the United Kingdom). NASCO has so far adopted one management measure – establishing the total catch for salmon in the waters off West Greenland.[97]

International Commission for the Conservation of Atlantic Tunas (ICCAT).[98] Like ICSEAF, the membership of ICCAT is at present open only to States. In 1979 France, at that time the only EEC Member State a member of ICCAT, proposed that the ICCAT Convention should be amended so as to permit the Community to become a member in its place. Because of East European objections, progress in acting on this proposal was slow, but in July 1984 a Protocol to the Convention was adopted which when it enters into force will permit the Community to become a member of ICCAT in place of its Member States.[99]

International Whaling Commission (IWC).[100] In August 1979 the Commission proposed that the Community should become a party, in place of its Member States, to the IWC Convention (to which at present only States may be parties) and/or any successor convention on cetaceans which might be negotiated.[101] At a meeting on October 29, 1979 the Council was unable to agree on this proposal because some Member States contested the Community's competence in matters of whaling.[102] Similar disagreement manifested itself at further Council meetings in June and July 1980,[103] and these differences of view appear still to be unresolved. In the absence of any progress on becoming a member of the IWC, the Community has sought and obtained observer status.[104]

In the international fishery commissions of which it is or will shortly become a member, the Community has a single vote, like each State member. The suggestions the Community has occasionaly made that voting in these bodies should be weighted have always been rejected by the other members. In the case of the Antarctic Commission, where both the Community and some individual EEC Member States are members, it is provided that while both the Community and its Member States each have one vote, the total number of votes they may cast may not exceed the number of EEC Member States that are members of the Commission, i.e. either the Community or, more likely, one of its Member States, will not be entitled to vote. As far as the budgets of the commissions are concerned, an equal apportionment of their cost among members might lead to an unjust benefit being conferred on the Community and large States. Thus, apart from IBSFC and the Antarctic Commission during the first five years of its life (where in each case the budget is equally apportioned among members), the apportionment of the cost of the budget is largely in proportion to each member's share of the catch in the commission's area of operation.

Other Bodies. There are a number of existing international fishery commissions to which one or more EEC Member States belong, but where there appear to be no plans at present to replace Member States' membership by

Community membership. These include the General Fisheries Council for the Mediterranean,[105] the Indo-Pacific Fisheries Commission,[106] the Inter-American Tropical Tuna Commission,[107] the Baltic Sea Salmon Standing Committee,[108] the Shellfish Commission for the Skagerrak and Kattegat,[109] FAO's Fishery Committee for the Eastern Central Atlantic,[110] FAO's Western Central Atlantic Fisheries Commission[111] and FAO's Indian Ocean Fishery Commission.[112] In many of these cases, membership by individual EEC Member States would seem to be incompatible with the long-term aspirations of the Community's Common Fisheries Policy, and it would accordingly seem necessary that in due course in these cases individual Member States' membership should be replaced by Community membership (although at the present time all these commissions are open only to membership by States). It should also be noted that with some of these commissions, e.g. the General Fisheries Council for the Mediterranean and the Western Central Atlantic Fisheries Commission, the Community has already obtained observer status.

Finally, the Community has become a party to two recent conventions which, while not predominantly concerned with marine resources, do have a bearing on fisheries management – the European Convention on the Conservation of European Wildlife and Natural Habitats, 1979[113] and the Convention on the Conservation of Migratory Species of Wild Animals, 1979.[114] In addition, the Convention on International Trade in Endangered Species of Wild Fauna and Flora is applied in the Community,[115] although the Community as such is not a party to the Convention.[116] It may also be asked whether it might not be desirable for the Community to seek to become a party to the one or two longer established multilateral agreements that are still of importance to fisheries and to which some or all of its Member States are parties, such as the 1967 Convention on Conduct of Fishing Operations in the North Atlantic[117] and the 1964 Convention on the International Council for the Exploration of the Sea,[118] accession to which is at present limited to States.

4. MANAGEMENT OF JOINT STOCKS[119]

As was pointed out in Chapter 1, many fish stocks do not confine themselves to the 200-mile zone of a single State, but migrate therefrom to the zone(s) of one or more other States and/or the waters beyond 200-mile limits. In relation to stocks migrating between the 200-mile zones of two or more States, the UN Convention on the Law of the Sea provides that the States concerned 'shall seek ... to agree upon the measures necessary to co-ordinate and ensure the conservation and development of such stocks' (Article 63(1)).

The Community shares a number of stocks with third States, notably Norway, Sweden, the Faroes, Spain (before its accession to the EEC) and

Canada and Iceland (before Greenland's withdrawal from the EEC). There are also shared stocks in the Baltic, which are managed by the International Baltic Sea Fishery Commission (discussed above). Undoubtedly, too, there are shared stocks in the Mediterranean and in the waters of the French overseas departments, but these appear so far to have been the object of little discussion or investigation.

Each of the reciprocal fisheries agreements that the Community has signed[120] provides that the Community and the third State concerned are to co-operate to ensure proper management of joint stocks. Such co-operation over management would seem to raise three main problems: (1) identifying joint stocks; (2) agreeing on conservation measures; and (3) allocating catches (a matter on which the UN Convention is conspicuously silent). Co-operation under the reciprocal fisheries agreements is so far most developed with Norway and Sweden. With each of these States the Community has since 1979 concluded a succession of annual arrangements. On the identification of joint stocks, agreement has largely been reached, although there is still disagreement between Norway and the EEC over whether Western mackerel is a joint stock, Norway taking the view that it is a joint stock, the Community that it is exclusive to the Community. In the absence of agreement on this matter, each party manages the stock autonomously.[121] In relation to stocks which are agreed to be joint, however, there is joint management. This takes the form of setting a TAC (based on the recommendations of the International Council for the Exploration of the Sea (ICES)), and allocating it between the parties. Although starting from ICES advice, Norway and the Community do not always find it very easy to agree on TACs because they have different management objectives: the Community in general wishes to stabilise fishing effort at existing levels whereas Norway wishes to reduce it.[122] As regards allocation of the TAC, the main criterion for allocation is the proportion of the stock which is of catchable size found in each party's zone.[123] The annual arrangements also introduce other limited conservation measures and, in the case of the arrangements between the EEC and Norway, provide that the parties are to consult on fishery regulations with a view to achieving a harmonisation of their regulatory measures. In addition, the EEC, Norway and Sweden have since 1979 reached trilateral agreement each year on arrangements for the Skagerrak and Kattegat. These arrangements are similar to the bilateral arrangements, but they contain more supplementary conservation measures. Before 1983 the above arragements did not always work particularly well, mainly because the Community was tardy in implementing, or failed to implement, its side of the arrangements, and because it failed to ensure that its fishermen observed the arrangements. Since 1983 the arrangements have worked much more smoothly except in the case of North Sea herring. Disagreement over how the total catch should be divided up between Norway and the EEC

(Norway claiming a greater share than the Community thought justified) resulted in no agreed TAC being set in 1984 or 1985: instead each party set an autonomous TAC. In 1986 an ad hoc agreement was reached on the TAC and its allocation, and a Joint Working Group set up to recommend a definitive formula for future allocation based on the zonal attachment of herring stocks.[124]

Before Greenland withdrew from the EEC, the Community enjoyed a certain amount of co-operation with Canada and Iceland over the management of what were then joint stocks. With Canada the Community agreed in 1979 and 1980 arrangements somewhat similar to those it has with Norway and Sweden.[125] Co-operation terminated in 1981, however, because of differences of view between Canada and the Community over management objectives.[126] In the case of Iceland, the Community, Iceland and Norway in 1982 signed an arrangement prohibiting fishing for capelin in the waters between Iceland, Greenland and Jan Mayen because of the poor state of the stock.[127] With Greenland now out of the Community, there are no joint stocks involving the Community and Canada and Iceland.

No arrangements over the management of joint stocks with the Faroes (mainly blue whiting) appear yet to have been discussed, nor has any action been taken in relation to the French overseas departments or in the Mediterranean. With the accession of Portugal and Spain to the EEC, the Community has acquired further joint stocks where action will need to be taken.

Viewing the position globally, there appears to have been a relative scarcity of practice in the management of joint stocks. While a good deal remains to be done, the EEC has already achieved considerable success with its joint stock management. It has thus made quite a significant contribution to State practice in this area, and has put some regional flesh on the bare bones of the UN Convention's provisions.

5. CONCLUSIONS

The EEC's external fisheries management policy has on the whole been relatively successful so far. The negotiation of access arrangements with third States is now nearly complete. A variety of techniques has been used to gain access. Whereas the UN Convention on the Law of the Sea envisages access being limited to the surplus catch, the Community has gained access to third States' waters not so much on the basis of the surplus catch as by a number of other principles – reciprocity; the payment of compensation; and exchanging access to third States' waters for more favourable access for third States' fishery exports to Community markets. Access to the waters of third States where Community vessels have traditionally fished has been maintained in most cases, although not surprisingly on a considerably reduced scale. On the other hand there has been a corresponding decline in fishing in Community waters by third States, particularly by the factory fleets of Eastern Europe. However, the speed at which access arrangements have been negotiated and brought into force has been affected by the disagreement over the internal Community regime which persisted until the beginning of 1983, and compares very unfavourably with the speed at which most other States have negotiated access arrangements. The delays caused by the Community have undoubtedly cost it some goodwill with the third States concerned, particularly Canada and Norway, and have possibly meant lower quotas in some third States' waters than might otherwise have been the case.

The Community has or is about to become a member of no less than seven international fishery commissions, and may possibly become a member of several other commissions in due course. This process was hindered, at least initially, by opposition from those Eastern European States which are members of the commissions in question. A point of some concern, which tends to undermine the credibility of the Community as a member of international fishery commissions, is the fact that the Community has been slow, or has even on occasions failed, to implement fishery measures adopted by the commissions which are binding on it. While the position was worse before 1983, there is still room for improvement, as the practice in relation to the Antarctic, Baltic and North-East Atlantic Commissions shows.

Where arrangements have been agreed for the management of joint stocks, such arrangements are now, after some pre-1983 difficulties, on the whole working well, and are an important example globally of what can be achieved in this area. Nevertheless, not all the stocks the Community shares with third States are subject to co-operative management and further arrangements therefore need to be developed.

As with its internal policy, the Community's external policy is still very under-developed as far as the Mediterranean is concerned. No agreements have been concluded with third States (particularly Tunisia and Yugoslavia) on access to fishing zones or management of joint stocks, nor has any move yet been made for the Community to become a member of the General Fisheries Council for the Mediterranean in place of its Member States.

The Community's external relations in the fisheries sector have thrown up one internal institutional problem for the Community. The arrangements made with third States in implementation of fisheries treaties – whether they be in relation to access arrangements, the management of joint stocks or measures adopted by international fishery commissions – are negotiated by the Commission on behalf of the Community. It is in the nature of such arrangements that once negotiated, they cannot readily be changed and they certainly cannot be amended unilaterally by the Community. Nevertheless, such arrangements require implementation into Community law, which means in principle, according to Article 43 of the EEC Treaty, that they must be adopted by the Council after consultation with the European Parliament. Since implementing arrangements cannot easily be modified, there is little point in the European Parliament proposing changes to them, and, not surprisingly, it has complained that it is being used simply as a rubber stamp.[128] Similarly, the Council can play no useful role in this procedure either, and its contribution so far has largely been limited to delaying the adoption of implementing measures. Of course, these problems are not unique to fisheries, and apply in other areas of the Community's external relations. Nor are these problems unique to the Community: with States, analogous problems arise in relation to negotiations conducted with other States by the executive which subsequently require the approval of the legislature. Nevertheless, in the case of measures which simply implement routine arrangements in fisheries matters with third States, there would seem to be a good case for depriving the European Parliament and Council of any role in the adoption of such measures. To a large extent the European Parliament has already been deprived of its role, because since the adoption of the Regulation establishing a Community System for the Conservation and Management of Fishery Resources in January 1983, more and more (but not all) external measures have been adopted by the Council acting under the simplified procedure, i.e. on a proposal from the Commission without requiring an opinion from the European Parliament (see pp. 39–41 above).[129] This process could reasonably be taken a step further, with all measures being adopted by the Commission (instead of the Council), although the management committee procedure should be used to retain an element of accountability. If this were done, it would mean not only that arrangements with third States would be implemented more swiftly than hitherto, but it would reduce the pressure of work on the Council and the European Parliament. An element of democratic accountability would still be retained, by the European Parliament, as happens now, being kept informed by the Commission of developments in this area and being able to question and criticise the Commission's activities.

NOTES

1. Participation by the Community in the United Nations Convention on the Law of the Sea, although relevant to the topic of this Chapter, is not dealt with, as it raises questions going far beyond fisheries; and as far as fisheries are concerned, it makes relatively little difference whether the Community and/or its Member States are parties to the Convention or not because, as suggested in Chapter 1, the provisions of the Convention dealing with fisheries have already largely become part of customary international law. For discussion of the Community's participation in the Convention, see – among a growing literature – K.R. Simmonds, 'The Community's Participation in the UN Law of the Sea Convention' in D.

O'Keeffe and H.G. Schermers (eds.), *Essays in European Law and Integration,* Deventer, 1982, pp. 179–195 and the papers by Treves, Vukas and Ederer in E.D. Brown and R.R. Churchill (eds.), *The U.N. Convention on the Law of the Sea: Impact and Implementation* (forthcoming).

2. Joined Cases 3, 4 and 6/76, *Officier van Justitie v. Kramer* [1976] E.C.R. 1279; [1976] 2 C.M.L.R. 440.

3. Art. 116 of the EEC Treaty (which provides that EEC Member States shall 'proceed within the framework of international organisations of an economic character only by common action') might at first sight be considered as a possible express treaty-making power (and, if so, relevant to the question of Community membership of international fishery commissions). However, the European Court, in Opinion 1/78, *Re the International Agreement on Natural Rubber,* [1979] E.C.R. 2871; [1979] 3 C.M.L.R. 639, made it clear that Art. 116 is not to be regarded as a treaty-making power (see grounds 50–51).

4. Case 22/70, *Re the European Road Transport Agreement: E.C. Commision v. E.C. Council* [1971] E.C.R. 263; [1971] C.M.L.R. 335.

5. *Ibid.,* pp. 274 and 354 respectively.

6. *Ibid.*

7. *Op. cit.* in n. 2, pp. 1309 and 469 respectively.

8. O.J. 1981 C105/1.

9. Opinion 1/76, *Re the Draft Agreement establishing a European Laying-Up Fund for Inland Waterway Vessels,* [1977] E.C.R. 741; [1977] 2 C.M.L.R. 279.

10. *Ibid.,* pp. 755 and 295 respectively.

11. *Ibid.*

12. *Op. cit.* in n. 4, pp. 274 and 355 respectively.

13. *Ibid.,* pp. 276 and 356 respectively.

14. T.C. Hartley, *The Foundations of European Community Law,* Oxford, 1981, p. 160. The same view is taken by A. Parry and J. Dinnage, *EEC Law,* 2nd edition, London, 1981, p. 446; and by the Commission – see its Answer to W.Q. 173/177, O.J. 1978 C72/1.

15. J.V. Louis and P. Brückner, *Relations Extérieures,* Vol. XII of Mégret et al (eds.), *Droit de la Communauté Economique Européenne,* Brussels, 1980, pp. 112–113, quoted in M.E. Martins Ribeiro, 'Compétence communautaire et compétence nationale dans le secteur de la pêche' (1982) 18 C.D.E. 144 at 182. A similar view is taken by Lachmann: see P. Lachmann, 'International Legal Personality of the EC: Capacity and Competence' [1984] L.I.E.I. 3 at 21.

16. But cf. the Commission's view given in evidence to a House of Lords Select Committee that the Community obtained exclusive treaty-making powers only at the beginning of 1979: see House of Lords Select Committee on the European Communities, *External Competence of the European Communities* HL Paper (1984–85) 236, p. 106.

17. According to (1983) 87 R.G.D.I.P. 413–4, quoting *Le Monde* of September 26, 1982.

18. Convention concerning Maritime Delimitation, 1984. J.O.R.F., October 6, 1985, p. 11, 600.

19. For further treatment of this question, see M. Leigh, *European Integration and the Common Fisheries Policy,* Beckenham, 1983, pp. 193–196; and J. Farnell and J. Elles, *In Search of a Common Fisheries Policy,* Aldershot, 1984, pp. 66–69.

20. Joined Cases 21–24/72, *International Fruit Co. N.V. v. Produktschap voor Groenten en Fruit (No. 3.)* [1972] E.C.R. 1219; [1975] 2 C.M.L.R. 1.

21. Hartley, *op. cit.* in n. 14, pp. 174–5, argues that the substitution principle should also apply to treaties concluded after the EEC Treaty, but before the Community obtained exclusive treaty-making powers in relation to the subject matter in question. Given that the substitution principle is essentially a corollary or extension of the principle of Community exclusivity in treaty-making, this seems a reasonable view.

22. Hartley, *op. cit.* in n. 14 pp. 175–6, argues that the substitution principle should apply to treaties to which only some (or even one) Member State(s) are parties. This seems rather doubtful: treaties to which only a few Member States are parties are probably better dealt with by Art. 234 (discussed below).

23. E.g. the Brussels Nomenclature Convention of 1950, Case 38/75, *Nederlandse Spoorwegen v. Inspecteur der Invoerrechten* [1975] E.C.R. 1439; [1976] 1 C.M.L.R. 167.

24. It is interesting to note that in Case 812/79, *Attorney General v. Burgoa* [1980] E.C.R. 2787; [1981] 2 C.M.L.R. 193, the Advocate General (but not the Court) discussed whether the substitution principle applied to the European Fisheries Convention of 1964. He came firmly to the conclusion that it did not. He also reached the same conclusion in respect of the Geneva Convention on Fishing and Conservation of the Living Resources of the High Seas in Joined Cases 180 and 266/80, *Tome v. Procureur de la République, Procureur de la République v. Yurrita* [1981] E.C.R. 2997.

25. *Op. cit.* in n. 24, pp. 2803 and 212 respectively.

26. Case 181/80, *Procureur Général v. Abelaiz-Emazabel* [1981] E.C.R. 2961 at 2982. See also *Burgoa, op. cit.* in n. 24, pp. 2807 and 215 respectively; *Tome* and *Yurrita, op. cit.* in n. 24, p. 3016; and Joined Cases 13–28/82, *Arantzamendi-Osa v. Procureur de la République* [1982] E.C.R. 3927.

27. For a full discussion of this question, see R.R. Churchill and N.G. Foster, 'European Community Law and Prior Treaty Obligations of Member States: the Spanish Fishermen's Cases' (1987) 36 I.C.L.Q. (forthcoming).

28. For the political background to access arrangements, see Leigh, *op. cit.* in n. 19, Chap. 6, and Farnell and Elles, *op. cit.* in n. 19, Chap. 3. For a more detailed legal account, see N. Nitsch, 'Les accords de pêche entre la Communauté et les états tiers' (1980) 240 R.M.C. 452.

29. The United States is treated here as a non-reciprocal State because it has been so considered by the Community. In fact, it would be more accurate to regard the United States as a reciprocal State since it engages in some fishing in Community waters (off French Guyana), as will be seen below.

30. Agreement between the Government of the United States of America and the European Economic Community concerning Fisheries off the Coasts of the U.S.A., Washington, February 15, 1977. In force June 9, 1977. O.J. 1977 L141/2. For an extended analysis of this Agreement, see D. Yandais, 'La Communauté et la pêche' (1979) 15 C.D.E. 185 at 203–213. This Agreement has been replaced by a similar agreement with the same title signed in 1984: O.J. 1984 L272/3. The latter agreement came into force on November 14, 1984 and will apply until July 1, 1989.

31. Quotas are allocated by the USA directly to individual Member States, rather than – as is the case under other agreements between the Community and third States – to the Community as such. For the reason why, see Leigh, *op. cit.* in n. 19, p. 127.

32. Canada-France. Agreement on their Mutual Fishing Relations, March 27, 1972. UN Legislative Series B/16, p. 570. With the change in status in 1985 of St. Pierre et Miquelon from an overseas department to an Annex IV territory, even this Canadian fishing is now not in Community waters.

33. Agreement on Fisheries between the Government of Canada and the European Economic Community, June 28, 1979. O.J. 1979 L312/2.

34. Agreement on Fisheries between the Government of Canada and the European Economic Community, December 30, 1981. O.J. 1981 L379/54. The Agreement runs until the end of 1987 and thereafter is terminable by either party on giving a year's notice.

35. EEC-Canada Agreement concerning their Fisheries Relations, December 30, 1981. O.J. 1981 L379/59.

36. For further details, see Leigh, *op. cit.* in n. 19, p. 132. On this question, and on EEC-Canada

fisheries relations generally, see also D. Barry, 'The Canada-European Community Long Term Fisheries Agreement: Internal Politics and Fisheries Diplomacy' (1985) 9 *Journal of European Integration 5*.

37. O.J. 1983 L371/35.

38. O.J. 1985 L29/9.

39. Agreement between the Government of the Republic of Senegal and the European Economic Community on Fisheries off the Coast of Senegal, Brussels, June 15, 1979. In force June 1, 1981. O.J. 1980 L226/18. For extensions of and amendments to the Agreement, see O.J. 1981 L220/34, L319/22 and L379/64; 1982 L234/8; 1984 L37/50; 1985 L361/87; and 1986 L75/29 and L168/22.

40. Agreement between the Republic of Guinea-Bissau and the European Economic Community on Fishing off the Coast of Guinea-Bissau, Brussels, February 27, 1980. In force December 17, 1981. O.J. 1980 L226/34. For extensions of and amendments to the Agreement, see O.J. 1982 L2/11, L126/16 and L247/33; 1983 L26/42 and 84/1; and 1986 L261/20.

41. Agreement between the European Economic Community and the Government of the Revolutionary People's Republic of Guinea on Fishing off the Guinean Coast, Conakry, February 7, 1983. In force February 19, 1986. O.J. 1983 L111/2. For extension of and amendments to the Agreement, see O.J. 1986 L80/52.

42. Agreement between the European Economic Community and the Government of the Republic of Equatorial Guinea on Fishing off the Coast of Equatorial Guinea, Malabo, June 15, 1984. In force December 3, 1984. O.J. 1984 L188/2.

43. Agreement between the European Economic Community and the Government of the Democratic Republic of Sao Tome and Principe on Fishing off Sao Tome and Principe, Brussels, February 1, 1984. In force April 18, 1985. O.J. 1984 L54/2.

44. Agreement between the European Economic Community and the Government of the Republic of Seychelles on Fishing off Seychelles, Brussels, May 23, 1985. O.J. 1985 L149/2.

45. Agreement between the European Economic Community and the Government of the Democratic Republic of Madagascar on Fishing off Madagascar, Antananarivo, January 28, 1986. In force May 21, 1986. O.J. 1986 L73/26.

46. As far as the cost of fishing is concerned, one estimate is that the licence fees amount to about one-third of the value of the catch: see Farnell and Elles, *op. cit.* in n. 19, p. 57.

47. Second Lomé Convention, Annex XVIII, O.J. 1980 L347/1; Third Lomé Convention, Arts. 55–59, O.J. 1986 L86/1.

48. Commission's Answer to W.Q. 1238/81, O.J. 1982 C38/14. See also E.P. Doc. 949/82, p. 38.

49. However, the Co-Operation Agreement signed between the EEC and Yugoslavia in 1980, O.J. 1983 L41/1, contains a very vague provision on fisheries. Article 11 states that the parties 'shall encourage exchanges of information on developments in their respective fisheries policies and the implementation of projects of mutual interest with the aim of promoting and strengthening co-operation in this sector.'

50. See COM's (78) 286 and 743; (79) 341 and 673; and (80) 310.

51. However, *Eurofish Report* No. 176 of April 12, 1984 reports the conclusion of a seven-year fisheries co-operation agreement between Italy and Yugoslavia under which Italian ship-builders will deliver 10 deep-sea fishing vessels to Yugoslavia: in exchange Italian fishermen will be allowed to fish in three areas of Yugoslav waters.

52. Commission's Answer to W.Q. 961/80, O.J. 1980 C312/15.

53. For details, see House of Lords Select Committee on the European Communities, *The Common Fisheries Policy* HL Paper (1984–85) 39, pp. 166–7, 170.

54. Reg. 373/77, O.J. 1977 L53/1.

55. However, in June 1985 an initial round of exploratory talks took place between the Community and Poland on possible future access arrangements: see *Bull. E.C.* 1985 No. 6, pp. 70–71.

56. The access of these third States is not provided by means of bilateral agreements, as one might expect, but autonomously by the Community by a succession of annual regulations.

57. Reg. 448/86, O.J. 1986 L50/34. This Reg. was due to expire on June 30, 1986. It is intended that in future access should not be regulated autonomously by the Community but should be on the basis of an agreement between the Community and Japan: see COM (86) 6.

58. However, German fishermen continued to fish in Icelandic waters until November 1977 under the terms of the 1975 Fisheries Agreement between Iceland and Germany ((1976) XV I.L.M. 43), and Belgian fishermen continue to fish in Icelandic waters under the terms of the 1975 Fisheries Agreement between Iceland and Belgium ((1976) XV I.L.M. 1), until the agreement is terminated by one party giving six months' notice. Icelandic fishermen were excluded from Community waters until August 1980, when they were admitted to fish until the end of 1980 for a 120,000 tonne quota of capelin in the 200-mile zone off Eastern Greenland north of 67°N, which was established on June 1, 1980. See Reg. 2167/80, O.J. 1980 L212/12. This arrangement has not been continued in subsequent years.

59. Agreement on Fisheries between the Government of Sweden and the European Economic Community, Brussels, March 21, 1977. In force April 7, 1981. O.J. 1980 L226/2.

60. Agreement on Fisheries between the Government of Denmark and the Home Government of the Faroe Islands and the European Economic Community, Brussels, March 15, 1977. O.J. 1980 L226/12.

61. Agreement on Fisheries between the Kingdom of Norway and the European Economic Community, February 27, 1980. In force June 16, 1981. O.J. 1980 L226/48.

62. Agreement on Fisheries between the Government of Spain and the European Economic Community, April 15, 1980. In force May 22, 1981. O.J. 1980 L322/3. For an excellent extended analysis of this Agreement, see J.L. Meseguer, 'Accord de pêche entre l'Espagne et la CEE' (1980) 241 R.M.C. 527 and (1980) 242 R.M.C. 589.

63. Agreement on Fisheries between the Government of Finland and the European Economic Community, Brussels, July 6, 1983. In force January 5, 1984. O.J. 1983 L192/9.

64. Ireland's opposition seems to have been used solely as a negotiating tactic (since Ireland has no interest in fishing in the waters of any of the countries concerned), in order to gain recognition for the needs of the Irish fishing industry: once it had received such recognition, its opposition ceased. The U.K. appears to have opposed conclusion of these agreements on the ground that to conclude them might prejudice the outcome of the negotiations over the Community's internal fisheries regime.

65. Norwegian Government, *Markedsutvalgets Rapport Nr. XVI om De Europeiske Fellesskap*, Oslo, 1982, p. 125. In the case of Sweden, since 1986 the Community has received additional access to Swedish waters over and above that covered by the balance in return for more reasonable access for Swedish fishery products to the markets of an enlarged Community under an exchange of letters initialled in February 1986 (not yet published): see COM (86) 323.

66. But note that under the EEC-Finland Agreement Finnish vessels were not to be permitted access to Community waters until the North Sea herring stock had recovered sufficiently to allow a TAC in excess of 100,000 tonnes to be set. In spite of the fact that a TAC in excess of 100,000 tonnes has been set for every year since 1983, Finnish vessels have not yet in practice been given access to Community waters.

67. Reg. 3734/85, O.J. 1985 L361/80, Art. 2(1). The 'measures and provisions governing fishing' are found in: (1) the licences issued to foreign vessels; (2) in the access regs. themselves; (3) in general EEC conservation measures applying in Community waters (see Chapter 4); and (4) in the limited legislation enacted by Member States.

68. *Ibid.*, Arts. 7 and 8. Note, however, that one of the penalties for infringement of the regs., revocation of the licence, lies solely with the Commission, and not with the authorities of Member States.

69. See COM (82) 338.
70. For examples, see Leigh, *op. cit.* in n. 19, pp. 195–196.
71. See O.J. 1982 L138/15; 1983 L205/1; 1984 L264/2; and *Bull. E.C.* 1985 No. 6, p. 71.
72. Agreement on Certain Measures for the Purpose of Promoting the Reproduction of Salmon in the Baltic Sea, Brussels, November 21, 1979. In force April 7, 1981. O.J. 1980 L226/8.
73. O.J. 1979 L297/24 and 1980 L160/50.
74. Farnell and Elles, *op. cit.* in n. 19, p. 58.
75. For more extended treatment of this topic, see A.W. Koers, 'The European Economic Community and International Fisheries Organisations' [1984] L.I.E.I. 113.
76. *Op. cit.* in n. 2, pp. 1311 and 470–1 respectively.
77. Unless such treaties also cover matters outside the Community's treaty-making competence, in which case a mixed agreement would be required.
78. Convention on Future Multilateral Co-Operation in the North-West Atlantic Fisheries. O.J. 1978 L378/16.
79. It is, however, interesting to note that when signing the Convention, Bulgaria, the German Democratic Republic and the U.S.S.R. each made a statement that their signature 'does not imply any change in [their] position . . . to different international organisations.'
80. See, for example, Regs. 2622/79 (conservation measures), 579/80 (scheme of joint international enforcement), 1728/83 (quotas for 1983) and 3114/84 (scientific observation programme), O.J. 1979 L303/1, 1980 L63/1, 1983 L169/9 and 1984 L292/7. But note that the Commission has proposed that the Community should denounce the joint enforcement scheme: see COM (86) 378.
81. Convention on Future Multilateral Co-Operation in North-East Atlantic Fisheries. Text in O.J. 1981 L227/22.
82. The Convention was approved on behalf of the Community by Dec. 81/608, O.J. 1981 L227/21.
83. Implemented in the Community by Reg. 1899/85, O.J. 1985 L179/2. This measure was implemented nearly six months after it became binding on the Community.
84. Established by the Convention on Fishing and Conservation of the Living Resources of the Baltic Sea and Belts, Gdansk, September 13, 1973. In force July 28, 1974. Text in O.J. 1983 L237/5.
85. COM (77) 582.
86. O.J. 1983 L237/9.
87. Reg. 1866/86, O.J. 1986 L162/1. The Council received the Commission's proposal in September 1985, nine months before its adoption.
88. Established by the Convention on the Conservation of Antarctic Marine Living Resources, Canberra, May 20, 1980. In force April 7, 1982. O.J. 1981 L252/27.
89. The Convention establishing the Commission was approved on behalf of the Community by Dec. 81/691, O.J. 1981 L252/26.
90. See the Final Act of the Conference on the Conservation of Antarctic Marine Living Resources, (1980) XIX I.L.M. 837 at 838–839.
91. Reg. 2245/85, O.J. 1985 L210/2, as amended by Reg. 2296/86, O.J. 1986 L201/2. Both Regs. were adopted four months after the measures in question became binding on the Community.
92. Established by the Convention on the Conservation of the Living Resources of the South-East Atlantic, Rome, October 23, 1969. In force October 24, 1971. 801 U.N.T.S. 101. Of EEC Member States, Belgium, France, the Federal Republic of Germany, Italy, Portugal and Spain are parties to the Convention.
93. OECD, *Review of Fisheries in OECD Member Countries 1980,* Paris, 1981, p. 254.
94. *Bull. E.C.* 1985, No. 12, p. 78.

95. Established by the Convention for the Conservation of Salmon in the North Atlantic Ocean, Reykjavik, March 2, 1982. In force October 1, 1983. O.J. 1982 L378/25.
96. The Convention was approved on behalf of the Community by Dec. 82/886, O.J. 1982 L378/24.
97. Implemented by Reg. 2305/84, O.J. 1984 L213/1.
98. Established by the International Convention for the Conservation of Atlantic Tunas, Rio de Janeiro, May 14, 1966. In force March 21, 1969. 673 U.N.T.S. 63. Of EEC Member States, France, Portugal and Spain are parties to the Convention.
99. Text of the Protocol in O.J. 1986 L162/41. Community accession to the Convention was approved by Dec. 86/238, O.J. 1986 L162/33.
100. Established by the International Convention for the Regulation of Whaling, Washington, December 2, 1946. In force November 10, 1948. 161 U.N.T.S. 72; 1949 U.K.T.S. 5. Of EEC Member States, Denmark, France, the Federal Republic of Germany, Ireland, Netherlands, Spain and the United Kingdom are parties to the Convention.
101. COM (79) 364.
102. *Bull. E.C.* 1979, No. 10, p. 52. Cf. also the discussion in Chapter 3, pp. 54–55.
103. See the Commission's Answer to W.Q. 730/80, O.J. 1980 C312/5.
104. Note also that to promote the conservation of whales, commercial imports of most primary whale products into the Community have been prohibited since January 1, 1982: see Regs. 348/81 and 3786/81, O.J. 1981 L39/1 (correction in L131/30) and L377/42. Cf. Dir. 83/129, O.J. 1983 L91/30, as extended by Dir 85/444, O.J. 1985 L259/70, which bans the commercial import of the skins of seal pups.
105. Established by the Agreement for the Establishment of a General Fisheries Council for the Mediterranean, Rome, September 24, 1949. In force February 20, 1952. 126 U.N.T.S. 237; 1952 U.K.T.S. 15. Of EEC Member States, France, Greece, Italy and Spain are parties to the Agreement. For further details of this and the other commissions mentioned here, see A.W. Koers, *International Regulation of Marine Fisheries,* London, 1973, especially Chapter II.
106. Established by the Agreement for the Establishment of the Indo-Pacific Fisheries Council, Banguio, February 26, 1948. In force November 9, 1948. 120 U.N.T.S. 59; 1949 U.K.T.S. 73. France and the United Kingdom are the only EEC Member States parties to the Agreement.
107. Established by the Convention for the Establishment of an Inter-American Tropical Tuna Commission, Washington, May 31. 1949. In force March 3, 1950. 80 U.N.T.S. 3. France is the only EEC Member State party to the Convention.
108. Established by the Agreement concerning the Protection of the Salmon Population in the Baltic Sea, Stockholm, December 20, 1962. In force March 1, 1966. UN Legislative Series B/15, p. 859. Denmark and the Federal Republic of Germany are the only EEC Member States parties to the Agreement.
109. Established by the Agreement concerning Measures for the Protection of the Stocks of Deep-Sea Prawns, European Lobsters, Norway Lobsters and Crabs, Oslo, March 7, 1952. In force January 26, 1953. 175 U.N.T.S. 205. Denmark is the only EEC Member State party to the Agreement.
110. Established by FAO in September 1967. Of EEC Member States, France, Greece, Italy, Spain and the United Kingdom are members of the Committee.
111. Established by FAO in November 1973. Of EEC Member States, France, Italy, Netherlands and the United Kingdom are members of the Commission.
112. Established by FAO in 1967. Of EEC Member States, France, Greece, Netherlands, Portugal and the United Kingdom are members of the Commission.
113. O.J. 1982 L38/3. Approved on behalf of the Community by Dec. 82/72, O.J. 1982 L38/1.
114. O.J. 1982 L210/11. Approved on behalf of the Community by Dec. 82/461, O.J. 1982 L210/10.

Both this and the previous Convention are mixed agreements, as they deal partly with matters outside the Community's competence. In furtherance of the latter Convention the Commission is carrying out work to conserve the monk seal: see COM(85) 532.

115. By virtue of Reg. 3626/82, O.J. 1982 L384/1. Text of the Convention in L384/7 (correction in 1983 L186/38). It is interesting to note that two EEC Member States (Greece and Ireland) have not yet ratified the Convention.

116. Though the Convention was amended in 1983 to allow the Community to become a party: see Cmnd. 9129 (1984). This amendment has not yet entered into force.

117. 1977 U.K.T.S. 40. This Convention was discussed briefly in the previous Chapter: see p. 150.

118. 652 U.N.T.S. 237; 1968 U.K.T.S. 67. The role and work of ICES were discussed briefly in the previous Chapter, see particularly p. 148.

119. For further discussion of this topic, see Farnell and Elles, *op. cit.* in n. 19, pp. 58–64.

120. See n's 59–63 above.

121. COM (82) 25.

122. See M.J. Holden, 'Management of Fisheries Resources: the Experience of the European Economic Community' in OECD, *Experience in the Management of National Fishing Zones,* Paris, 1984, p. 113 at 115–6.

123. Norwegian Government, *Markedsutvalgets Rapport Nr. XIV om De Europeiske Fellesskap,* Oslo, 1980, p. 104.

124. See the Commission's Answer to W.Q. 2547/85, O.J. 1986 C156/20. This ad hoc agreement was, however, achieved at the cost of setting a TAC double the size recommended by ICES.

125. See Agreed Record of Consultations with Canada in COMs (79) 74 and (80) 126.

126. See Farnell and Elles, *op. cit.* in n. 19, p. 60.

127. *Bull. E.C.* 1982 No. 7/8, p. 46.

128. See, for example, the European Parliament's Resolution of July 11, 1980, O.J. 1980 C197/88.

129. It is unlikely that the European Parliament is happy with this development. In its opinion on NAFO quotas for 1981 (O.J. 1981 C90/108), Parliament said that the Commission should not be able to bind the Community without the Council or Parliament being informed, while in its opinion on the NEAFC Convention (O.J. 1981 C90/115), Parliament requested the Commission to inform it and the Council of NEAFC recommendations as soon as the EEC was notified of them in order to allow objections to be made within the specified time limits. Parliament proposed an additional article to the Dec. concluding the Convention embodying this request, but it was not accepted by the Council. A similar position was taken by Parliament in its opinion on the Baltic Convention (O.J. 1983 C242/128).

CHAPTER 6

Structural policy

Structural policy, in the Community jargon, refers broadly speaking to the catching side of the fishing industry. Management of, and the conditions of access to, the resource base have already been examined in the two previous Chapters. This Chapter will therefore be concerned with the other, basically socio-economic, aspects of the catching side of the fishing industry, including the capacity and efficiency of fishing fleets; what one might call their infrastructure (such as ports and processing and marketing facilities); the working conditions of fishermen; and questions related to these matters. That there should be a Community structural policy for the fishing industry is implied by Article 39 of the EEC Treaty, which speaks of the objectives of the Common Fisheries Policy as including increasing productivity and ensuring a fair standard of living for fishermen (cf. the discussion in Chapter 2 at pp. 23–25 above). Concrete proposals for a Community structural policy were contained in the Commission's 1966 'Report on the Situation in the Fisheries Sector of EEC Member States and the Basic Principles for a Common Policy'.[1] These proposals were given partial effect to in Regulation 2141/70 laying down a Common Strutural Policy for the Fishing Industry (hereafter referred to as the Structural Regulation).[2]

Article 9 of the Structural Regulation suggests that the aims of the Community's structural policy should be 'to promote the rational development of the fishing industry within the framework of economic growth and social progress and to ensure an equitable standard of living' for fishermen. In particular, the Community should aim at increasing 'productivity through restructuring of fishing fleets and other means of production, in keeping with technical progress, and intensification of the search for new fishing grounds and new methods of fishing'; adapting and developing production, processing and marketing conditions to market requirements; and improving the standard and conditions of living of fishermen. A basic question – which has also arisen in a similar fashion with agriculture[3] – is whether such objectives should be achieved essentially through the Community co-ordinating national structural policies or whether the Community should aim at its own full-blooded structural policy to replace national policies. Given the diversity of the fishing industries of the EEC both between and within Member States (see the discussion in Chapter 1 at pp. 8–10), and the different approaches of Member States in this area (ranging from the traditional interventionist approach of the French authorities to structural policy to the German tradition of leaving such matters to the industry),[4] it is scarcely surprising that originally the Community limited its role to one of seeking to co-ordinate national policies. In more recent years, however, and no doubt in part at least as a result of its having obtained the primary responsibility for managing fishery resources, the Community has begun to move more towards having its own comprehensive policy. It has done so in a number of ways. First, it has embarked on an extensive programme of Community aid to the fishing industry: by controlling the way in which this money is spent, the Community influences the content of national policies. Secondly, the Commission has proposed a wide-ranging set of measures relating to employment and social policy in the fishing industry. Finally, the Community authorities have in recent years adopted a much stricter approach to controlling national financial aids to the fishing industry. Each of these matters will be examined in turn. First, however, it is necessary to say something about the general way in which the Community seeks to co-ordinate the individual structural policies of its Member States.

1. CO-ORDINATION OF NATIONAL STRUCTURAL POLICIES

Article 5 of the Structural Regulation provides that Member States 'shall co-ordinate their structural policies for the fishing industry'. The Regulation does not, however, specify any very definite means by which such co-ordination is to be effected. It lays down a number of obligations, all of which are relevant to such co-ordination, but which do not, even when taken together, amount to any real co-ordination. First, Member States are required each year to notify the Commission of 'the structural situation'; 'liaison between structures of the fishing industry and market policy'; proposed measures for structural improvement; and 'projects for research and scientific and technical assistance adopted by the public authorities or financially assisted by them' (Article 5(1)). Secondly, Member States must send the Commission certain documents concerning proposed structural improvements for the fishing industry. The Commission *may* express its opinion on these documents, and *must* do so if requested by a Member State (Article 10). Thirdly, the Commission is required to submit a report each year to the European Parliament and the Council on structures for the fishing industry. Article 6(2) sets out a number of matters with which this Report must deal. These include: a review of the structural situation of the fishing industry and the policies followed by Member States: an account of the measures adopted by Member States and an assessment of their effectiveness; information concerning co-ordination on a Community scale of structural policies; and a review of the situation in each Member State. In practice the Commission has failed to observe this obligation to submit annual reports properly, if at all. According to the European Parliament, as of December 1980 the Commission had not submitted a single report.[5]

Article 11 of the Structural Regulation sets up a Standing Committee for the Fishing Industry, consisting of representatives of EEC Member States meeting under the chairmanship of a representative of the Commission. The Committee's general function is 'to promote the co-ordination of structural policies for the fishing industry and to ensure close and constant co-operation between Member States and the Commission.' The Commission's more specific functions are set out in Article 12. These include: ensuring that Member States and the Commission are kept mutually informed of structural policies and fishery measures; studying the structural policies of Member States; helping the Commission prepare its annual report on structures for the fishing industry; and giving opinions on structural problems of the fishing industry when so requested by the Commission. Under the various programmes of Community financial assistance to the fishing industry, the Committee is also to be consulted by the Commission before the latter makes grants of Community aid.

The result of these provisions is that no direct co-ordination of national structural policies has occurred or is likely to occur. At best a certain amount of indirect co-ordination has taken place. More effective than the above provisions in leading to the co-ordination of national policies, although again such co-ordination is indirect, are the Community's programmes of financial assistance to the fishing industry and its control over national aids to the fishing industry.

2. COMMUNITY AID TO THE FISHING INDUSTRY

There are at present a considerable number of Community programmes of financial assistance to the fishing industry, as well as some programmes which have already expired. These programmes provide aid for a number of different purposes – adjusting capacity to catch potential; building and modernising vessels; developing aquaculture; and improving processing and marketing facilities. The way in which each of these matters is the subject of Community aid will now be examined in turn.

a) Adjusting Capacity to Catch Potential

It was pointed out in Chapter 1 (see p. 14) that the general introduction of 200-mile limits in the mid- and late 1970s meant that there was both overcapacity in the Community's fishing fleets (i.e. there were considerably more vessels than were required to catch the quantity of fish available to the Community), and that there were many distant-water vessels which no longer had any distant-water fishing open to them and which were ill-suited for fishing in near and middle waters. From the outset the Commission recognised that this situation meant economic inefficiency in the fishing industry and that it would be likely that TACs and other conservation measures would be harder to enforce than if the fleet were smaller. The Commission therefore produced a series of proposals aimed at adjusting the capacity of the Community fleet to the catches available to it. Not until October 1983, however, was the Council able to agree on these proposals. In the interval, as Table 3 shows, there was a considerable decrease in the overall capacity of the Community fleet, measured in terms of tonnage (engine power is a more accurate indicator of capacity than tonnage, but detailed figures do not appear to be available). The decrease was particularly marked in the case of distant-water vessels, especially of France, West Germany and the United Kingdom. This fairly marked adjustment in capacity, largely the product of market forces, was to some extent cushioned by financial aid granted by individual Member States.

The measures adopted by the Council in October 1983 comprise a Directive concerning Certain Measures to Adjust Capacity in the Fisheries Sector[6] and a Regulation on Measures to Encourage Exploratory Fishing and Co-Operation through Joint Ventures in the Fishing Sector.[7] The Directive provides that the Community will reimburse Member States for 50 per cent of their costs in introducing programmes for the temporary laying-up and scrapping of vessels. The programme for the laying-up of vessels involves Member States in paying to the owners of vessels over 18 metres a daily laying-up premium, calculated on the basis of a maximum of 12 per cent of the cost or insured value of the vessel for an average annual period of fishing of 250 days, where owners are prepared to lay-up their vessels for at least 45 days a year. The scrapping programme involves paying owners of vessels over 12 metres, whose characteristics make it difficult to adapt them to the types of fishing available to the Community in the medium term, a grant if the owners are prepared to withdraw their vessels permanently from the Community fishing fleet either by scrapping them, selling them to a third State or assigning them to purposes other than fishing e.g. work in the offshore oil industry. It was originally estimated that these two programmes would cost the Community 44 million and 32 million ECU respectively: on the accession of Portugal and Spain to the Community these figures were increased to 60 and 46 million.[8] Unlike the Commission's original proposals,[9] the Directive contains no provision for the Community to contribute to the cost of encouraging early retirement, the cost of unemployment benefit for fishermen made unemployed as a result of implementation of the Directive, or the cost of information campaigns to promote the consumption of lesser-known species of fish.

Table 3. Change in capacity of EEC fleets, 1976–85.

	Total number of motorised vessels			Total tonnage ('000 GRT) of motorised vessels		
	1976	*1983*	*1985*	*1976*	*1983*	*1985*
Belgium	253	201	197	24.0	22.3	23.1
Denmark	7,430	3,347	3,295	149.1	119.5	129.2
France	12,967	11,939	12,940	275.8	172.9	229.4
W. Germany	1,294	688	952	141.3	79.8	57.7
Greece	N/A	5,111[1]	N/A	N/A	172.2[1]	N/A
Ireland	1.237	1,566	N/A	27.7	35.5	N/A
Italy	21,227	22,981	19,410	269.6	316.8	267.8
Netherlands	1,025	1,041	N/A	90.4	131.1	N/A
United Kingdom	6,703	6,490	7,595	247.3	177.4	160.7
Portugal	5,161	5,948	7,123[2]	195.0	183.6	193.2[2]
Spain	17,148	17,740	17,749	807.4	698.8	678.9

[1] Figures are for 1982; [2] Figures are for 1984.
Source: OECD's Annual *Reviews of Fisheries in OECD Member Countries.*

It is difficult to establish what the practical results of the Directive have so far been. The Commission has approved the programmes for implementing the Directive which all Member States except Ireland, Portugal and Spain have put forward, but its decisions granting such approval[10] give no details of these programmes. The Commission is also required to publish in the *Official Journal* a list of all vessels permanently withdrawn from the Community fishing fleet as a result of the implementation of the Directive. So far one such list has been published.[11] This shows that 2 Danish vessels, totalling 421.8 GRT, and 54 British vessels, totalling 15,994.5 GRT, have been withdrawn. This compares with the approximately 142,000 GRT[12] that the Community apparently envisages should be withdrawn.

Whatever may have been the results of the temporary laying-up programme in practice, in theory at least the programme would seem to raise some problems. The preamble to the Directive justifies the programme as being necessary while fish stocks are being built up through Community conservation measures so that Member States can retain 'production capacity at the level needed for optimal exploitation of the reconstituted stocks at a later date.' This justification is based on two questionable assumptions: first, that stocks will be 'reconstituted' within the relatively short period of three years that the programme is scheduled to last; and secondly, that at the time the Directive was adopted capacity was indeed at the level needed for future optimal exploitation (and in any case what does the Council mean by 'optimal'?). The programme would also seem to require considerable resources to be properly enforced, because a check should be kept that vessels are actually laid up at the times that they said they would be under the programme. It has been suggested, too, that the size of the laying-up premium (and scrapping grant) has not been sufficiently attractive to fishermen.[13] Finally, as Butlin points out,[14] temporary laying-up is likely to cause a lay-up/price cycle. As vessels are laid up, the supply of fish will be reduced (this assumes, of course, that a large number of vessels are in fact laid up) and prices will rise. This price rise will then encourage back into fishing vessels which are laid up (including possibly some which might have been prepared to withdraw from the fleet permanently). This increase in capacity is then likely to lead to an increase in supplies, thus causing a drop in prices and a loss of revenue to vessels. This will encourage vessels to start laying-up again, and so the whole cycle will begin anew.

The other Community measure to adjust capacity to catch potential, Regulation 2909/83, is not concerned (as the Directive is) with reducing capacity, but to redeploy capacity which would otherwise be excessive. Two forms of redeployment are to be financially assisted under the Regulation – exploratory fishing voyages, both in Community waters and elsewhere, for species or in areas which have previously been under-utilised,[15] and joint ventures with third States in the Mediterranean or West Africa. In the case of the former, the Community will reimburse Member States 50 per cent of their costs in paying vessels undertaking exploratory voyages a redeployment premium, based on the difference between operating costs and revenue from catches. To be eligible for such a premium, vessels must be over 24 metres in length, make voyages that last for at least 30 days a year, and have an observer on board or during the preparation and evaluation of the results of the voyage. In the case of joint ventures, the Community will reimburse Member States for 50 per cent of their expenditure in granting a co-operation premium to their fisher-men taking part in joint ventures. Such a premium is not to exceed 25 ECU per GRT for a period of three months in the case of vessels transferred temporarily to take part in fishing under a joint venture, or 400 ECU per GRT in the case of vessels permanently transferred. Vessels fishing under joint ventures must not fish in Community waters. It was originally estimated that Community expenditure would amount to 11 million ECU in the case of exploratory voyages and 7 million ECU in the case of joint ventures: these figures were increased to 13 million and 10 million ECU on the accession of Portugal and Spain to the Community.[16]

The Regulation has so far had little practical application. No money has been spent on joint ventures. It has been suggested that this is partly because it is more straightforward for owners to withdraw their vessels permanently from the Community fleet under the Directive, and partly because the areas in which joint ventures are eligible for Community aid (the Mediterranean and West Africa), while being areas of traditional Community interest, are not perhaps the areas of greatest opportunity.[17] In the case of exploratory voyages, five Member States – Denmark, France, West Germany, Italy and the Nether-lands – have received support from the Community for voyages undertaken by their vessels.[18] This has so far involved the Community in expenditure of about 1.7 million ECU. It has been suggested that more use of Community finance for exploratory voyages has not been made because the financing arrange-ments are complex and the Community may have underestimated the costs which have to be covered to encourage such voyages, especially where the catch may not have any commercial value. Furthermore limiting Community aid to vessels over 24 metres may have been unduly restrictive.[19]

No assessment of the effect of the Directive and Regulation on the overall capacity of the Community fishing fleet – or of what sort of arrangements should follow after the expiry of these instruments at the end of 1986 – can be made until the Community's programmes of aid for constructing and moderni-sing vessels have been considered. Before doing so, however, it is perhaps appropriate at this stage to say just a few words about one of the Community's most recent programmes of aid which is designed in part to deal with some of the consequences of reducing the capacity of the Community's fleet. Regulation 3638/85[20] provides that funds are to be made available from the European Regional Development Fund to stimulate the creation of new employment in 'certain areas adversely affected by the implementation of the Community fisheries policy' where employment opportunities are limited. These areas are specified in Article 2(2) of the Regulation and are the districts around most of the ports for distant-water fleets in France, West Germany and the United Kingdom and Bornholm and North Jutland in Denmark (but do not, it should be noted, include any areas in Portugal or Spain).

b) The Construction and Modernisation of Vessels

There have been a variety of Community programmes providing financial assistance for the construction and modernisation of fishing vessels. Before 1980 aid could be given by the Guidance Section of the European Agricultural Guidance and Guarantee Fund (EAGGF) under Regulation 17/64[21] for any project which was both aimed at an adaptation or improvement of fishing necessitated by the economic consequences of implementing the Common Fisheries Policy and which offered an adequate guarantee of lasting economic benefit. Such aid was normally not to exceed 25 per cent of the cost of the project. Between 1971 and 1977 65.2 million ECU was granted under this provision for the modernisation and construction of vessels (as well as a further 2.6 million ECU for port infrastructure).[22]

During this same period there was also a specialised programme of Community aid directed at converting vessels in the salt cod-fishing industry.[23] The need for such a conversion scheme stemmed from the lifting of duties on imports of salt cod coming into the Community from third States. This produced competition for the Community salt cod-industry which it was ill-equipped to face. It was therefore felt that it would be advantageous to encourage the fishermen involved to switch to other techniques – in particular, deep-freezing on board – and to fish for other species, especially tuna which was in short supply.[24] Under this programme EAGGF funds (up to 25 per cent of each project) were made available for projects to restructure production, processing and marketing activities in the cod fishing sector and to finance the cost of further training for workers affected by structural reconversion in this sector. Between 1972 and 1977 a total of 9.8 million ECU (out of 10.2 million budgeted) was spent by EAGGF on a dozen projects in France and West Germany.[25]

The third programme of aid for constructing and modernising vessels was concerned with restructuring the inshore fishing industry. Originally proposed by the Commission in November 1975,[26] the programme was adopted by the Council in July 1978[27] but with a rather different emphasis from the Commission's original proposal. Whereas the latter had contained elements aimed at contracting the inshore fishing industry (e.g. scrapping old boats, pensioning off fishermen over 55), the programme actually adopted appears designed to encourage the expansion of the industry. The programme was of an interim nature pending the adoption of a comprehensive programme for restructuring the industry generally: originally adopted only for 1978, the programme was subsequently extended to the end of 1982.[28] Under the programme EAGGF was authorised to spend up to 95 million ECU in the period 1978–82 on the development of inshore fishing in regions where fishing potential made this possible and on the development of aquaculture in regions which were particularly suited to this activity. For the purposes of the programme, the development of inshore fishing meant the purchase or construction of new fishing vessels between 6 and 24 metres in length and the modernisation or conversion of existing vessels of the same size for the purpose of rationalising fishing operations, better preserving catches or saving energy. Aid from EAGGF took the form of a capital subsidy not exceeding 25 per cent (50 per cent in certain disadvantaged areas[29]) of the total investment: the Member State concerned had to finance at least 5 per cent of the total investment, while the beneficiary had to finance at least 50 per cent (25 per cent in the disadvantaged areas). Details of the aid granted under this programme – and, it may be noted, requests for aid exceeded by nearly three times the total amount of money available[30] – are shown in Table 4. According to the Commission, by 1981 the programme had led to about 6 per cent (by tonnage) of the inshore fleet being renewed.[31]

Table 4. Community aid for the construction and modernisation of fishing vessels.

	Under the inshore fishing programme		Under regulation 2908/83, 1983–85	
	Number of projects	Amount of aid (million ECU)	Number of projects	Amount of aid (million ECU)
Belgium	6	0.9	42	8.3
Denmark	113	4.6	280	11.3
France	93	11.4	193	20.8
West Germany	58	4.8	71	6.0
Greece	105	7.3	122	9.9
Ireland	162	16.7	41	2.5
Italy	258	15.0	467	26.9
Netherlands	33	3.0	41	2.3
United Kingdom	216	18.0	273	19.1
Total EEC	1044	81.7	1530	107.1

Source: OECD's Annual *Reviews of Fisheries in OECD Member Countries.*

The principal current programme of Community assistance for modernising and constructing fishing vessels is Regulation 2908/83 on a Common Measure for Restructuring, Modernising and Developing the Fishing Industry and for Developing Aquaculture,[32] adopted at the same time as the Directive and Regulation concerned with adjusting fleet capacity to catch potential (discussed above). The Regulation provides that Community financing is to be provided for the purchase or construction of new vessels and the modernisation or conversion of existing vessels (the aim of such restructuring being an increase in productivity and hence fishermen's incomes); the development of aquaculture (discussed below); and the construction of artificial strucures to encourage the restocking of inshore waters in the Mediterranean. Unlike the Commission's proposal, the Regulation contains no provision for Community aid for building or modernising centres for training and research. As a first step in obtaining community aid, Member States must submit to the Commission for its approval a multiannual guidance programme (which is a set of objectives relating to the three matters for which financial provision is made by the Regulation, together with a statement of the means for attaining these objectives). Such a programme must seek to attain the long-term objective of 'a satisfactory balance between the fishing capacity to be deployed by the production facilities covered by the programme and the stocks which are expected to be available during the period of validity of the programme'. In considering whether to approve a programme, the Commission must take into account the following factors: production potential, measures for the conservation and management of fish stocks, demand for the products concerned, and the 'guidelines of the Common Fisheries Policy' (what these guidelines are is nowhere specified).

Once a programme has been approved by the Commission (in consultation with the Standing Committee for the Fishing Industry), applications may be made for individual investment projects to receive Community aid. To qualify for such aid, a project must be consistent with the guidelines laid down by the relevant multiannual guidance programme; offer a satisfactory guarantee of yielding a profit; relate to vessels between 9 and 33 metres in length; and contribute to the lasting structural improvement aimed at by the programme. In the case of conversion or modernisation, a project must be substantial (generally involving expenditure of at least 20,000 ECU), and must be undertaken to rationalise fishing operations, improve conditions for storing the catch, or save energy. Where the Commission is faced with applications for more aid than is available under the programme (and so far applications have exceeded three-fold the aid available), priority is to be given, in the case of buying or building new vessels, to projects which replace old, lost or withdrawn vessels or based in areas where fishing is traditionally an important economic activity; and, in the case of conversion or modernisation, to projects which are concerned with fuel economy, improving the processing of catches or which are 'co-ordinated in their economic and technical aspects' (whatever that may mean).

For projects which have been approved, Community aid takes the same form as under the Inshore Fishing Programme discussed above, although to the disadvantaged areas (for which the Community grant is 50 per cent) have been added Portugal and parts of Spain (including the Canary Islands, which are otherwise outside the scope of EEC fisheries law – see Chapter 3).[33] The cost to the Community of aid under this Regulation (which is due to expire at the end of 1986) was originally estimated as being 156 million ECU, of which 118 million was intended for vessels, 34 million for aquaculture and 4 million for artificial reefs. On the accession of Portugal and Spain to the Community the total amount of aid available under the Regulation was increased to 230 million ECU, though it is not specified how this total is to be allocated among the three areas of operation of the Regulation.[34] As Table 4 shows, up to the end of 1985 107.1 million ECU had been spent on 1,530 projects (of which 676 involved new vessels and 854 modernised vessels). In addition a further 5.8 million ECU was spent on 18 projects for artificial reefs in French and Italian waters.

All the Member States have drawn up multiannual guidance programmes for vessel construction and modernisation which have been approved by the Commission.[35] In most cases the aim is to maintain capacity at 1982/83 levels by offsetting additions to the fleet with withdrawals and by not increasing engine power in the case of vessel modernisations. In the case of the Netherlands and Spain, the aim is actually to reduce capacity to the catches available. In nearly every case in approving these programmes the Commission has said that the Member State concerned should introduce a permanent system for monitoring capacity. In addition to stabilising or reducing capacity, most of the programmes are also aimed at improving working and safety conditions on vessels.

The Fisheries Working Group of the European Parliament has criticized the minimum and maximum lengths of the vessels for which aid is available. Vessels under 9 metres are important in some peripheral areas. Conversely vessels over 33 metres are required for fishing in certain waters and at certain times of the year. There are also safety implications in an ageing fleet of vessels over 33 metres. The Working Group has also said that there is a feeling in the fishing industry that the granting of aid is something of a lottery. The Commission's criteria in selecting applications are perceived as unclear. Application forms are also regarded as cumbersome, and aid is often slow in reaching its beneficiary.[36]

Aid for modernising and constructing fishing vessels is also available from other Community sources. First, the Integrated Mediterranean Programmes, adopted in 1985,[37] provide for aid to develop the fishing industry in the South of France, much of Italy and the whole of Greece. This aid is to be used for restructuring, converting and modernising fishing fleets; improving infrastructure and port installations; developing aquaculture; improving storage and processing facilities; encouraging the sale of fishery products (in particular by advertising campaigns); and intensifying research and vocational training. The Programmes last for seven years and total Community aid during this period is envisaged as being 4,100 million ECU by way of grants and 2,500 million ECU by way of loans. Of this amount the Commission intends that 466 million ECU should be spent on fisheries.[38] Community aid is normally not to exceed 70 per cent of the cost of a project.

A second additional source of finance, admittedly for a very limited geographical area, is the Integrated Development Programme for the Western Isles of Scotland,[39] which provides aid for improving landing stages and other onshore facilities for the inshore fishing industry and for developing aquaculture. Finally, fisheries projects may also be eligible for aid from the European Investment Bank, the European Regional Development Fund and the European Development Fund,[40] but aid from these sources excludes any concurrent aid from EAGGF.[41]

The various programmes of aid described above have led to a lot of older vessels, especially in the inshore fleet, being replaced or modernised. This is obviously desirable for reasons of efficiency and safety, as well as having beneficial effects for regional policy, since much of the aid has gone to the poor peripheral regions of the Community. But the main question to be asked in evaluating the various Community measures of financial aid for the construction and modernisation of vessels is the effect of such measures on the capacity of the Community fishing fleet. There seems little doubt that before 1983 the various Community measures did increase the capacity of the non-distant-water part of the fleet, both in overall terms and for particular sectors of the fleet.[42] It is harder to say what the effect has been since 1983. While the general aim of the various multiannual guidance programmes approved under Regulation 2908/83 is to maintain the size of fishing fleets at a stable level (but whether this level is above or below optimum capacity probably no one knows), the effect of the aid under the other measures discussed (such as the Integrated Mediterranean Programmes) would seem to be to increase capacity. It is true that the rather incomplete and probably not wholly accurate figures in Table 3 suggest a decline in the capacity of some national fleets between 1983 and 1985, but other national fleets have clearly increased in size, and in any case there may well be overcapacity in certain sectors of the fleets of the former. Nor is tonnage more than a rough guide to capacity: many vessels may not have increased in size but may have increased their fish-catching capacity through the acquisition of more effective fishing gear and equipment and an increase in engine size.

A first need, therefore, before deciding on what measures (if any) should follow Regulation 2908/83 on its expiry at the end of 1986, is for the Community authorities to determine what the present Community capacity is and its relationship to the optimum level of capacity, as the Fisheries Working Group of the European Parliament has recommended.[43] Of course, ascertaining either of these things is far from straightforward. In the case of the former, apart from the problems of defining capacity (alluded to at the end of the previous paragraph), there is the further difficulty that there are not full statistics on all Member States' fleets nor, where there are statistics, are they always in comparable form. As regards measuring the optimum level of capacity, such a level is determined by the size of catches available, something which is obviously very difficult to predict and which in any case varies from year to year. Nevertheless, the Community authorities have to make rough calculations on these two matters. Only when this information is known, can a meaningful decision be taken as to the aims of any future Community programmes of aid – whether they should be contraction, modernisation, or possibly even in some sectors expansion.

The Community also needs to start thinking now about how, once the capacity of Community fleets is roughly at an optimum level, it can be kept at that level: if no action is taken, capacity will almost certainly (as suggested in Chapter 1, see p. 4) start to increase again. While the European Parliament has begun to think about this problem,[44] there is no evidence that the Commission has: in a Commission 'Communication on Guidelines and Initiatives for the Development of the Common Fisheries Policy' published in June 1986,[45] there is no mention of the matter, although if the Commission was considering the question, one would presumably have expected some discussion of it in this document.

Action to keep capacity at a stable level could, of course, be taken by individual Member States rather than the Community. Indeed some Member States are already taking some action of this kind: for example, in the United Kingdom if a vessel holding a licence for a pressure stock (i.e. a stock for which the United Kingdom quota is likely to be fully exploited) withdraws, the licence is returned to the Government and not reissued.[46] However, it is probably desirable that action to keep capacity at a stable level should be taken, additionally or alternatively, by the Community. If action is not taken by the Community and only by some Member States, this is likely to lead to differences in compliance with TACs and quotas. The more rational fleets are likely to observe their quotas, while those national fleets with excess capacity are likely to exceed their quotas. This situation is clearly a recipe for breeding mistrust between the different national fishing industries. And if quotas are greatly exceeded, then TACs will be exceeded, with the consequences of overfishing, reduced supplies and increased prices and/or imports.

It is of course obvious that the introduction of Community measures to stabilise capacity (such as limited entry or individual vessel quotas) poses formidable problems. It would amount to the Community saying which vessels and fishermen should be allowed to continue to fish. Apart from the problem of choosing the criteria for such a selection (something which it would be immensely difficult for the Community to agree on), such action would amount to a degree of central Community direction alien to the philosophy of most Member States and most fishermen. On the other hand, it is possible to imagine something less centrally *dirigiste*. Since the level of desirable capacity is governed by the resources available, and since the resources available to each Member State are largely determined by the Community's TAC and quota system, then the Community need do no more than set the total capacity available to each Member State. Individual Member States could then decide how and by what means to allocate their allotted capacity between their vessels and fishermen.

c) Developing Aquaculture

Compared with countries such as Japan and Norway, aquaculture in the Community is – or at least was until very recently – under-developed. There is thus considerable scope for developing aquaculture. This would be beneficial in a number of ways. First it would contribute to making up the shortfall in Community supplies of fish from Community sources, thus reducing imports. It is unlikely, however, that aquaculture would ever do more than make up a relatively small proportion of such shortfall, partly because the shortfall is so large compared with the present production of aquaculture and partly because the shortfall relates to species like cod and tuna which are not suitable for farming. A second benefit is that aquaculture, producing high-value species like salmon, turbot and shellfish for which the Community market is relatively limited, offers considerable possibilities for export, especially to the markets of North America and Japan. Thirdly, aquaculture offers possibilities of employment in many of Europe's poorest peripheral regions where unemployment is high but conditions for aquaculture ideal.

Given these advantages of aquaculture, and the fact that starting up or expanding an aquaculture installation is something of commercial risk, it is not surprising that the Community has offered financial support to aquaculture under a number of programmes. First, aid (up to 25 per cent of the cost of a project) was available before 1978 under Regulation 17/64. Between 1971 and 1977 5.53 million ECU worth of aid was given to aquaculture.[47] Secondly, under the Inshore Fishing Industry Programme (discussed above) aid from EAGGF, in the form of a grant of 25 per cent of the cost of a project (50 per cent in the disadvantaged areas), was available for the development of aquaculture in regions which were particularly suited to this activity. As can be seen from Table 5, under this Programme just over 23 million ECU was spent on 109 projects. The third, and currently major source, of Community finance is Regulation 2908/83 (discussed above), under which 34 million ECU has been set aside for aquaculture for the period 1983–86. Aid takes the same form as under the Inshore Fishing Industry Programme. As with the construction and modernisation of vessels, Member States must submit for the Commission's approval a multiannual guidance programme, the object of which must be a substantial and economically profitable production of fish, crustaceans and molluscs. The Commission has so far approved those programmes submitted to it,[48] except for those parts of programmes containing proposals for the fresh-water culture of trout and carp: the Commission has withheld approval for these because it does not think there is a market for any further production of these species. The amount of aid given under Regulation 2908/83 up to the end of 1985 is shown in Table 5. Apart from Regulation 2908/83, aid for aquaculture is also available under the Integrated Mediterranean Programmes and the Integrated Development Programme for the Western Isles of Scotland (discussed in the previous sub-section). The result of all this Community aid has no doubt been an increase in aquaculture production, but the writer has unfortunately been unable to discover any figures indicating the size of this increase.

Table 5. Community aid for aquaculture.

	Under the inshore fishing programme		Under regulation 2908/83, 1983–85	
	Number of projects	Amount of aid (million ECU)	Number of projects	Amount of aid (million ECU)
Belgium	–	–	–	–
Denmark	4	0.3	17	1.1
France	7	2.3	10	2.5
West Germany	–	–	1	0.1
Greece	5	1.3	4	1.4
Ireland	19	3.4	17	2.8
Italy	39	13.3	27	9.0
Netherlands	2	0.4	15	1.1
United Kingdom	33	2.1	14	0.7
Total EEC	109	23.1	105	18.7

Source: OECD's Annual *Reviews of Fisheries in OECD Member Countries.*

d) Processing and Marketing

It is clearly of benefit to fishermen if the processing and marketing of fish (particularly of under-utilised species) can be improved and developed. To this end there have been various programmes of Community aid. Prior to 1978 aid was available under Regulation 17/64 from EAGGF, and pursuant to this provision some 12.6 million ECU worth of aid was given for marketing.[49] Since 1978 the main source of Community aid for processing and marketing has been Regulation 355/77.[50] Under this provision (which is scheduled to last until 1995) aid may be given by the Guidance Section of EAGGF to develop or rationalise the treatment, processing or marketing of fisheries products. Such aid shall not normally exceed 25 per cent (35 or 50 per cent in certain disadvantaged regions) of the cost of the project, while the beneficiary must contribute at least 50 per cent (less in the disadvantaged regions) to the cost and the relevant Member State at least 5 per cent. Since 1980 projects have had to be part of a programme put forward by a Member State and approved by the Commission. Aid will not be given for projects directed principally at the marketing and processing of fish products other than those for human con-sumption, but consideration may be given to investments concerned ex-clusively with the handling, processing or marketing of waste from fish prod-ucts. Priority is given to projects which relate to the marketing or processing of under-utilised species; which involve technological innovation; which involve the reconversion of factories for the processing of fish products for purposes other than human consumption to operations relating specifically to human consumption; which reduce the seasonality or irregularity of production of processed fish; or which improve hygiene conditions. Between 1978 and 1985 just over 90 million ECU worth of aid was granted under Regulation 355/77 for 439 projects, as can be seen from Table 6.

The entry into the Community of Portugal and Spain with their large and efficient sardine canning industries, threatens the continued economic viability of many sardine canning plants in the pre-existing Community. To help such plants meet this threat the Council in December 1985 adopted a three-year programme of assistance.[51] Under this programme the Community will pay 50 per cent of the expenditure involved in one of the following forms of action:

1. research and/or manufacture of new products or products derived from sardines, more suited to the requirements of the market and whereby the markets of canning plants may be broadened;
2. promoting the consumption of sardines and sardine-based products;
3. improving marketing and distribution;
4. improving the quality of production and the productivity of existing plants;
5. converting plants from canning sardines to processing other fishery prod-ucts of Community origin;

6. closing plants.

It is estimated that this aid will total 10 million ECU.

As with the construction and modernisation of vessels and as with aquaculture, Community aid for processing and marketing is also available under the Integrated Mediterranean Programmes. In addition, the European Regional Development Fund and the European Investment Bank also make grants and loans for investments in processing and marketing: for example in 1985 the Bank lent more than 15 million ECU for small and medium-sized investments to improve operating and marketing conditions in coastal areas eligible for regional aid.[52]

Having looked at Community financial aid to the fishing industry, we must now turn to examine the second element – or more realistically a potential element – in the Community's structural policy – the Commission's proposals, and the very limited Council action so far, in relation to employment and social policy in the fishing industry.

3. EMPLOYMENT AND SOCIAL POLICY

In its report on the Basic Principles for a Common Fisheries Policy, published in 1966, the Commission suggested that the Policy should embrace working and social conditions in the fishing industry, and it discussed at some length the kinds of measures which might be adopted.[53] However, neither the Commission's draft regulations of 1968 nor the regulations adopted in 1970 (nor their consolidating successors) deal with the question of social policy at all (although it is true that Article 9 of the Structural Regulation speaks of measures

Table 6. Community expenditure on projects under Regulation 355/77, 1978–85.

Member State	Number of projects	Amount of aid (million ECU)
Belgium	18	2.1
Denmark	78	6.7
France	24	5.5
West Germany	38	3.5
Greece	11	3.1
Ireland	44	15.2
Italy	77	39.2
Netherlands	22	2.1
United Kingdom	127	13.4
Total EEC	439	90.8

Source: OECD's Annual *Reviews of Fisheries in OECD Member Countries.*

being adopted to improve, in step with technical progress, 'the standard and conditions of living of the population which depends on fishing for its livelihood'). Although the Commission's fishery management proposals of September 1976 contain a fleeting reference to social policy,[54] it was not until 1980 that the Commission took up the question of social conditions in the fishing industry in a comprehensive manner, having earlier been pressed to do so by the European Parliament.[55]

In November 1980 the Commission sent to the Council a 'Communication on the Social Aspects in the Community Sea Fishing Sector.'[56] This document contains the guidelines for a social action programme and deals with four questions: vocational training, employment, safety and health at work, and working conditions. As regards vocational training, the Commission proposes that there should be established a joint approach in developing such training and there should be introduced a Community action programme designed to back up certain specific aspects of this approach. In the first instance these aims would be sought to be realised by means of a Council Resolution. This would call on Member States to ensure that fishermen obtain appropriate vocational training; specify the minimum period of training and the training programmes involved; provide refresher courses for instructors and the access of fishermen to continuous training; and make a forecast of training requirements. Much of this action to be taken by Member States would be eligible for aid from the European Social Fund. The Resolution would also call on the Commission to define back-up measures for training. Such measures would *inter alia* define the qualifications required to become a professional fisherman; set up common vocational training programmes; encourage an exchange of information between Member States; develop and use modern teaching aids; and provide for the training of instructors.

While the development of vocational training will help improve employment prospects, other measures are necessary. These measures, according to the Commission, should be aimed at identifying the employment situation in fisheries, balancing the vacancies offered and the labour available, maintaining or creating jobs for fishermen in disadvantaged regions and helping young people find work. While the Commission envisages that all these measures would be taken by Member States, presumably some of them (though the Commission does not say so) would be eligible for aid from the European Social Fund.

To improve safety and health in the fishing industry, the Commission proposes that the rules relating to the construction and equipment of fishing vessels should be improved; there should be a study of the causes of accidents; health care on board ship should be improved (e.g. by making it compulsory for all vessels to carry a medicine chest); training should include theoretical and practical instruction on safety, health and the prevention of accidents; and assistance and rescue at sea should be made more effective and co-ordinated at a Community level. The Commission said it would publish a draft directive to give effect to these proposals.

Finally, as regards working conditions, the Commission is of the view that it is not appropriate at present to take uniform action at Community level because of the wide variations in working conditions throughout the EEC and the changes taking place in the structure of the fleets. Instead, Member States should encourage the two sides of the fishing industry to reach agreement on such matters as remuneration (including possibly a guaranteed wage), hours of work (including minimum periods of rest), holiday entitlement, job security and organisation of work.

Insofar as any of the above guidelines for a social action programme require the adoption of Community measures, the Commission will put forward proposals after having consulted the Member States and the Joint Committee on Social Problems in Sea Fishing (on which see p. 34 above).

Although these rather bland proposals by the Commission for a Community social policy in the fishery sector were welcomed by the European Parliament[57] and Economic and Social Committee[58] (though neither body thought the Commission had gone far enough), the Commission has not yet – nearly six years later – followed up its guidelines with any concrete implementing proposals, nor has the Council adopted the one concrete proposal in the Commission's 1980 Communication – the Draft Resolution on a Common Training Policy for the Fisheries Sector.

Although it has taken no action on the Commission's 1980 proposals, the Council has taken one action in the general area of the working conditions of fishermen, albeit of a very modest character. In 1980 it recommended that Member States should ratify the 1977 Torremolinos Convention for the Safety of Fishing Vessels by July 31, 1982.[59] In fact only three Member States – Belgium, France and the United Kingdom-ratified the Convention by the specified date. In reaction to this poor response, the Commission in 1984 put forward a draft Decision under which not only would those Member States that had not ratified the Convention be required to do so by the middle of 1986 but Member States would also be required to apply the Convention's provisions from the beginning of 1987 even if the Convention had not entered into force on that date.[60] The latter step was necessary, thought the Commission, because unco-ordinated application of the Convention was likely to affect competition conditions within the Community and render the safety measures taken by some Member States ineffective. Although the Commission's proposal has been approved by the European Parliament[61] and Economic and Social Committee,[62] it has not (yet) been adopted by the Council.

In spite of the fact that no action has been taken on the Commission's 1980 proposals, it should be noted that in practice some Community aid for the training of fishermen is already given under the Social and Regional Development Funds, and the 1984 Budget contained for the first time an appropriation on 'Actions leading towards the Development of a Common Fisheries Training Policy.'[63]

The reasons for the Council's complete inaction on the Commission's 1980 proposals are not entirely clear. Presumably some of the reasons are the increased Community expenditure that would result from the Commission's proposals and a certain reluctance on the part of some Member States for ideological reasons to see the Community getting too involved in questions of employment policy. The same symptoms can be seen in the Council's rejection of the social aspects of the Commission's restructuring proposals. And yet one would have thought that an active and progressive social policy was an important and necessary component of the thriving and profitable fishing industry which the Community through its management and restructuring policies is seeking to realise.

4. CONTROL OF NATIONAL AIDS TO THE FISHING INDUSTRY

The final element in the Community's structural policy is the control it exercises over national financial aids to the fishing industry. Until the adoption in 1983 of comprehensive programmes of aid from the Community for restructuring fishing fleets, individual Member States gave various kinds of aid to try to help their fishing industries through the difficulties they were then facing (described in Chapter 1: see pp. 10–11). Even after 1983 many of these national aids have been continued. Such aids have taken and continue to take a variety of forms – fuel subsidies, operating subsidies, aids for the building or scrapping of vessels, and so on. Any detailed survey of these aids lies outside the scope of this book.[64] The aim here is to try to establish how far national aids to the fishing industry are permissible and are controlled under Community law.

Clearly if national aids are unco-ordinated they may lead to Community fishing fleets, viewed as a whole, being restructured in an undesirable and unbalanced manner. Furthermore, national aids such as fuel subsidies may lead to unfair competition between fishing vessels. Such unfair competition is all the more undesirable and its effects more greatly felt as a result of the right of equal access to maritime zones and the fact that there is a common market in fishery products. The Commission showed itself especially aware of this latter problem in its 1966 Report on the Basic Principles for a Common Fisheries Policy.[65] Both in this Report and in one of its 1968 draft regulations the Commission called for a harmonisation of certain types of national aid and a prohibition of other types. The actual regulations adopted in 1970 and their consolidating successors, however, adopt a more modest and less clear-cut approach.

Article 8(1) of the Structural Regulation provides that Member States may grant financial aid in so far as the operations to which this relates contribute to the achievement of increased productivity through the restructuring of fishing fleets and other means of production, adaptation of production and marketing conditions to market requirements, or improved standards of living for those dependent on fishing for their livelihood. Article 8(2) of the 1976 Structural Regulation, blindly echoing Article 9(2) of the 1970 Regulation, provides that common rules fixing the conditions for granting such aid were to be laid down by the Council before June 1, *1971*. In fact, apart from aid to producers' organisations, which is dealt with by Regulation 3796/81 on the Common Organisation of the Market in Fishery Products[66] (the Marketing Regulation) and its predecessor Marketing Regulations, and is discussed in the next Chapter, no common rules laying down conditions for granting aid have been adopted.[67]

In the absence of such common rules, except for aid to producers' organisations, the position is as follows. According to Article 42 of the EEC Treaty the general provisions of the Treaty dealing with State aids (i.e. Articles 92–94) only apply to the production of and trade in agricultural products (which include fishery products) to the extent determined by the Council. Such a determination has been made by Article 28 of the Marketing Regulation which provides that 'Articles 92, 93 and 94 of the Treaty shall apply to the production of and trade in' fishery products.[68] Article 92 provides that in general State aid which distorts or threatens to distort competition and which affects trade between Member States is not permitted. Exception may be made, *inter alia,* for aid to promote the economic development of areas where the standard of living is abnormally low or where there is serious under-employment, or for aid to facilitate the development of certain economic activities or areas, 'where such aid does not adversely affect trading conditions to an extent contrary to the common interest.' Under Article 93 the Commission is to keep all State aids under review: any aid which it considers impermissible it may require the Member State in question to abolish, and if the latter fails to do so, the Commission may refer the case to the European Court. The Commission must be informed in advance of all plans to grant aid.

The result of the above provisions is, therefore, that if State aid to the fishing industry does not fall foul of the prohibition in Article 92 and provided that the conditions of Article 8(1) of the Structural Regulation are satisfied, such aid will be permitted. Under both Article 93 and Article 10 of the Structural Regulation the Commission must be notified in advance of any proposals for such aid.[69]

We must now turn to see how the Commission has in practice exercised its powers under Articles 92–94 and applied the criteria of Article 8(1) of the Structural Regulation in relation to State aid to the fishing industry, and to try to establish what kinds of aids the Commission regards as permissible and what kinds of aid are impermissible. The Commission's attitudes and policy have evolved and changed somewhat over a number of years, and it is therefore desirable to adopt an historical approach and consider a number of phases where the Commission's policy has become established. The first such phase is the period of the mid-1970s, following the enormous increase in fishing vessel fuel prices as the price of oil soared after the Arab-Israeli war in 1973. A number of Member States had introduced fuel subsidies for their vessels. At the request of the Council, the Commission in June 1974 published a report in which it stated that State aids designed to alleviate the adjustment of fishing vessels to increased fuel costs were only permissible if such aids were for a strictly limited period of time and ended at the latest by June 30, 1975 (a time limit later extended to December 31, 1975). In addition, such aid should not exceed 50 per cent of the increase in the price of fuel in the Member State concerned.[70]

The second phase is the period 1976–80. Following the general extension of fishing limits to 200 miles and the consequent difficulties for certain sectors of Community fishing fleets, and in the absence of Community restructuring measures, most EEC Member States introduced a number of State aids for their fishing industries. The initial reaction of the Commission was that in view of the serious difficulties facing the fishing industry, and in spite of the dangers to a common policy which such national measures might eventually represent, it would not object to these measures in so far as they were of an interim nature and would not jeopardise the application of a common structural policy at a later stage.[71] However, no doubt as a result of the inability of the Council to agree on Community structural measures and the increasingly distorted effect on competition of national aids (some of which had been in existence for two or three years), the Commission in July 1980 announced that it was going to take a tougher line in future in monitoring State aids to the fishing industry.[72]

At the same time the Commission laid down some preliminary guidelines as to the criteria it would use in reviewing State aids. These guidelines are now only of historic interest and therefore will not be summarised, as they have been replaced by definitive guidelines, issued by the Commission in October 1985.[73] These guidelines begin by setting out some general principles and then go on to assess the compatibility with Community law of each specific type of potential State aid. As far as the general principles are concerned, State aids will only in principle be permissible if they are in accordance with the objectives of the Common Fisheries Policy as set out in Article 39 of the EEC Treaty (see pp. 23–25 above), do not obstruct the operation of Community rules and are not conservative in effect, i.e. they must lead to increased rationalisation and efficiency and not simply reduce the recipient's operating costs or increase his income. In particular, aid must provide an incentive for development and adaptation measures which cannot be undertaken under normal market circumstances because of insufficient flexibility in the sector and the limited financial capacity of those employed in it. It must result in lasting improvements so that the fishing sector can continue to develop solely on the basis of market earnings. Its duration must therefore be limited to the time needed to achieve the desired improvements and adaptations.

In examining aid schemes, the Commission will also take account of the size in absolute or relative terms of the overall support granted by the Member State concerned to the fisheries sector in the light of its impact on competition and trade between Member States.

The guidelines then go to explain how these principles apply to, and the likely attitude of the Commission to, the various categories of aid. This section of the guidelines is far too detailed for any summary to be attempted here. The final section of the guidelines deals with questions of procedure. It reminds Member States of their obligation to notify the Commission of all State aids, and warns them that any aid granted illegally may have to be repaid as well as possibly affecting the amount of Community aid granted to Member States.

In line with the new and stricter approach to State aid to the fishing industry which it adopted in 1980, the Commission has since that year opened the procedure under Article 93 on about 20 occasions. In most of the cases the proceedings were terminated with a finding that the aid in question was permissible or had been discontinued, but on six occasions the Commission has ordered the Member State concerned to put an end to the aid in question. These latter concern fuel subsidies granted by Belgium, France and Italy;[74] an operating subsidy granted by the United Kingdom in 1980 and 1981 to fishing vessel owners to help tide them through the crisis facing the fishing industry;[75] aid granted by the United Kingdom to producers' organisations to enable them to maintain their autonomous system of withdrawal prices;[76] and various marketing aids granted by France.[77]

There is little doubt that up until the early 1980s the Community through the Commission had little control over State aids to the fishing industry, in part at least because Member States failed to observe their obligations under Article 93 to notify the Commission of aid and to refrain from paying out aid which was under investigation by the Commission. This situation was causing both a development of the Community fishing industry potentially inimical to the desired overall structure of the industry as well as unfair competition, thus preventing the building up of mutual confidence between national fishing industries without which a Common Fisheries Policy cannot hope to operate effectively and successfully. With the adoption from 1983 onwards of extensive programmes of Community aid the need for, and temptation to provide, national financial aids has decreased, and the Commission appears to have got better control over those national aids that are still being provided, although the Commission still has to get to grips with the provision of aid in Portugal and Spain which is extensive (for example, in 1984 Spain gave 23.8 million pesetas worth of aid to its fishing industry, of which 7 million alone was a fuel subsidy)[78] and there are forms of aid (such as tax concessions) which are difficult to detect if not notified. In this latter respect the Commission's intention, stated in its 1985 guidelines, to take a tougher line when aid is not notified is to be welcomed. But assuming aids are notified, and then controlled by the Commission in accordance with its guidelines, there should be an overall improvement in the structure of the Community fishing industry, and a reinforcement of the objectives the Community has sought to achieve through its own programmes of financial assistance.

5. CONCLUSIONS

Through its programmes of financial assistance and its supervision of State aids, the Community is moving towards, though it has not yet achieved, a full-blooded structural policy of its own (as opposed merely to co-ordinating national policies). In terms of the objectives of such a policy, which were discussed at the beginning of this Chapter, increased productivity is likely to result from the Community's programmes of financial assistance, and the same programmes have led to some adaptation and development of processing and marketing facilities. While increased productivity should improve the standard of living of fishermen, no Community action has yet been taken to improve working conditions of fishermen.

A good deal remains to be done therefore. Apart from taking action on working conditions, the Community institutions need to get to grips with the problem of eliminating such excess capacity as still exists (thus improving productivity) and then making sure capacity does not increase beyond any increase in catch potential. There is probably also a need for more Community aid for infrastructure for fishing fleets (not just in the Mediterranean as at present), as well as a need for more aid for Portugal and Spain, which either arrived too late in the Community to benefit much from many of the Community's financial aid programmes or which are ineligible under continuing programmes (notably the Integrated Mediterranean Programmes).

NOTES

1. COM (66) 250, substantially reproduced in J.O. 1967, p. 862.
2. O.J. S. Edn. 1970 (III), p. 703. This Reg. was replaced in 1976 by the almost identical Reg. 101/ 76, O.J. 1976 L20/19.
3. See F.G. Snyder, *Law of the Common Agricultural Policy*, London, 1985, Chap. 7.
4. For a comparison of British and French approaches to this question, see M. Shackleton, 'The Politics of Fishing in Britain and France: Some Lessons for Community Integration' (1985) 9 *Journal of European Integration* 29.
5. Resolution of December 19, 1980, O.J. 1980 C346/112. Cf. O.J., Debates of the European Parliament No. 190, April 1975, p. 21, where the Commission blamed the non-appearance of the report on staff shortages and other difficulties.
6. Dir. 83/515, O.J. 1983 L290/15. For detailed rules relating to the application of the Dir., see Dec. 85/474, O.J. 1985 L284/1.
7. Reg. 2909/83, O.J. 1983 L290/9. For detailed rules relating to the implementation of the Reg., see Dec. 85/475, O.J. 1985 L284/8.
8. Dir. 85/590, O.J. 1985 L372/49. It is also worth noting that under a draft EEC-Spain Agreement (text in O.J. 1984 C298/6) the Community would have contributed 28.5 million ECU to Spain to reduce the capacity of its fleet *before* accession. The agreement, however, was never approved by the Council.
9. O.J. 1977 C278/15; amendments in O.J. 1978 C148/4 and COM (80) 787.
10. See O.J. 1984 L18/39, L64/12, L131/42, L196/54 and L322/13; 1985 L59/24, L252/28 and L287/ 31; and 1986 L205/50.
11. O.J. 1986 C140/3.
12. This figure is arrived at by dividing the total Community aid envisaged (46 million ECU) by the maximum amount of Community assistance per GRT prescribed by the Directive (325 ECU).
13. E.P. Doc. A2–40/86, p. 25; House of Lords Select Committee on the European Communities, *The Common Fisheries Policy* HL Paper (1984–85) 39 pp. 51 and 189 (but see p. 116 for a different view); and the Economic and Social Committee's Own-Initiative Opinion of February 27, 1985, O.J. 1985 C104/12.
14. J.A. Butlin, 'Do We really have a Common Fisheries Policy?' *Fisheries Economics Newsletter* No. 15, May 1983, p. I at VIII-IX.
15. Such species and areas are defined in Reg. 1248/84, O.J. 1984 L120/12.
16. Reg. 3727/85, O.J. 1985 L361/56.
17. E.P. Doc. A2–40/86, p. 25. So, too, the Economic and Social Committee, *op. cit.* in n. 13, which also feels the level of aid offered is not sufficient to act as an incentive.
18. See *Bull. E.C.* 1985 No. 2, p. 46; No. 3, p. 49; and No. 7/8, p. 69, and O.J. 1986 L233/13.
19. *Loc. cit.* in n. 17.
20. O.J. 1985 L350/17.
21. O.J. S. Edn. 1963–64, p. 103.
22. OECD, *Financial Support to the Fishing Industry*, Paris, 1980, pp. 157 and 159.
23. Reg. 2722/72, O.J. S. Edn. 1972 (December 28–30), p. 31, supplemented by Regs. 1462/73 and 645/74, O.J. 1973 L145/11 and 1974 L78/19.
24. R. Fennell, *The Common Agricultural Policy of the European Community*, London, 1979, pp. 211–212.
25. OECD, *op. cit.* in n. 22, pp. 155 and 159.
26. O.J. 1976 C6/2. The Commission published a revised proposal in June 1978 – see O.J. 1978 C148/4.
27. Reg. 1852/78, O.J. 1978 L211/30.

28. Regs. 592/79, 1713/80, 2992/81 and 31/83, O.J. 1979 L78/5, 1980 L167/50, 1981 L299/24 and 1983 L5/1.
29. Greece, Greenland, Ireland, the Mezzogiorno, Northern Ireland and the French overseas departments.
30. Commission's Answer to W.Q. 1126/83, O.J. 1984 C24/26.
31. Commission's Answer to W.Q. 730/82, O.J. 1982 C245/16.
32. O.J. 1983 L290/1. Detailed rules implementing this Reg. are contained in Regs. 3166/83 and 378/84, O.J. 1983 L316/1 and 1984 L46/11.
33. These additions were made by Regs. 3733/85 and 2972/86, O.J. 1985 L361/78 and 1986 L279/1.
34. Reg. 3733/85, *op. cit.*
35. See O.J. 1985 L44/44 and C173/2 (Belgium) and L157 for the programmes of the other pre-1986 Member States, and O.J. 1986 L205/46 and L279/46 (for Portugal and Spain respectively).
36. *Op. cit.* in n. 17, pp. 23–25. The Economic and Social Committee, *op. cit.* in n. 13, has also suggested that the 33-metre maximum length should be relaxed.
37. Reg. 2088/85, O.J. 1985 L197/1.
38. *Op. cit.* in n. 17, p. 22.
39. Reg. 1939/81, O.J. 1981 L197/6.
40. As examples of aid from these sources, the European Investment Bank in 1975 lent FF. 50 million for the modernisation of the French fishing fleet (see O.J. 1975 C122/17), while the European Development Fund in 1983 granted 2.97 million ECU for developing the fishing industry in French Guyana (see *Eurofish Report* No. 169, p. BB6). For information on aid given by the European Regional Development Fund to the fishing industry, see O.J. 1980 C156/31.
41. Reg. 729/70, O.J. S. Edn. 1970 (I), p. 218, Art. 1(3).
42. As an example of the latter, the Court of Auditors points out in its third Annual Report that much of the aid under Regulation 17/64 went to the construction and modernisation of vessels for herring fishing. At the same time, the Community was imposing significant restrictions on herring fishing for conservation reasons. As a result, many of the vessels receiving Community aid had very limited scope for fishing. See O.J. 1980 C342/1 at 86–87.
43. *Op. cit.* in n. 17.
44. See its Resolution of May 16, 1986, O.J. 1986 C148/132.
45. COM (86) 302.
46. House of Lords, *op. cit.* in n. 13, p. 92.
47. *Loc. cit.* in n. 22.
48. See O.J. 1985 L157, pp. 4, 9, 14, 20, 26, 35, 41 and 46; 1986 L171/63 and L205/44.
49. *Loc. cit.* in n. 22.
50. O.J. 1977 L51/1, as amended. Detailed rules for the implementation of the Reg. are contained in Regs. 1685/78 and 2515/85, O.J. 1978 L197/1 and 1985 L243/1. See also O.J. 1983 C152/2 for a list of criteria for the choice of projects to be financed under Reg. 355/77.
51. Reg. 3722/85, O.J. 1985 L361/36.
52. Commission of the European Communities, *The Common Fisheries Policy,* European File 10/86, p. 9.
53. *Op. cit.* in n. 1, pp. 878–882.
54. COM (76) 500, p. 18.
55. See its Resolutions of December 16, 1977 and May 11, 1979, O.J. 1978 C6/125 and 1979 C140/115.
56. COM (80) 725.
57. Resolution of December 18, 1981, O.J. 1982 C11/208.
58. Opinion in O.J. 1981 C189/1.

59. O.J. 1980 L259/29.
60. O.J. 1984 C183/17.
61. Resolution of February 14, 1985, O.J. 1985 C72/110. In its Resolution the European Parliament also called on the Commission to propose Community safety codes for all vessels over 12 metres (the Convention applies only to vessels over 24 metres).
62. O.J. 1984 C307/3.
63. Commission's Answer to W.Q. 1476/83, O.J. 1984 C109/10. It should be noted, too, that the multiannual guidance programmes under Regulation 2908/83 (discussed above at p. 213) are aimed in part at – and may, therefore attract Community finance for – improving working and safety conditions on vessels.
64. For a detailed survey of State aids, see OECD, *op. cit.* in n. 22, OECD, *Problems of Trade in Fishery Products,* Paris, 1985, pp. 80–87, and the OECDs annual *Review of Fisheries in OECD Member Countries.*
65. *Op. cit.* in n. 1.
66. O.J. 1981 L379/1.
67. The Commission did, in fact, forward to the Council in November 1973 a draft Reg. laying down conditions for granting aid (O.J. 1973 C110/64), but this proposal was never adopted by the Council. The reg. would have specified the types of aid permissible, and the conditions under which they could be granted.
68. The ambit of this phrase is not entirely clear. 'Production' of fishery products clearly includes the actual catching of fish, but does it include their marketing? If not, and if marketing falls outside the concept of 'trade' (as seems likely), it would mean that Arts. 92–94 would not apply to State aids given for the marketing of fish. It would be anomalous if Arts. 92–94 applied to all State aids to the fishing industry except those concerned with marketing, and in fact the practice of the Commission is to regard marketing aids as subject to Arts. 92–94.
69. In practice most Member States have not observed this obligation – at least prior to 1980. See COM (80) 240, pp. 113–114.
70. Norwegian Government, *Rapport om De Europeiske Fellesskap i annet halvar 1973 og aret 1974,* Oslo, 1975, p. 46.
71. *Twelfth General Report on the Activities of the European Community in 1978,* Brussels, 1979, pp. 190–191. Many of the State aids which the Commission decided not to oppose were similar to the proposals it had made itself for Community structural measures.
72. COM (80) 240, pp. 112–116.
73. Guidelines for the Examination of State Aids in the Fisheries Sector, O.J. 1985 C268/2.
74. Decs. 83/246 and 83/312–314, O.J. 1983 L137/28 and L169/29, 32 and 35. The failure of France to comply with the decision concerning its fuel subsidy led to the matter being referred to the European Court and France being adjudged in breach of its Community obligations: see Case 93/84, *Commission v. France* [1985] 3 C.M.L.R. 169.
75. Dec. 83/315, O.J. 1983, L137/38.
76. Dec. 85/425, O.J. 1985, L241/20.
77. Dec. 86/186, O.J. 1986, L136/55.
78. OECD, *Review of Fisheries in OECD Member Countries 1984,* Paris, 1985, p. 15.

CHAPTER 7

The common organisation of the market in fishery products

The marketing and trade aspects of the Common Fisheries Policy have hitherto attracted far less political and academic attention than the management and structural sides of the policy. Yet for the fishing industries of the EEC, these aspects are at least as important as the management and structural policies. As was pointed out in Chapter 1, Articles 39–43 of the EEC Treaty require the Community institutions to establish a common organisation of the market in fishery products, and a Regulation establishing such an organisation was adopted by the Council in October 1970.[1] Following the enlargement of the Community in 1973, a number of amendments were made to this Regulation. A revised, consolidated Regulation on the Common Organisation of the Market in Fishery Products replaced the original Regulation in 1976.[2] This regulation was in turn replaced by a new Regulation in 1981[3] (hereafter referred to as the Marketing Regulation), designed to correct the deficiences which had been revealed in the operation of the 1976 Regulation, particularly after fishing limits were extended to 200 miles in 1977. Finally, in the latest step in the evolution of this side of EEC fisheries law, the 1981 Regulation has been amended by the 1985 Iberian Act of Accession.[4] In this Chapter the basis of discussion will be the 1981 Regulation as amended, but reference will be made to its two predecessors where appropriate. In many respects the 1981 Regulation (like its predecessors) is a framework one, and a large number of subsidiary regulations providing for its detailed implementation and application have been adopted and are referred to, where appropriate, in the course of this and the following Chapter.

Before the EEC was established, individual national markets for fishery and agricultural products were usually managed, and not left to the free and unrestricted operation of market forces. The EEC has continued with managed markets for both fisheries and agriculture, rather than the free markets which it has aimed to create for other sectors of the economy. The reason for this special treatment lies partly in the nature of the markets (which are characterised by seasonal fluctuations in supply and the perishable nature of many agricultural and fishery products), and partly in the fact that there is a large number of producers (i.e. farmers and fishermen), many of them very small concerns, who cannot, unorganised and alone, secure the prices, and therefore the income, that will enable them to stay in business. Thus the aim of the common organisation of the market in fishery products is to 'encourage market stability',[5] and so create a better standard of living for fishermen. The means adopted by the Community institutions to achieve this aim and manage the market in fishery products[6] are a common price system, common marketing standards, producers' organisations and common rules governing trade with third countries. The last of these is discussed in Chapter 8: the other mechanisms for managing the market form the subject of this Chapter and will each be considered in turn. Finally in this Chapter, the division of competence between the Community and its Member States in fish marketing matters will be considered. The reason why this question is considered at the end of the Chapter, rather than at the beginning (as in Chapters 4 and 5) is because it is more easily understood after the Community's role in marketing has been explained.

1. COMMON PRICE SYSTEM

The common price system is concerned with the formation of prices at the first-hand sale of fish, i.e. from the producer (fisherman) to the wholesaler or retailer. The Community system is not concerned with prices at any of the subsequent stages of marketing. Most first-hand sales of fish for human consumption in the Community take place through auctions. The common price system modifies the normal free market mechanism, where the price is fixed purely by the levels of supply and demand. It does this, not by providing a guaranteed price (as happens in some sectors of agriculture, such as cereals), but by providing that where prices fall below a certain level, fish is to be withdrawn from the market: the decrease in supply which thus results should, according to the normal operation of supply and demand, lead to the price rising again.[7] Within this basic mechanism different details have been laid down for various categories of fish: the reason for these differences is partly to concentrate market support on the most important species and partly because of the differing degrees to which the Community is self-sufficient in fish. We will now look at each of these categories in turn.

(i) Products listed in Annex I(A), (D) and (E) of the Marketing Regulation

These products are fresh or chilled herring, sardines, dogfish, redfish, cod, saithe, haddock, whiting, ling, mackerel, anchovies, plaice, hake, megrim, Ray's bream, monkfish, shrimps, crabs and Norway lobsters. Together they account for a large proportion of Community production of fish for human consumption (about 50 per cent before the Community's most recent enlargement). For these products three kinds of prices are established – guide prices; withdrawal prices (for products listed in Annex I(A) and (D); and Community selling prices (for products in Annex I(E), viz. crabs and Norway lobsters). The chief function of guide prices is to determine the level of withdrawal and Community selling prices: to some extent, too, guide prices indicate the desired price for the product in question. The function of withdrawal prices is to fix the price level at which fish will be withdrawn from the market, thus leading to a stabilisation of the market. Community selling prices serve a similar function in respect of crabs and Norway lobsters.

Under Article 10 of the Marketing Regulation the Council, acting by a qualified majority on a proposal from the Commission, is each year to fix guide prices for the products listed in Annex I(A), (D) and (E). Guide prices are to be based on the average of prices recorded on representative wholesale markets or at representative ports during the preceding three years,[8] together with an assessment of production and demand prospects. In fixing guide prices, the Community institutions must also take account of the need to

234

stabilise prices and avoid the formation of surpluses, help support fishermen's incomes and consider consumers' interests. In practice the Council fixes guide prices, expressed in ECUs, at the end of the calendar year preceding the year to which they relate.

Under Article 8 of the Marketing Regulation producers' organisations may, but are not obliged to, fix withdrawal prices. If a producers' organisation does decide to fix withdrawal prices, then if the first-hand market prices of fish for human consumption fall below the level of withdrawal prices, that fish may be withdrawn from the market by the producers' organisation. The organisation must dispose of the fish thus withdrawn from the market in such a way as not to interfere with the normal marketing of the fish in question. This usually means that such fish is distributed free to deserving individuals and institutions (such as schools and hospitals) or is converted to meal or oil to be used for animal feed.[9] Where fish is withdrawn from the market, the producers' organisation must grant its members compensation in respect of fish conforming to the EEC's common marketing standards. This compensation, it should be noted, is not the same as the withdrawal price, but is related to the price of the market outlet which is actually found for the fish withdrawn from the market. To finance these withdrawal arrangements, producers' organisations are to create intervention funds financed by a levy on sales or alternatively they may have recourse to an equalisation system. Any producers' organisation intending to operate a withdrawal system must inform its national authorities (who in turn are to inform the Commission) of the products covered by the system, the period of time during which withdrawal prices are applicable and the levels of such prices.[10]

Although in principle producers' organisations are, as we have just seen, responsible for financing withdrawal arrangements, under Article 13 of the Marketing Regulation part of their expenditure on these arrangements will be reimbursed by the national authorities of Member States provided certain conditions are fulfilled. First, the withdrawal prices operated by the producers' organisation must be the same as or very close to the withdrawal prices laid down by the Commission each year.[11] The latter prices must be between 70 per cent and 90 per cent of the guide price, multiplied by a quality conversion factor.[12] In areas which are distant from the main centres of consumption in the Community, withdrawal prices are set at a lower level.[13] The reason for the regionalisation of withdrawal prices, a concept introduced by the 1972 Act of Accession at the request of Norway and the United Kingdom, is that when there is excess supply of fish, it is always peripheral markets which will suffer first, because of their distance from the main centres of consumption. The second condition for obtaining reimbursement is that the products withdrawn from the market conform to Community marketing standards. Thirdly, the compensation granted by the producers' organisation to its members must not exceed Community withdrawal prices nor be less than certain prescribed levels.[14] Fourthly, withdrawal prices must normally be applied to each category of product marketed. The final condition is that the fish withdrawn from the market is disposed of for purposes other than human consumption or in such a way as not to interfere with the normal marketing of the product in question.[15] Provided that all these conditions are met, and in practice most producers' organisations operate these official withdrawal arrangements, the national authorities must reimburse the producers' organisation (unless withdrawals are below a minimum quantity to be fixed). The level of such reimbursement varies, ranging between 0 and 85 per cent of the withdrawal price, depending on the amount of fish withdrawn: the more fish that is withdrawn, the lower the reimbursement, and once more than 20% of the annual amount put up for sale is withdrawn, no reimbursement is made – the object being to influence producers' organisations to take steps to ensure that supply corresponds as closely as possible to demand.[16]

It should be noted that withdrawal arrangements only operate where there is an appropriate producers' organisation in existence. Where there is no such organisation, or for fishermen who do not belong to an existing organisation, there is no possibility of withdrawal arrangements. As will be seen, neither the formation of producers' organisations, nor membership by individual fishermen of existing organisations, is compulsory.

The idea behind withdrawal prices, as explained earlier, is that they should help to stabilise prices. By withdrawing supplies from the market, the price should then – according to the normal operation of the laws of supply and demand – rise again. Of course, this will only work if most fish is marketed through producers' organisations, which alone can operate withdrawal arrangements. Although there is no compulsion to form or belong to a producers' organisation, most fishermen do in fact belong to such organisations,[17] and as will be seen in section 3 below, there are provisions which make it possible to compel non-members of producers' organisations to observe the withdrawal arrangements operated by the latter. In the early years of the common organisation of the market, market prices for most species remained above withdrawal prices, so that withdrawal arrangements did not operate to any great extent. In the late 1970s and early 1980s, however, prices dropped, and considerable quantities of fish were withdrawn from the market. In September 1981 the European Parliament adopted a Resolution in which it deplored the fact that in 1980 more than 100,000 tonnes of fish were withdrawn from the market and destroyed, and it called on the Council to put an end to this 'scandalous destruction of highly valuable foodstuffs.'[18] The changes made by the 1981 Regulation should help to avoid such large withdrawals in future. First, as we have already seen, there is the degressive system of Member States' reimbursements to producers' organisations for withdrawals of fish:

under the 1976 Regulation reimbursement was fixed at a uniform and fairly high level. Secondly, the 1981 Regulation has introduced a system of carry-over premiums.

The aim of this system is to encourage producers' organisations to carry over more highly-valued products withdrawn from the market and put them back on the market again later, instead of destroying them or reducing them to meal and oil as has usually been the case. This 'carrying-over' may be done by means of processing for human consumption or storage. Under Article 14 of the Marketing Regulation and its implementing legislation,[19] a carry-over premium may be paid to producers' organisations in respect of most Annex I(A) and (D) products[20] which have been withdrawn from the market provided that they have been supplied by a member producer, meet certain quality, size and presentation requirements, are processed by means of freezing, salting or drying, and are stored for a specific period.[21] The premium will be granted only for quantities not exceeding 15 per cent of the annual amount put up for sale. The premium is to be fixed by the Commission each year, but may not exceed the amount of the actual cost of processing and storage or 50 per cent of the Community withdrawal price for the product in question. A special carry-over premium is laid down for a four-year period (which expires at the beginning of 1987) for sardines and anchovies caught in the Mediterranean and intended for the processing industry (i.e. basically canning).[22] This is designed to meet the particular difficulties faced by this sector of the fishing industry (rapidly fluctuating prices and severe competition from imports from third States) and the fact that producers' organisations have been slow to develop in the Mediterranean.

The Iberian Act of Accession has introduced a further kind of carrying-over system for the products listed in Annex I(E), viz. crabs and Norway lobsters. Under a new article added to the Marketing Regulation (Article 14(A)), Member States are to grant a storage premium to those producers' organisations which instead of selling crabs and Norway lobsters below the Community selling price (which is determined by the Commission each year in the same way as withdrawal prices), store them for sale later when prices pick up. To be eligible for the premium, producers' organisations must meet certain conditions as to quality, marketing and storage. The premium is payable only for quantities which do not exceed 20% of the total annual quantity offered for sale.[23]

(ii) Products listed in Annex II

The products listed in Annex II are all products in frozen form: sardines, sea bream, squid, cuttlefish and octopus. For these products the Council fixes guide prices each year in the same way as it does for the products listed in

Annex I. In theory withdrawal arrangements could also operate in the same way as for Annex I products, except that there is no provision for Member States to reimburse producers' organisations for expenditure incurred on withdrawal arrangements, but in practice they do not because of the system of private storage aid laid down in Article 16 of the Marketing Regulation. Under this provision, where the price for an Annex II product falls below 85 per cent of the guide price for a period during which a trend towards a disturbance of the market is apparent, private storage aid may be granted to producers by Member States, provided that products conform to marketing standards when placed on the market again.[24] Such aid may not exceed actual storage costs and interest charges. Detailed rules relating to the granting of storage aid are laid down in Regulation 696/71.[25] Under this Regulation, aid may only be given for the storage of products which have been frozen on board a vessel registered in an EEC Member State. To qualify for aid, a producer must conclude a standard type of contract relating to the storage with the competent authorities of his Member State. The aim of this contract is to ensure the proper preservation of the products being stored and to allow effective supervision of storage operations by the Member State. In practice prices of Annex II products have held up well, and between 1973 and 1982 inclusive it was necessary to have recourse to private storage aid only in two years – 1975 and 1976.

Storage is essentially a specialised form of withdrawal, possible in this instance because the fish in question are frozen, and serving the same function of stabilising prices by reducing supplies. Unlike the normal withdrawal arrangements, producers' organisations have no role to play here.

(iii) Tuna intended for the canning industry

Under Article 17 of the Marketing Regulation, the Council fixes each year a Community producer price for tuna (of all species) intended for the canning industry. This price is calculated in much the same way as guide prices for Annex I and II products. Under Article 17(1) compensation shall be granted 'if necessary' to Community producers of tuna. The circumstances in which such compensation is to be granted are set out in Regulation 1196/76.[26] There are essentially two conditions which must be met before compensation becomes payable. First, the quarterly average Community market price for tuna and the free-at-frontier price[27] for imports of tuna must both at the same time be less than 90% of the Community producer price. Secondly, the situation on the Community market must be the result of the level of prices on the world market and the drop in price on the Community market must not be due to an abnormal increase in quantities caught by Community vessels. If both these conditions are met, compensation becomes payable. Such compensation is not to exceed the difference between the Community producer price and either the price actually obtained by the Community producer or the quarterly average Community market price, whichever is the higher.

The intention of this system of compensation is to offset any disadvantages which the Community import system might present for Community fishermen fishing for tuna. Since Community production of tuna is inadequate, and in order to keep the tuna canning industry supplied, Community customs duties on tuna have been suspended. Thus, a fall in import prices could threaten the incomes of Community tuna fishermen. In practice, this has not happened to any great degree, and therefore little use has been made of these compensation arrangements.

(iv) Salmon and Lobsters

The 1981 Regulation introduced special price provisions for salmon and lobsters. Article 18 provides that 'compensation shall be granted if necessary to Community producers' of salmon and lobsters. The Council, acting on a proposal from the Commission, is to adopt general rules for granting such compensation. No such rules have yet been adopted (nor, it appears, proposed), so that it is impossible at the present time to say what form such compensation might take. Nor is it immediately obvious why the possibility of such compensation has been introduced for two products which traditionally have been able to command high and stable prices. Presumably the reason is to provide an additional measure of protection to Community producers from the threat of cheap imports.

(v) Other fish

There are a number of other fishery products not falling in any of the above categories which are of commercial importance. They include carp, eels, trout, halibut, mullet, sea bream, all fish which is dried, salted, smoked or in brine, some frozen fish, some shellfish, species such as sandeels and Norway pout fished for industrial purposes, and fish meal and flour. There are no Community price rules for these products, although there is nothing to prevent producers' organisations from establishing their own withdrawal arrangements: any expenditure on such arrangements, however, will not be eligible for reimbursement by Member States, and indeed their reimbursement by Member States would be contrary to Community Law (see the discussion in section 5 below). Nor is there anything to prevent the Council acting directly under Articles 42 and 43 of the EEC Treaty and adopting *ad hoc* rules where this proves necessary. This happened in 1975 when the Council introduced a temporary system of aid for the private storage of frozen tuna and frozen cod and saithe fillets because the markets price for these products had fallen to abnormally low levels and it was becoming difficult to dispose of this fish.[28] The reason for the absence of normal Community rules is presumably because the markets for many of these products are small and relatively stable: some products, such as halibut and trout, have traditionally fetched a high price because demand is strong and supplies limited. There is thus no need for market-support measures. In addition, some of these products, such as fish meal and flour and dried and smoked fish, are not in this state at the first stage of marketing, which is when Community pricing arrangements operate.

As far as fish meal and oil are concerned, it is of interest to note that the Joint Declaration on the Fisheries Sector, attached to the 1972 Act of Accession, states that the Community institutions:

> will examine the problems of the fish meal and fish oils sector with a view to adopting measures which might prove necessary in that sector in respect to the raw material used. These measures should meet the need for protection and rational use of the sea's biological resources while avoiding the creation or retention of insufficiently profitable production units.

This provision was adopted largely at the request of Norway. The Norwegian Government had argued that since fish meal is largely used as feed stuff and is in competition with, and therefore affected by the price of, vegetable-based feed stuffs, and since the latter are regulated by a common organisation of the market, it would be reasonable and desirable to have a common organisation of the market for fish meal. The fact that Norway did not in the end join the EEC is probably the reason why the Community institutions have not yet, as far as the writer is aware, carried out the examination provided for in the Declaration; although given its interest in industrial fishing, one might have thought that Denmark would have pushed for some action in this area.

(vi) Integration of Portugal and Spain into the Community's Price System

While Portugal and Spain have in general been integrated into the Community's price system since the date of their accession, an exception has been made as regards sardines and anchovies. This is to help sardine producers in the Community as previously constituted adjust gradually to the increased competition resulting from the inclusion in the Community of Portugal and Spain, both large and efficient catchers and processors of sardines and anchovies. Thus, Community guide prices for Atlantic sardines are to be aligned gradually with Iberian guide prices and will not become fully applicable in Portugal and Spain until 1995: likewise, in the case of Spain, guide prices for anchovies are to be gradually aligned, the process to be completed by 1990.[29] In addition, during the period of price alignment for sardines, producers of sardines in the

Community as previously constituted are to be paid a compensatory indemnity: in the case of Atlantic sardines this indemnity is the difference between the actual sales price and a defined minimum price, in the case of Mediterranean sardines the difference between withdrawal prices for Atlantic sardines in the old Community and such prices in the new Member States.[30]

(vii) General measures relating to prices

Regulation 1883/78 as amended[31] provides that the Guarantee Section of the European Agricultural Guidance and Guarantee Fund (EAGGF) is to reimburse Member States for the expenditure they incur (a) in reimbursing producers' organisations for the latter's expenditure on withdrawal arrangements; (b) in paying out carry-over and storage premiums; (c) in private storage aid; (d) in compensation to tuna producers; and (e) in the free distribution of products which have been withdrawn from the market. In this connection the 1981 Marketing Regulation has introduced an interesting and important provision. Article 26(2) provides that EAGGF reimbursement is available only in respect of quantities within the limits of a Member State's quotas. This provision is not very clearly drafted. Assuming that the reference to quantities is to the total quantity marketed rather than the total withdrawn, and that Member States must still reimburse producers' organisations if quotas are exceeded (for otherwise producers' organisations would be penalised for something for which they are not individually responsible), this provides a financial incentive to Member States to make sure they observe the quotas allocated to them.

In 1985 the Commission attempted for the first time to link reimbursement from EAGGF with the observance of quotas when it withheld reimbursement relating to withdrawals in 1981 from Denmark, France, Ireland, the Netherlands and the United Kingdom on the ground that these five Member States had exceeded certain of their quotas.[32] The Commission has chosen a singularly inappropriate instance to inaugurate the use of such a power. First, the only quotas relating to 1981 are those contained in Commission proposals: as we saw in Chapter 2 (p. 42 above) while the Commission in its declaration of July 1981 regards these proposals as binding, it is far from certain that this is the case. Secondly, if the Commission's action is based on Article 26(2), it is applying the article retrospectively as it did not come into force until June 1, 1982: if the Commission is not acting under Article 26, it is difficult to see from where its claimed power derives. Not surprisingly, therefore, the Commission's decisions in withholding reimbursement have been challenged on these grounds by the Member States concerned, and at the time of writing these challenges were awaiting determination by the European Court.[33] It is to be hoped that in future the Commission will act more circumspectly. If it applies

Article 26(2) properly, then this – coupled with the fact that no reimbursement is payable where more than 20% of the catch is withdrawn or more than 15% carried over – should succeed in avoiding what some commentators have seen as a potential conflict between the Community's management policy (which aims at conserving resources) and its marketing policy (which links price support to the quantity of fish landed).[34]

The amounts expended by EAGGF on reimbursement for intervention arrangements, even when quite large amounts of fish were being withdrawn, are very small in terms of the total Community budget – from 1975 to 1982 inclusive they averaged just over 10 million ECU a year[35] – and represent less than 0.1 per cent of the total budget and a good deal less than one per cent of the expenditure on the price support measures of the Common Agricultural Policy.

Article 29 of the Marketing Regulation provides that where the price of fish rises above guide prices (in the case of Annex I or II products) or the Community producer price for tuna by a percentage which the Council is to determine, and where this situation is likely to persist and is disturbing the market, 'appropriate measures may be taken to remedy the situation.' The Council has yet to determine the percentage by which prices must rise before this provision comes into operation, nor has it adopted any other rules for the detailed application of this Article. The reason for this is presumably because only very infrequently, if ever, have market prices significantly exceeded guide prices since the first Marketing Regulation was adopted in 1970, and thus disturbed the market.

(viii) Assessment of the Common Price System

The revised pricing arrangements for fisheries products established by the 1981 Marketing Regulation came fully into operation only on January 1, 1983. It is therefore rather early to make any considered assessment of them, and in any case it remains to be seen how the arrangements will function after the accession of Portugal and Spain to the Community at the beginning of 1986. Nevertheless, one or two preliminary observations can be made. The new arrangements attempt to deal with two of the complaints made about the pre-1983 system – that it was too inflexible and that is resulted in too much fish being withdrawn from the market and wasted.[36] The 1981 Regulation deals with the first criticism by introducing new and more flexible criteria for the calculation of guide prices and by allowing producers' organisations to depart from Community withdrawal prices within certain margins while still being entitled to reimbursement from the Community via Member States.[37] It deals with the second criticism by making such reimbursement degressive and by introducing carry-over premiums. The effect of these changes in practice has been a general reduction in the amount of fish being withdrawn. Whereas in 1982 138,875 tonnes of fish were withdrawn, in 1983 and 1984 the amounts of fish withdrawn were 87,217 and 75,938 tonnes respectively.[38]

A third complaint directed against the Community's pricing arrangements for fish, particularly in the United Kingdom since the mid-1970s, is that guide and withdrawal prices have been set at too low levels and therefore fishermen have not been getting an adequate return.[39] To some extent this criticism has been acknowledged by the Community institutions: in the early 1980s guide and withdrawal prices were significantly increased, and subsequently these prices have been raised each year roughly in line with inflation. On the other hand, it needs to be borne in mind that if guide and withdrawal prices are set at too high levels, more fish will be withdrawn from the market and probably not used for human consumption. Furthermore, the returns to fishermen are not necessarily correspondingly increased with high withdrawal prices: in respect of fish actually sold there is a good price and a good return to fishermen, but in respect of fish withdrawn and not carried over, compensation will be relatively small. As Young demonstrates, the level at which withdrawal prices will maximise fishermen's incomes depends on the elasticity of demand for fish for human consumption at the auction market level, the rate at which compensation declines as withdrawals increase, and the total supply of fish to the auction market in a given period.[40] Furthermore, the question of guide and withdrawal prices should not be looked at in isolation. One reason why fish prices dropped in the late 1970s and early 1980s was because of competition from imports. As we shall see in Chapter 8, the 1981 Marketing Regulation has introduced more effective measures to deal with imports. It must also be remembered that fish is in competition with other food stuffs, particularly meat and poultry, so that if the price of fish rises in relation to its competitors, less fish will be bought. It is especially important to keep this factor in mind, given the long-term trend in most Member States of declining fish consumption: indeed this trend in many ways lies at the heart of the recent weakness in prices. As far as obtaining a decent income for fishermen is concerned, prices are only one aspect of the matter. Just as important are increasing the economic efficiency of fishing vessels and maintaining fish stocks in a healthy state.

In fixing prices the Community institutions have to take into account the interests not only of fishermen but also of consumers and fish processors. For the consumer, the price arrangements of the Marketing Regulation are reasonably satisfactory – certainly far more satisfactory than the pricing arrangements of the Common Agricultural Policy for most sectors of agriculture. The wholesale price of fish is probably little higher than it would be in an unregulated market, and while it may be that the price of fish in shops is higher in relation to quayside prices than it should be, this is not the responsibility of the

Community. As far as fish processors are concerned, their interest is in a regular supply of fish at reasonable wholesale prices. For those processors who do not buy their fish directly under contract from fishermen, and that is most processors outside the fish meal and oil industry and those large firms of processors owning their own vessels, the Community's pricing arrangements appear to work reasonably satisfactorily; but equally important for most of them are import arrangements, since not all the fish that they require can be met by Community production. Finally, for the Community taxpayer, accustomed to financing butter mountains and wine lakes, the position in relation to fish is far better than with agriculture, for, as we have seen, the sums required to finance the Community's price support arrangements for fish are miniscule compared with those required to finance price support under the Common Agricultural Policy.

Finally, whatever may be the merits or otherwise of the Community's price system in principle, it should be noted that the Court of Auditors, in its review of the common organisation of the market in fishery products carried out in 1984, found considerable deficiencies in the practical implementation of the Community's rules concerning prices by producers' organisations and the national authorities of the Member States.[41]

2. COMMON MARKETING STANDARDS

As we have seen, Community marketing standards play quite an important role in the operation of the common price system for fish. Guide and withdrawal prices are framed with reference to the common marketing standards, the price varying according to the quality grade of the fish. Furthermore, withdrawal compensation is normally only payable in respect of fish which conforms to Community marketing standards. Apart from their role in the operation of the Community's common price system, common marketing standards also have the object of helping 'to improve the quality of fish marketed and thus facilitate their sale,'[42] as well as 'keeping products of unsatisfactory quality off the market and facilitating trade relations based on fair competition, thus helping to improve the profitability of production.'[43]

Under Article 2 of the Marketing Regulation the Council may lay down common marketing standards for any fisheries products to which the Regulation applies. Such standards may cover classification by quality, size or weight, and packing, presentation and labelling. Acting under this provision the Council has so far laid down marketing standards for certain kinds of fresh and chilled fish[44] and for shrimps, crabs and Norway lobsters.[45] These standards grade fish according to their size and freshness (which is determined by the appearance, condition and smell of the fish). Such grading is done by the industry, in collaboration with experts designated for this purpose by the trade organisation concerned. Fish may not be sold or marketed unless it conforms to these standards. An exception is made for small quantities of fish sold by inshore fishermen direct to retailers or consumers, where common marketing standards do not apply. The standards do, however, apply to fish imported from third countries intended for human consumption.

Article 4 of the Marketing Regulation states that products for which common marketing standards have been laid down shall be liable to inspection by Member States to ensure their conformity with these standards, and all infringements are to be penalised. Detailed rules are to be laid down for the application of this provision. Such rules were not adopted until December 1985,[46] in spite of the fact that such rules were also called for by the 1970 and 1976 Marketing Regulations.

The common marketing standards which have so far been adopted in most cases replace pre-existing national standards. The Community's standards have been criticised for their complexity.[47] For example, cod has to be graded into three categories of freshness and five of size, giving 15 possible grades. Because of this complexity, there is some evidence that the grading system is not being meticulously observed.[48] Furthermore, the complexity of the system adds to the cost of production, while there is no evidence that corresponding benefits flow to the consumer. On the other hand, marketing standards give some support to the Community regulations on minimum fish sizes adopted for conservation purposes (see Chapter 4), by providing that fish below such sizes shall not be marketed for human consumption.

3. PRODUCERS' ORGANISATIONS

As we saw when looking at the EEC's common price system for fishery products, producers' organisations play a central role in the practical working of the system because it is they who are actually responsible for the operation of withdrawal arrangements. In addition, they help to improve marketing by carrying this out on behalf of their members. More generally, it is hoped that the formation of producers' organisations will help to overcome the traditional fragmentation of much of the fishing industry.

Articles 5–8 of the Marketing Regulation deal with the establishment of producers' organisations and their recognition for the purposes of the operation of the common organisation of the market in fishery products. A producers' organisation is defined in Article 5(1) as 'any recognised organisation or association of such organisations, established on producers' own initiative for the purpose of taking such measures as will ensure that fishing is carried out along rational lines and that conditions for the sale of the products are improved.' To be considered as a producers' organisation for the purposes of the Community marketing system, an organisation must be officially recognised as such.[49] To obtain recognition, a producers' organisation must fulfil the following conditions:

1. Its activities must cover fresh, chilled or frozen fish; dried, salted or smoked fish, or fish in brine; or crustaceans and molluscs.
2. It must require its members (a) to dispose of their catches through the organisation, unless catches are disposed of otherwise in accordance with common rules established in advance; and (b) to apply, with regard to production and marketing, rules which have been adopted by the organisation with the aim of improving product quality and adapting the volume of supply to market requirements.[50]
3. It must be sufficiently active economically.[51]
4. It must not discriminate between Community fishermen within an 'economic area', particularly on the grounds of nationality or place of establishment.
5. It must have the necessary legal status under national legislation.
6. It must include in its rules an obligation to keep separate accounts for activities for which recognition is granted and provisions to ensure that members wishing to leave the organisation are free to do so, provided that they have been members for three years since the organisation was recognised and provided that they give a year's notice of their intention to leave.
7. It must not hold a dominant position on the common market unless necessary in pursuance of the objectives in Article 39 of the EEC Treaty.

If all these conditions are satisfied, an organisation will be recognised as a producers' organisation. If, after having been recognised, an organisation no longer meets all these conditions, recognition must be withdrawn. Conferring and withdrawing recognition is done by the national authorities of Member States, because they are in a better position than the Community institutions to check that an organisation fulfils the necessary conditions. Nevertheless, a Member State must inform the Commission on each occasion when it grants or withdraws recognition. The Commission publishes from time to time a list of producers' organisations which have been recognised. In mid-1985 93 producers' organisations had been recognised throughout the EEC as then constituted: 1 in Belgium, 3 in Denmark, 19 in West Germany, 27 in France, 2 each in Ireland and the Netherlands, 16 in Italy, 18 in the United Kingdom and 5 in Greece.[52] It can be seen that there is a good deal of variation between Member States. In Denmark, for example, there was until 1983 a single, nation-wide organisation covering all types of fishermen (about 90 per cent of all owners of fishing vessels), whereas in the four large Member States there are separate organisations for the different sectors of the industry (inshore, deep sea etc.). The percentage of fishermen belonging to producers' organisations also varies

246

considerably between Member States. Whereas in 1982 in Greece and Italy only 6% and 35% respectively of fish caught for human consumption was caught by members of producers' organisations, in Ireland and Belgium the corresponding figures were 73% and 90%: for the Community as a whole the figure was 50%.[53]

There is no compulsion on fishermen to form producers' organisations. Nevertheless, their formation is encouraged, and this encouragement is made tangible in the form of financial assistance. Each of the Marketing Regulations has provided Community aid for the formation of producers' organisations. Under Article 6 of the 1981 Regulation, Member States may make aid available to producers' organisations formed after the entry into force of that Regulation, i.e. January 3, 1982.[54] Aid may be granted, on a decreasing scale and within certain limits, for the three years following the recognition of the organisation, or for five years on a greater scale in the case of producers' organisations formed within five years of the entry into force of the Regulation where such formation brings about 'an improvement in production and marketing structures by comparison with the existing situation:' this latter alternative is aimed particularly at Greece where at the time of the adoption of the 1981 Regulation there were no producers' organisations.[55] Member States are to be re-imbursed for half of this aid from the Guidance Section of EAGGF. In addition to this form of aid, Article 6(4) provides that for the five years following the creation of intervention funds to finance a producers' organisation's withdrawal arrangements, a Member State may make aid available to the organisation, either directly or through credit institutions, in the form of loans on special terms to cover part of the anticipated cost of intervention. All aid given by Member States to producers' organisations must be notified to the Commission. Between 1971 and 1981 inclusive the Community spent a total of 0.9 million ECU on aid to producers' organisations[56] – a very modest sum in the context of total Community expenditure.

One problem with the fact that neither the formation nor membership of producers' organisations is compulsory, is that measures taken by producers' organisations to stabilise markets may not, and indeed in practice often have not, achieved their full effect because sales by fishermen who do not belong to producers' organisations may have and have had a disrupting influence on price formation.[57] Articles 7 and 8 of the 1981 Marketing Regulation (which have no corresponding provisions in the earlier Regulations) attempt to deal with this problem.[58] Where a producers' organisation is considered to be representative of production and marketing along a particular stretch of coast, the Member State concerned may (but need not) oblige fishermen not members of the organisation who market their catch on that stretch of coast to comply with the organisation's rules on marketing and withdrawal and to pay the fees paid by members. Such arrangements must not lead to an infringement of EEC competition rules. A Member State which has introduced such an arrangement may indemnify non-member fishermen for any fish not marketed or withdrawn up to 60 per cent of the withdrawal price: such indemnities are reimbursable by EAGGF. Clearly the effectiveness of these provisions will depend on the extent to which Member States exercise their option to compel non-members to observe the rules of producers' organisations. What the practice has been so far, the writer has unfortunately been unable to ascertain.

As we have seen, there is no compulsion for fishermen to form producers' organisations although in fact a considerable number of such organisations have been formed. Fishermen still contemplating whether to form a producers' organisation will have to balance the advantages of such an organisation (the possibility of operating withdrawal arrangements, financial assistance) against the disadvantages. These include membership levies for individual fishermen and considerable administrative burdens for the organisation. As regards the latter, the methods of calculating compensation arising from the operation of withdrawal arrangements are not simple, and detailed records have to be kept of these operations. In addition, efforts must be made to ensure fishing is carried out in a rational way and that marketing conditions for members' catches are improved. Furthermore, non-member fishermen will have to take into account the measures that can be taken under Articles 7 and 8 of the Marketing Regulations.

4. MISCELLANEOUS MATTERS

There are a number of further, miscellaneous matters with which the Marketing Regulations deals, which need to be considered.

(i) Equal Access to Ports

Article 27(2) provides that:

> Member States shall take the necessary steps to ensure that all fishing vessels flying the flag of one of the Member States enjoy equal access to ports and first-stage marketing installations together with all associated equipment and technical installations.

Given that there is a right of equal access to each Member State's maritime zones, that there is a common market in fishery products and the perishable nature of most fishery products, it follows fairly naturally that there should be a right of equal access to ports. Indeed, without such a right the operation of the common market would be frustrated. The right also helps processors to obtain a regular supply of fish.

Like the right of access to maritime zones (discussed in Chapter 4), the right of access to ports is not a right of free access, but of equal access. This means that a Member State must grant the same access to a particular port to vessels from other Member States, as it grants to its own vessels. In other words, it may not restrict access to its ports on the basis of nationality, although it may limit access on the basis of objective factors, such as the size of vessel or the type of catch.

(ii) Communications between Member States and the Commission

Article 31 provides that 'Member States and the Commission shall communicate to each other the information necessary for the implementation' of the Marketing Regulation. Detailed rules for the communication and distribution of such information are to be laid down. As yet, no such rules have been adopted except as regards the communication of withdrawal arrangements (see text at n. 10 above).

(iii) The application of EEC competition rules to the marketing of fish products

Article 1 of the Marketing Regulations says, somewhat laconically, that the common organisation of the market in fishery products shall comprise *inter alia* 'common rules on competition'. The remainder of the Marketing Regulation, apart from its provisions on State aids to producers' organisations which we have looked at in this Chapter and Article 28 on State aids generally which we looked at in the previous Chapter, contains no provisions relating to 'common rules on competition', or, more specifically, about the way in which EEC competition rules (contained in Articles 85–90 of the EEC Treaty) apply to the marketing of fish products. The position is therefore governed by the general provisions of Community law.

Article 42 of the EEC Treaty provides that EEC competition rules 'shall apply to production of and trade in agricultural products only to the extent determined by the Council'. The Council in fact made such a determination in Regulation 26 of 1962.[59] Article 1 of this Regulation provides that Articles 85–90 of the Treaty, and their implementing legislation, apply to production of or trade in the products listed in Annex II to the EEC Treaty, which include fishery products, subject to some exceptions set out in Article 2 of the Regulation. Thus EEC competition rules in principle apply to fisheries in the same way as they apply to most other sectors of the economy. However, because of the multipartite structure of the fishing industries in EEC Member States, it seems unlikely in practice that EEC competition rules will have any application to the marketing of fish products, at least at the wholesale stage (which is all that we are concerned with – the position may be different at subsequent stages), although as pointed out above, Article 7 of the Marketing Regulation does envisage the possibility of producers' organisations being caught by the competition rules.

5. THE DIVISION OF COMPETENCE BETWEEN THE COMMUNITY AND
   ITS MEMBER STATES IN RELATION TO MARKETING

As we have seen, the Community not only has competence to regulate the marketing of fish products, but has also adopted a wide range of marketing measures. The question naturally arises as to whether Member States have retained any competence to regulate the marketing of fish, for example by price support measures or by setting marketing standards for species of fish not covered by Community standards. No answer to this question is given by the Marketing Regulation. One possible answer in seeking to establish Member States' competence might be to apply the European Court's case law in respect of Member States' competence to adopt fishery management measures (see Chapter 4), and say that Member States no longer have any competence to regulate marketing, except insofar as powers are delegated to them by the Community. However, this is probably not the correct answer, as the Court's case law in relation to management competence has been very much influenced by Article 102 of the Act of Accession, which obviously has no relevance to marketing. Another possible answer might be to look at the Court's case law concerning Member States' competence in relation to agricultural marketing where common organisations of the market have been established under the Common Agricultural Policy.[60] In its case law the Court has distinguished between national measures affecting price formation and other marketing measures. In relation to the former, the Court has held that Member States are precluded from taking any measures which affect price formation at producer level, but may take measures affecting price formation at later marketing stages provided that there is no jeopardising of the functioning of the common organisation of the market in question.[61] As regards other marketing measures, Member States may adopt such measures provided they do not jeopardise the operation or aims of the common organisation of the market.[62]

The Commission, in a Decision of October 1985 under Article 93(2) of the EEC Treaty ordering France to abolish various Government price support measures to French producers' organisations which were not only incompatible with the Community's pricing system but by giving French fishermen a competitive advantage over other Community fishermen were impermissible State aids, took the view that the above-mentioned principles relating to national agricultural marketing measures applied equally to the marketing of fish.[63] However, in its judgment in *De Boer v. Produktschap voor Vis en*

Visprodukten[64] given a few days earlier, the Court appears to have taken a narrower view. The case concerned the compatibility with Community law of Dutch rules which required herring caught by Dutch vessels to be processed in such a way as to be sold as *maatjesharing,* a traditional Dutch delicacy: these rules were being challenged by De Boer which had processed its herring differently. The Court began by observing that under the Marketing Regulation producers' organisations could adopt marketing rules for their members (Article 5), but that the powers of Member States were restricted to the possibility of requiring non-members to comply with such rules (Article 7). It therefore followed, said the Court, that the Community rules on production and marketing no longer leave Member States 'any power to adopt rules on the treatment and processing of fishery products by the fishermen established in their territory.'[65]

Although this decision is limited to rules concerning processing, by taking as its point of departure the role of producers' organisations in marketing, it would seem to suggest that Member States have lost any competence to adopt rules relating to the first-stage marketing of fish. Thus, for example, if marketing standards were thought desirable in a Member State for species not covered by existing Community rules, it would seem that only producers' organisations could introduce the standards desired. An interesting question is whether the Government or Parliament of that State could require producers' organisations to adopt such standards. It seems likely that this would be regarded by the European Court as an impermissible interference with the autonomy producers' organisations are clearly intended to enjoy under the Marketing Regulation.[66] On the other hand, where the Marketing Regulation requires Member States to take implementing action, for example reimbursing producers' organisations or enforcing marketing standards, Member States are obviously able to adopt any legislation which may be thought necessary to carry out such implementing action.

6. CONCLUSIONS

Of the three principal matters dealt with by the Marketing Regulation, the encouragement of producers' organisations is the most welcome. Such encouragement should lead to the fishing industry becoming better organised and represented. In the long term it may lead to more rational marketing through supply matching demand and possibly also to better observance of quotas. For students of public law, producers' organisations also represent an interesting example of a governmental function being carried out by purely private bodies. As far as marketing standards are concerned, such standards are clearly required in order to ensure that fish sold to the consumer is of good quality – and without fish being of good quality, the present decline in the demand for fish will not be reversed. However, the present Community marketing standards are probably more complex than their purpose warrants.

As regards the third major concern of the Marketing Regulation, the common price system, this seems in practice to have had relatively little impact on the price of fish.[67] This may not be welcomed by fishermen, but it is in the interests of consumers and fish processors. Equally the common price system has done little to provide support for or increase fishermen's incomes, which is one of its aims. The experience of the Common Agricultural Policy suggests that price mechanisms should not be designed primarily with the aim of supporting producers' incomes because this leads to inefficiency and unfairness: consumers pay more for food than would otherwise be the case (and poor consumers, for whom spending on food constitutes a higher proportion of their expenditure, pay disproportionately more), while the benefits of higher prices go as much, if not more, to large, rich farmers as to poor, struggling ones.

The way to promote fishermen's incomes is, first, through restructuring, to make the industry more efficient; secondly, by good management of the stocks, to ensure that sufficient quantities of fish are there to be caught by fishermen; and thirdly, to promote demand.[68] While such promotion is better undertaken by national bodies (and most Member States have fish promotion campaigns), rather than the Community itself, Community funds should be made available for the national promotional bodies (indeed such funds are already available under the Integrated Mediterranean Programmes and for promoting sardines: see the previous Chapter). On the other hand, there seems little point in spending Community funds on promoting the consumption of fish, and thus by definition trying to persuade people to eat less meat, when meat production in the EEC is not only financed by the Community, but thanks to that financing is considerable in excess of existing demand (witness the Community's frozen beef mountain). A rational Community food policy, the mere mention of which is no doubt purely wishful thinking, would seek, on grounds both of health and economic and food efficiency, to promote greater consumption of fish, fruit and vegetables and less consumption of meat and dairy products – the very things in greatest over-production in the Community at present.

NOTES

1. Reg. 2142/70, O.J. S. Edn. 1970 (III), p. 707.
2. Reg. 100/76, O.J. 1976 L20/1.
3. Reg. 3796/81, O.J. 1981 L379/1. This Reg. has applied since June 1, 1982, apart from some of its pricing provisions (Arts. 13 and 14), application of which was deferred until January 1, 1983 by Reg. 1865/82, O.J. 1982 L206/1.

4. O.J. 1985 L302/1.
5. Reg. 3796/81, Recital 7.
6. The actual fishery products subject to the common organisation of the market are listed in Art. 1(2) of Reg. 3796/81. They include: (a) fresh and frozen fish; (b) dried, salted and smoked fish, and fish in brine; (c) crustaceans and molluscs; (d) fish, crustaceans and molluscs unfit for human consumption; (e) prepared or preserved fish; (f) prepared or preserved crustaceans and molluscs; (g) fish meal and flour. Note that the Reg. covers fresh-water fish, and not just salt-water fish. Fats and oils of fish and marine mammals come under the common organisation of the market in oil and fats, see Reg. 136/66, O.J. S. Edn. 1965–66, p. 221.
7. It should also be noted that the EEC influences prices in Community markets by reducing competition from imports – a matter discussed in the next Chapter.
8. For a list of such markets and ports, see Reg 3598/83, O.J. 1983 L357/17, as amended by Regs. 3473/85 and 2326/86, O.J. 1985 L333/10 and 1986 L202/23. The period of three years may be criticised as being too long in times of rapid inflation.
9. Reg. 1501/83, O.J. 1983 L152/22.
10. Detailed application of this notification system is laid down in Reg. 3599/83, O.J. 1983 L357/22.
11. This means not more than 10 per cent below the Community withdrawal price or 5 per cent above: see Art. 13(1) of Reg. 3796/81. These margins are to allow seasonal fluctuations in price to be taken into account.
12. For further details as to how this is fixed in practice, see Art. 12 of Reg. 3796/81, and the current annual withdrawal price regulation. For a detailed explanation, with a practical example, of how conversion factors are applied, see OECD, *Problems of Trade in Fishery Products,* Paris, 1985, pp. 382–3.
13. For a list of such areas and the way in which this level is calculated, see the current annual wihdrawal price regulation.
14. See Art. 13(1) and (3) of Reg. 3796/81.
15. For detailed application of this provision, see Reg. 1501/83, *op. cit.* in n. 9.
16. For further factors to be taken into account in calculating the level of reimbursement, see Art. 13(4) and (5) of Reg. 3796/81: and for the detailed implementation of the provisions relating to reimbursement, see Regs. 2202/82 and 3137/82, O.J. 1982 L235/1 and L335/1, and Reg. 3165/84, O.J. 1984 L297/14.
17. According to the Commission in 1980 about 70 per cent of the products listed in Annex I(A) and (D) was marketed through producers' organisations: see COM (80) 724.
18. 1981 O.J. C260/81.
19. Reg. 2203/82 and 3321/82, O.J. 1982 L235/4 and L351/20. The latter has been amended by Reg. 3587/85, O.J. 1985 L343/16 and the 1985 Act of Accession, Annex I, XV, point 7.
20. Specified more precisely in Reg. 2203/82, Art. 2 and Annex (as amended by the 1985 Act of Accession, Annex I, XV, point 5).
21. Art. 14(1) of Reg. 3796/81. Details of the conditions are spelt out in Reg. 2203/82, Art. 2 and Reg. 3321/82, Arts. 3 and 4.
22. Art. 14(3) and (4) of Reg. 3796/81, together with its implementing legislation – Regs. 2204/82 and 3138/82, O.J. 1982 L235/7 and L335/9, as amended by Regs. 3160/84, 3624/84, 3646/84 and 3728/85, O.J. 1984 L333/40, L335/2 and 57 and 1985 L361/57; and 1985 Act of Accession, Annex I, XV, point 6. Under the 1976 Regulation special provision was made for sardines and anchovies by means of intervention prices.
23. Detailed rules for the implementation of these provisions are laid down in Reg. 314/86, O.J. 1986 L39/8.
24. Although this requirement is laid down in Art. 16, there are in fact no Community marketing standards for Annex II products. Storage aid is not available for frozen sardines in respect of which a carry-over premium has been paid.

25. O.J. S. Edn. 1971 (I), p. 187.
26. O.J. 1976 L133/1. Further implementing measures are contained in Regs. 3510/82 and 2469/86, O.J. 1982 L368/27 and 1986 L211/19.
27. The concept of free-at-frontier prices is discussed in the next Chapter.
28. Regs. 1629/75 and 1647/75, O.J. 1975 L165/14 and 56.
29. 1985 Act of Accession, Arts. 169–172 and 356–9.
30. Regs. 3117/85, 3459/85 and 3460/85, O.J. 1985 L297/1 and L332/16 and 19.
31. O.J. 1978 L216/1: amendments in Regs. 1303/81 and 1716/84, O.J. 1981 L130/2 and 1984 L163/1.
32. Decs. 85/451, 456, 458, 464 and 466, O.J. 1985 L267/10, 24, 30, 46 and 52.
33. Case 325/85, *Ireland v. Commission;* Case 326/85, *Netherlands v. Commission;* Case 336/85, *French Republic v. Commission;* Case 346/85, *United Kingdom v. Commission;* and Case 348/85, *Denmark, v. Commission;* O.J. 1985 C357/2, 3, 5 and 6.
34. See, e.g. S. Cunningham and J.A. Young, 'The EEC Common Fisheries Policy: Retrospect and Prospect' *National Westminster Bank Quarterly Review,* May 1983, p. 2 at 8.
35. OECD, *Review of Fisheries in OECD Member Countries 1982,* Paris, 1983, p. 266.
36. Even if withdrawn fish is processed into animal feed, this still represents a waste, because it is an inefficient and expensive way of producing animal protein for human consumption when the fish could have been so used in the first place.
37. It may be that still more flexibility needs to be built in to the guide and withdrawal price system in order to take account of the fact that prices vary widely in the Community because of different consumer tastes: e.g. in 1976 the price of mullet was 20 times higher in France than in the United Kingdom, while in 1977 the price of cod in the United Kingdom was double that in West Germany. See E.P. Doc. 560/80, p. 36.
38. Court of Auditors, 'Special Report on the Common Organisation of the Market in Fishery Products', O.J. 1985 C339/1 at 6. It would seem that the system of carry-over premiums is very little responsible for this reduction because at the time little use had been made of the system, *ibid.,* p. 12. See also the Commission's response to the Court's Report, *ibid.,* p. 16.
39. It seems that withdrawal prices, while acting as a reserve price at fish auctions and thus in theory independent of the actual price realised, do in practice influence the level of prices obtained. See Fifth Report from the House of Commons Expenditure Committee, *The Fishing Industry,* HC Paper (1977–78) 356, Vol. II, p. 278. (Memorandum by Mr. A. Laing).
40. T. Young, 'Market Support Arrangements for Fish: The Withdrawal Price Scheme', Sea Fish Industry Authority Occasional Paper Series No. 1 1984.
41. *Op. cit.* in n. 38, pp. 11–13.
42. Reg. 103/76, *op. cit.* in n. 44, recital 4.
43. Marketing Reg., recital 8.
44. Reg. 103/76, O.J. 1976 L20/29, as amended by Regs. 3049/79, 273/81, 3166/82, 3250/83 and 3396/85, O.J. 1979 L343/22, 1981 L30/1, 1982 L332/4 (as corrected in L354/36), 1983 L321/20 and 1985 L322/1, and the 1985 Act of Accession, Annex I, XV, point 2. The species of fish covered by this Reg. are herring, sardines, dogfish, redfish, cod, saithe, haddock, whiting, ling, mackerel, anchovies, plaice, hake, megrim, Ray's bream and monkfish.
45. Reg. 104/76, O.J. 1976 L20/35, as amended by Regs. 3575/83 and 3118/85, O.J. 1983 L356/6 and 1985 L297/3, and the 1985 Act of Accession, Annex I, XV, point 3. For implementation of Reg. 104/76 see Reg. 1048/86, O.J. 1986 L96/14. In 1971 the Commission proposed that common marketing standards should also be adopted for frozen fish of those species for which standards already exist in their fresh state, and also for frozen squid, cuttlefish and octopus. This propoal was never adopted by the Council. See EEC Commission, *Fifth General Report on the Activities of the Communities 1971,* p. 240.
46. Reg. 3703/85, O.J. 1985 L351/63.
47. White Fish Authority, *Annual Report 1971–72,* pp. 1 and 4–5; Laing, *op. cit.* in n. 39, pp. 279–80.

48. See, for example, the Court of Auditors Report, *op. cit.* in n. 38, p. 10.
49. The rules on the recognition of producers' organisations contained in the Marketing Reg. have been supplemented by Regs. 105/76 and 2062/80, O.J. 1976 L20/39 and 1980 L200/82. The latter has been amended by Reg. 1995/84, O.J. 1984 L186/23.
50. Detailed guidance on such rules is contained in Art. 5 of Reg. 2062/80, as amended. This condition (2) has frequently not been observed in practice by recognised producers' organisations: see the Court of Auditors Report, *op. cit.* in n. 38, pp. 10–11.
51. More precise content is given to this condition by Arts. 1 and 3 of Reg. 2062/80, as amended.
52. O.J. 1985 C347/2.
53. Court of Auditor's Report, *op. cit.* in n. 38, p. 11.
54. Detailed rules for the application of this provision are contained in Regs. 3140/82, 1452/83 and 671/84, O.J. 1982 L331/7, 1983 L149/5 and 1984 L73/28.
55. Under the Iberian Act of Accession a five-year period for aid also applies to Portuguese producers' organisations formed within five years of the date of accession: see Annex XXXII, Point VIII, 1.
56. *Loc. cit.* in n. 35.
57. The Court of Auditors even goes as far as 'to question the use of a minimum selling price [i.e. the Community withdrawal price] which is not applied to all operators and which therefore only concerns part of the market': *op. cit.* in n. 38, p. 14.
58. Detailed rules for the application of these provisions are contained in Regs. 1772/82 and 3190/82, O.J. 1982 L197/1 and L338/11.
59. O.J. S. Edn. 1959–62, p. 129.
60. On this topic, see P. Baumann, 'Common Organisations of the Market and National Law' (1977) 14 C.M.L. Rev. 303; G. Beradis, 'The Common Organisation of Agricultural Markets and National Price Regulations' (1980) 17 C.M.L. Rev. 539; and J. Usher, *European Community Law and National Law. The Irreversible Transfer?* London, 1981, pp. 43–55.
61. E.g. Case 31/74, *Filippo Galli* [1975] E.C.R. 47; [1975] 1 C.M.L.R. 211; Case 65/75, *Riccardo Tasca* [1976] E.C.R. 291; [1977] 2 C.M.L.R. 183.
62. E.g. Case 51/74, *Hulst v. Produktschap voor Siergewassen* [1975] E.C.R. 79; [1975] 1 C.M.L.R. 236; Case 111/76, *Officier van Justitie v. Beert van den Hazel* [1977] E.C.R. 901; [1980] 3 C.M.L.R. 12; Case 83/78, *Pigs Marketing Board v. Redmond* [1978] E.C.R. 2347; [1979] 1 C.M.L.R. 177. But as regards both price and other marketing measures the Court in its most recent case law is moving away from the 'jeopardising' or compatibility test towards Community exclusivity: see J.A. Usher, 'The Scope of Community Competence – its Recognition and Enforcement' (1985) XXIV J.C.M.S. 121 at 123–127.
63. Dec. 86/186, O.J. 1986 L136/55 at 60.
64. Case 207/84, Judgment of October 3, 1985 (not yet reported).
65. Para. 33.
66. However, it seems that in the absence of Community rules Member States may still legislate for health controls on fish, since in a recent case the Court did not question the permissibility in principle of such national rules: see Case 247/84, *Motte,* Judgment of December 10, 1985 (not yet reported).
67. Although more research on this question is required before any very definite conclusions can be reached. See Young, *op. cit.* in n. 40.
68. A similar point is made by Cunningham and Young, *op. cit.* in n. 34, p. 12.

CHAPTER 8

Trade in fishery products

In Chapter 1 it was pointed out that EEC Member States engage in a considerable amount of trade in fishery products, both amongst themselves (such trade being facilitated by the right of equal access to ports, discussed in the previous Chapter) and with third States. The purpose of this Chapter is to examine the legal rules governing such trade. We will look first at the rules governing trade between Member States (intra-Community trade), and then at the rules governing trade between the EEC and third States.

1. INTRA-COMMUNITY TRADE

Regulation 3796/81 (the Marketing Regulation) contains no provisions dealing with trade between Member States. However, Article 38(2) of the EEC Treaty makes it clear that where a regulation laying down a common organisation of the market for a particular sector of agriculture contains no rules relating to intra-Community trade, the general provisions of the EEC Treaty governing trade between Member States (Articles 9–17 and 30–37) apply. That this is the position as regards intra-Community trade in fishery products has been confirmed in Recital 35 of the Marketing Regulation and by the European Court in the *Kramer* case.[1]

Before examining the general rules of the EEC relating to intra-Community trade, it is necessary to determine first to what products these rules apply. Article 9(2) of the EEC Treaty provides that the rules apply, first, to 'products originating in Member States', and, secondly, to 'products coming from third countries which are in free circulation in Member States'. The latter products are considered to be in free circulation 'if the import formalities have been complied with and any customs duties or charges having equivalent effect which are payable have been levied in that Member State, and if they have not benefited from a total or partial drawback of such duties or charges' (Article 10(1)). More important for our present purposes is to determine what products are considered as 'originating in Member States'. Can fish caught at sea, often a long way from the coasts of Member States, be considered as 'originating' in those States? Rather curiously perhaps, neither the EEC Treaty nor secondary legislation define what products are considered as 'originating in Member States'. Regulation 802/68[2] provides that, for the purposes of trade with third countries, fish caught by a vessel registered or recorded in a Member State and flying its flag are to be regarded as originating in that Member State. It is not unreasonable to suggest that a similar definition should apply to fish which are the subject of intra-Community trade. Support for this view is afforded by Regulation 137/79.[3] This Regulation provides for a special form of documentation to be used when a vessel of one Member State lands its catch in another Member State, when the catch is transshipped from one EEC vessel to another and then landed in a Member State, or when an EEC vessel lands the catch in a country outside the EEC, whence it is transported to the Community. The purpose of this system of documentation is to provide proof that such catches originate in Member States or are in free circulation in Member States.[4]

The rules on intra-Community trade do not apply to fishery products which are manufactured or obtained from products not originating in Member States or in free circulation therein, since Article 27(1) of the Marketing Regulation provides that such products shall not be admitted to free circulation within the Community.

For fishery products which do originate in Member States or which are in free circulation within the Community, the most important rules governing their trade between Member States are as follows.[5] First, as a result of Articles 13–16 of the EEC Treaty, Articles 31–38 of the 1972 Act of Accession and Article 64 of the 1979 Greek Act of Accession, all customs duties on fisheries products and charges having equivalent effect[6] have been abolished as between EEC Member States.[7] Nor may any such duties or charges be re-introduced (Article 12 of the EEC Treaty). Secondly, in order to prevent the prohibition on customs duties and charges having equivalent effect from being circumvented by the imposition of taxes, Article 95 of the EEC Treaty provides that no Member State shall impose, either directly or indirectly, on the product of any other Member State any internal taxation of any kind in excess of that imposed directly or indirectly on similar domestic products; nor may it impose any internal taxation of such a kind as to afford indirect protection to other products.[8] If a Member State does tax imports in such a way as not to infringe Article 95, the Member State from which the goods are exported may reimburse its exporters for the import tax levied: such reimbursement, however, must not exceed the amount of any tax paid (Article 96). Lastly, as a result of Articles 30 and 32–34 of the EEC Treaty, Article 42 of the 1972 Act of Accession and Article 35 of the Greek Act of Accession, all quantitative restrictions and measures having equivalent effect on imports have been abolished as between EEC Member States;[9] nor – according to Article 31 of the EEC Treaty – may such restrictions and measures be re-introduced.[10] While the concepts of quantitative restrictions and measures having equivalent effect may be relatively easy to define in general terms,[11] it is by no means always obvious in practice whether a particular measure adopted by a Member State amounts to a quantitative restriction or a measure having equivalent effect, and thus to determine whether the adoption of such a measure constitutes an infringement of that Member State's Community obligations. Not surprisingly, therefore, this question has led to a considerable number of cases coming before the European Court. We will limit our consideration of these cases to the handful that have concerned fisheries.

In the *Kramer* case[12] the Court was faced with the argument that catch quotas imposed by the Netherlands for the purposes of fisheries conservation constituted a quantitative restriction or a measure having equivalent effect. The Court rejected this suggestion. It began by observing that catch quotas were concerned with production, whereas the prohibition on quantitative restrictions and equivalent measures was concerned with a different stage of the economic process, namely marketing. The Court then went on to state that:

Measures for the conservation of the resources of the sea through fixing catch quotas and limiting the fishing effort, while restricting 'production' in the short term, are aimed precisely at preventing such 'production' from being marked by a fall which would seriously jeopardise supplies to consumers. Therefore, the fact that such measures have the effect, for a short time, of reducing the quantities that the States concerned are able to exchange between themselves, cannot lead to these measures being classified among those prohibited by the Treaty, the decisive factor being that in the long term these measures are necessary to ensure a steady optimum yield from fishing.[13]

While in cases involving agriculture the Court has held that limitations on production do amount to quantitative restrictions or equivalent measures,[14] its finding in the *Kramer* case that fishery quotas do not constitute such measures is particularly to be welcomed, given the need for effective measures to conserve fish stocks. The Court's decision seems to result more from its finding that the Dutch quotas did not affect the common organisation of the market in fishery products, and less from the distinction it draws between the production and marketing stages of the economic process.

In *Commission v. United Kingdom*,[15] a case concerned with the validity of a number of United Kingdom fishery conservation measures, the Commission argued that one of these measures, which restricted the number of ports at which Irish fishermen could land herring caught in United Kingdom waters, was contrary to Community law because it amounted to a measure equivalent in effect to a quantitative restriction. The United Kingdom argued in its defence that its legislation was not such a measure: the reason for the limitation of landing ports was to ensure effective control of its conservation measures. While the Advocate General tended towards agreeing with the Commission, the Court found it was not necessary to consider the question and determined the validity of the United Kingdom legislation on other grounds. Thus the question of whether a Member State which limits the ports at which catches can be landed for the purposes of verifying compliance with conservation measures, infringes the EEC Treaty's provisions on quantitative restrictions and equivalent measures has been left open. Limiting the ports at which catches may be landed is generally considered to be one of the more effective methods of ensuring that conservation methods are complied with, and indeed, the Commission at one time proposed that such a system of control should be introduced on a Community basis, although this proposal was not in the end adopted. While a Community system to limit the ports at which catches may be landed is probably lawful,[16] *Commission v. United Kingdom* suggests that a national system would fall foul of Community law because it would amount to a quantitative restriction or equivalent measure.[17]

A rather different potential restriction on trade was at issue in *United Foods and Van den Abeele v. Belgian State.*[18] This case concerned Belgian legislation requiring imported fish to be subject to a public health inspection. The Court held that in the absence of common or harmonised rules relating to health controls on fish, national rules amounted to a measure equivalent in effect to a quantitative restriction. However, such rules would be saved by Article 36 (the public health exception), provided, as Article 36 requires, they did not 'constitute a means of arbitrary discrimination or a disguised restriction on trade.' Whether the Belgian rules at issue did amount to arbitrary discrimination or a disguised restriction on trade, the European Court did not and could not decide, as this case was a preliminary ruling. Nevertheless, it suggested that certain aspects of the Belgian rules – such as the requirement of advance notification of importation, restrictions on the time and place when controls could be carried out, and the necessity for health controls to have been carried out in the exporting country – went beyond what was permissible under Article 36.

Health controls were also at issue in *Motte.*[19] Here the question arose as to whether Belgian rules prohibiting the adding of colourants to potted roe imported from a Member State where the addition of such colourants was permitted, was compatible with Community law. The Court held such rules were prima facie contrary to Article 30 and would only be saved if justified under the public health exception of Article 36. In determining whether the rules were so justified (and this the European Court could not do, as this was again a preliminary ruling), the following factors should be considered: whether it was really necessary to add colourants to the food stuff in question; the scientific evidence as to the health risks of the additives at issue; and, generally, whether the national rules were, in accordance with the principle of proportionality, restricted to what was necessary to attain the legitimate aim of protecting health.

Finally, it may be of interest to mention two cases which never reached the stage of being referred to the European Court. First, in the early 1970s France operated a system of import certificates for fish, which also appeared to imply the levying of a special tax. The Commission pointed out to the French Government that this system was contrary to Community law, and in 1974 the French Government undertook to abolish the system.[20] Secondly, in 1982 the Commission began Article 169 proceedings against France, alleging that its rules on health inspection for imported fish were contrary to Community law.[21] The case appears to have been settled without being referred to the Court, but what the terms of the settlement were the writer unfortunately does not know.

The effect of the above provisions is that trade in fishery products between EEC Member States may not be made subject to any customs duties or charges having equivalent effect, nor to any discriminatory tax treatment, nor may quantitative restrictions or measures having equivalent effect be imposed on such trade. While this is the theory, it seems that in practice trade is not so free, and that fishery products, like most other goods, are subject from time to time to obstacles as they move from one Member State to another.[22] Thus, trade in fishery products, like trade in other products, would benefit if the Community's ambitions to remove all obstacles to trade and create a genuine internal market by 1992 were realised.[23]

2. TRADE BETWEEN THE EEC AND THIRD STATES[24]

As we saw in Chapter 1, the EEC is nowhere near self-sufficient in fish. This contrasts with most sectors of agriculture, where the Community is completely, or almost completely, self-sufficient. Thus it is not thought necessary to give fishermen the same degree of protection against imports from third countries, or the same degree of assistance in exporting, as is given to producers in most sectors of agriculture. Nevertheless, Community fishermen are protected to some extent against competition from imports by means of customs duties and a system of reference and free-at-frontier prices, as well as by some other, more limited, measures. They also receive some assistance in exporting fish through export refunds.

The rules governing trade in fisheries products with third countries are contained not only in the Marketing Regulation, but also in general Community legislation relating to trade and in a number of commercial and association agreements with third States, concluded under Articles 113 and 238 of the EEC Treaty.[25] In adopting this legislation and entering into these agreements, the Community has had to have regard to the relevant provisions of the General Agreement on Tariffs and Trade (GATT), by which the Community is bound, having taken over the obligations of its Member States in this regard by virtue of the substitution principle (see Chapter 5, section 1).[26]

(i) The Regulation of Imports

a) Customs Duties. In principle, customs duties are payable on most fishery products. These duties – the common customs tariff (CCT) – are set out in Part II of the Annex to Regulation 950/68.[27] Since the CCT is frequently revised, an amended version of the Annex is published each year. For fish, crustaceans and molluscs (other than those in a prepared or preserved state) the CCT ranges between 3 and 25 per cent (see Chapter 3 of the CCT). For other fisheries products covered by the Marketing Regulation duties range as follows: for products unfit for human consumption (Chapter 05.15) nil; for prepared fish, crustaceans and molluscs (Chapters 16.04 and 16.05) from 6 to

30 per cent; and for fish flour and meal (Chapter 23.01) from 0 to 2 per cent. By virtue of Article 19(2) of the Marketing Regulation, the general rules relating to the interpretation and application of the CCT contained in Regulation 950/68 apply to fisheries products.

It was said that customs duties are payable on most fishery products 'in principle'. This is because there are now so many exceptions that the application of the CCT, so far from being the general rule, has in practice become the exception.

First, customs duties are in many cases suspended, totally or partially, on a permanent or a seasonal basis, because catches by Community fishing vessels are inadequate for the needs of consumers and processors in the Community. Thus Article 20 of the Marketing Regulation[28] suspends duties totally on tuna imported for the canning industry for the whole of the year, and Annex VI suspends duties on herring and sprats for several months of the year. In addition, there are a vast number of other regulations, too numerous to list, suspending customs duties, either totally or partially, for a limited period because of a shortage of supplies in the Community. In many of these cases this is done by setting a quota, representing the estimated Community shortfall of supplies, for which customs duties are suspended. Finally, in the event of an emergency caused by supply difficulties on the Community market or the fulfilment of international commitments, Article 20(2) of the Marketing Regulation empowers the Commission, acting in accordance with the Management Committee procedure, wholly or partly to suspend the CCT on any fishery products. These powers, introduced by the 1981 Marketing Regulation, have not yet been used.

Secondly, fish caught by a Community vessel in the waters of a third State under an agreement between the Community and that third State and processed in that third State, or fish transshipped to a Community vessel in such a third State's waters, may be imported into the Community wholly or partially free of customs duties.[29]

Thirdly, customs duties on imports of fishery products from many third countries have either been totally abolished or substantially reduced.[30] Third countries enjoying this benefit include those non-European territories for whose external relations EEC Member States are responsible which are listed in Annex IV of the EEC Treaty;[31] the 66 or so developing African, Caribbean and Pacific (ACP) States parties to the Lomé Convention;[32] those developing countries benefiting from the system of generalised preferences;[33] the Faroes;[34] the Canary Islands, Ceuta and Melilla;[35] two EFTA Member States, Iceland[36] and Norway;[37] and a number of Mediterranean States – Algeria,[38] Morocco,[39] Tunisia,[40] Egypt,[41] Turkey,[42] and Malta.[43] In the case of a number of these third countries (the Faroes, Iceland, Norway and Turkey), the reduction or abolition of customs duties is dependent on these countries observing the EEC's reference prices. In the case of tinned sardines imported from Algeria, Morocco, Tunisia and Turkey, the reduction or abolition of customs duties is dependent on these countries observing agreed minimum prices (the system of reference prices does not apply to tinned sardines).[44] Furthermore, in many cases the EEC is entitled to impose quantitative restrictions on fishery products imported from third countries at reduced or nil duties.

In the case of virtually all third countries enjoying the benefit of reduced or nil duties, the arrangements providing this benefit contains rules of origin which *inter alia* are aimed at ensuring that the vessels catching the fish subject to this preferential customs treatment have a genuine connection with the third country concerned, and are not mere flags of convenience. These rules are quite strict. To take the provisions for Norway, which are fairly typical: a vessel must be registered in Norway, fly the Norwegian flag and be at least 50 per cent owned by Norwegian or EEC nationals or companies. In addition, the captain, officers and three-quarters of the crew of the vessel must possess Norwegian or an EEC nationality.[45] These rules may be contrasted with the position in relation to the access of third country vessels to EEC waters, where there are no provisions designed to ensure that vessels have a genuine connection with the third country concerned. The reason for this difference is that if there were no rules of origin for imported products, trade advantages could be obtained by a third State not enjoying preferential access to Community markets through the use of a flag of convenience of a third State which did enjoy such access. In the case of the access of a third State's vessels to Community waters, on the other hand, it makes no real difference to the Community whether vessels from that State have a genuine connection with it or not, since the number of vessels granted access and/or the amount of fish they can catch is strictly limited.

Finally, it is of interest to note that in three cases – Iceland, Norway and Greenland – the reduction of customs duties has been coupled with the question of access to fishing grounds.[46] In the case of Iceland, Article 2 of Protocol 6 to the EEC – Iceland Free Tade Agreement[47] provides that the EEC reserves the right not to begin the reduction in customs duties provided for in the Protocol 'if a solution satisfactory to the Member States of the Community and to Iceland has not been found for the economic problems arising from the measures adopted by Iceland concerning fishing rights.' At the time the Free Trade Agreement came into force, in April 1973, the United Kingdom and the Federal Republic of Germany were both in dispute with Iceland over the latter's action in extending its fishing limits to 50 miles on September 1, 1972. The EEC therefore invoked Article 2 to suspend the application of Protocol 6, and it was only when both disputes had been settled, in June 1976, that the EEC allowed customs duties on imports of fish from Iceland to be reduced as provided for in Protocol 6.[48] This Protocol is so worded that it appears that once the scheduled reduction of customs duties has begun, it is not possible to re-suspend this reduction, even though there might be some renewed disagreement between Iceland and EEC Member States over access to Icelandic fishing limits.[49] In the case of Norway, the Exchange of Letters attached to the EEC-Norway Free Trade Agreement[50] provides that the reduction of customs duties by the EEC is 'subject to the maintenance of present conditions of general competition in the fishery sector'. This provision was invoked when Norway established trawler-free zones beyond its then 12-mile exclusive fishing zone at the beginning of 1975. It was agreed that the establishment of these zones did not so affect the conditions of competition in the fisheries sector that it should lead to any alterations in the reduction of customs duties, but it appears that EEC representations did lead to Norway modifying the areas of these zones from those originally proposed.[51] On the other hand, the provision in the Exchange of Letters does not appear to have inhibited Norway from extending its fishing limits to 200 miles at the beginning of 1977, nor has this action affected its tariff concessions. The reason for this is presumably because EEC Member States extended their limits to 200 miles at the same time, even though the alteration in the conditions for fishing which this has produced for Norway is not covered by the Exchange of Letters. Finally, in the case of Greenland the maintenance of imports of fishery products from Greenland free of customs duties is dependent on the access of Community vessels to Greenland's 200-mile fishing zone remaining 'satisfactory'.[52]

b) Reference and Free-at-frontier Prices. Even if they applied fully, customs duties on their own would not be sufficient to give Community fishermen adequate protection from adverse competition from imports. The Marketing Regulation (in Article 21) has therefore introduced a system of reference and free-at-frontier prices which apply to fishery products imported from third countries. Reference prices act as a kind of minimum import price, and are designed to prevent disturbances to the stability of markets which might be caused by abnormally low-priced imports.

Reference prices are fixed each year for the products listed in Annexes I,[53] II,[54] III,[55] IVB[56] and V[57] to the Marketing Regulation.[58] For products for which withdrawal or Community selling prices are fixed, the reference price is the same as those prices. For the frozen products listed in Annexes I, IVB and V, the reference price is determined on the basis of the reference price for the fresh product, taking account of processing costs and the 'need to ensure a relationship of prices in keeping with the market situation.' For the products listed in Annex II, the reference price is normally 85 per cent of the guide prices set for those products. For tuna the reference price is based on representative c.i.f. import prices over a three-year period.

For all products for which a reference price is fixed, a free-at-frontier price is laid down. For the products listed in Annex I (A), (D) and (E), the free-at-frontier price is based on the price recorded at a specific marketing stage for the imported product on representative import markets or in representative ports of import, less any customs duties paid and the costs of unloading and transport from the Community frontier to those markets or ports. For other products the free-at-frontier price is based on the price recorded for the usual commercial quantities which are imported into the Community, less any customs duties paid and the costs of unloading and transport.[59]

When the free-at-frontier price for a given product imported from a third country remains lower than the reference price for at least three successive market days and if significant quantities of such products are being imported, then one or more of three types of corrective action may be taken by the Commission in accordance with the Management Committee procedure (and in the intervals between the periodic meetings of the Management Committee the Commission can take temporary action on its own). First, autonomous suspension of the CCT for the products in question may be lifted. Secondly, in the case of the products listed in Annex I (A), (C), (D) and (E) and Annexes II, IV and V, 'imports may be subjected to the requirement that the free-at-frontier price . . . is at least equal to the reference price.' Thirdly, in the case of herring and tuna, imports may be subjected to a countervailing charge, provided that this complies with GATT rules on binding. Such a countervailing charge is to be equal to the difference between the reference price and the free-at-frontier price, and is added to any customs duties which may be payable. A countervailing charge may not be imposed on third States which undertake not to sell their imports below reference prices. The only measures so far taken under these powers are a Regulation of May 1983 which for a 6-week period subjected imported hake to the condition that free-at-frontier prices must be at least equal to the reference price,[60] and a Regulation of May 1986 which made the import of squid from Poland and the USSR subject to the same condition for a 4-month period.[61]

The system of reference and free-at-frontier prices contained in the 1981 Marketing Regulation is rather different from that of the two previous Marketing Regulations. While reference prices and free-at-frontier prices (known as entry prices in the earlier Regulations) are calculated in much the same way (though they cover a rather wider range of products), the action which can be taken where the free-at-frontier price falls below the reference price is rather different. Under the 1976 Marketing Regulation the action which could be taken was either to suspend imports (which in practice happened on about half-a-dozen occasions) or to impose a countervailing charge, the provisions relating to which (although never applied in practice) were similar to the 1981 Regulation.

The system of reference and entry prices in the 1976 Marketing Regulation was heavily criticised in the late 1970s and early 1980s for being inadequate to deal with the flood of low-priced, often heavily subsidised, imports coming into the Community at that time which were undercutting Community fishermen. The problem was particularly bad in the United Kingdom, because the high price of sterling made the British market very attractive. There seem to have been three main reasons for the ineffectiveness of the 1976 system. First, reference prices were set at a low level, thus making it unlikely that entry prices would drop below reference prices and activate the mechanisms to protect the Community market. To try to remedy this situation, reference prices were substantially raised in May 1980 and this increase has been maintained subsequently. The second reason for the ineffectiveness of the 1976 system is that reference prices were often not observed where there was an obligation on certain third States to do so in return for tariff concessions:[62] furthermore, the complexity of the system made it difficult to monitor their observance. The 1981 Marketing Regulation does not really address itself to these problems. The third reason for the ineffectiveness of the 1976 Regulation is that under it measures to suspend imports could only be taken by the Council: this usually took time. There is now a wider and more flexible range of measures; and these can be taken by the Commission, which can act much more quickly. Such measures, unlike those of the 1976 Regulation which in practice involved solely the suspension of imports, do not lead to a complete loss of supplies to the Community market from imports, which would be contrary to the interests of processors and consumers (especially in view of the fact that the Community now imports a higher proportion of its fish supplies than formerly): on the other hand, they do at the same time give some protection to Community fishermen. The 1981 Regulation is therefore an improvement in this respect on its predecessor; but it will be necessary to monitor its operation in practice, especially after the enlargement of the Community at the beginning of 1986, to see whether it has cured all the ills of the 1976 Regulation relating to reference and entry prices. Finally, one general feature inherent in the reference price system has been criticised on economic grounds by Cunningham and Young. They point out that reference prices act as minimum prices 'which the exporter must charge, even if he might be quite content with a lower profit margin and the increased competitiveness thereby gained. The net result of this situation is that the consumer of imported products is taxed to the benefit of exporting nations. Moreover, this represents revenue to the Community which could easily be captured by the simple application of a levy, while still maintaining the import price at the same level and preventing the disruptive effects of imports being supplied to the Community at below the reference price.'[63]

A special system of reference prices operates for carp and trout (the latter being added by the 1981 Marketing Regulation). Under Article 22 of the Regulation a reference price for carp and trout may be laid down each year. In practice, such prices have been laid down for carp each year since 1974 (but no such prices have yet been laid down for trout). The reference price for carp is fixed on the basis of the average of producer prices recorded during the three years preceding the year for which the reference price is to be set.[64] If the free-at-frontier price[65] is lower than the reference price, imports are to be subjected to a countervailing charge, which is calculated in a similar manner to that used in the general system of reference and free-at-frontier prices. A countervailing charge is not to be applied to third countries which guarantee that for the carp they export to the Community, the price plus the customs duty actually levied is not less than the reference price and also that deflections of trade will be avoided. In practice, it does not appear to have been necessary yet to introduce countervailing charges on imported carp.

For fisheries products other than those just discussed, there is no sysem of reference and free-at-frontier prices, but as we shall see in a moment, there are other means by which imports of such products can be controlled. In any case, such products are, in general, of less commercial importance than those covered by the reference and free-at-frontier price system, and the markets for such products are generally more stable.[66]

c) Other Measures to Control Imports. The Marketing Regulation provides a number of other means by which imports can be controlled. First, Article 23 deals with imports of fish for inward processing arrangements. The latter term refers to customs arrangements whereby raw materials from third countries are imported for the purpose of processing without payment of customs duties, and the processed product is then immediately exported outside the Community.[67] Under Article 23 the Council may in certain cases, to the extent necessary for the proper working of the common organisation of the market in fishery products, prohibit, in whole or in part, the use of inward processing arrangements in respect of fish, crustaceans or molluscs, where these products are to be dried, salted, pickled, smoked, prepared or preserved. As yet, the Council does not appear ever to have made use of these powers.

In practice, more important powers to restrict imports are contained in Article 24 of the Marketing Regulation. This provides that if the Community market in one or more of the products to which the Marketing Regulation applies[68] experiences or is threatened with serious disturbances which may endanger the objectives of the Common Fisheries Policy,[69] appropriate measures may be applied to trade with third countries until such disturbances or the threat of such disturbances have ceased. Such measures are to be taken by the Commission acting on its own initiative or at the request of a Member State. Any measures adopted by the Commission may be referred by any

Member State to the Council within three working days of their adoption. The Council, meeting without delay, may, by qualified majority, amend or repeal the Commission's measures. These powers, it should be noted, are additional to the powers contained in the provisions concerning reference and free-at-frontier prices.

The powers provided by Article 24 (and the corresponding provision in the earlier Marketing Regulations) have only been used five times in practice so far. In February 1975, following a general ban on all imports of fish into France introduced unilaterally by the French Government in response to a strike by French fishermen in protest against the difficult market situation, Article 24 was used to ban imports into France of tuna for the canning industry and frozen hake fillets. The ban on hake imports lasted until May 1975 and that on tuna imports until May 1976.[70] Secondly, imports into Italy of frozen squid of the species not covered by a ban introduced under the reference and entry price system were suspended from all third countries except Greece between November 1977 and April 1978, except for imports which observed specified minimum import prices.[71] Thirdly, imports into Italy of clams were suspended from all third countries between February and June 1981.[72] Fourthly, following a drastic fall in the price of frozen squid on the Community market in 1984 as a result of substantially increased imports (mainly from Poland), a ban on imports of frozen squid from Poland was imposed for the last three months of 1984, although an exception was made for imports whose free-at-frontier price was not less than the reference price.[73] In 1985 Poland agreed informally to continue to observe reference prices and to limit its exports to the Community to 10,000 tonnes.[74] It is odd that this action was taken under Article 24 when it could have been taken under the general powers relating to reference prices, as was in fact done when the problem arose again in 1986 (see above). The final use so far made of Article 24 relates to the import of yellowfin tuna into France. In 1985 the French authorities, concerned about the impact of greatly increased yellowfin tuna imports into France on French tuna fishermen, asked the Commission to suspend imports. The Commission refused this request, and instead introduced in November 1985 as a preventative measure an early warning system to monitor the quantities of yellowfin tuna imported into France.[75] This system has been continued throughout most of 1986.[76]

The question of when it is appropriate to use Article 24 arose in an acute form in 1980, when a sharp difference of opinion between the European Parliament and Commission was revealed. In May 1980 the Commission was asked in the European Parliament why it had not taken action under Article 24 to deal with cheap imports of fish which had flooded Community markets in the early part of 1980. The Commission replied that it did not believe that the time had come for applying Article 24, nor had any Member State suggested that it should be applied. To deal with possible disturbances to Community markets from cheap imports, the Commission had decided to raise reference prices and to propose that autonomous customs reductions should not be continued after July 1, 1980 for a number of products. The Commission thought that these measures would be sufficient to stabilise markets.[77] Not satisfied with this answer, the European Parliament adopted a resolution calling on the Commission to adopt without delay the necessary protective measures under Article 24 and calling on both the Commission and the Council to take all possible measures to remedy the situation, including raising withdrawal prices and revising customs duties.[78]

Further provisions dealing with the control of imports are contained in Article 19 of the Marketing Regulation. In general, unless the Council specifically decides otherwise, the levying of any charge having an effect equivalent to customs duties and the application of any quantitative restrictions are prohibited. However, Article 19(4) provides that until Community arrangements for the import of canned sardines and tuna are adopted,[79] Member States may retain the quantitative restrictions that they applied to imports of these products from third States at the time when the Regulation entered into force, i.e. February 3, 1982.[80]

Finally, in the unlikely event that the above powers should prove inadequate to control imports, recourse could be had to the Community's general anti-dumping legislation.[81] Under this the Community is empowered to apply an anti-dumping duty to any product dumped on Community markets or to impose a countervailing duty on subsidised products where the entry of such products on Community markets causes injury to Community producers. Protective measures can also be taken under the Regulation on Common Rules for Imports[82] and the Community's New Commercial Policy Instrument.[83]

(ii) The Regulation of Exports

The reduction or abolition of customs duties on imports of fishery products from certain third countries, discussed above, are unilateral concessions by the Community: the third countries concerned have not made any corresponding reductions in the customs duties they levy on fishery products imported from the Community. Nevertheless, with most of these countries, as well as with many other third countries, the Community enjoys most-favoured-nation treatment in relation to customs duties on its goods exported to these countries, i.e. it enjoys for each product the lowest rate of duty which the country concerned levies on imports of that product.

The Community gives some encouragement of its own to exporters of fishery products to third countries through export refunds. Article 25 of the Marketing Regulation[84] provides that in order to allow fishery products caught by Community vessels to compete with comparable products on world markets where Community prices are higher than world prices, the Community may grant export refunds to subsidise the price difference. Export refunds are fixed about every three months by the Commission in consultation with the Management Committee for Fishery Products. In so doing, the Commission is required to take particular account of the need to establish a balance between the use of Community basic products in the manufacture of processed goods for export to third countries and the use of third country products brought in under inward processing arrangements, in order that the former are not placed at a disadvantage in comparison with the latter which would encourage Community processing industries to give preference to raw materials imported from third countries. The levels at which export refunds are set can be varied according to the destination of the products concerned, and even be not applied at all in respect of exports to certain countries.[85]

Refunds can be granted only in respect of products whose export is 'economically important', and this condition has meant that in practice little use has been made of export refunds. In the early 1970s the export of dried and frozen cod was considered economically important and therefore eligible for support, but with the decline in Community distant-water fishing as the result of the world-wide extension of fishing limits to 200 miles, and the consequent drastic drop in the Community's cod catch, this export has long since ceased to be important and attract refunds. In the late 1970s and early 1980s, the export of mackerel and dried and salted saithe qualified for refunds, but these were abolished on November 1, 1983 because the Community price for these products was no longer higher than the world price.[86] Since that date no export refunds have been made, but this situation may alter with the accession of Portugal and Spain, although the Community's position as a net importer of fish suggests that the use of export refunds is unlikely to become widespread in the foreseeable future.

When export refunds have been in operation, one problem has been what appears to be fraud. This has notably been the case in relation to exports of mackerel from the Netherlands. In 1981, for example, the Netherlands caught 37,000 tonnes of mackerel and imported a further 35,450 tonnes, yet managed to export nearly 192,000 tonnes (on most of which export refunds were claimed)![87] The Commission subsequently withheld payment of most of the export refunds claimed,[88] but this action has been challenged by the Dutch Government in legal proceedings which at the time of writing were pending before the European Court.[89]

It should be noted that unlike price support arrangements, which are tied to observance of quotas (see p. 240 above), no such linkage is made in the Marketing Regulation as regards export refunds, nor could it so easily be made, as exports from one Member State could include fish imported into that

State from another Member State (as appears to be the case with the Netherlands) or fish caught in the previous year which had been frozen and stored. It seems, however, that a linkage between export refunds and quotas has been asserted by the Commission in the litigation referred to above. The point will no doubt be clarified once the Court gives its judgment.

3. CONCLUSIONS

As far as intra-Community trade is concerned, there are in theory no longer any barriers to such trade (apart from some temporary restrictions between Portugal and Spain and the rest of the Community). Nevertheless, as indicated above, obstacles to intra-Community trade do from time to time manifest themselves. Most such obstacles appear to involve health controls on imported fish, and it may well be that if the Community were to adopt common rules on health controls – as advocated by the European Parliament[90] – many existing obstacles to intra-Community trade would disappear.

As regards trade with third States, given the Community's lack of self-sufficiency in fish, the present fairly liberal trading regime obviously makes sense for consumers and fish processors, who require a regular supply of fish which Community fishermen are not always in a position to provide. At the same time the present regime does provide some measure of protection for Community fishermen against damaging competition from imports. The 1981 Marketing Regulation has certainly struck a better balance between the interests of consumers, processors and fishermen than its predecessors: whether the balance is now about right, and each of these groups' interests sufficiently taken care of, can only really be judged when the system has been in operation for some time and its functioning in the enlarged Community observed.

NOTES

1. Joined Cases 3, 4 and 6/76, *Officier van Justitie v. Kramer* [1976] E.C.R. 1279 at 1312; [1976] 2 C.M.L.R. 440 at 472.
2. O.J. S. Edn. 1968 (I), p. 165.
3. O.J. 1979 L20/1, as amended by Reg. 3415/85, O.J. 1985 L324/12.
4. On the other hand, fish which are caught by a non-Community vessel, the nets then being transferred to a Community vessel, are regarded as not originating in a Member State: Case 100/84, *Commission v. United Kingdom* [1985] 2 C.M.L.R. 199.
5. It is beyond the scope of this book to give anything other than a brief sketch of these rules. For a more detailed treatment, see D. Wyatt and A. Dashwood, *The Substantive Law of the EEC*, London, 1980, Chapters 9-12 and P. Oliver, *Free Movement of Goods in the EEC*, London, 1982.

6. The European Court has defined such charges as including 'any pecuniary charge, however small and whatever its designation and mode of application, which is imposed unilaterally on domestic or foreign goods by reason of the fact that they cross a frontier, and which is not a customs duty in the strict sence, . . . even if it is not imposed for the benefit of the State, is not discriminatory or protective in effect and if the product on which the charge is imposed is not in competition with any domestic product', Case 24/68, *Commission v. Italy* [1969] E.C.R. 193 at 201; [1971] C.M.L.R. 611 at 623. For an example of such a charge in the field of fisheries trade, see the charges for health inspections on imported fish at issue in *United Foods and Van den Abeele v. Belgian State, op. cit.* in n. 18.

7. Except as between Portugal and Spain and the rest of the EEC where customs duties are to be abolished by January 1, 1993. An exception is made for sardines (and also, in the case of Portugal, anchovies and tuna) where customs duties are not to be abolished until 1996 (although, in the case of Portugal, certain quantities of preserved or prepared sardines, tuna and mackerel may be exported duty-free to the rest of the Community as from the date of accession). During this period, if imports of sardines lead to a disturbance of the market, minimum import prices can be imposed. See the 1985 Act of Accession, Arts. 170, 173, 357, 360 and 362, O.J. 1985 L302.

8. Art. 95 has been in issue on at least one occasion as regards trade in fishery products. In 1984 the Commission brought an action against France before the European Court under Art. 169 arguing that France was in breach of Art. 95 by imposing different rates of charges on domestic and imported products in respect of fees for the health inspection of oysters, mussels and shellfish (Case 98/84, O.J. 1984 C139/4). The case was subsequently withdrawn (O.J. 1985 C178/6), so presumably France abolished its different rates of charge.

9. Except that imports into Portugal and Spain from the rest of the EEC, and imports into the EEC of canned tuna and sardines from Spain, may be quantitatively restricted until 1993. See 1985 Act of Accession, Arts. 174, 175 and 361. For detailed implementation, see Regs. 254/86 and 546/86, O.J. 1986 L31/13 and L55/47.

10. But note that under Art. 36 the provisions of Arts. 30–34 do not preclude prohibitions or restrictions on trade justified on grounds of public morality, public policy, public security, the protection of health, the protection of national treasures, or the protection of commercial and industrial property. Of these, only the protection of health would seem relevant to trade in fisheries products.

11. The European Court has defined quantitative restrictions as 'measures which amount to a total or partial restraint of . . . imports, exports, or goods in transit' (Case 2/73, *Geddo v. Ente Nazionale Risi* [1973] E.C.R. 865 at 879; [1974] 1 C.M.L.R. 13 at 42), and measure having equivalent effect as 'all trading rules enacted by Member States which are capable of hindering, directly or indirectly, actually or potentially, intra-Community trade' (Case 8/74, *Procureur du Roi v. Dassonville* [1974] E.C.R. 837 at 852; [1974] 2 C.M.L.R. 436 at 453–4).

12. *Op. cit.* in n. 1.

13. *Ibid.,* pp. 1313 and 472 respectively.

14. E.g. Case 190/73, *Officier van Justitie v. Van Haaster* [1974] E.C.R. 1123; [1974] 2 C.M.L.R. 521.

15. Case 32/79, [1980] E.C.R. 2403; [1981] 1 C.M.L.R. 219.

16. The Community institutions have the competence to adopt legislation which restricts trade between Member States provided that this is in the Community interest. See Oliver, *op. cit.* in n. 5, pp. 36–42.

17. Unless possibly it fell within the doctrine of the *Cassis de Dijon* case-Case 120/78, *Rewe v. Bundesmonopolverwaltung für Branntwein* [1979] E.C.R. 649; [1979] 3 C.M.L.R. 494. In this case the Court accepted that national legislation which hindered trade would not be contrary to Art. 30 if such legislation was required to safeguard the public interest.

18. Case 132/80, [1981] E.C.R. 995; [1982] 1 C.M.L.R. 273.
19. Case 247/84, Judgment of December 10, 1985 (not yet reported).
20. See the Commission's Answer to W.Q. 78/73, O.J. 1973 C68/13.
21. See the Commission's Supplementary Answer to W.Q. 1143/80, O.J. 1982 C245/1.
22. See, for example, the extraordinary list of obstacles put in the way of Danish imports by the Italian authorities catalogued by Mr. Kirk in W.Q. 1600/81. In its Answer, the Commission was unable to say at the time whether these Italian measures were contrary to Community law: see O.J. 1982 C111/9.
23. Single European Act, Arts. 13–19, *Bull. E.C.* Suppl. 2/86, and COM(83)80.
24. Note that imports from Portuguese and Spanish joint ventures with third States are regarded as coming from outside the Community, though the 1985 Act of Accession, Arts. 168 and 355, establishes a seven-year period for such imports to be adapted to the general trading regime with third States.
25. It follows from the discussion in section 1 of Chapter 5 that the competence to negotiate commercial agreements (including those concerned with tariffs and trade in fisheries products) is one which vests exclusively in the Community. Although the discussion in Chapter 5 was solely in the context of the Community's implied treaty-making powers, the same principle of Community exclusivity applies also in the case of express treaty-making powers: see Opinion 1/75, *Re the OECD Understanding on a Local Cost Standard* [1975] E.C.R. 1355; [1976] 1 C.M.L.R. 85.
26. See Joined Cases 21–24/72, *International Fruit Co. N.V. v. Produktschap voor Groenten en Fruit (No. 3)* [1972] E.C.R. 1219; [1975] 2 C.M.L.R. 1. For a survey of the relevant provisions of GATT, see OECD, *Problems of Trade in Fishery Products,* Paris, 1985, pp. 89–94, 133–135 and 316–324.
27. O.J. S. Edn. 1968 (I) p. 275. Portugal and Spain have been given a seven-year period in which to adapt their tariffs to the CCT – 1985 Act of Accession, Arts. 173(4) and 360(4).
28. As amended by Reg. 3655/84, O.J. 1984 L340/1.
29. Iberian Act of Accession, Protocol 4 and Reg. 568/86, O.J. 1986 L55/103.
30. For a table showing the preferential tariff treatment applied by the Community to third countries, see O.J. 1984 C22/1.
31. Dec. 86/283, O.J. 1986 L175/1, Art. 70, and Reg. 486/85, O.J. 1985 L61/4, Art. 7. All customs duties on fishery products from Annex IV territories are abolished. For the list of Annex IV territories, see Chapter 3, section 2. In the case of Greenland see also the Protocol on Special Arrangements for Greenland and Reg. 225/85, O.J. 1985 L29/7 and 18.
32. Third Lomé Convention, O.J. 1986 L86/1, Art. 130 and Annex XIII, and Reg. 486/85, *op. cit.* in n. 31, Art. 7. All customs duties on fishery products from the ACP States are abolished.
33. Governed by a series of annual regs. Duties are completely abolished for the 38 or so least developed developing countries, and reduced for other developing countries. Many of the developing countries covered by this scheme will, in fact, enjoy equal or greater benefit from some of the other measures listed here, notably the Lomé Convention.
34. Regs. 2051/74 and 3184/74, O.J. 1974 L212/33 and L344/1. Duties on most fishery products have been reduced by 80 per cent.
35. 1985 Act of Accession, Protocol 2, Art. 3. Customs duties are to be abolished by 1993 (1996 in the case of sardines).
36. EEC-Iceland Free Trade Agreement 1972, Protocol No. 6, O.J. S. Edn. 1972 (December 31) p. 4, as amended by Reg. 1976/76, O.J. 1976 L217/1. Duties have been abolished for some fishery products and reduced for others.
37. Exchange of Letters attached to the EEC-Norway Free Trade Agreement 1973, O.J. 1973 L171/2, and Reg. 102/76, O.J. 1976 L20/23. Duties have been substantially reduced for most fishery products.

38. EEC-Algeria Co-Operation Agreement 1976, O.J. 1978 L263/2, Arts. 15 and 18. Duties on most fishery products have been abolished.
39. EEC-Morocco Co-Operation Agreement 1976, O.J. 1978 L264/2, Arts. 15 and 19. Duties on most fishery products have been abolished.
40. EEC-Tunisia Co-Operation Agreement 1976, O.J. 1978 L265/2, Arts. 15 and 18. Duties on most fishery products have been abolished.
41. EEC-Egypt Co-Operation Agreement 1977, O.J. 1978 L266/2, Art. 17. Duties on shrimps and prawns have been reduced by 50 per cent.
42. Reg. 1180/77, O.J. 1977 L142/10, Arts. 1, 3 and 11; Reg. 3590/82, O.J. 1982 L375/1; and Reg. 3721/84, O.J. 1984 L343/6. Duties on most fishery products are reduced, and some completely abolished.
43. A series of annual regs. abolish customs duties on imports of fish meal and flour from Malta.
44. However, this system is dependent on the adoption of the necessary technical rules which has not in fact yet been done. Pending such adoption, the Community applies a tariff quota regime.
45. Reg. 102/76, *op. cit.* in n. 37, Annex.
46. Cf. also the EEC-Canada Fisheries Agreement (discussed in Chapter 5) under which the access of EEC fishing vessels to Canadian waters is contingent upon tariff quotas for Canadian fishery exports to the EEC.
47. *Op. cit.* in n. 36.
48. Decs. 73/62 and 73/70, O.J. 1973 L98/30 and L181/21; and Reg. 1440/76, O.J. 1976 L161/1.
49. As there has in fact been since the beginning of 1977. See Chapter 5.
50. *Op. cit.* in n. 37.
51. See O.J. 1975 C99/5 and M. Leigh, *European Integration and the Common Fisheries Policy,* Beckenham, 1983, p. 68.
52. Protocol on Special Arrangements for Greenland, *op. cit.* in n. 31.
53. The products listed in Annex I are fresh or chilled herring, sardines, dogfish, redfish, cod, saithe, haddock, whiting, ling, mackerel, anchovies, plaice, hake, megrim, Ray's bream and monkfish; frozen herring; and shrimps, crabs and Norway lobsters.
54. The products listed in Annex II are frozen sardines, sea bream, squid, cuttle-fish and octopus.
55. The products listed in Annex III are all species of tuna.
56. The products listed in Annex IVB are frozen or salted redfish, cod, saithe, haddock and whiting; and frozen ling, mackerel, plaice, hake, dogfish, herring, megrim, Ray's bream, monkfish, crabs and Norway lobsters.
57. The products listed in Annex V are frozen or salted cod, mackerel and hake (of species not covered by Annex IVB); and frozen or salted pollack, flounder and shrimps. These products are not produced in the Community but are in direct competition with Community products.
58. Portugal and Spain have been given a seven-year period in which to adjust to Community reference prices: see 1985 Act of Accession, Arts. 176 and 363.
59. Detailed rules for the calculation of free-at-frontier prices are laid down in Reg. 3191/82, O.J. 1982 L338/13, as amended by Reg. 3474/85, O.J. 1985 L333/16.
60. Reg. 1142/83, O.J. 1983 L124/19.
61. Reg. 1327/86, O.J. 1986 L117/17.
62. See the statement by the United Kingdom Minister of Agriculture, Fisheries and Food in H.C. Deb., June 25, 1981, col. 371. In a debate in the European Parliament in February 1981 one Member, Mr. Provan, stated that the British Government had reported imports of fish coming into the United Kingdom at below reference prices on 22 occasions: on some occasions these imports had been at 45 per cent below the reference price. See Debates of the European Parliament, February 12, 1981, O.J. Annex No. 1–266, p. 245.
63. S. Cunningham and J.A. Young, 'The EEC Common Fisheries Policy: Retrospect and Prospect' *National Westminster Bank Quarterly Review,* May 1983, p. 2 at 8.

64. Detailed rules for calculating this reference price are laid down in Reg. 1985/74, O.J. 1974 L207/30, as amended by Regs. 1701/78 and 2046/85, O.J. 1978 L195/14 and 1985 L193/15.

65. As to how this is calculated, see Reg. 1985/74, *op. cit.* in n. 64.

66. Although one should note that in recent years Community lobster fishermen have complained that they are being drastically undercut by massively-subsidised imported lobsters from Canada. Under the 1981 Marketing Regulation their plight may to some extent be mitigated if a deficiency payment scheme is introduced (see the previous Chapter).

67. See Dir. 69/73, O.J. S. Edn. 1969 (I), p. 75. In the case of fishery products, the quantity of raw materials which, for the purpose of inward processing arrangements, is not subject to customs duties or equivalent charges must 'correspond to the conditions under which the processing operation in question is actually to be effected' (Art. 23(2) of the Marketing Reg.).

68. For details of these products, see Chapter 8, n. 6.

69. Set out in Art. 39 of the EEC Treaty. See Chapter 2, section 1.

70. Regs. 460/75, as amended, 816/76 and 986/76, O.J. 1975 L51/15 and 1976 L94/7 and L113/24.

71. Regs. 2619/77 and 897/78, O.J. 1977 L304/37 and 1978 L117/61.

72. Reg. 337/81, O.J. 1981 L37/17. Before the Reg. expired, an arrangement was reached with Thailand, the main exporter of clams to the Community, the purpose of which was to set export conditions which would prevent a recurrence of the market disturbances in 1980 and early 1981 which had originally led the Community to take action. See *Bull E.C.* 1981 No. 6, p. 46.

73. Reg. 2779/84, O.J. 1984 L261/9.

74. Commission's Answer to W.Q. 2850/85, O.J. 1986 C182/58.

75. Reg. 3150/85, O.J. 1985 L299/9.

76. Regs. 293/86 and 1156/86, O.J. 1986 L35/7 and L105/25.

77. O.J. Annex No. 1–256, pp. 31–32 and 271–276.

78. Resolution of May 23, O.J. 1980 C147/117. The Commission and the Council did not respond to this request.

79. The Commission proposed such arrangements for canned sardines in 1976 (O.J. 1976 C200/1), but they were not adopted by the Council. The arrangements proposed would have taken the form of minimum import prices and import licences. The Commission withdrew its proposal in 1980: see COM (80) 724, p. 7.

80. The 1985 Act of Accession authorises Portugal and Spain to maintain their quantitative restrictions on imports of other kinds of fishery products from third States until 1993 – Arts. 176 and 363.

81. Reg. 2176/84, O.J. 1984 L201/1.

82. Reg. 288/82, O.J. 1982 L35/1, as corrected in L260/16 and L351/35.

83. Reg. 2641/84, O.J. 1984 L252/1.

84. Detailed rules for the implementation of this Art. are laid down in Regs. 192/75, 110/76, 686/78 and 148/83, O.J. 1975 L25/1, 1976 L20/48, 1978 L93/12 and 1983 L18/9.

85. Note that export refunds do not apply to sales of fish to foreign fish factory ships in Community waters (much mackerel in the United Kingdom is sold this way). See the Commission's Answer to W.Q. 808/81, O.J. 1981 C267/60.

86. Reg. 3090/83, O.J. 1983 L301/65.

87. See the Commission's Answer to W.Q. 671/83, O.J. 1983 C315/6.

88. Dec. 85/464, O.J. 1985 L267/46.

89. Case 326/85, *Netherlands v. Commission,* O.J. 1985 C357/2. A similar point is at issue in Case 332/85, *Federal Republic of Germany v. Commission,* O.J. 1985 C357/3. The Commission has also withheld export refunds for 1982 claimed by the Netherlands and Ireland – and the Commission's decisions have again been challenged before the European Court: see Cases 237/86 and 239/86, O.J. 1986 C258/7 and C260/16.

90. Resolution of February 10, 1983 on Community Fisheries Policy in the Mediterranean, O.J. 1983 C68/74.

CHAPTER 9

Some concluding observations – the Community as a regulatory body

At the beginning of this book it was pointed out that if a fishery is unregulated, the probable consequence is both over-exploitation of the stock and a level of fishing effort that is well above the economic optimum. To prevent such biological and economic waste, it is therefore desirable to regulate a fishery. Put very simply, this involves essentially that measures (such as TACs and gear restrictions) should be taken to ensure that the amount and size of fish being caught is not such as to endanger the long-term well-being of the stocks, and that the size of the fishing fleet is no greater than that capable of taking the amount of fish available. In the case of fisheries falling within the fishing limits of EEC Member States, the EEC (rather than the individual Member States) is primarily responsible for such regulation. How far is the EEC succeeding in achieving the two broad goals of regulation just described (which are also goals that the Community has set itself)?

As regards the first of these goals, maintaining the long-term well-being of fish stocks, it was suggested in Chapters 4 and 5 that in the case both of stocks exclusive to EEC waters and stocks shared with third States such as Norway, the Community has since 1983 had a relatively successful system of management. While TACs have been set, for socio-economic reasons, at levels higher than those recommended by fishery scientists, it seems that on the whole (though it may be a little early to reach a definite conclusion) the levels are not so high as to endanger the long-term well-being of fish stocks: rather the consequence is that it will take longer to build up over-exploited stocks to a level around MSY than it would have done had the advice of fishery scientists been strictly followed. The major problem in this area of regulation is one of enforcement. Greater compliance with Community management measures, particularly with technical conservation measures, is required.

In relation to the second major goal of regulation, adjusting capacity to catch potential, the picture is less clear. Undoubtedly the capacity of the Community fleet has been reduced since the general introduction of 200-mile fishing limits in the North Atlantic at the beginning of 1977, although this is due more to the operation of market forces than any positive (and cushioning) action taken by the Community, but no one seems really to know whether the capacity of the Community fleet is now at roughly the optimum level or whether capacity needs further to be reduced. Nor has the Community made any real effort yet to get to grips with the problem of the natural tendency for capacity, once it has been reduced to around the optimum level, to start to increase again. If this is not done, and capacity does begin significantly to increase, this will not only lead to a less economically healthy fishing industry, but risks jeopardising the success the Community has achieved with managing stocks, because a larger fleet is less likely to comply with catch limits and gear regulations.

Apart from managing fish stocks and seeking to adjust capacity to catch potential, the Community has also taken other steps to regulate the fishing industry and promote its economic well-being. Thus, Community financial aid is available for modernising vessels, improving marketing and, to a limited extent, for promoting increased consumption of fish (see Chapter 6). These measures, together with managing stocks, adjusting capacity and promoting producers' organisations for fishermen, are more likely and should be used (it was suggested at the end of Chapter 7) to improve the standard of living of fishermen, rather than the arrangements for price support which the Community has adopted. Such arrangements appear in practice to have had a marginal impact on the price of fish (and, fortunately for the Community taxpayer, on the Community budget): on the other hand, one positive benefit of these arrangements is that they are a means for ensuring compliance with quotas. In addition to the various measures mentioned above, the Community also promotes the economic well-being of fishermen through its rules on trading with third States, which protect Community fishermen to some extent from competition from imports. Fortunately, however, these rules do not seem to be so restrictive as to hinder the interests of processors and consumers. On the other hand, amidst these relative successes, it must be pointed out that the Community's social policy programme for the fishing industry is woefully under-developed.

These few broad-brush conclusions about the effectiveness so far of the Community's regulation of marine fisheries are all that will be offered here, since more detailed conclusions have already been presented at the end of the preceding five chapters. This account of EEC fisheries law will end by making a few rather more general observations about the Community's regulation of marine fisheries as a regulatory system. Although fisheries as the object of regulation are unique compared with other objects of governmental regulation because of their common property nature, the means and techniques of fisheries regulation are not unique, and therefore the comments that follow may be not without some relevance and interest for other areas (such as agriculture and trade) where the Community has a regulatory role.

Various techniques may be used to regulate fisheries (or any other economic activity for that matter). While, to the lawyer at least, the most obvious technique may be legal rules, prescribing or prohibiting certain types of conduct (referred to below as direct regulation), there is also a number of other techniques, such as grants, taxes and persuasion through information (referred to as indirect regulation). In seeking to regulate marine fisheries and the fishing industry, the Community uses both direct and indirect regulation. In the case of the fishing operation itself, regulation is direct, through Community rules relating to TACs and quotas, technical conservation measures and access. In the case of structural questions, on the other hand, Community regulation is largely indirect, through financial assistance and control on national subsidies. With marketing and trade, regulation is both direct and indirect. In relation to marketing, the Community lays down detailed rules concerning marketing standards, but operates much less directly in relation to prices, leaving it up to individual fishermen whether to form producers' organisations, and if they do, whether to operate the Community's pricing arrangements, which in any case only indirectly influence the price of fish. With trade the Community only intervenes directly on the infrequent occasions when it requires imports to observe reference prices or prohibits imports. Its main regulatory input is to influence trading activities indirectly through the adoption, suspension or abolition of customs duties and the use of reference and free-at-frontier prices, and through paying export refunds.

The experience of the Community with fisheries regulation shows that for some activities at least indirect regulation (i.e. using financial tools, rather than legal rules, to influence conduct in a desired direction) may be at least as effective as direct regulation. This suggests therefore that when the Community is faced with any new question requiring regulation, it should consider very carefully whether direct or indirect regulation, or some combination, is the most appropriate form of regulation, rather than simply assuming, as most lawyers probably would (and remember that a high proportion of Commission officials, even outside the Legal Service, have a legal training), that direct regulation should always be used in preference to indirect regulation. Of course, even where regulation is indirect, the various forms of such regulation (grants, taxes, etc.) are often laid down in legislation, so that the result is that with a system that uses both direct and indirect forms of regulation (as the Community's regulatory system for fisheries does), there is, as we have seen in this book, a mass of rules and regulations.

A major matter for any fisheries manager – or for any regulatory body – is communication with the addressees of its regulations. Unless there is proper, and two-way, communication between a regulatory body and those whom it is seeking to regulate, its regulations are likely at best to be only partially successful. In the context of Community fisheries regulation the question of communication is particularly important in the case of resource management and structural measures, where the regulations are numerous and frequent and the addressees of such regulations (individual fishermen) number tens of thousands; and rather less of a problem, although still important, in the case of marketing and trade, where there are fewer addressees of the regulations (mainly producers' organisations and the national authorities of the Member States). Communication of fisheries regulations involves, at least, three inter-related issues: knowledge, comprehensibility and acceptability.

As far as knowledge is concerned, it is obvious that Community fisheries regulations have no chance of being complied with if fishermen do not know about them. Community fisheries regulations, like all Community legislation, are published in the *Official Journal of the European Communities*. Presumably no Community fisherman reads the *Official Journal* regularly (unless seeking a cure for insomnia). Even for the lawyer and bureaucrat the *Official Journal* is not the easiest of sources to use because of its bulk (the Legislation series appears practically daily), the fact that individual issues are not arranged according to subject matter, and the fact that its indices often appear late and are not always accurate (though it must be admitted in relation to this last question that there has been a significant improvement recently). If fishermen do not read the *Official Journal,* they are presumably informed of the exist-ence and content of EEC regulations by their national Ministry of Fisheries (through local officials, probably) and by the specialist press. It would be interesting to know how efficient and speedy these channels of communication are: as far as the writer is aware, no research has been done on this matter.[1]

The fact that fishermen have become aware of the existence of Community regulations is not the end of the matter, of course. They still have to read the regulations (or a ministerial or press précis). The likelihood of their reading the regulations depends, in part, on the accessibility of the language in which the regulations are drafted (a point considered below), and also in part on the bulk and number of the regulations. The more regulations there are, the less likely it is that fishermen will read them (or all of them). Most fishermen in any case will by temperament and training not want to spend much time reading regulations. As far as bulk is concerned, the Community's fisheries regu-lations, though considerable in number, are probably not excessively bulky (except perhaps for the regulations dealing with marketing and arrangements for Spain and Portugal), compared with such major Western fishing States as Norway, Canada and the USA.[2] It must be remembered, however, that a Community fisherman fishing in Community waters is governed not only by Community regulations but also by rules promulgated by national authorities. Such rules may come from a variety of bodies: in the United Kingdom, for instance, fisheries regulations are contained in Acts of Parliament, Statutory

Instruments made by ministers, bye-laws made by local sea Fisheries Committees for inshore waters, and rules about obtaining grants made by the Sea Fish Industry Authority. Such a variety of bodies makes for further difficulties for fishermen seeking simply to discover the existence of potentially relevant regulations. When these national regulations are added to Community rules, the Community fishermen is undoubtedly faced with quite a bulky collection.

The matter is made worse when the rules are subject to frequent revision or amendment. In the case of Community rules, this was particularly the case for fishery management measures before 1983 when there was a mass of short-term measures subject to frequent revision or renewal. Even after 1983 there are still areas where the regulations are frequently amended. Thus, for example, the annual TAC and quota regulations are usually amended several times a year, while to have an up-to-date text of the Technical Conservation Measures Regulation (Regulation 171/83) it is necessary to look at not only the original Regulation but also a further six amending Regulations and the Iberian Act of Accession. There is obviously scope for improvement here. It was suggested at the end of Chapter 4 that minor adjustments to TACs during the year were probably unnecessary and that for some stocks TACs could be set at less frequent intervals than a year. In the case of amendments to the Technical Conservation Measures Regulation, the Enforcement Regulation and other management Regulations, there is a good case for saying that when the Regulation is amended, a revised version of the Regulation incorporating the amendments should be published at the same time. In general, the Commission and Council would do well to legislate only when regulations really are necessary. This is a point which the Commission, at least, appears to recognise, because in reply to a question in the European Parliament in 1983 it said that the criteria which motivate it to propose fisheries legislation are the seriousness of the problem which is intended to be solved, the practicability of any solution, and its likely effectiveness, taking into consideration the difficulties and costs of enforcement.[3]

Turning from the question of knowledge of Community regulations to the question of their comprehensibility, it is obvious that the easier the regulations are to understand, the greater the chances of their being observed by fishermen. Clear drafting is also important for those national authorities that have to implement and enforce Community rules. From the vast mass of Community legislation on fisheries it is difficult to make any meaningful generalisations about the quality of drafting. Nevertheless it may be worth making one or two impressionistic observations. Although the language of Community legislation is not exciting and in fact is frequently pretty turgid (as Advocate General Mancini wittily remarks in a recent case, he doubts whether 'Marguerite Yourcenar or Graham Greene would be prepared to read each morning a piece or two of Community legislation 'pour prendre le ton', as Stendhal used to read Articles of the Code Civil'[4]), from the point of view of an English lawyer Community legislation at least avoids the lengthy sentences and frequent subordinate clauses with which his national legislation abounds and which renders that legislation frequently difficult to understand. Unlike English legislation, Community legislation does not usually attempt to provide for every eventuality and therefore is less detailed and cluttered than its English counterpart. Against these virtues must be set some defects. In places Community fisheries legislation is at times vague and imprecise, e.g. the formula for allocating quotas (see p. 115) and the provisions identifying the beneficiaries of the 12-mile zone (see p. 135). Such vagueness, whilst not excusable, can often be explained as the result of political compromise and a need to express what may not be total agreement on a sensitive issue in less than completely clear-cut terms. On other occasions, where the political need for equivocation does not lie behind the language, Community legislation seems wilfully and unnecessarily obscure (e.g. the criterion for Community aid for modernising fishing vessels that projects be 'co-ordinated in their economic and technical aspects', see p. 213) or perverse. A good example of the latter is Article 166 of the Iberian Act of Accession, which provides that the special arrangements laid down by the Act regarding the access of Spanish fishermen to Community waters are to remain in force 'until the date of expiry of the period laid down in Article 8(3) of Regulation (EEC) No. 170/83.' Turning to Article 8(3) one finds that the period referred to there is the 10 years 'following December 31, 1992'. Surely it would have been possible for Article 166 simply to have said that the arrangements last until December 31, 2002, rather than engaging in a cumbersome piece of cross-referencing? These examples show that there is plenty of scope for the Community legislator – Commission, Council and Parliament – to improve the drafting of Community legislation for the future. The Community legislator should also realise, and give more thought to the fact, that apart from the question of the language of individual provisions of Community fisheries law, such provisions when taken together often amount to a collection of rules of considerable complexity, as Table 2 (in Chapter 4) shows.

Even if Community regulations are known to Community fishermen and are framed in easily understandable language, that will not in itself make the regulations more acceptable to Community fishermen. To increase the chances of the regulations being more acceptable, and thus the chances of their being more strictly observed, it is necessary for there to be consultation between the Community and fishermen when regulations are being drawn up. A frequently expressed opinion is that there needs to be much more consultation than there is at present between the Community (particularly the Commission) and fishermen over proposed Community regulations;[5] and indeed lack of consultation and communication between fishery managers and fishermen is seen as a general problem, and not confined to the Community.[6] More consultation would not only be likely to increase the chances of Community regulations being more acceptable to fishermen, and therefore better observed, it might well also improve their drafting.

However, while increased consultation is desirable, the Community must realise that as a group fishermen are less easy to consult with than many other occupations and groups because of fishermen's geographical and cultural isolation, their inarticulateness, their generally poor organisation, and the fact that fishermen (even from a single Member State) do not share a common view on every issue.[7] From the point of view of fishermen the structure of the Community may cause confusion about where they should seek consultation and concentrate their lobbying activities. Should it be the Commission, European Parliament, Economic and Social Committee or the national fisheries minister who meets in Council? With limited financial resources this may be a real problem for fishermen's organisations. Asked to advise, one would suggest that effort be concentrated on the first and last of the bodies mentioned.

Turning from the question of the communication of regulations to the regulatory body itself, the Community as a fisheries regulatory body is diffuse and multipartite. While the Commission and the Council are the main Community organs involved in fisheries regulation, many other Community bodies also play a greater or a lesser role. These include the various committees which advise the Commission, the European Parliament and its Fisheries Working Group, the Economic and Social Committee and its Section for Agriculture, the working parties of the Committee of Permanent Representatives, and the two Management Committees (see further Chapter 2). It must also be remembered that various national ministries and other public bodies in the Member States are involved in the implementation and enforcement of the regulations. Apart from making it difficult for fishermen to know how best to communicate with the Community as a fisheries regulator (as pointed out above), this diffusive structure makes the Community a very bureaucratic body and probably reduces its efficiency. Since agreement on a Community management system at the beginning of 1983, the most obvious signs of inefficiency have been slowness in adopting various measures relating to conservation and enforcement (see Chapter 4) and in implementing the recommendations of international fishery commissions (Chapter 5), and complaints over the processing of applications for Community structural aid (Chapter 6). In addition, bearing in mind the wide range of functions which the Commission is required to perform under the various areas of the Common Fisheries Policy and the vast amount of information which the Commission receives and is required to process, the outsider is bound to wonder if the Commission has sufficient staff for the job. The European Parliament, at least, is of the view that the

Commission is under-staffed.[8] Could lack of staff be the reason for the inefficiencies of the Commission just alluded to and the explanation for why it has failed to produce the annual reports required under the Management and Structural Regulations (see p. 154 and 205 above)?

Since 1983 the Community has achieved much, by establishing a basic regulatory regime for the fishing industry which has so far shown itself capable of operating in practice relatively smoothly and effectively. Thus a stable framework, which should last at least until 2002, has been secured, and this should allow the Community's fishing industry to plan for the future with confidence and certainty, something which was impossible during the decade of uncertainty and change before 1983. While the basic framework has been established, there is still a need to improve many of the details of the regime (as indicated in earlier Chapters) and, as suggested in this Chapter, a need to try to improve the efficiency of the regulatory body (the Community) and the way in which it communicates with the fishing industry.

NOTES

1. It would seem that at least on some occasions these channels are less effective than they might be. For a good example, see the confusion over the closure of the North Sea sprat fishery in October 1983, reported by D.I.A. Steel in 'Fisheries Policy and the EEC: The Democratic Influence' (1984) 8 *Marine Policy* 350 at 352. And see also the Commission's rather complacent response in its Answer to W.Q. 1438/83, O.J. 1984 C122/1.
2. In Norway about 200 fisheries regulations are issued each year, and the regulations are frequently referred to as 'a jungle'.
3. Commission's Answer to W.Q. 161/83, O.J. 1983 C257/7.
4. Case 100/84, *Commission v. United Kingdom* [1985] 2 C.M.L.R. 199 at 204.
5. See, e.g., the European Parliament's Resolution of May 16, 1986, O.J. 1986 C148/130; E.P. Doc. A2–40/86, p. 17; D.I.A. Steel, 'Restricting Entry in the EEC: Present Possibilities and Future Plans' in G. Ulfstein, P. Andersen and R. Churchill (eds.), *Proceedings of the European Workshop on the Regulation of Fisheries* (forthcoming).
6. See, e.g., FAO, *Expert Consultation on the Regulation of Fishing Effort*, FAO Fisheries Report No. 289 (1983), p. 21 and D.B. Thomson, 'Fishermen and Fisheries Management' in *ibid.*, Suppl. 2 (1985), p. 21.
7. For fuller discussion of these questions, see Thomson, *op. cit.*, pp. 33–35.
8. Resolution of May 16, 1986, *op. cit.* in n. 5.

Bibliography on the Common Fisheries Policy and EEC Fisheries Law

(Note: this Bibliography does not include official publications in serial form (e.g. the Commission's Communications to the Council), nor does it include case notes.)

R. Allen, 'Fishing for a Common Policy' (1980) XIX J.C.M.S. 123–139.

Anon., 'De Libertate Maris Communitatis' Editorial Comments in (1983) 20 C.M.L. Rev. 7–11.

Anon. (ed.), *Norge i Europa – Fisket, Naturgrunnlaget og salget,* Oslo, 1971.

Anon. (ed.), *Norge i Europa – Fisket og grensene,* Oslo, 1971.

G. Apolllis, 'La réglementation des activités halieutiques dans l'acte d'adhésion de l'Espagne et du Portugal à la CEE' [1985] A.F.D.I. 837–867.

G. Apollis, 'Le régime communautaire d'accès aux lieux de pêche et aux stocks halieutiques' [1983] A.F.D.I. 646–673.

T. Ballarino, 'Il diritto di pesca e la Comunità Economica Europea' (1986) 27 *Studi Marittimi* 45.

D. Barry, 'The Canada-European Community Long-Term Fisheries Agreement: Internal Politics and Fisheries Diplomacy' (1985) 9 *Journal of European Integration* 5–28.

A. Beghé Loreti, 'I diritti della Spagna in tema di pesca anteriormento alla conclusione dell'accordo CEE/Spagna' [1983] *Diritto Comunitario e degli Scambi Internazionali* 444–464.

J-P. Beurier, 'La conservation des stocks halieutiques et la CEE' (1979) 22 *German Yearbook of International Law* 221–238.

P. Birnie, 'The History of the EEC Common Fisheries Policy' in Fifth Report from the Expenditure Committee, *The Fishing Industry,* H.C. Paper (1977–78) 356, Vol. I, pp. 92–118.

D. Boos, 'La politique commune de la pêche, quelques aspects juridiques' (1983) 269 R.M.C. 404–416.

M. Brouir, 'Le réglement du Conseil de la CEE de 1970 sur les pêcheries' (1973) 9 C.D.E. 20–37.

E.D. Brown, 'British Fisheries and the Common Market' (1972) 25 *Current Legal Problems* 37–73.

J.F. Buhl, 'The European Economic Community and the Law of the Sea' (1982) 11 O.D.I.L. 181–200.

J.A. Butlin, 'Do We Really have a Common Fisheries Policy?' *Fisheries Economics Newsletter,* No. 15, May 1983, pp. II–X.

M. Bywater, 'La mer européenne: patrimonie communautaire ou resources cotières' (1976) 201 R.M.C. 487–92.

R.R. Churchill, 'Revision of the EEC's Common Fisheries Policy' (1980) 5 E.L.R. 3–37 and 95–111.

R.R. Churchill, 'The EEC's Common Fisheries Policy' (1979) 2 *Marine Policy Reports* 1–5.

R.R. Churchill, 'The EEC's Contribution to 'State' Practice in the Field of Fisheries' in E.D. Brown and R.R. Churchill (eds.), *The UN Convention on the Law of the Sea: Impact and Implementation* (forthcoming).

R.R. Churchill, 'The EEC Fisheries Policy – Towards a Revision' (1977) 1 *Marine Policy* 26–36.

Commission of the European Communities, *The European Community's Fishery Policy,* Periodical 1/1985, Luxembourg, 1985.

S. Cunningham, 'EEC Fisheries Management – A Critique of Common Fisheries Policy Objectives' (1980) 4 *Marine Policy* 229–235.

S. Cunningham, M.R. Dunn and D. Whitmarsh, *Fisheries Economics: An Introduction,* London, 1985, pp. 211–220.

S. Cunningham and J.A. Young, 'The EEC Fisheries Policy: Retrospect and Prospect', *National Westminster Bank Quarterly Review,* May 1983, pp. 2–14.

P. Daillier, 'La CEE et le respect des droits acquis' [1979] *Annuaire de Droit Maritime* 211–222.

P. Daillier, 'Le régime de la pêche maritime des ressortissants espagnols sous jurissdiction des Etats Membres de la CEE' (1982) 256 R.M.C. 187–193.

P. Daillier, 'Les Communautés Européennes et le Droit de la Mer' (1979) 79 R.G.D.I.P. 417–473.

A. Del Vecchio, 'In tema di incidenza della normativa comunitaria sui trattati in materia di pesca fra Stati membri della CEE e Stati terzi' in B. Conforti (ed.), *La Zona Economica Esclusiva,* Milan, 1983, pp. 187–200.

A. Del Vecchio, 'Sull' incidenza della normativa comunitaria sui trattati in materia di pesca fra Stati membri della CEE e Stati terzi' (1982) 65 *Rivista di Diritto Internazionale* 571–582.

P.J. Derham, 'The Problems of Quota Management in the European Community Concept' in FAO, *Report of the Expert Consultation on the Regulation of Fishing Effort,* FAO Fisheries Report No. 289 (1985), Supplement 3, pp. 241–50.

D.J. Driscoll and N. McKellar, 'The Changing Régime of North Sea Fisheries' in C.M. Mason (ed.), *The Effective Management of Resources: The International Politics of the North Sea,* London, 1979, pp. 125–167.

B. Dynna, 'Fiskerisektoren i EF-forhandlingene' in V. Angell and J.J. Holst (eds.), *EF-Norges vei?* Oslo, 1972, pp. 31–49.

A.M. El-Agraa, 'The Common Fisheries Policy' in A.M. El-Agraa (ed.) *The Economics of the European Community,* 2nd ed., Deddington, 1985, pp. 205–208.

A.C. Evans, 'Fishery Conservation and EEC Law' [1982] *Scots Law Times* 109–111

J. Farnell and J. Elles, *In Search of a Common Fisheries Policy,* Aldershot, 1984.

C.A. Fleischer, 'L'accès aux lieux de pêche et le traité de Rome' (1971) 141 R.M.C. 148–156.

D. Freestone and A. Fleisch, 'The Common Fisheries Policy' in J. Lodge (ed.), *Institutions and Policies of the European Community,* London, 1983, pp. 77–84.

H. Frost, 'Fisheries Management and Uncertainty within the EEC' (1984) 1 *Marine Resource Economics* 97–103.

R. Garron, *Le Marché Commun de la Pêche Maritime,* Paris, 1971.

P. Gueben and M. Keller-Noellet, 'Aspects juridiques de la Politique de la Communauté Economique Européenne en matière de pêche' (1971) 144 R.M.C. 246–258.

G. Guillaume, 'Le droit de la pêche au sein de la Communauté Economique Européenne' (1982) 4 *Derecho Pesquero* 37–47.

M. Hardy, 'External Aspects of the Fisheries Policy of the European Community' in D.M. Johnston (ed.), *Regionalisation of the Law of the Sea,* Cambridge, Mass., 1978, pp. 73–81.

M. Hardy, 'Regional Approaches to Law of the Sea Problems: the European Community' (1975) 24 I.C.L.Q. 336–348.

M. Hardy, 'The EEC, the Law of the Sea and Future Fishing Arrangements in the Economic Zone' in M.M. Sibthorp and M. Unwin (eds.), *Oceanic Management: Conflicting Uses of the Celtic Sea and Other Western U.K. Waters,* London, 1977, pp. 152–163.

M. Hardy, 'The Fisheries Policy of the European Community' in E. Miles and J.K. Gamble (eds.), *Law of the Sea: Conference Outcomes and Problems of Implementation,* Cambridge, Mass., 1977, pp. 3–24.

D. Hedges, 'La Pêche dans la Communauté, Quelques Difficultés' (1977) 211 R.M.C. 449–451.

E. Hiester, 'The Legal Position of the European Community with regard to the Conservation of the Living Resources of the Sea' [1976] L.I.E.I. 55–79.

R. Hofmann, 'Zur Rechtsprechung des EuGH in Fischereifragen' (1981) 41 *Zeitschrift für Ausländisches Offentliches Recht und Völkerrecht* 808–824.

M.J. Holden, 'Management of Fishery Resources: The EEC Experience' in OECD, *Experiences in the Management of National Fishing Zones,* Paris, 1984, pp. 113–120.

M.J. Holden, 'The Procedures followed and the Problems met by the European Economic Community in implementing the Scientific Recommendations of the International Council for the Exploration of the Sea on Total Allowable Catches' in FAO, *Report of the Expert Consultation on the Regulation of Fishing Effort,* FAO Fisheries Report No. 289 (1985), Supplement 3, pp. 231–239.

House of Lords Select Committee on the European Communities, *EEC Fisheries Policy,* H.L. Paper (1979–80) 351.

House of Lords Select Committee on the European Communities, *The Common Fisheries Policy,* H.L. Paper (1984–85) 39.

M.W. Janis, 'The Development of European Regional Law of the Sea' (1973) 1 O.D.I.L. 275–289.

U. Jenisch, 'Zur Anwendung des Europäischen Rechts in den Meereszonen der EG-Staten' (1979) 22 *German Yearbook of International Law* 239–254.

A.W. Koers, 'Internal Aspects of the Common Fisheries Policy of the European Community' in D.M. Johnston (ed.), *Regionalisation of the Law of the Sea,* Cambridge, Mass., 1978, pp. 81–88.

A.W. Koers, 'Participation of the European Economic Community in a New Law of the Sea Convention' (1979) 73 A.J.I.L. 426–443.

A.W. Koers, 'The EEC's Common Fisheries Policy and UNCLOS III' in F. Laursen (ed.), *Towards a New Internationl Marine Order,* The Hague, 1982, pp. 111–118.

A.W. Koers, 'The European Economic Community and International Fisheries Organisations' [1984] L.I.E.I. 113–131.

A.W. Koers, 'The European Economic Community and the Sea' in L.M. Alexander (ed.), *The Law of the Sea: The United Nations and Ocean Management,* Kingston, Rhode Island, 1971, pp. 277–93.

A.W. Koers, 'The External Authority of the EEC in Regard to Marine Fisheries' (1977) 14 C.M.L. Rev. 269–301.

A.W. Koers, 'The Fisheries Policy' in Commission of the European Communities (ed.), *Thirty Years of Community Law,* Luxembourg, 1983, pp. 467–475.

A. Laing, 'The Common Fisheries Policy of the Six' (1971–2) 1 *Fish Industry Review* 8–18.

F. Laursen, 'EEC Fisheries Management: A Comment' in G. Ulfstein, P. Andersen and R. Churchill (eds.), *Proceedings of the European Workshop on the Regulation of Fisheries* (forthcoming).

M. Leigh, *European Integration and the Common Fisheries Policy,* Beckenham, 1983.

F. Leita and T. Scovazzi (eds.), *Il Regime della pesca nella Comunità Economica Europea,* Milan, 1979.

F. Leita, 'La CEE e la pesca nel Mediterraneo' in B. Conforti (ed.), *La Zona Economica Esclusiva,* Milan, 1983, pp. 81–96.

P. Lemaître, 'Une dernière difficulté pour les problèmes d'adhésion: les questions du droit de pêche' (1971) 146 R.M.C. 313–317.

K.G. Lundby, 'EF og Norge; Gjensidige Fiskeriforbindelser' in NFFR, *Fiskerinaeringen: Lov, Forvaltning, Organisasjon,* Trondheim, 1983, pp. 88–103.

G. Mackay, 'The UK Fishing Industry and EEC Policy' (1981) 132 *The Three Banks Review* 48–62.

M.E. Martins Ribeiro, 'Compétence communautaire et compétence nationale dans le secteur de la pêche' (1982) 18 C.D.E. 144–185.

J.L. Meseguer, 'Accord de pêche entre l'Espagne et la CEE' (1980) 241 R.M.C. 527–534, (1980) 242 R.M.C. 589–594.

F. Montag, 'Der Widerstand Grossbritanniens gegen die Schaffung einer Europäischen Fischereiordnung' [1982] *Europarecht* 63–74.

N. Nitsch, 'Les Accords de Pêche entre la Communauté et les Etats Tiers' (1980) 240 R.M.C. 452–473.

G. Olmi, 'Agriculture and Fisheries in the Treaty of Brussels of January 22, 1972' (1972) 9 C.M.L. Rev. 293–321.

E. Peyroux, 'Incidences du nouveau droit de la mer sur le régime des pêches des Neuf' (1977) 13 R.T.D.E. 53–78.

E. Peyroux, 'Les difficultés actuelles de la politique commune des pêches' (1979) 15 R.T.D.E. 269–289.

E. Peyroux, 'Problèmes juridiques de la pêche dans le Marché commun' (1973) 9 R.T.D.E. 46–64.

C. Philip, 'Note sous les arrêts du 8 décembre 1981 de la Cour de Justice des Communautés européennes dans les affaires 180/80, 266/80 et 181/80' [1981] A.F.D.I. 322–9.

O. Quintin, 'La politique commune de la pêche depuis l'adhésion' (1974) 172 R.M.C. 68–73.

P.D. Reynolds, 'The EEC and the Law of the Sea' (1977) 1 *Marine Policy* 118–131.

J. Sack, 'La nouvelle politique commune de la pêche' (1983) 19 C.D.E. 437–449.

T. Scovazzi, 'Competenze degli stati membri della CEE in materia di conservazione della risorse ittiche' (1979) 18 *Diritto Comunitario e degli Scambi Internazionali* 57–68.

T. Scovazzi, 'Comunità europea e convenzioni stipulate dagli Stati membri in materia di pesca' (1982) 21 *Diritto Comunitaria e degli Scambi Internazionali* 459.

T. Scovazzi, 'Le Régime de la Pêche dans la Communauté Economique Européenne' (1982) 5 *Derecho Pesquero* 69–80.

T. Scovazzi, 'Problemi della regolamentazione comunitaria della pesca marina' (1978) 61 *Rivista di Diritto Internazionale* 28–44.

A.L. Seager, 'Fishing in Troubled Waters: The Approach of the ECJ to Fishing Problems' [1980] *Scots Law Times* 105–110.

M. Shackleton, 'Fishing for a Policy? The Common Fisheries Policy of the Community' in H. Wallace, W. Wallace and C. Webb (eds.), *Policy Making in the European Community*, 2nd ed., Chichester, 1983, pp. 349–371.

M. Shackleton, 'The Politics of Fishing in Britain and France. Some lessons for Community Integration' (1985) 9 *Journal of European Integration* 29–54.

K.R. Simmonds, 'Fisheries Cases: the Ruling of the European Court and the External Legal Capacity of the EEC' in *International Law and Economic Order: Essays in Honour of F.A. Mann,* Munich, 1977, pp. 399–407.

R. Simonnet, 'Competences of the European Economic Community in the Field of Fisheries' in FAO, *Report of the Expert Consultation on the Conditions of Access to the Fish Resources of the Exclusive Economic Zones,* FAO Fisheries Report No. 293, Rome, 1983, pp. 183–187.

R. Simonnet, 'L'intégration européenne des pêcheries communautaires: la politique commune des pêches' (1967) 101 R.M.C. 241–249.

J. Soubeyrol, 'La pêche espagnole dans la zone communautaire' (1986) 1 *Espaces et Ressources Maritimes* 31–68.

J. Soubeyrol, 'Les droits de pêche des Espagnols dans les zones maritimes gérées par la CEE: état actuel et perspectives' (1978) 14 R.T.D.E. 193–203.

M. Spada, 'Tutela del mare e disciplina della pesca nella recente legislazione nazionale e comunitaria' [1984] *Rivista di Diritto Europeo* 159–171.

D.I.A. Steel, 'European Community Fisheries and the Wider Opportunity – the Challenge of Enlargement'. Paper given at Greenwich Forum XI, *Into the 1990s: Private Enterprise and Public Control in the Management of North Sea Resources,* Edinburgh, 1985.

D.I.A. Steel, 'Fisheries Policy in the EEC: The Democratic Influence' (1984) 8 *Marine Policy* 350–353.

D.I.A. Steel, 'Restricting Entry in the EEC: Present Possibilities and Future Plans' in G. Ulfstein, P. Andersen and R. Churchill (eds.), *Proceedings of the European Workshop on the Regulation of Fisheries* (forthcoming).

D.I.A. Steel, 'The EEC and the Progress of Fisheries Negotiations – January to May 1977' (1977) 4 *Maritime Policy and Management* 425–430.

C. Swords, 'External Competence of the European Economic Community in Relation to International Fisheries Agreements' [1979] L.I.E.I. 31–64.

T. Treves, 'La Communauté Européenne et la Zone Economique Exclusive' [1976] A.F.D.I. 653–677.

T. Treves, 'The EEC and the Law of the Sea: How Close to One Voice?' (1983) 12 O.D.I.L. 173–189.

C. Vallée, 'Sur quelques poursuites engagées contre des pêcheurs espagnols ayant pratiqué la pêche dans les eaux territoriales ou dans la zone économique de la France' (1979) 83 R.G.D.I.P. 220–245.

Y. Van der Mensbrugghe, 'The Common Market Fisheries Policy and the Law of the Sea' (1975) VI N.Y.I.L. 199–228.

D. Vignes, 'La Création dans la Communauté au cours de l'automne 1976 et de l'hiver 1977 d'une zone de pêche s'étendant jusqu'à 200 milles' in *Mélanges Fernand Dehousse,* Brussels, 1979, Vol. 2, pp. 323–332.

D. Vignes, 'La Réglementation de la Pêche dans le Marché Commun au regard du Droit Communautaire et du Droit International' [1970] A.F.D.I. 829–840.

D. Vignes, 'The EEC and the Law of the Sea' in R.R. Churchill et al. (eds.), *New Directions in the Law of the Sea,* Vol. III, London, 1973, pp. 335–347.

D. Vignes, 'The Problem of Access to the European Economic Community's Fishing Zone as the Cornerstone for the Adoption of a Common Fisheries Policy' in C.L. Rozakis and C.A. Stephanou (eds.), *The New Law of the Sea,* Amsterdam, 1983, pp. 83–96.

U. Villani, 'L'adozione della nuova politica comunitaria della pesca' (1984) 21 *Studi Marittimi* 127–136.

A. Volle and W. Wallace, 'How Common a Fisheries Policy?' (1977) 33 *The World Today* 62–72.

R. Wainwright, 'Common Fisheries Policy – the Development of a Common Régime for Fishing' (1981) 1 *Yearbook of European Law* 69–91.

R. Wallace, 'Special Economic Dependency and Preferential Rights in respect of Fisheries: Characterisation and Articulation within the European Communities' (1984) 21 C.M.L. Rev. 525–37.

D.C. Watt, 'The EEC and Fishing – New Venture into Unknown Seas' (1977) 48 *Political Quarterly* 328–336.

White Fish Authority, *Fisheries of the European Community,* Edinburgh, 1978.

White Fish Authority, *The Sea Fisheries of the European Community in the Context of Enlargement,* Edinburgh, 1978.

K. Winkel, 'Equal Access of Community Fishermen to Member State Fishing Grounds' (1977) 14 C.M.L. Rev. 329–337.

M. Wise, *The Common Fisheries Policy of the European Community,* London, 1984.

D. Yandais, 'La communauté et la pêche' (1978) 14 C.D.E. 158–201 and (1979) 15 C.D.E. 185–244.

T. Young, *Market Support Arrangements for Fish: The Withdrawal Price Scheme,* Sea Fish Industry Authority, Fishery Economics Research Unit, Occasional Paper Series No. 1, 1984.

Index